KINGS
OF THE
BROKEN WHEEL

Book 8 in the *ELFQUEST* Reader's Collection

Poughkeepsie
New York

KINGS OF THE BROKEN WHEEL

Reprinting **Elfquest: Kings of the Broken Wheel**
comic book issue numbers 5 through 9
as published 1991 - 1992

Story by Wendy & Richard Pini

Art by Wendy Pini

About the ELFQUEST Reader's Collection

The twenty year — and ongoing — saga that is Elfquest has been told in many different comic book titles. The Elfquest Reader's Collection is our attempt to collect all the core stories in book form, so that readers new and old can follow the entire tale from its beginnings on up to the most recent work.

As planned the Elfquest Reader's Collection series will include the following volumes:

#1 - Fire and Flight
#2 - The Forbidden Grove
#3 - Captives of Blue Mountain
#4 - Quest's End
      The story of Cutter, chief of the Wolfriders, and his tribe as they confront the perils of their primitive world, encounter new races of elves, and embark on a grand and dangerous quest to unveil the secret of their past.

#5 - Siege at Blue Mountain
#6 - The Secret of Two-Edge
      The adventures of the Wolfriders some years after the end of the first quest, as they face the machinations of a villainess from their past and her enigmatic half-elf, half-troll son.

#7 - The Cry from Beyond
#8 - Kings of the Broken Wheel
      The Wolfriders face their most daunting challenge when one of their number kidnaps Cutter's mate and children into future time, to prevent the accident that first brought the elves to this world.

#8a - Dreamtime
      The visions of the Wolfriders as they slept for ten thousand years, waiting for the time when Cutter and his family can be united once more.

#9 - Rogue's Challenge
      Tales of the "bad guys" who have caused the Wolfriders so much trouble over the centuries.

#9a - Wolfrider!
      The tale of Cutter's sire Bearclaw, and how he brought two things to the Wolfriders — the enmity of humans and a monstrous tragedy, and a chief's son like no elf the tribe had ever known.

#10 - Shards
#11 - Legacy
#11a - Huntress
#12 - Ascent
#12a - Reunion
      Cutter and family are together again, but now a ruthless human warlord threatens the elves' very existence. The Wolfriders must become two tribes — one to fight a terrible war, the other to flee to ensure that the tribe continues. Volume #10 sets the stage; volumes #11 and #11a follow Cutter's daughter Ember as she leads the Wild Hunt elves into new lands; volumes #12 and #12a take Cutter and his warriors into the flames of battle.

#13 - the Rebels
#13a - Skyward Shadow
#14 - Jink!
#14a - Mindcoil
      In the far future of the World of Two Moons, human civilization has covered the planet — and the elves have disappeared. Where did they go? Volumes #13 and #13a follows a group of young adventurers as they seek the answer. Volumes #14 and #14a tell the story of a mysterious woman who is more than she seems — for she may be the last surviving descendant of the missing elves.

KINGS OF THE BROKEN WHEEL

Book 8 in the *ELFQUEST* **Reader's Collection**

Published by Warp Graphics, Inc.
under its Wolfrider Books imprint.

Entire contents
copyright © 1998
Warp Graphics, Inc.
All rights reserved worldwide.

Elfquest and the Warp Wolf logos are
registered trademarks, and all other
Elfquest characters, names, logos,
situations and all related indicia and their
distinctive likenesses are trademarks of
Warp Graphics, Inc.
43 Haight Avenue
Poughkeepsie, New York 12603

ISBN 0-936861-62-2
Printed in USA

Visit www.elfquest.com
For catalog, call toll-free 877-WOLFRIDER
(outside the USA, 203-863-1926)

Comments on the Quest

BY JAMES GURNEY

Fantasy springs from all sorts of soil. Some writers and artists were raised in the misty haunts of England. I happened to be even luckier, for I spent my formative years in the ideal breeding ground for the imagination: Suburbia. My house was properly stuccoed, my lawn well-cropped, my driveway gently sloping. My home had the requisite bleakness and I the requisite loneliness to nurture a wandering spirit.

Out behind our back fence was a narrow vacant lot owned by the phone company. It was cut off from the rest of the neighborhood. The phone company never exercised its rights to this plot of ground, except to store a few old cable spools and shipping pallets and other castoffs. Over the years my family enlarged the passageway in our back fence and began to domesticate the territory, which I called "Yonderland." We planted some rows of corn, abandoned a few bikes to rust, and nailed together a fort or two.

Way off in a weedy corner there was a curious old piece of junk that someone had left lying on the ground. It was made of big black timbers, bolted together with heavy metal straps. My brother said it was a hatch-cover from a pirate ship. My sister believed it was the lid from a giant's footlocker. I maintained it was a door from a castle, and that it blew here in a tornado. None of us could lift or budge it. The more I looked at it, the more I became convinced it was a door, a door facing down into the ground. With hardly an awareness of it, my mind began working on the idea that it was an entryway to another world. Whoever succeeded in opening it would discover an old, chipped, marble stairway leading down into dark parlors. I saw it all in my mind every night before falling asleep. I knew that if I had a good flashlight and a long afternoon I might explore far enough underground to find luminous gardens and waterfalls. I pictured myself returning home after an adventure in Yonderland. I would cross my back yard, slide open the glass doors, enter the warmth of my house, and sit down to macaroni and cheese with my family. And then I would unload my pockets full of emeralds and Mayan amulets.

I never did succeed in prying open that

doorway. Now I wouldn't want to try. Dreaming is the better part of living. Reality never holds a candle to fantasy. The worlds that we carry in our hearts are the only ones worth inhabiting in the long run. That other world of stucco houses and manicured lawns and plastic signs is just a passing illusion, useful to us because it provides an occasional glimpse of more permanent things. People under the age of twenty, the better part of our population, already know that fantasy is more real than reality. Hopefully, the rest of us have not forgotten.

Thoughtful psychologists and earnest critics might say that dreams of other worlds represent a need to escape from the harsh realities of a troubled family or a disintegrating society. Fantasy, they would argue, is a form of escapism, a disengagement from the duties of living.

In fact, the opposite is true. Fantasy is, or should be, engaging. It should ask us to participate. It should allow us to try on different hats, to say things we couldn't ordinarily say, to witness the world from different points of the compass. Those lucky people who triumph over bleakness by practicing at living imaginary lives are the best adapted to surviving in our fast-changing world. If any are doomed to drown in the fluctuations of real life, it is those who have allowed actuality to overwhelm possibility, those who have turned their backs on the potency of the question "What if...?"

There is hardly a soul alive who has not once believed in a Yonderland of one

kind or another. For me the doorway was in a vacant lot. For you it may have been in an old coat closet, or in a quiet circle of trees in a forest, or in a friend's treehouse. Or the doorway may have been through books. Yonderland may have been resurrected in the guise of Middle Earth, Oz, Narnia, Slumberland or the Secret Garden. These places are more than idle fancies. They have shaped the collective dreaming of all mankind and have become the mythologies of our times.

The world of Elfquest has already taken its place among the best of these Yonderlands. Nothing I could say in praise of it could raise it any higher. It has the unity of vision that could only be born from the dynamic of a creative partnership which has seen the idea through from the first hazy concepts batted across the dinner table to the pound and a half of beautiful color pages that you hold in your hands. It succeeds in the peculiar alchemy of all good fantasy, allowing each of us as a reader to participate in a collaboration with Wendy and Richard Pini, to conjure a world beyond that printed on the pages.

As you prepare to visit or revisit the wonderful adventures of Cutter and Leetah and all the Wolfriders and trolls and preservers, prepare to enter a world — the World of Two Moons — more real than our own.

BY RICHARD & WENDY PINI

One of the most satisfying comments we've ever received about Elfquest came from a professional animator who compared the story you've been reading to Disney's Snow White. This person made the observation based not only on the art, which is designed with animation in mind, but also on the more primal or mythic qualities of the story. This, safe to say, made us feel very proud.

Joseph Campbell, certainly this century's most gifted student and synthesist of myths and legends, called mythology the encoding of rituals. Rituals are those behaviors by which all people, but particularly "primitive" groups, strive to cope with and survive in the world. Myths are then a kind of cookbook for living: In this situation do the following things, but in that situation do these others. And the instructions in the cookbook take the form of epic stories and poems passed from generation to generation because, after all, it's far easier to remember a rousing tale than a dry list of things to do.

Often, the recipes contained within the myths had to do with rites of passage: the initiation of a young boy into the mysteries of manhood and the hunt, the dawning of awareness in a young girl that she is the carrier and nurturer of new life, the crossing over of the invisible but undeniable line between life and death. Because primitive peoples meshed much more successfully with the world around them, were far more sensitive to its needs and rhythms, they made certain that the lessons of passage were powerful and certain to have the desired effect. Initiation rituals were intense, sometimes painful or terrifying. They were assuredly unforgettable.

In becoming civilized, in our attempt to tame the world, we have turned our backs on the power of myth. Even the rites of passage have been diluted, their potency lost. The traumatic descent with the tribal shaman into the painted hunting cave or kiva — guaranteed to teach a youngster the ways of the tribe — has been replaced with the gift-giving of the bar-mitzvah or the gentle slap on the face of confirmation. Professor Campbell, when asked if there were any modern mythologies, replied that the world now changes too quickly for ritual to "stick" and accumulate into a body of myth. The tribe no longer exists, with its unity of purpose. There are no longer any universally accepted tribal cookbooks to turn to for the wisdom to cope with modern day concerns and problems, so people must now find smaller, individual myths to take within themselves and use.

Actually, small myths have existed for almost as long as the large ones. They've been called fables or fairy-tales, and they are bite-sized myths. They are the babes from whose mouths the beginning of wisdom comes. If myth and its attendant ritual is the entire cookbook for survival, then fables are individual recipes, little lessons on a single timeless theme. But fables have fallen on hard times too these days, despite their timelessness.

Who today takes any lesson — on envy from "The Fox and the Grapes," or on compassion from "The Lion and the Mouse"? Who remembers that "Little Red Riding Hood" is really about the rite of passage from girl- to womanhood? Disney's superb imagery aside, who recalls that "Snow White" is actually a pretty scary tale of youth struggling to cope with the pain of growing up and leaving the home? Fairy-tales seem to be passé these days, and yet everyone goes through the same passages, just as our Neanderthal ancestors did. We all grow up, we all experience jealousy and pride, we all struggle with one deep thing or another. While we may no longer believe in the bogeyman as a motivation to learn life's lessons, we still need the rituals of passage, those recipes that provide a touchstone here and there on the journey through life. We need to be able, occasionally, to point to someone else's story and say, "Ah, yes, I know that feeling. I identify."

The truest, most enduring fantasies are those that speak some kind of personal truth, even though it is cloaked in symbols. When we began Elfquest in 1978 as a mom-and-pop independent comic book, we knew that the story was about Cutter, eleventh chief of the Wolfriders, and his quest to find the elves' ancestral home. We had little idea, however, that over the course of telling the story we would tap into as many personal — to us and to readers — questions and truths as we seem to have done. It wasn't a studied and deliberate effort! But perhaps simply in the course of living life and surviving the world we collected a boxful of recipes that found their way into the adventures of this elfin tribe. Certainly there are fragments of us, large or small, in every character and our experiences, reflected in a ripply mirror, are the experiences of the elves.

It's not something that we set out to do, but perhaps Elfquest has become a fairy-tale for these times. We seem to have stumbled into one of the old caves where the scent of smoky torches lingers and faint chanting echoes can yet be heard. The bones and chipped flints still possess the ancient slow magic. Let it reach, past the headlines and hurry, into you.

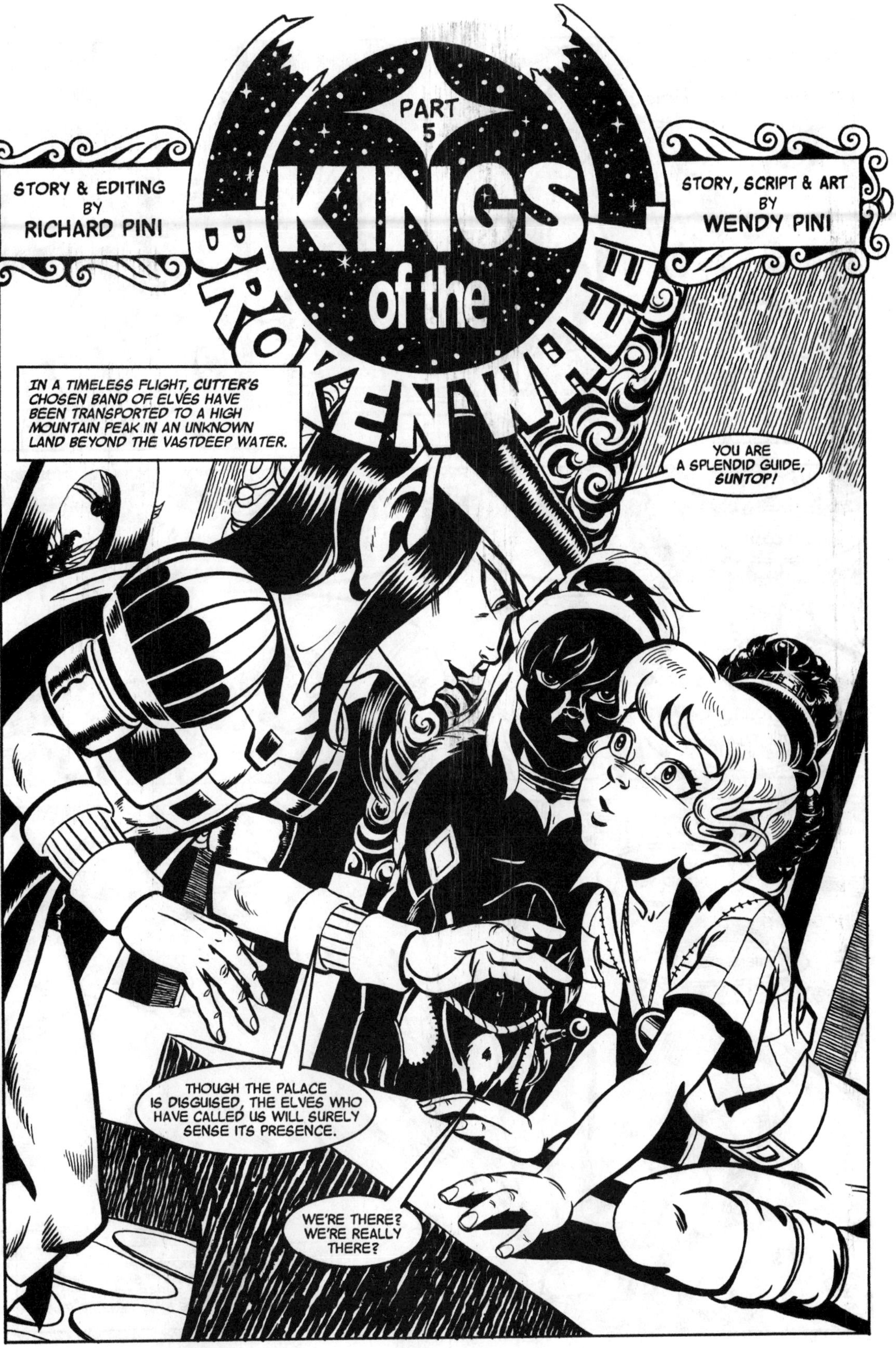
PART 5
KINGS of the BROKEN WHEEL
STORY & EDITING BY RICHARD PINI
STORY, SCRIPT & ART BY WENDY PINI
IN A TIMELESS FLIGHT, CUTTER'S CHOSEN BAND OF ELVES HAVE BEEN TRANSPORTED TO A HIGH MOUNTAIN PEAK IN AN UNKNOWN LAND BEYOND THE VASTDEEP WATER.
YOU ARE A SPLENDID GUIDE, SUNTOP!
THOUGH THE PALACE IS DISGUISED, THE ELVES WHO HAVE CALLED US WILL SURELY SENSE ITS PRESENCE.
WE'RE THERE? WE'RE REALLY THERE?

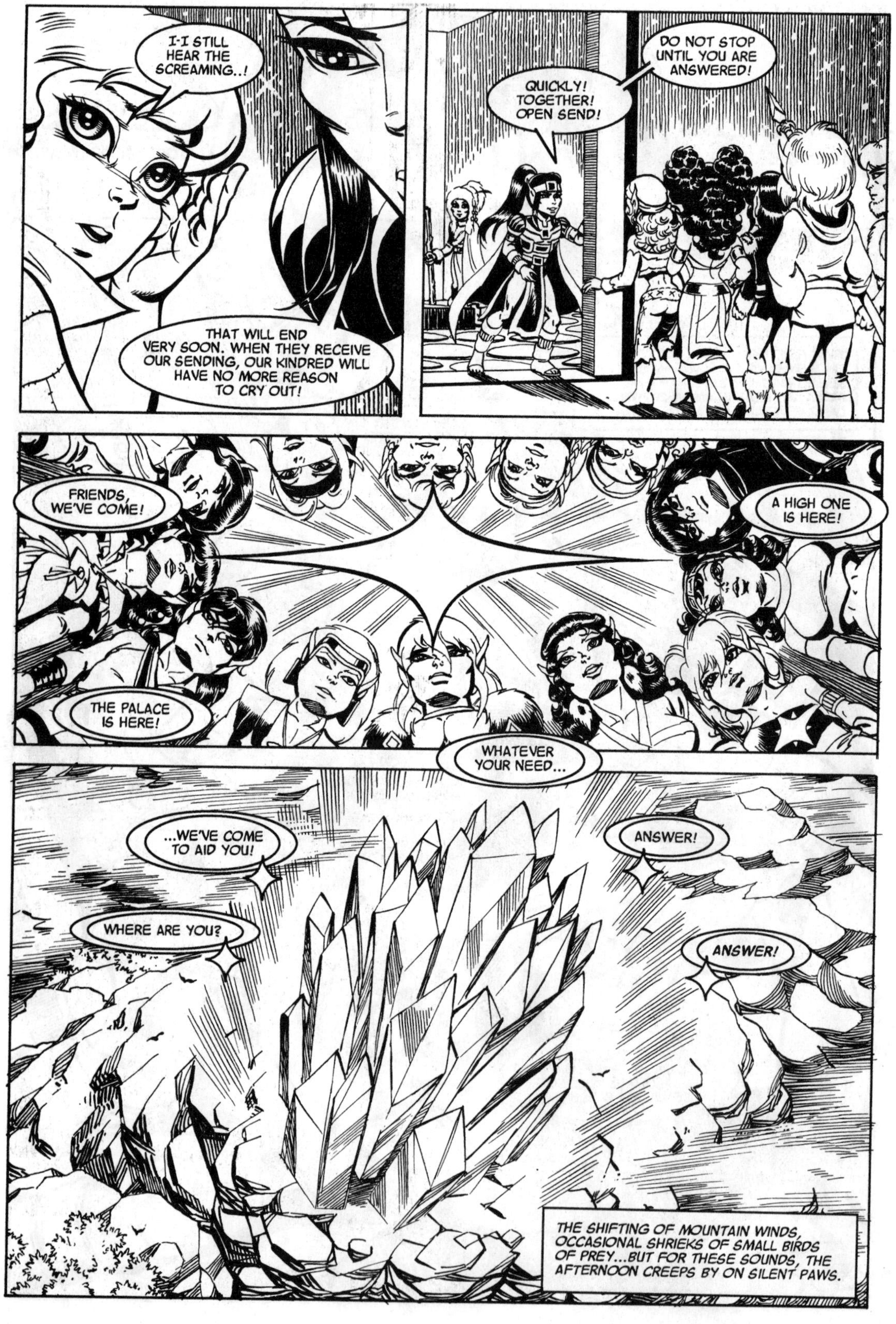
I-I STILL HEAR THE SCREAMING..!
THAT WILL END VERY SOON. WHEN THEY RECEIVE OUR SENDING, OUR KINDRED WILL HAVE NO MORE REASON TO CRY OUT!
QUICKLY! TOGETHER! OPEN SEND!
DO NOT STOP UNTIL YOU ARE ANSWERED!
FRIENDS, WE'VE COME!
A HIGH ONE IS HERE!
THE PALACE IS HERE!
WHATEVER YOUR NEED...
...WE'VE COME TO AID YOU!
ANSWER!
WHERE ARE YOU?
ANSWER!
THE SHIFTING OF MOUNTAIN WINDS, OCCASIONAL SHRIEKS OF SMALL BIRDS OF PREY...BUT FOR THESE SOUNDS, THE AFTERNOON CREEPS BY ON SILENT PAWS.

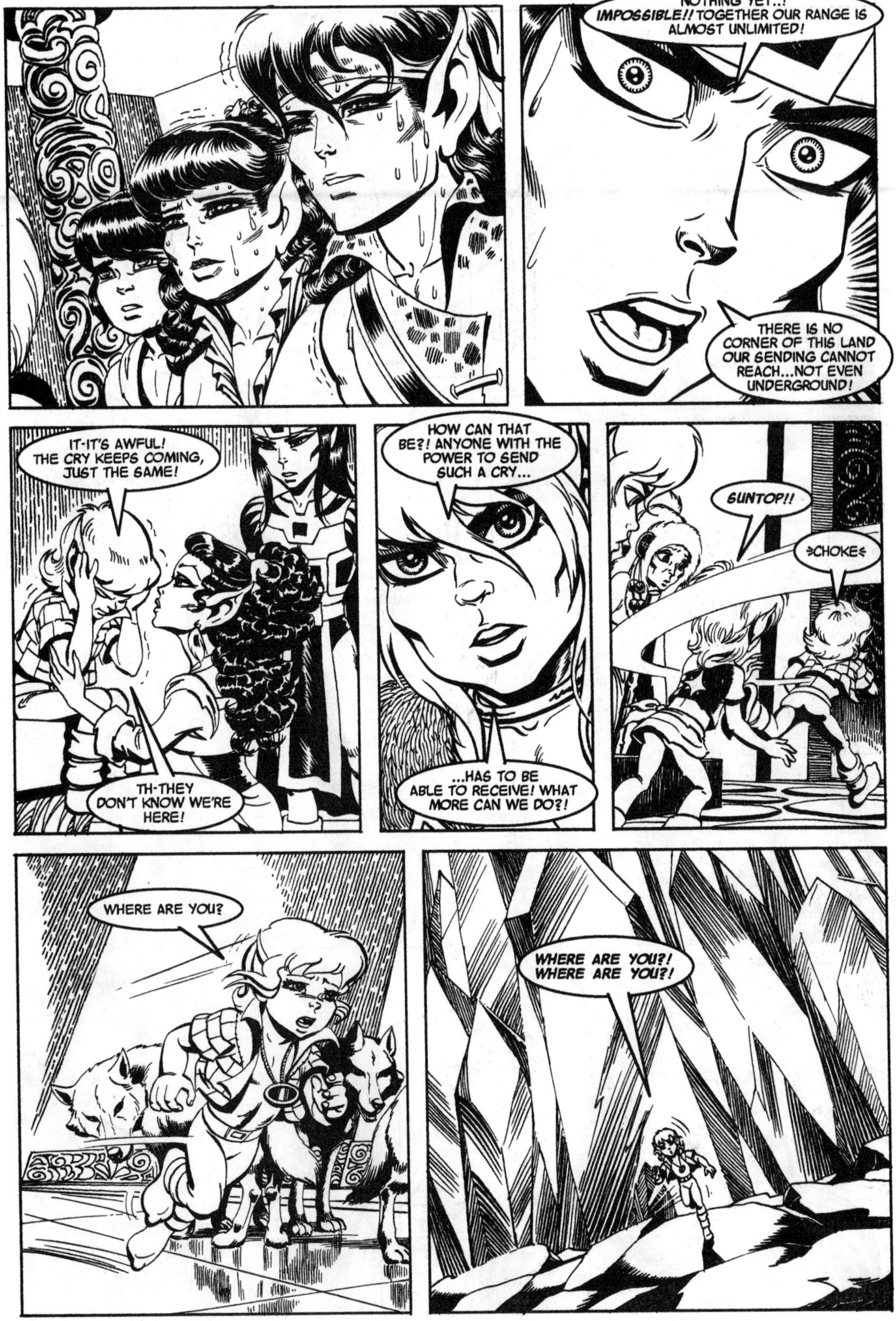
NOTHING YET..!
IMPOSSIBLE!! TOGETHER OUR RANGE IS ALMOST UNLIMITED!
THERE IS NO CORNER OF THIS LAND OUR SENDING CANNOT REACH...NOT EVEN UNDERGROUND!
IT-IT'S AWFUL! THE CRY KEEPS COMING, JUST THE SAME!
TH-THEY DON'T KNOW WE'RE HERE!
HOW CAN THAT BE?! ANYONE WITH THE POWER TO SEND SUCH A CRY...
...HAS TO BE ABLE TO RECEIVE! WHAT MORE CAN WE DO?!
SUNTOP!!
CHOKE
WHERE ARE YOU?
WHERE ARE YOU?!
WHERE ARE YOU?!

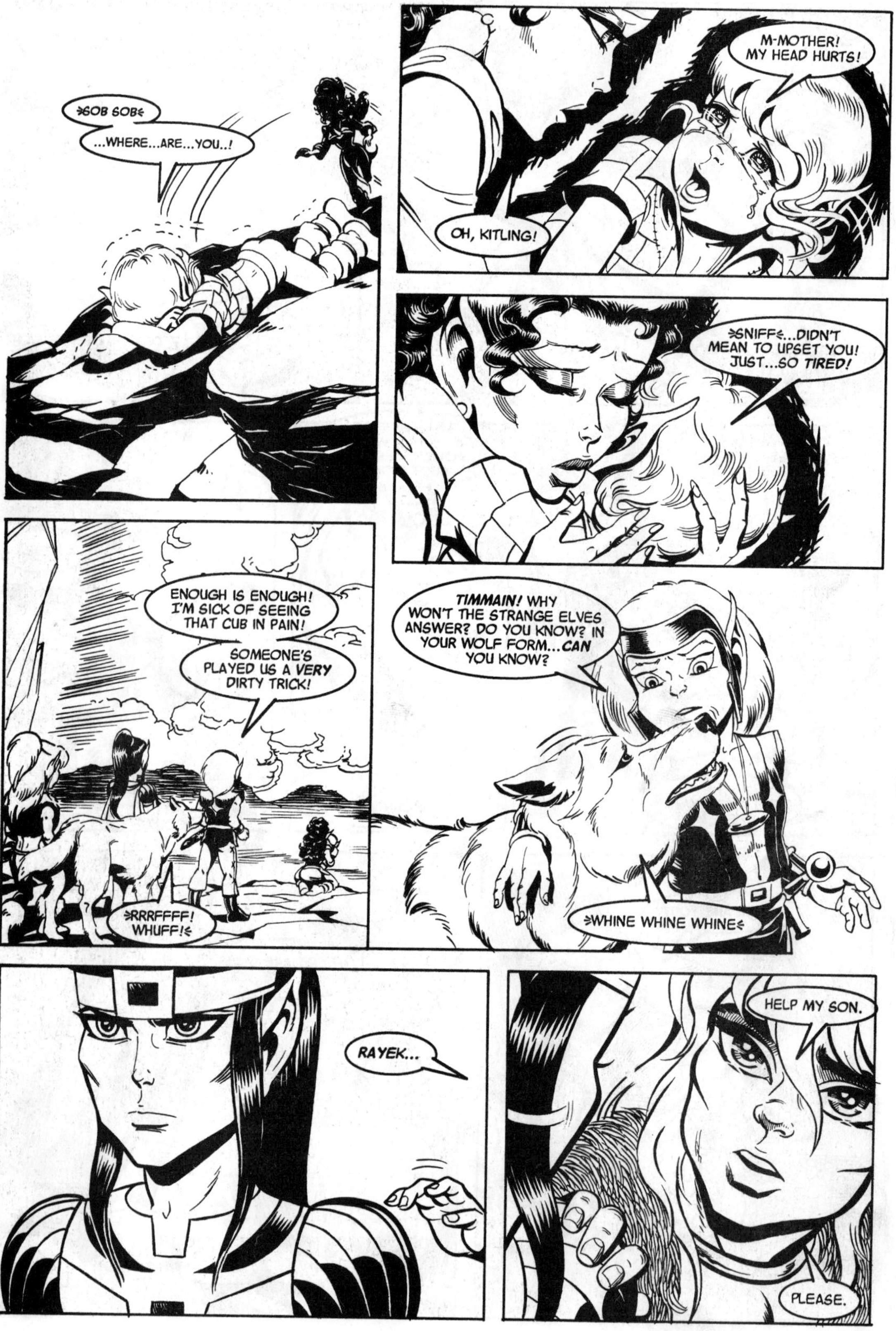

SOB SOB
...WHERE...ARE...YOU..!
M-MOTHER! MY HEAD HURTS!
OH, KITLING!
SNIFF...DIDN'T MEAN TO UPSET YOU! JUST...SO TIRED!
ENOUGH IS ENOUGH! I'M SICK OF SEEING THAT CUB IN PAIN!
SOMEONE'S PLAYED US A VERY DIRTY TRICK!
RRRFFFF! WHUFF!
TIMMAIN! WHY WON'T THE STRANGE ELVES ANSWER? DO YOU KNOW? IN YOUR WOLF FORM...CAN YOU KNOW?
WHINE WHINE WHINE
RAYEK...
HELP MY SON.
PLEASE.

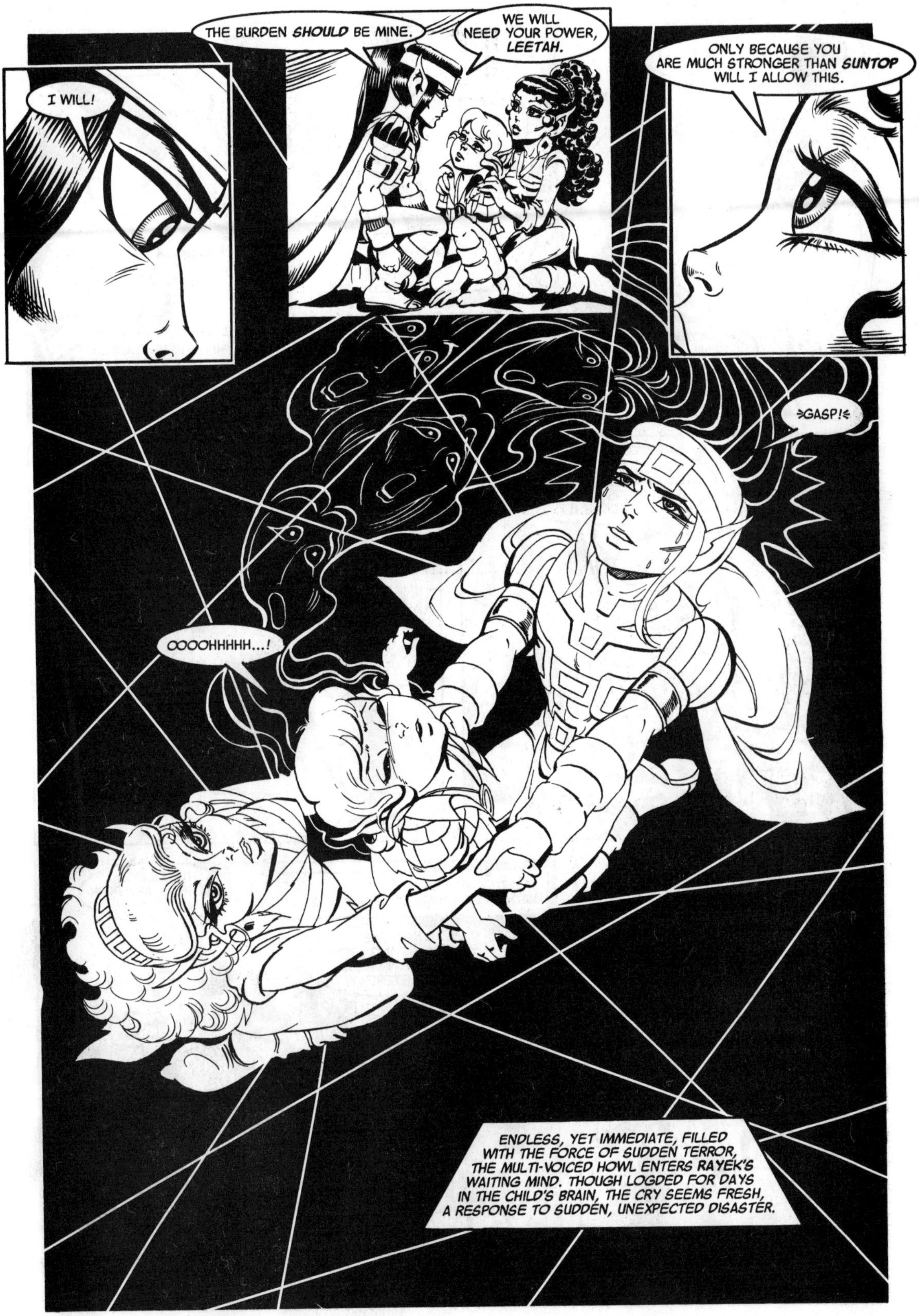
I WILL!
THE BURDEN SHOULD BE MINE.
WE WILL NEED YOUR POWER, LEETAH.
ONLY BECAUSE YOU ARE MUCH STRONGER THAN SUNTOP WILL I ALLOW THIS.
≥GASP!≤
OOOOHHHHH...!
ENDLESS, YET IMMEDIATE, FILLED WITH THE FORCE OF SUDDEN TERROR, THE MULTI-VOICED HOWL ENTERS RAYEK'S WAITING MIND. THOUGH LOGDED FOR DAYS IN THE CHILD'S BRAIN, THE CRY SEEMS FRESH, A RESPONSE TO SUDDEN, UNEXPECTED DISASTER.

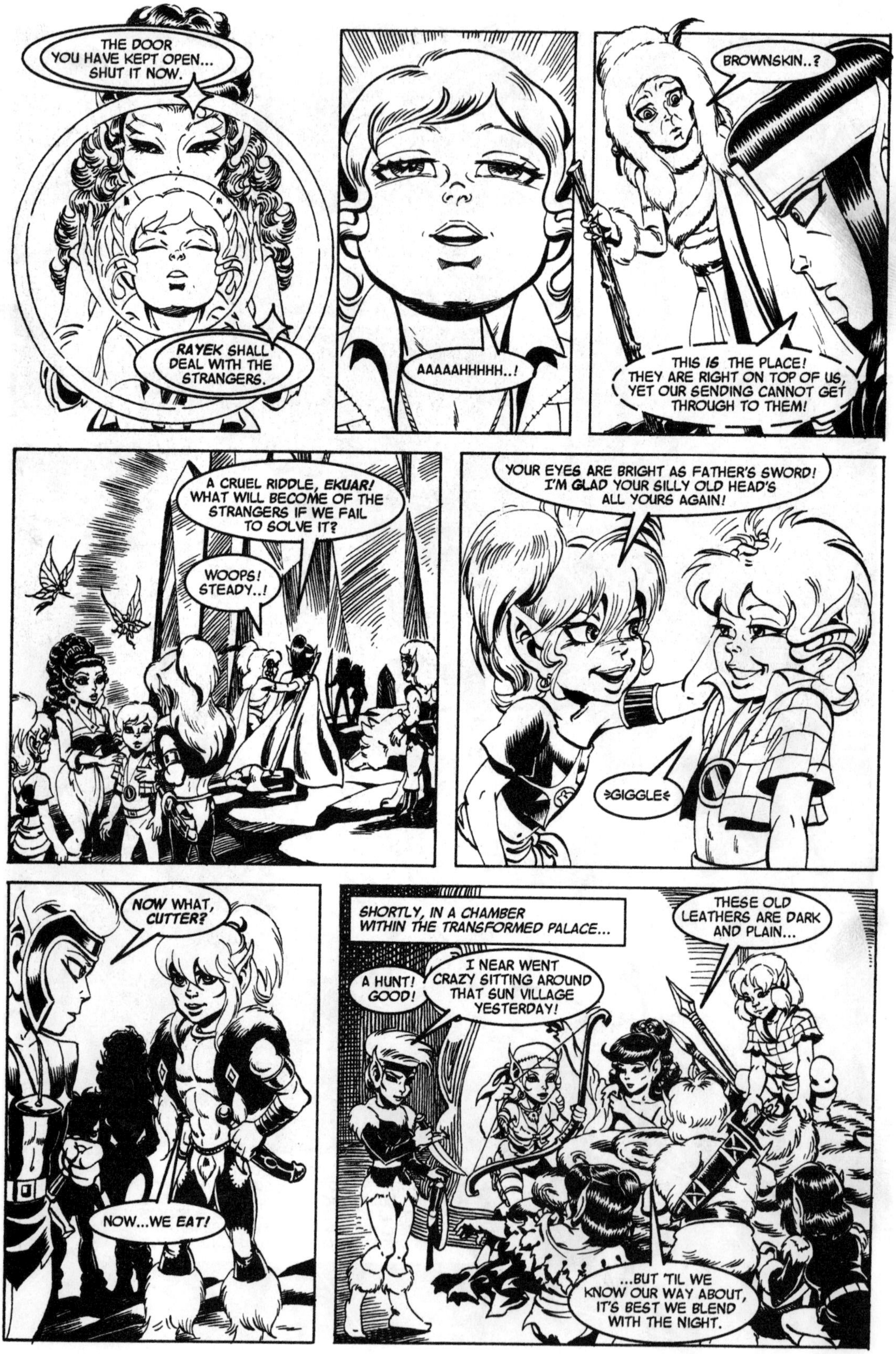
THE DOOR YOU HAVE KEPT OPEN... SHUT IT NOW.
RAYEK SHALL DEAL WITH THE STRANGERS.
AAAAAHHHHH..!
BROWNSKIN..?
THIS IS THE PLACE! THEY ARE RIGHT ON TOP OF US, YET OUR SENDING CANNOT GET THROUGH TO THEM!
A CRUEL RIDDLE, EKUAR! WHAT WILL BECOME OF THE STRANGERS IF WE FAIL TO SOLVE IT?
WOOPS! STEADY..!
YOUR EYES ARE BRIGHT AS FATHER'S SWORD! I'M GLAD YOUR SILLY OLD HEAD'S ALL YOURS AGAIN!
GIGGLE
NOW WHAT, CUTTER?
NOW...WE EAT!
SHORTLY, IN A CHAMBER WITHIN THE TRANSFORMED PALACE...
THESE OLD LEATHERS ARE DARK AND PLAIN...
A HUNT! GOOD!
I NEAR WENT CRAZY SITTING AROUND THAT SUN VILLAGE YESTERDAY!
...BUT 'TIL WE KNOW OUR WAY ABOUT, IT'S BEST WE BLEND WITH THE NIGHT.

AND SOON...
AAAAAYYYYYOOOOOAAAHHH!
I AM GLAD YOU AND CHOPLICKER CHOSE TO STAY HERE WITH ME, EMBER.
WELL...THEY TOLD ME I'D BETTER CHOOSE TO!
DON'T BE SCARED, SHENSHEN. WE WOLFRIDERS SAY THE BEST WAY TO GET TO KNOW A NEW PLACE IS TO HUNT IT!

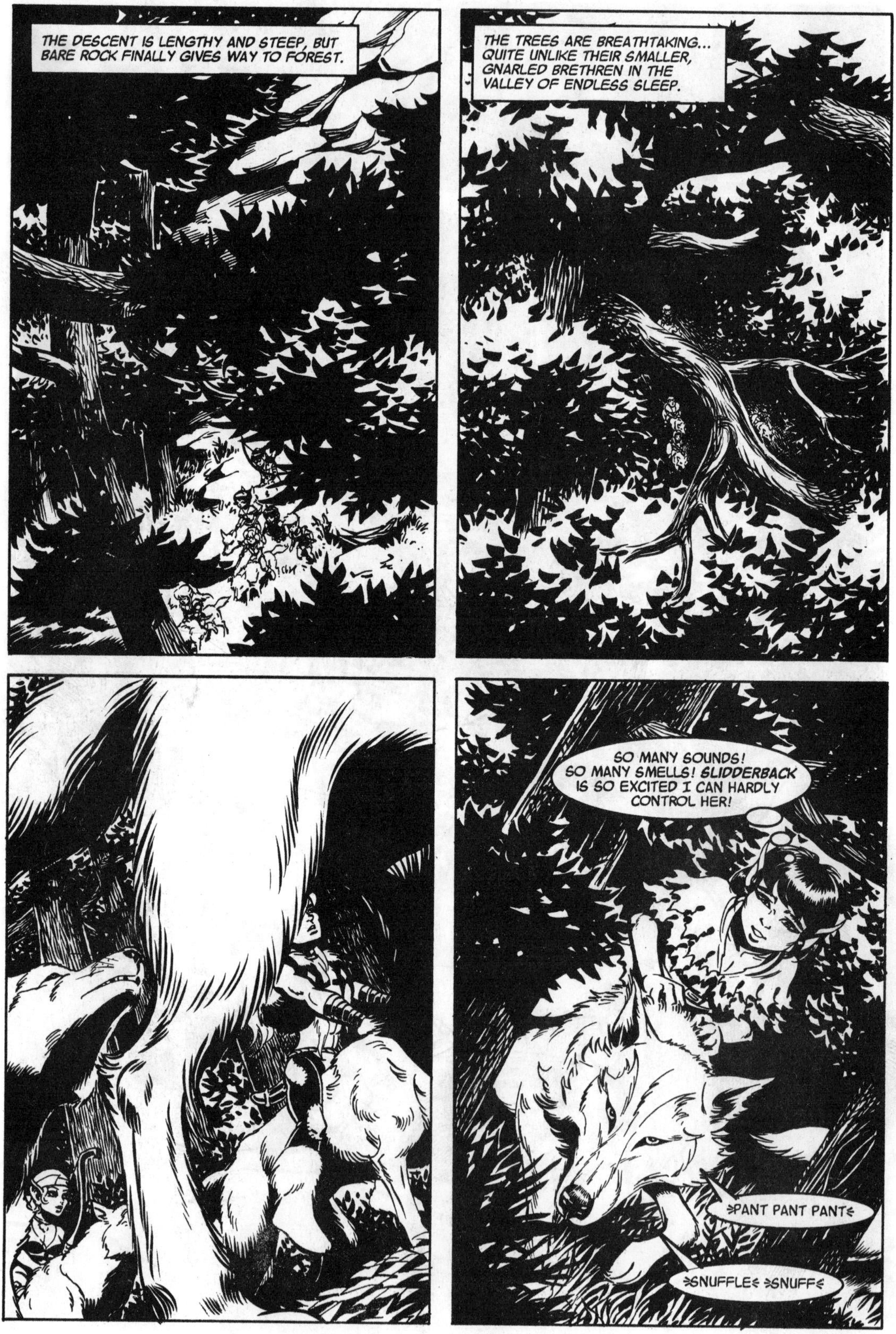
THE DESCENT IS LENGTHY AND STEEP, BUT BARE ROCK FINALLY GIVES WAY TO FOREST.
THE TREES ARE BREATHTAKING... QUITE UNLIKE THEIR SMALLER, GNARLED BRETHREN IN THE VALLEY OF ENDLESS SLEEP.
SO MANY SOUNDS! SO MANY SMELLS! SLIDDERBACK IS SO EXCITED I CAN HARDLY CONTROL HER!
PANT PANT PANT
SNUFFLE SNUFF

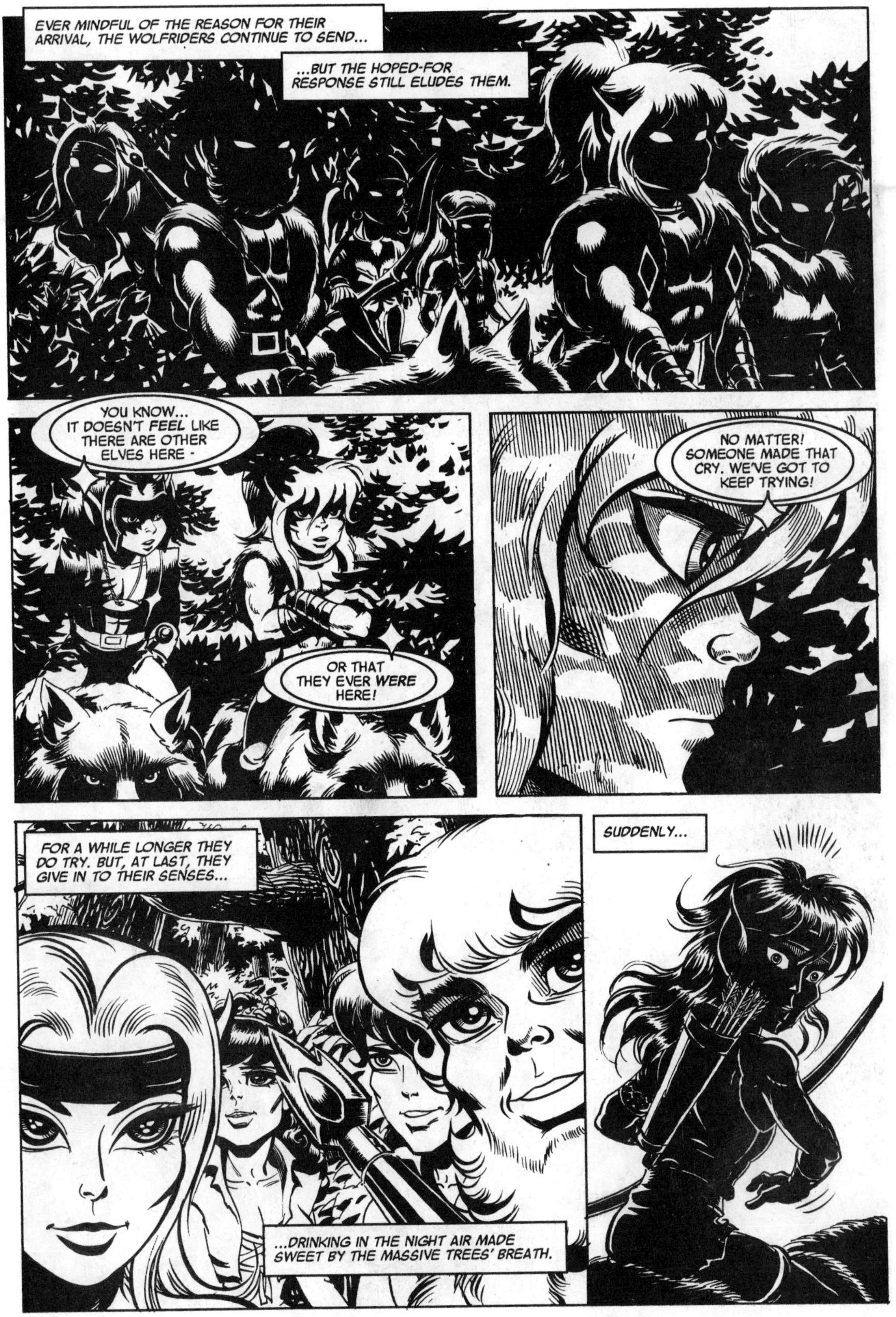
EVER MINDFUL OF THE REASON FOR THEIR ARRIVAL, THE WOLFRIDERS CONTINUE TO SEND...
...BUT THE HOPED-FOR RESPONSE STILL ELUDES THEM.
YOU KNOW... IT DOESN'T FEEL LIKE THERE ARE OTHER ELVES HERE -
OR THAT THEY EVER WERE HERE!
NO MATTER! SOMEONE MADE THAT CRY. WE'VE GOT TO KEEP TRYING!
FOR A WHILE LONGER THEY DO TRY. BUT, AT LAST, THEY GIVE IN TO THEIR SENSES...
...DRINKING IN THE NIGHT AIR MADE SWEET BY THE MASSIVE TREES' BREATH.
SUDDENLY...

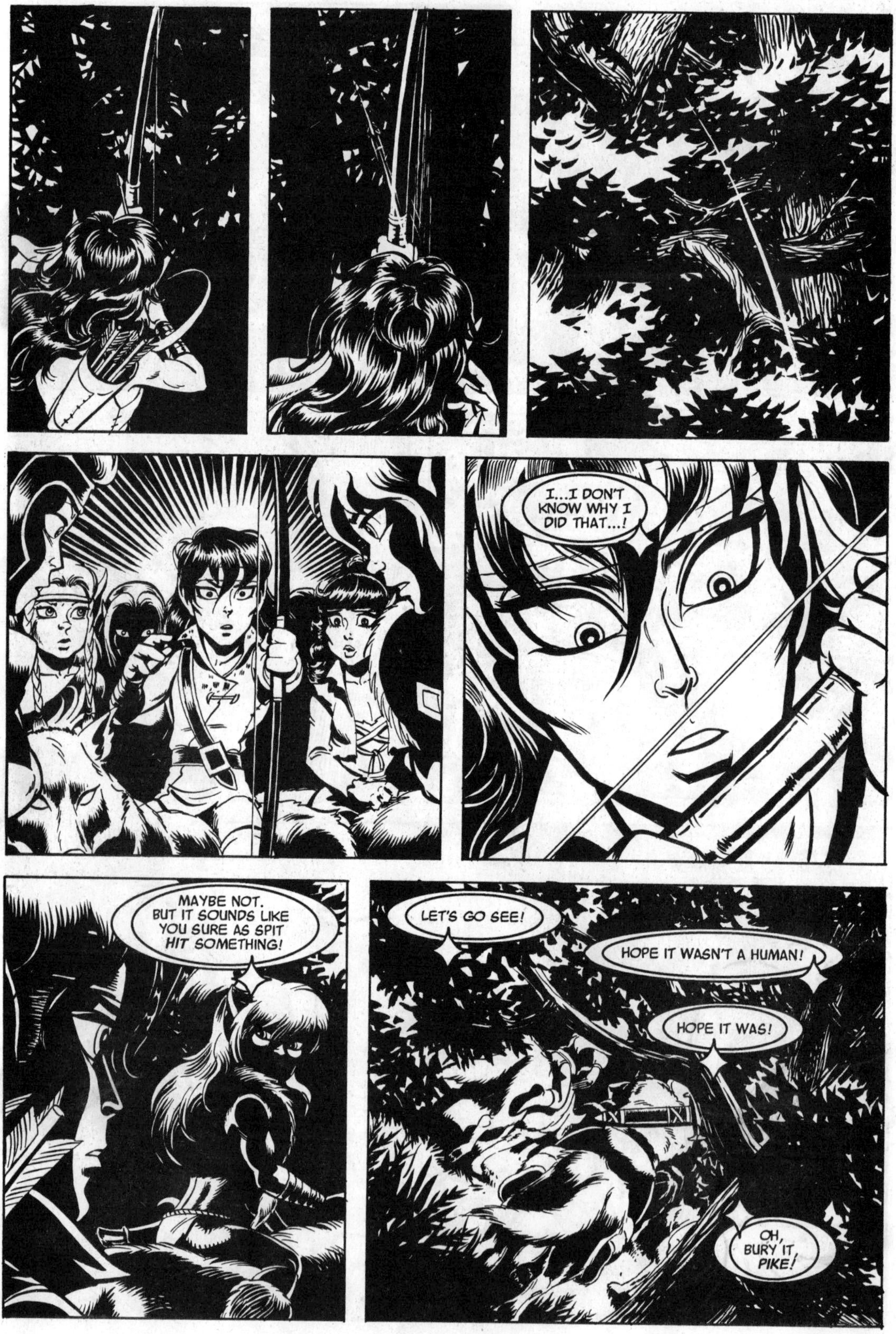
I...I DON'T KNOW WHY I DID THAT...!
MAYBE NOT. BUT IT SOUNDS LIKE YOU SURE AS SPIT HIT SOMETHING!
LET'S GO SEE!
HOPE IT WASN'T A HUMAN!
HOPE IT WAS!
OH, BURY IT, PIKE!

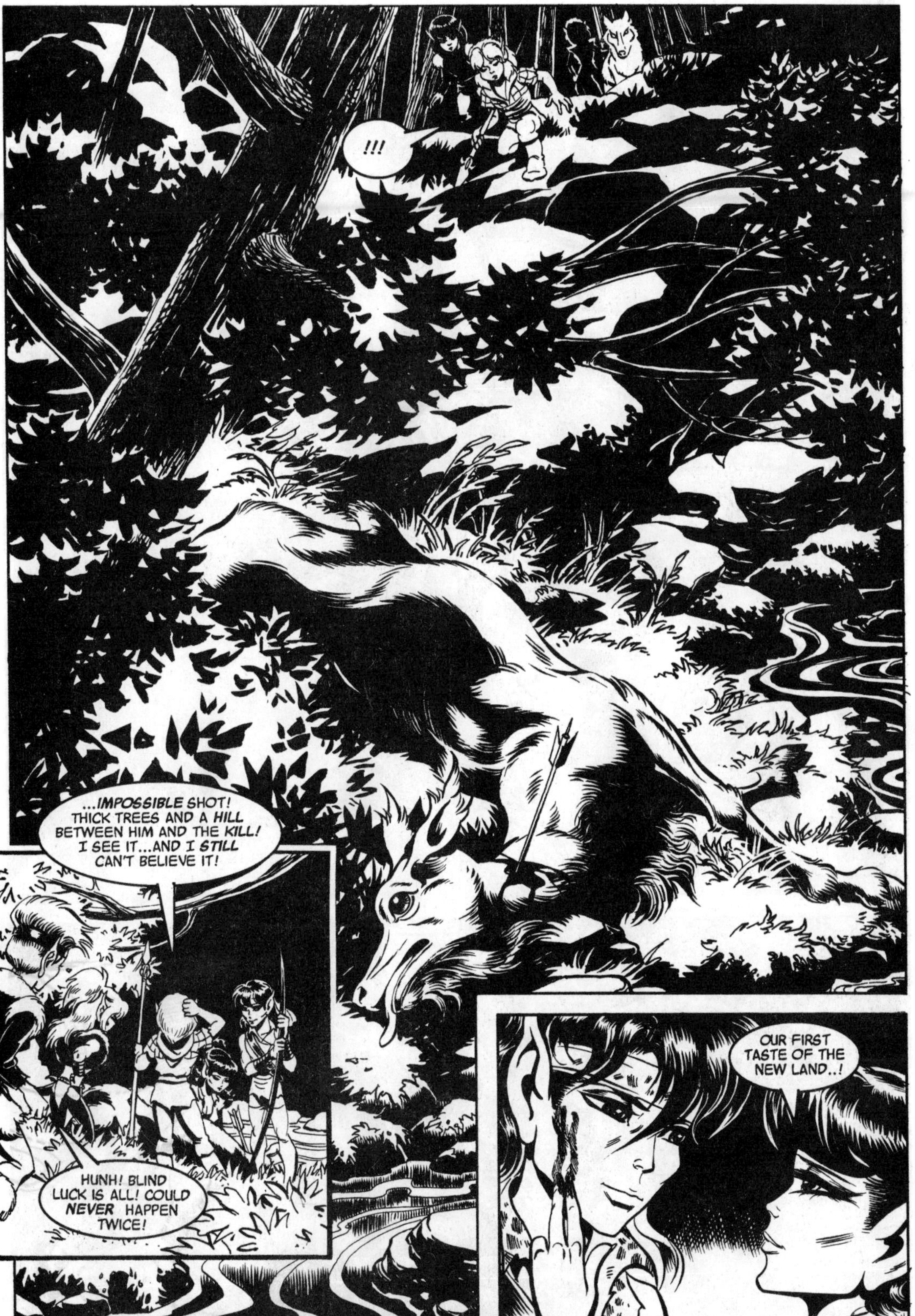
!!!
...IMPOSSIBLE SHOT! THICK TREES AND A HILL BETWEEN HIM AND THE KILL! I SEE IT...AND I STILL CAN'T BELIEVE IT!
HUNH! BLIND LUCK IS ALL! COULD NEVER HAPPEN TWICE!
OUR FIRST TASTE OF THE NEW LAND..!

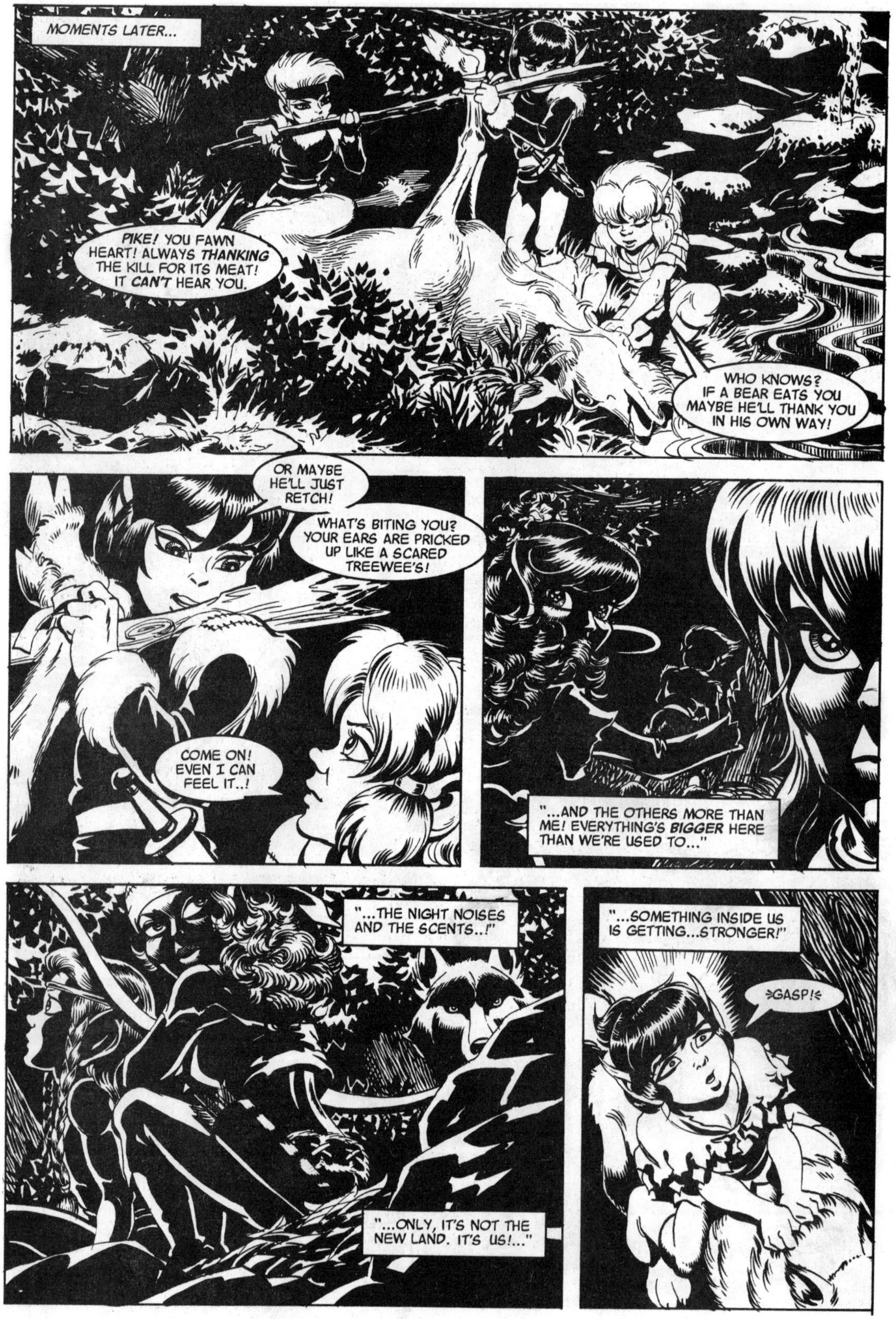
MOMENTS LATER...
PIKE! YOU FAWN HEART! ALWAYS THANKING THE KILL FOR ITS MEAT! IT CAN'T HEAR YOU.
WHO KNOWS? IF A BEAR EATS YOU MAYBE HE'LL THANK YOU IN HIS OWN WAY!
OR MAYBE HE'LL JUST RETCH!
WHAT'S BITING YOU? YOUR EARS ARE PRICKED UP LIKE A SCARED TREEWEE'S!
COME ON! EVEN I CAN FEEL IT..!
"...AND THE OTHERS MORE THAN ME! EVERYTHING'S BIGGER HERE THAN WE'RE USED TO..."
"...THE NIGHT NOISES AND THE SCENTS..!"
"...ONLY, IT'S NOT THE NEW LAND. IT'S US!..."
"...SOMETHING INSIDE US IS GETTING...STRONGER!"
>GASP!<

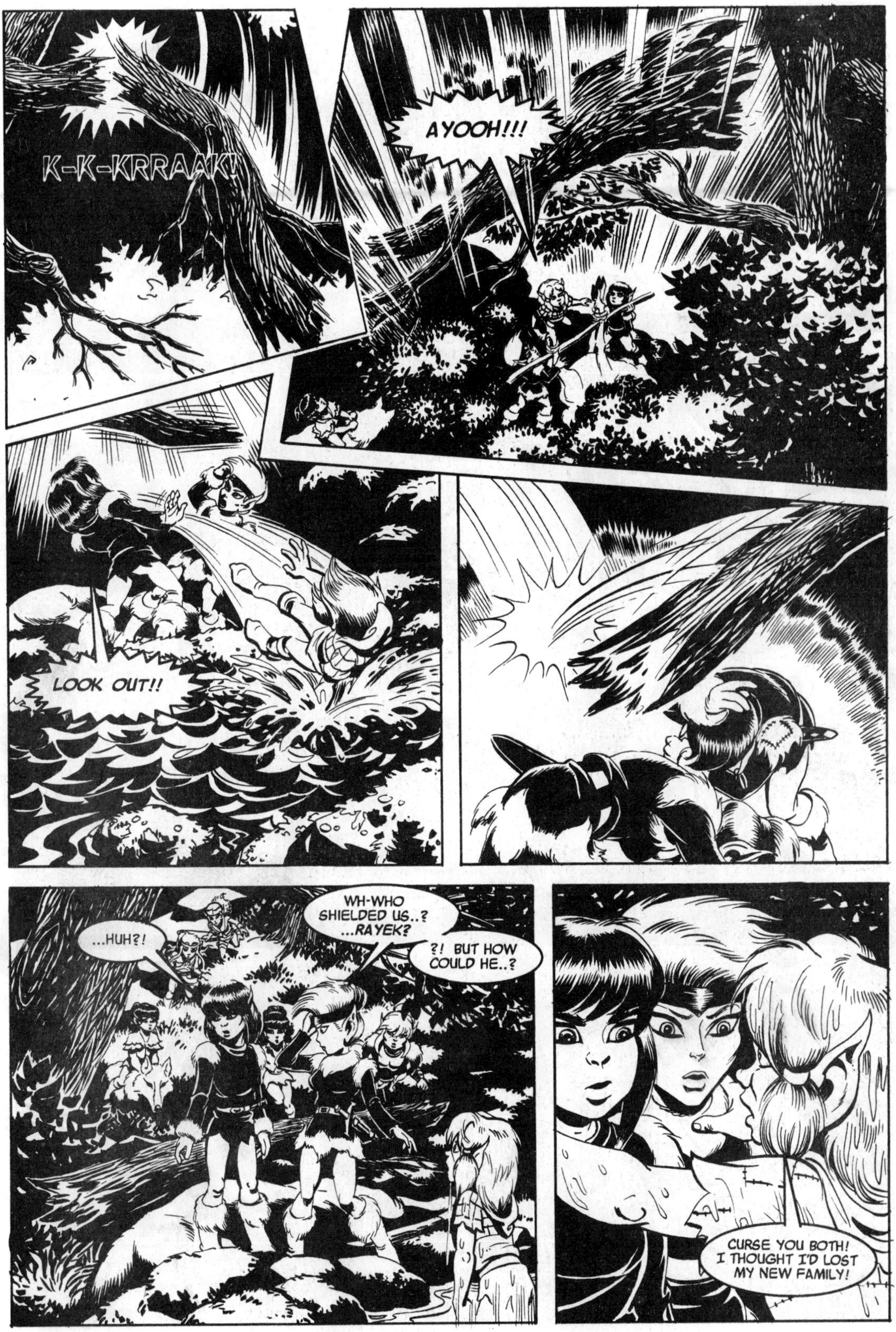
K-K-KRRAAK!
AYOOH!!!
LOOK OUT!!
...HUH?!
WH-WHO SHIELDED US..? ...RAYEK?
?! BUT HOW COULD HE..?
CURSE YOU BOTH! I THOUGHT I'D LOST MY NEW FAMILY!

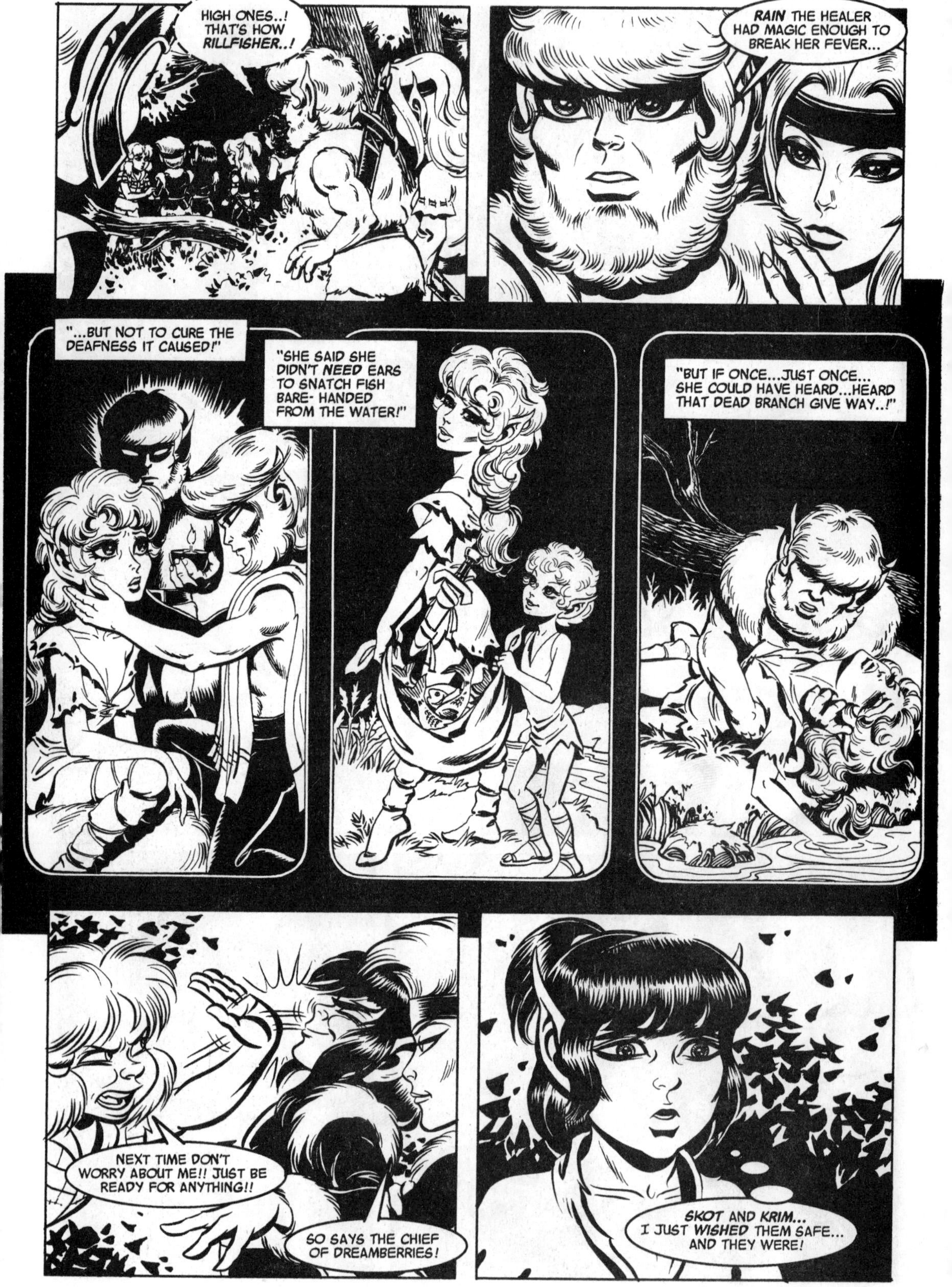
HIGH ONES..! THAT'S HOW RILLFISHER..!
RAIN THE HEALER HAD MAGIC ENOUGH TO BREAK HER FEVER...
"...BUT NOT TO CURE THE DEAFNESS IT CAUSED!"
"SHE SAID SHE DIDN'T NEED EARS TO SNATCH FISH BARE- HANDED FROM THE WATER!"
"BUT IF ONCE...JUST ONCE... SHE COULD HAVE HEARD...HEARD THAT DEAD BRANCH GIVE WAY..!"
NEXT TIME DON'T WORRY ABOUT ME!! JUST BE READY FOR ANYTHING!!
SO SAYS THE CHIEF OF DREAMBERRIES!
SKOT AND KRIM... I JUST WISHED THEM SAFE... AND THEY WERE!

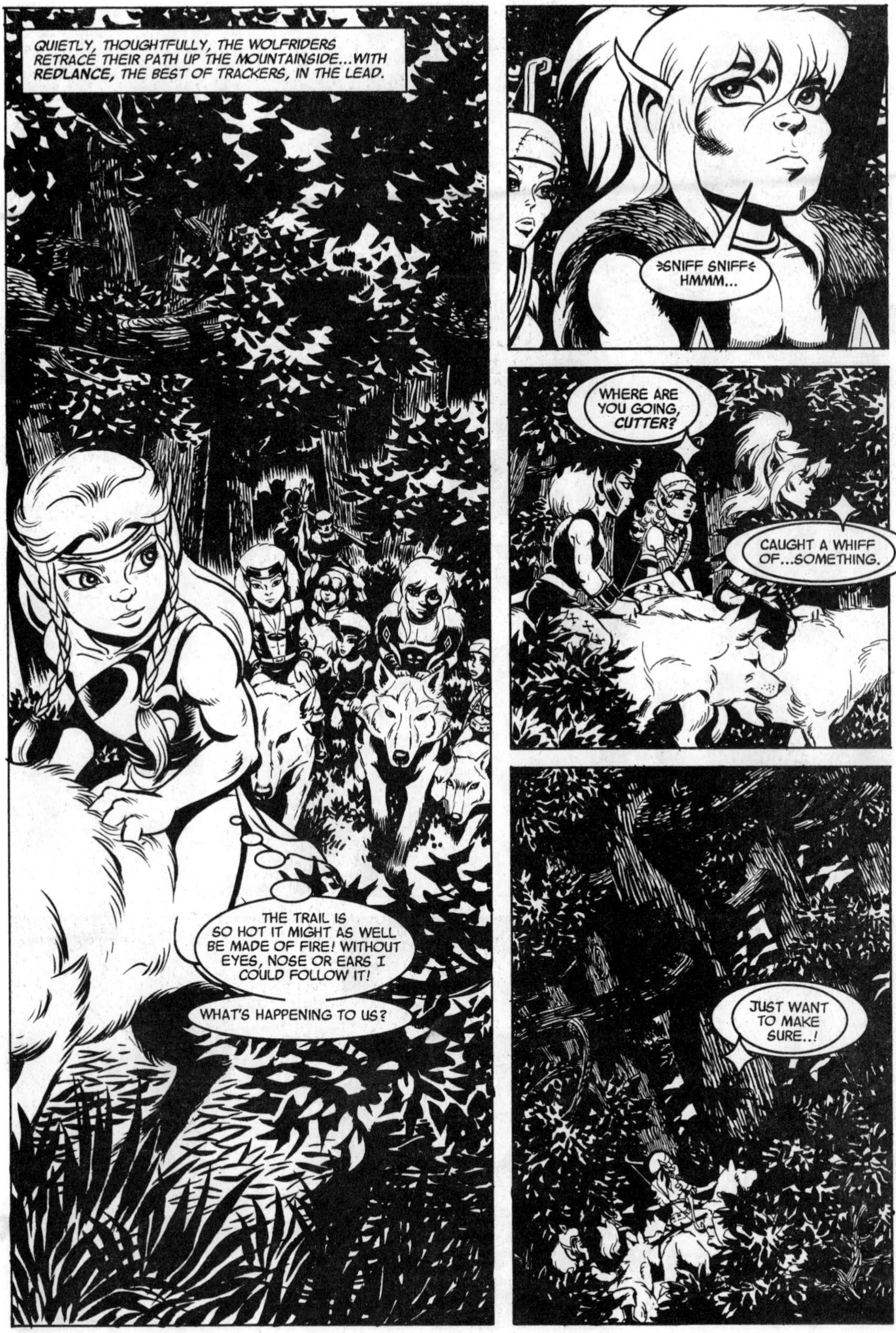
QUIETLY, THOUGHTFULLY, THE WOLFRIDERS RETRACE THEIR PATH UP THE MOUNTAINSIDE...WITH REDLANCE, THE BEST OF TRACKERS, IN THE LEAD.
THE TRAIL IS SO HOT IT MIGHT AS WELL BE MADE OF FIRE! WITHOUT EYES, NOSE OR EARS I COULD FOLLOW IT!
WHAT'S HAPPENING TO US?
≥SNIFF SNIFF≤ HMMM...
WHERE ARE YOU GOING, CUTTER?
CAUGHT A WHIFF OF...SOMETHING.
JUST WANT TO MAKE SURE..!

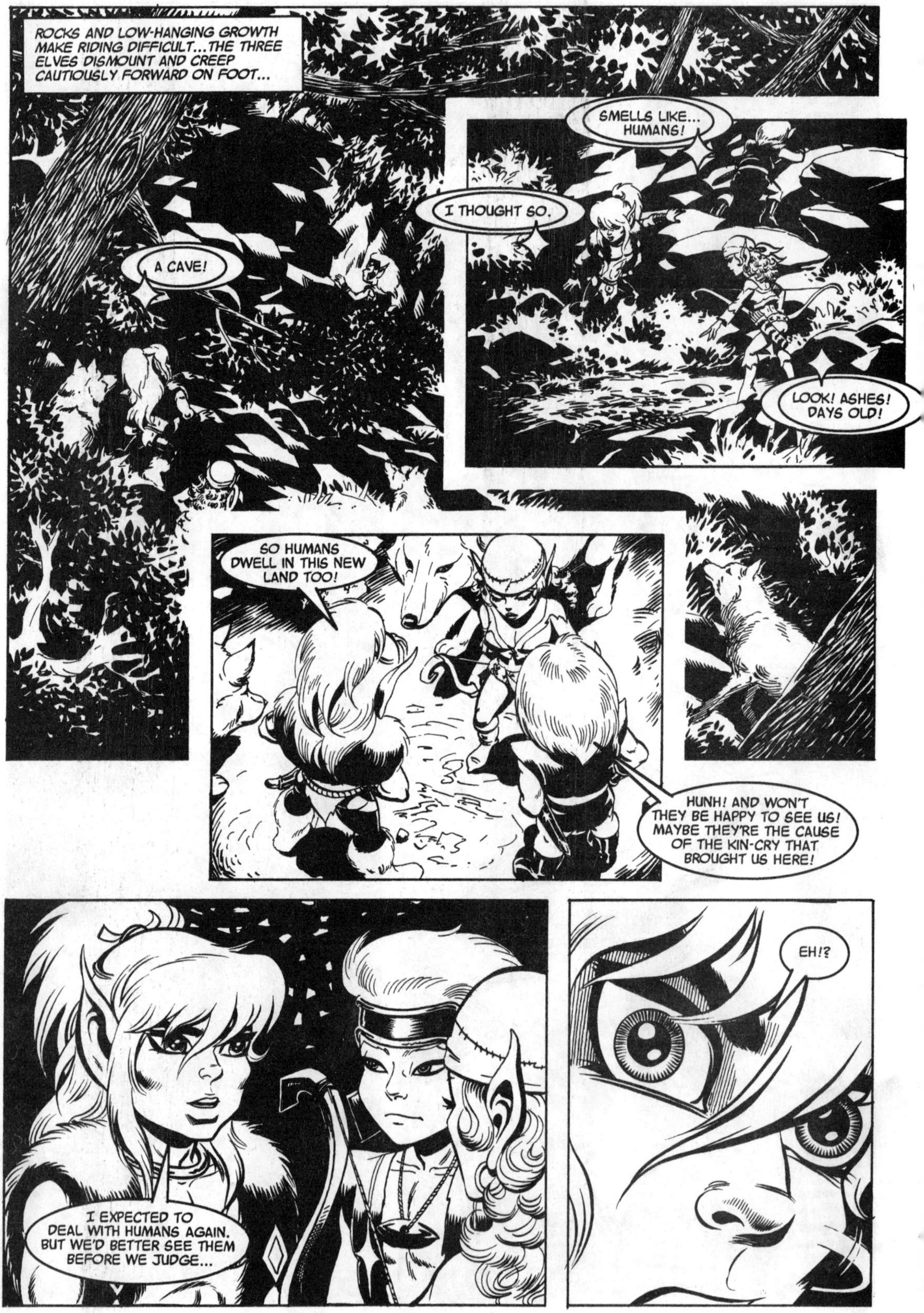
ROCKS AND LOW-HANGING GROWTH MAKE RIDING DIFFICULT...THE THREE ELVES DISMOUNT AND CREEP CAUTIOUSLY FORWARD ON FOOT...
A CAVE!
SMELLS LIKE... HUMANS!
I THOUGHT SO.
LOOK! ASHES! DAYS OLD!
SO HUMANS DWELL IN THIS NEW LAND TOO!
HUNH! AND WON'T THEY BE HAPPY TO SEE US! MAYBE THEY'RE THE CAUSE OF THE KIN-CRY THAT BROUGHT US HERE!
I EXPECTED TO DEAL WITH HUMANS AGAIN. BUT WE'D BETTER SEE THEM BEFORE WE JUDGE...
EH!?

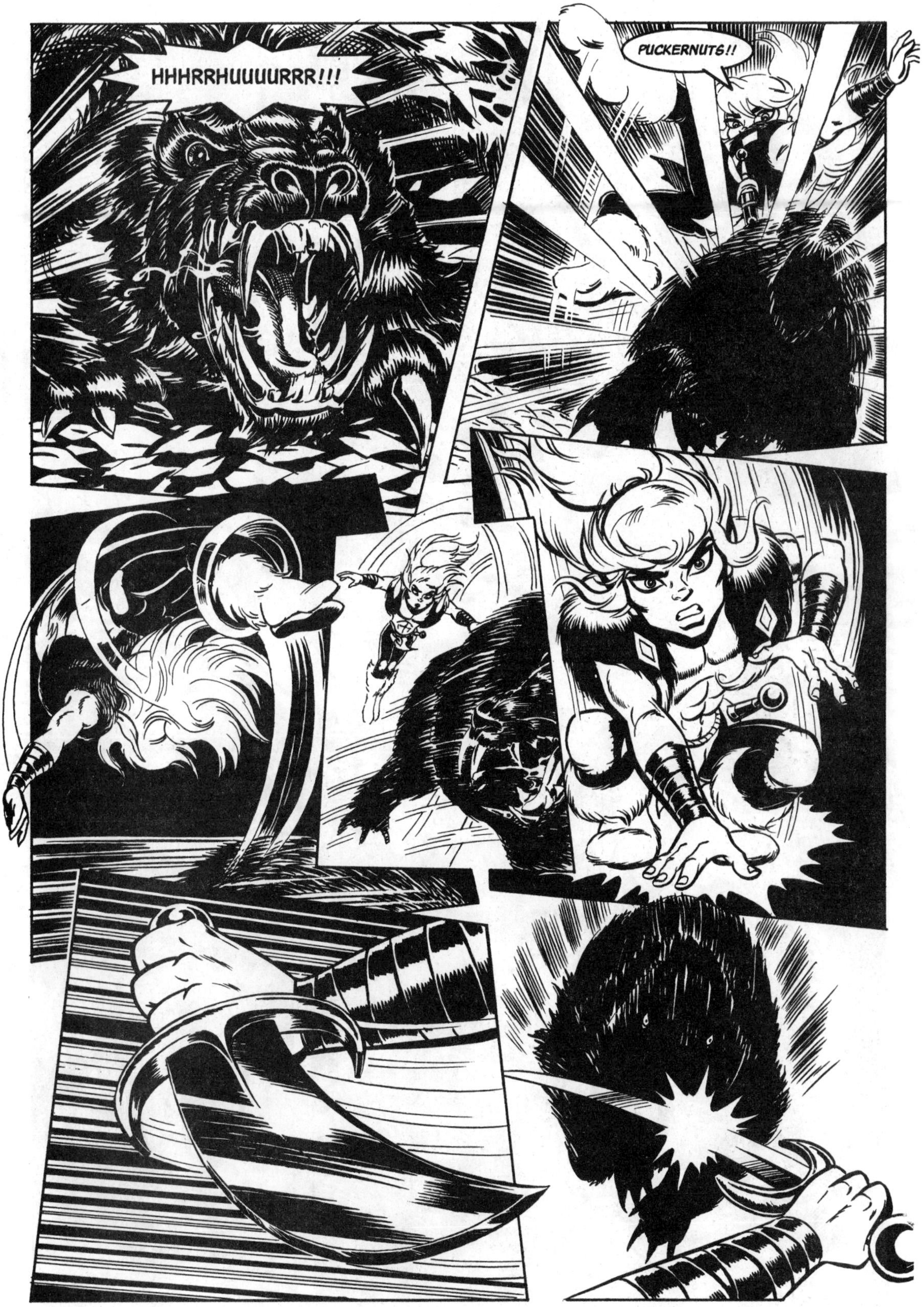
HHHRRHUUUURRR!!!
PUCKERNUTS!!

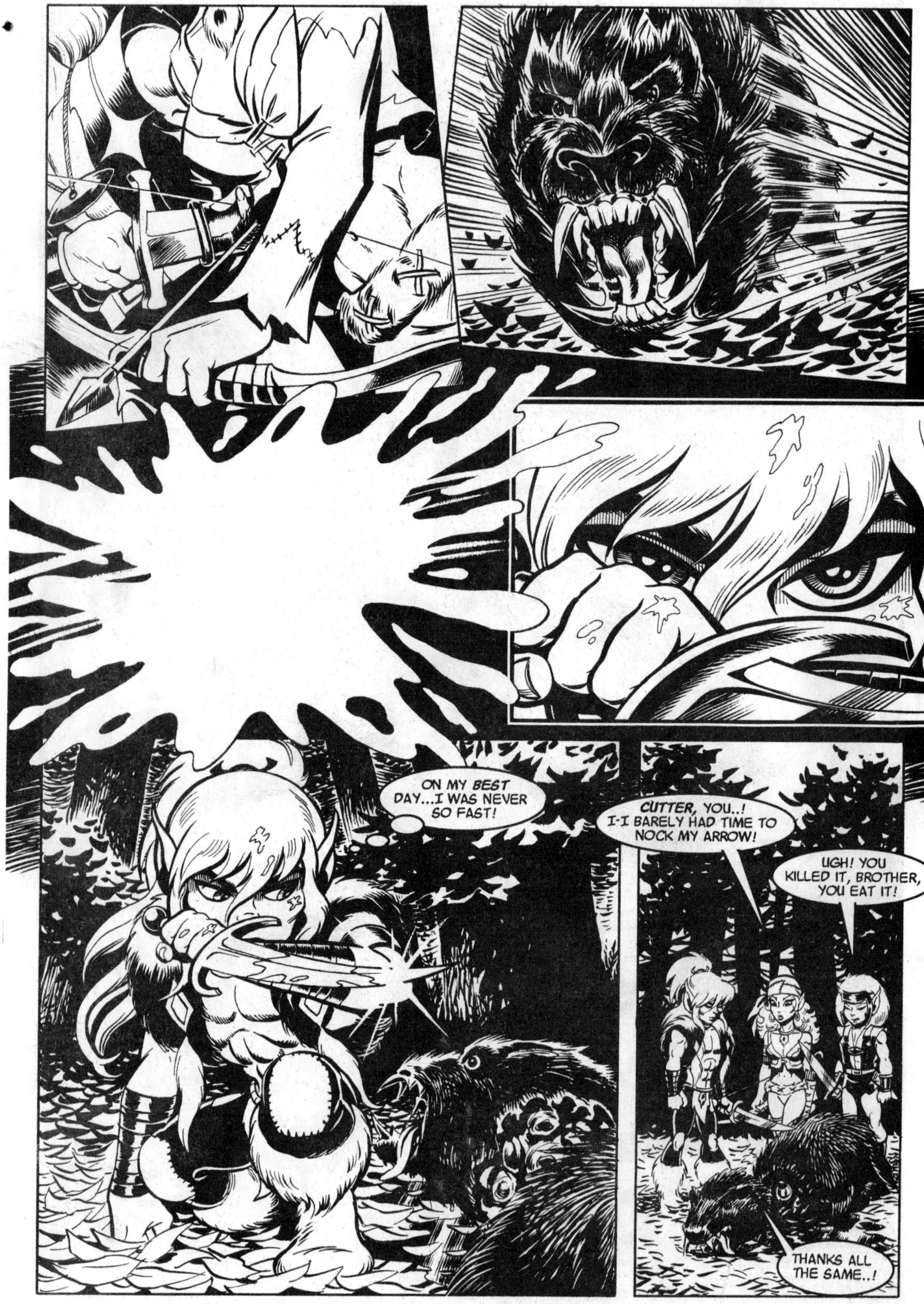
ON MY BEST DAY...I WAS NEVER SO FAST!
CUTTER, YOU..! I-I BARELY HAD TIME TO NOCK MY ARROW!
UGH! YOU KILLED IT, BROTHER, YOU EAT IT!
THANKS ALL THE SAME..!

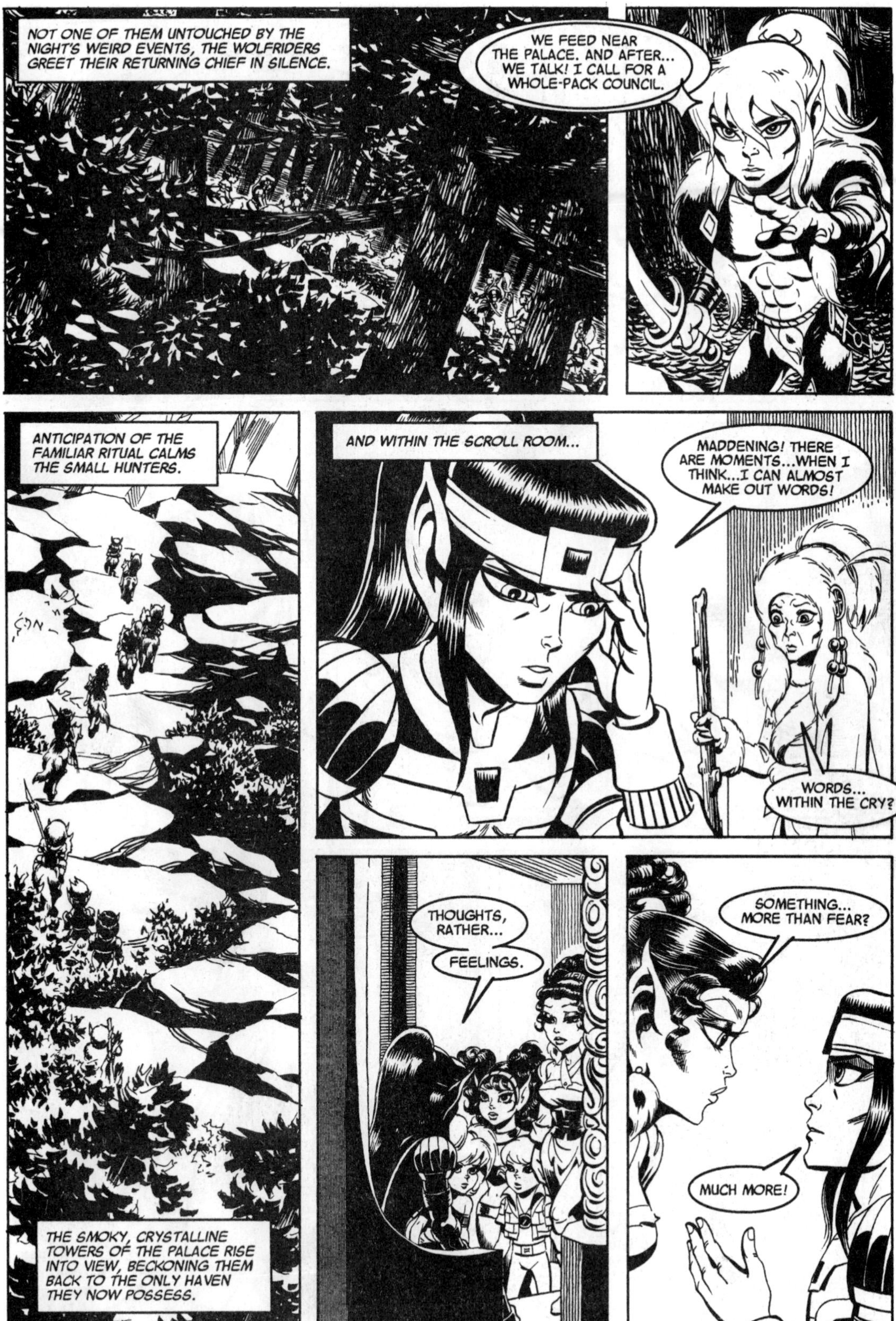
NOT ONE OF THEM UNTOUCHED BY THE NIGHT'S WEIRD EVENTS, THE WOLFRIDERS GREET THEIR RETURNING CHIEF IN SILENCE.
WE FEED NEAR THE PALACE. AND AFTER... WE TALK! I CALL FOR A WHOLE-PACK COUNCIL.
ANTICIPATION OF THE FAMILIAR RITUAL CALMS THE SMALL HUNTERS.
THE SMOKY, CRYSTALLINE TOWERS OF THE PALACE RISE INTO VIEW, BECKONING THEM BACK TO THE ONLY HAVEN THEY NOW POSSESS.
AND WITHIN THE SCROLL ROOM...
MADDENING! THERE ARE MOMENTS...WHEN I THINK...I CAN ALMOST MAKE OUT WORDS!
WORDS... WITHIN THE CRY?
THOUGHTS, RATHER...
FEELINGS.
SOMETHING... MORE THAN FEAR?
MUCH MORE!

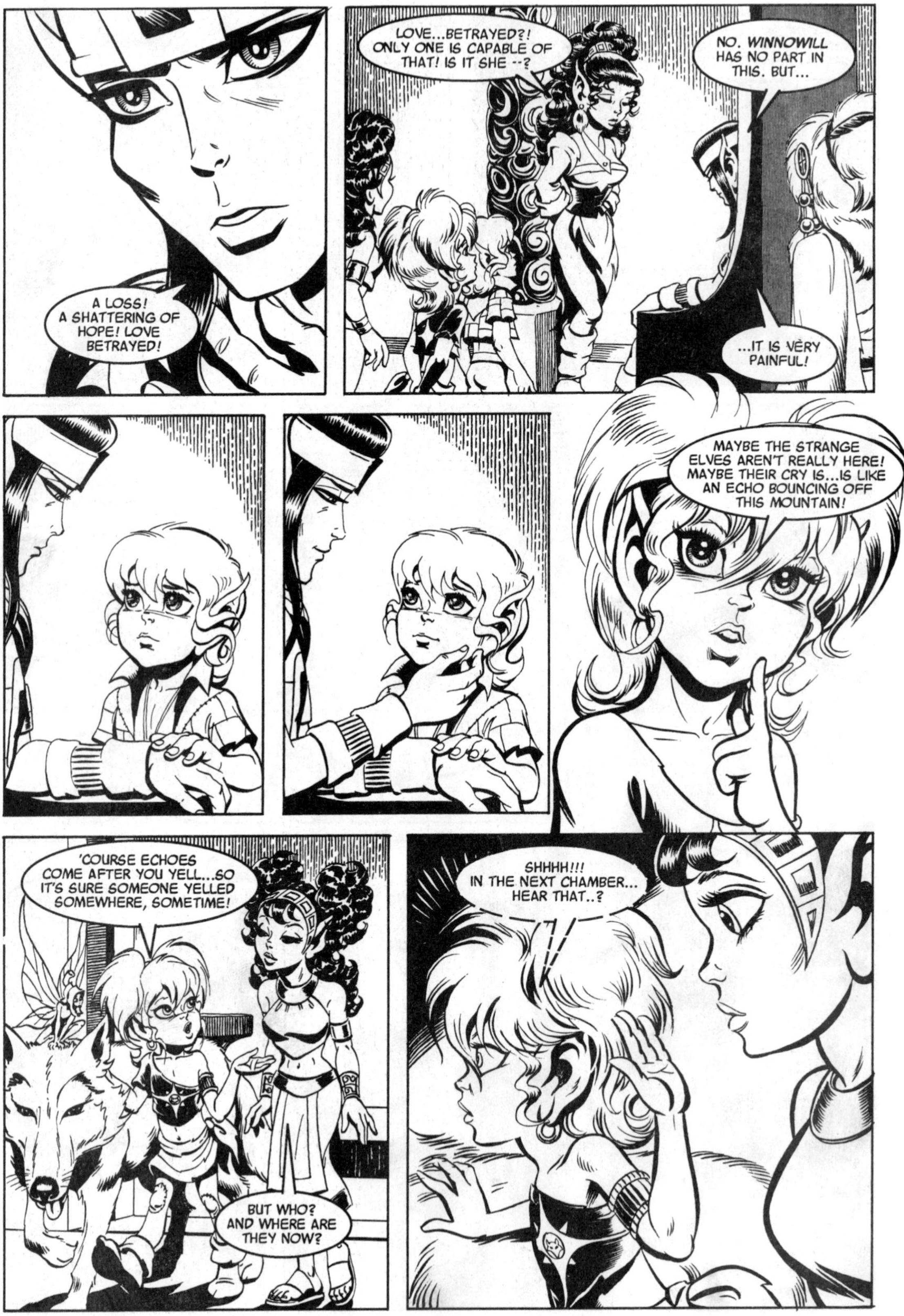
A LOSS! A SHATTERING OF HOPE! LOVE BETRAYED!
LOVE...BETRAYED?! ONLY ONE IS CAPABLE OF THAT! IS IT SHE --?
NO. WINNOWILL HAS NO PART IN THIS. BUT...
...IT IS VERY PAINFUL!
MAYBE THE STRANGE ELVES AREN'T REALLY HERE! MAYBE THEIR CRY IS...IS LIKE AN ECHO BOUNCING OFF THIS MOUNTAIN!
'COURSE ECHOES COME AFTER YOU YELL...SO IT'S SURE SOMEONE YELLED SOMEWHERE, SOMETIME!
BUT WHO? AND WHERE ARE THEY NOW?
SHHHH!!! IN THE NEXT CHAMBER... HEAR THAT..?

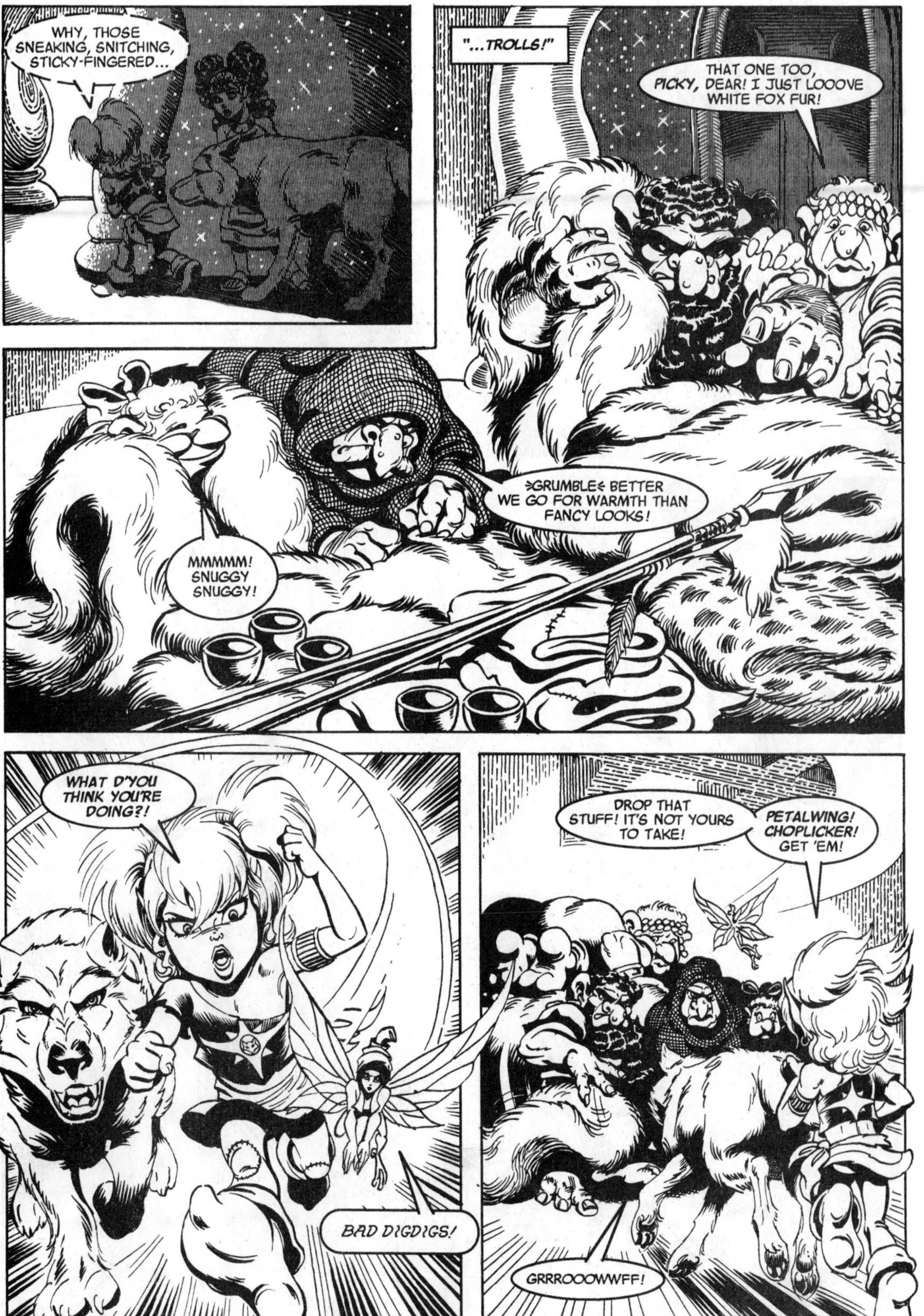
WHY, THOSE SNEAKING, SNITCHING, STICKY-FINGERED...
"...TROLLS!"
THAT ONE TOO, PICKY, DEAR! I JUST LOOOVE WHITE FOX FUR!
MMMMM! SNUGGY SNUGGY!
>GRUMBLE< BETTER WE GO FOR WARMTH THAN FANCY LOOKS!
WHAT D'YOU THINK YOU'RE DOING?!
BAD DIGDIGS!
DROP THAT STUFF! IT'S NOT YOURS TO TAKE!
PETALWING! CHOPLICKER! GET 'EM!
GRRROOOWWFF!

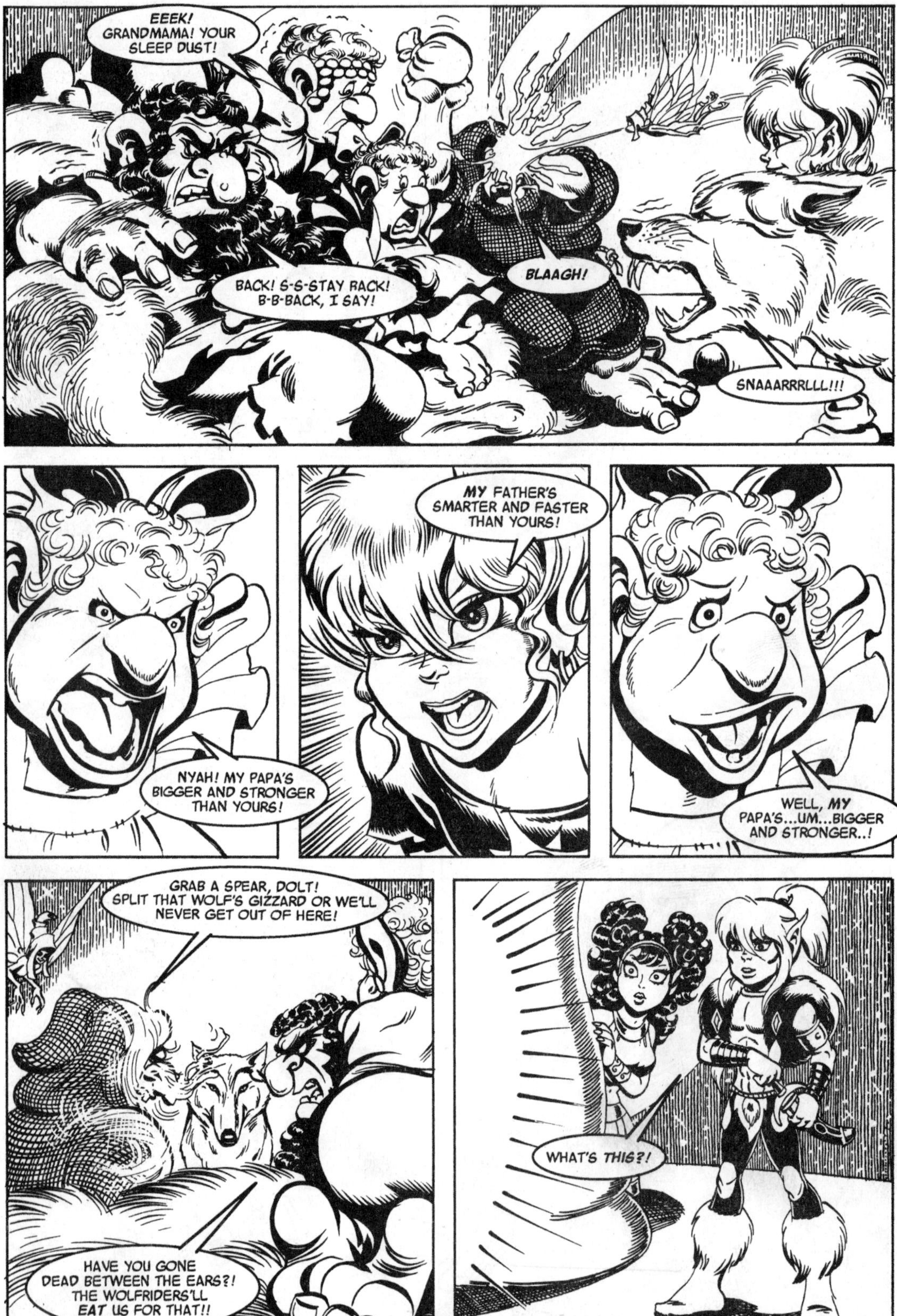
EEEK! GRANDMAMA! YOUR SLEEP DUST!
BACK! S-S-STAY BACK! B-B-BACK, I SAY!
BLAAGH!
SNAAARRRLLL!!!
NYAH! MY PAPA'S BIGGER AND STRONGER THAN YOURS!
MY FATHER'S SMARTER AND FASTER THAN YOURS!
WELL, MY PAPA'S...UM...BIGGER AND STRONGER..!
GRAB A SPEAR, DOLT! SPLIT THAT WOLF'S GIZZARD OR WE'LL NEVER GET OUT OF HERE!
HAVE YOU GONE DEAD BETWEEN THE EARS?! THE WOLFRIDERS'LL EAT US FOR THAT!!
WHAT'S THIS?!

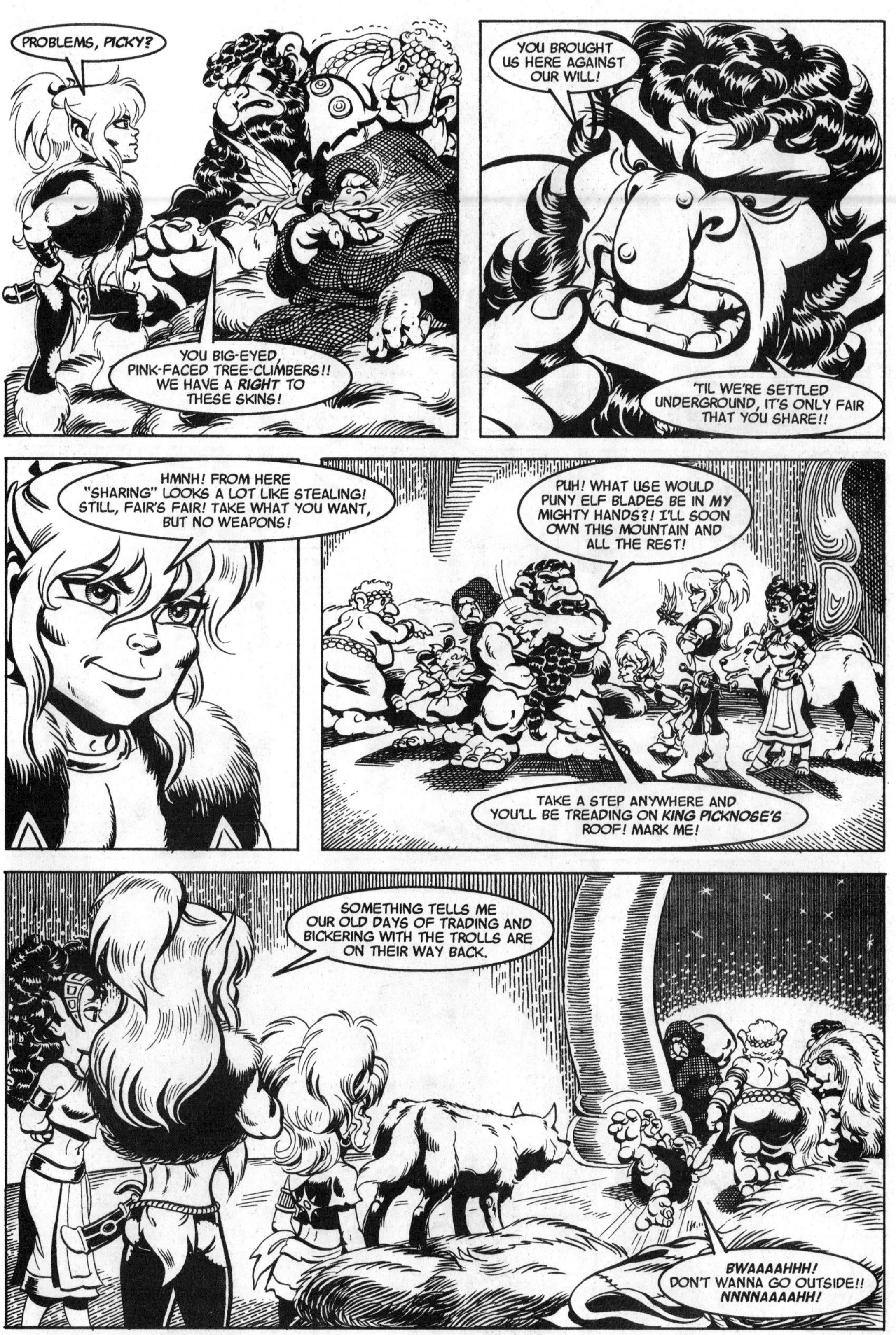
PROBLEMS, PICKY?
YOU BIG-EYED, PINK-FACED TREE-CLIMBERS!! WE HAVE A RIGHT TO THESE SKINS!
YOU BROUGHT US HERE AGAINST OUR WILL!
'TIL WE'RE SETTLED UNDERGROUND, IT'S ONLY FAIR THAT YOU SHARE!!
HMNH! FROM HERE "SHARING" LOOKS A LOT LIKE STEALING! STILL, FAIR'S FAIR! TAKE WHAT YOU WANT, BUT NO WEAPONS!
PUH! WHAT USE WOULD PUNY ELF BLADES BE IN MY MIGHTY HANDS?! I'LL SOON OWN THIS MOUNTAIN AND ALL THE REST!
TAKE A STEP ANYWHERE AND YOU'LL BE TREADING ON KING PICKNOSE'S ROOF! MARK ME!
SOMETHING TELLS ME OUR OLD DAYS OF TRADING AND BICKERING WITH THE TROLLS ARE ON THEIR WAY BACK.
BWAAAAHHH! DON'T WANNA GO OUTSIDE!! NNNNAAAAHH!

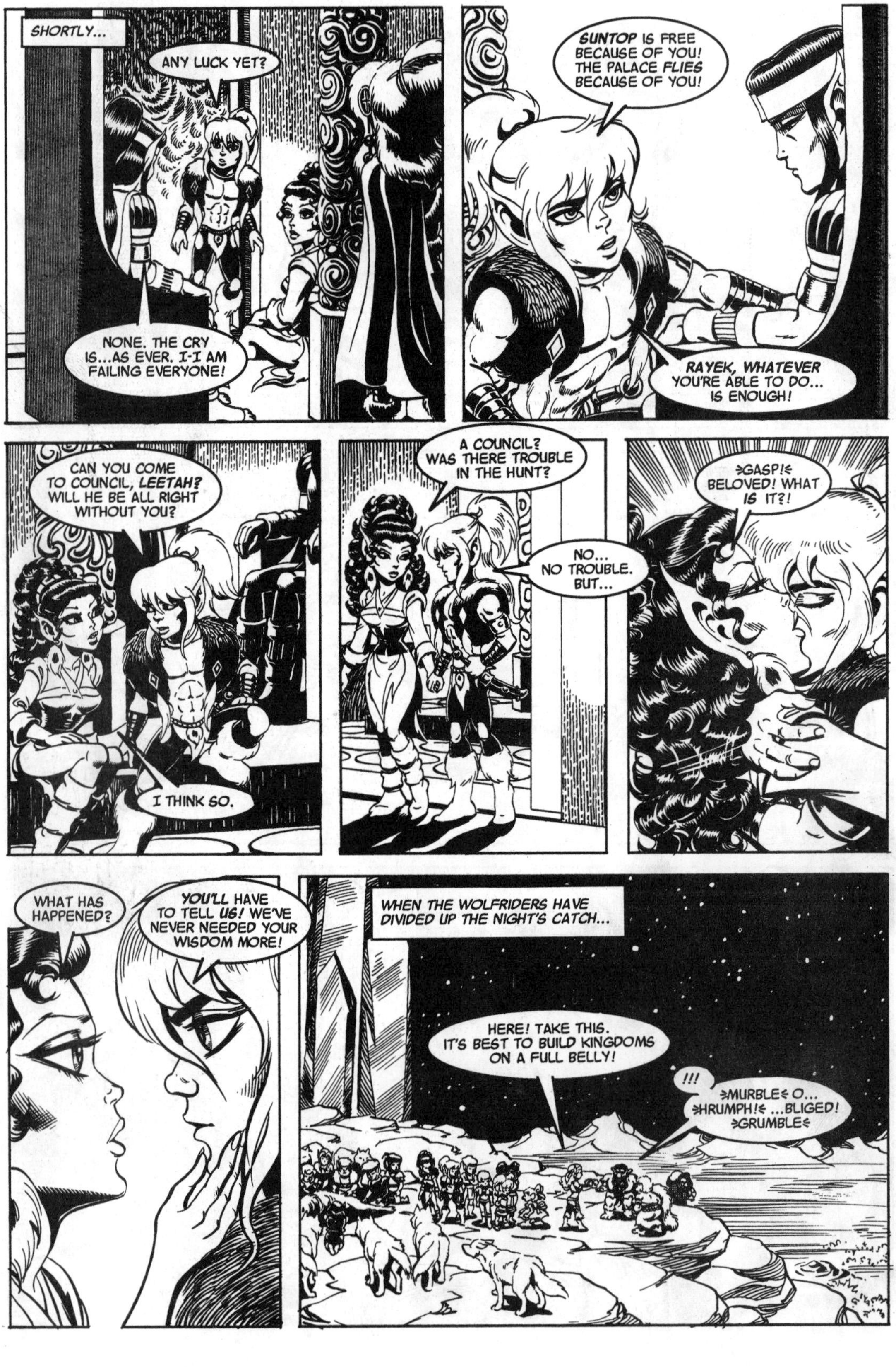
SHORTLY...
ANY LUCK YET?
NONE. THE CRY IS...AS EVER. I-I AM FAILING EVERYONE!
SUNTOP IS FREE BECAUSE OF YOU! THE PALACE FLIES BECAUSE OF YOU!
RAYEK, WHATEVER YOU'RE ABLE TO DO... IS ENOUGH!
CAN YOU COME TO COUNCIL, LEETAH? WILL HE BE ALL RIGHT WITHOUT YOU?
I THINK SO.
A COUNCIL? WAS THERE TROUBLE IN THE HUNT?
NO... NO TROUBLE. BUT...
≥GASP!≤ BELOVED! WHAT IS IT?!
WHAT HAS HAPPENED?
YOU'LL HAVE TO TELL US! WE'VE NEVER NEEDED YOUR WISDOM MORE!
WHEN THE WOLFRIDERS HAVE DIVIDED UP THE NIGHT'S CATCH...
HERE! TAKE THIS. IT'S BEST TO BUILD KINGDOMS ON A FULL BELLY!
!!!
≥MURBLE≤ O... ≥HRUMPH!≤ ...BLIGED! ≥GRUMBLE≤

AAAWWWAAAAAHHHH!!! NOOOO! WON'T GO! WON'T GO!
GIGGLE
WHIMPER WHIMPER
BAAAAWWWWW!!!!
BAAAWWW...
AAWW...
AWW...
AW.......
UNOBTRUSIVELY, THE HEALER OBSERVES THE WOLFRIDERS AS THEY FEAST AND NOTES NO OUTWARD SIGN OF CHANGE.
BUT LEETAH KNOWS WHAT SHE HERSELF HAS SENSED SINCE HER FIRST FLIGHT IN THE PALACE.
LATELY I HAVE FELT AN INCREASE OF POWER AND CLARITY. HAVE ANY OF YOU..?
WASHING OVER THE INCOMPLETE QUERY COMES A FLOOD OF ANSWERS.

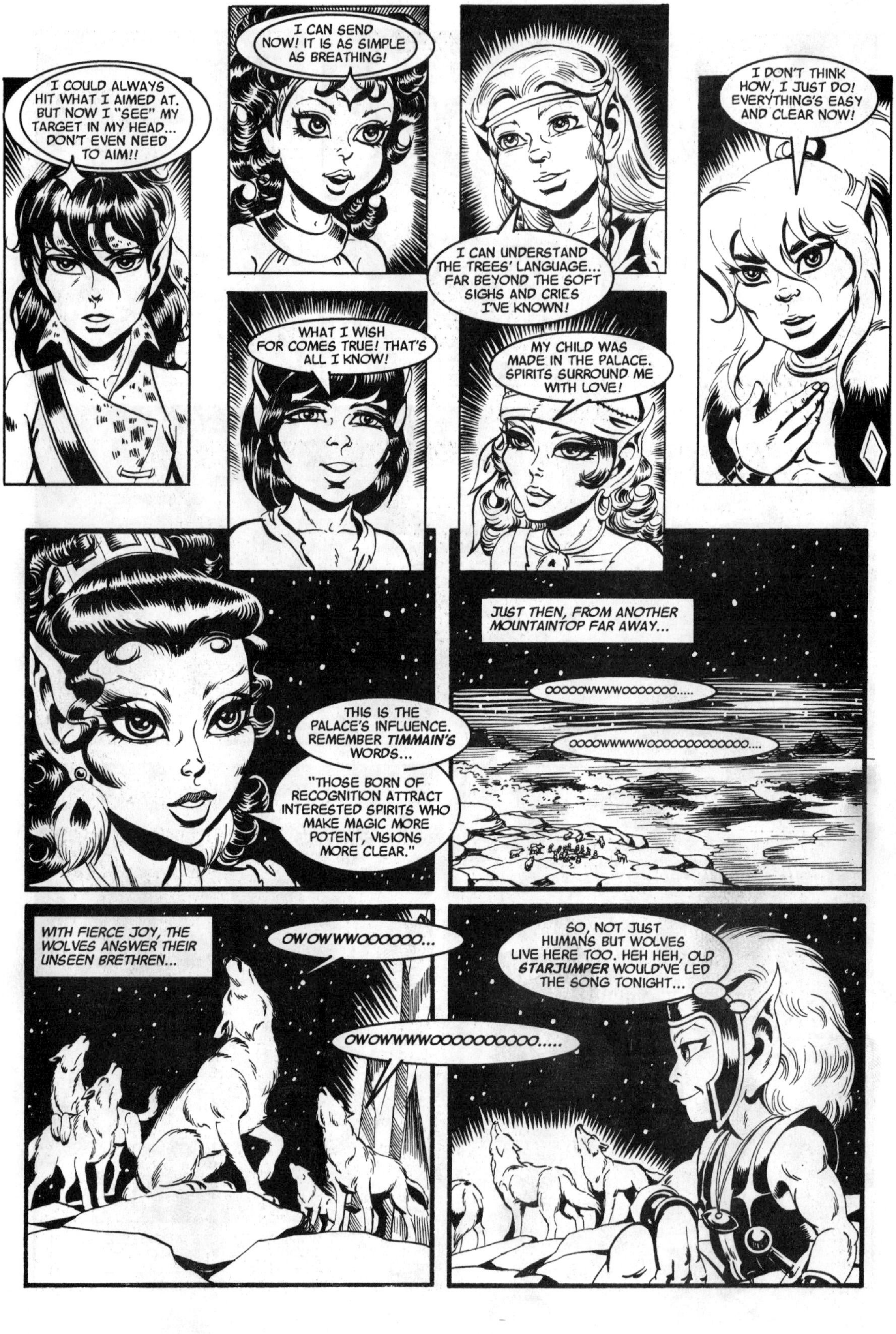

I COULD ALWAYS HIT WHAT I AIMED AT. BUT NOW I "SEE" MY TARGET IN MY HEAD... DON'T EVEN NEED TO AIM!!
I CAN SEND NOW! IT IS AS SIMPLE AS BREATHING!
I CAN UNDERSTAND THE TREES' LANGUAGE... FAR BEYOND THE SOFT SIGHS AND CRIES I'VE KNOWN!
I DON'T THINK HOW, I JUST DO! EVERYTHING'S EASY AND CLEAR NOW!
WHAT I WISH FOR COMES TRUE! THAT'S ALL I KNOW!
MY CHILD WAS MADE IN THE PALACE. SPIRITS SURROUND ME WITH LOVE!
THIS IS THE PALACE'S INFLUENCE. REMEMBER *TIMMAIN'S* WORDS...
"THOSE BORN OF RECOGNITION ATTRACT INTERESTED SPIRITS WHO MAKE MAGIC MORE POTENT, VISIONS MORE CLEAR."
JUST THEN, FROM ANOTHER MOUNTAINTOP FAR AWAY...
OOOOOWWWOOOOOOOO.....
OOOOWWWWWOOOOOOOOOOOOOO....
WITH FIERCE JOY, THE WOLVES ANSWER THEIR UNSEEN BRETHREN...
OWOWWWOOOOOO...
OWOWWWWOOOOOOOOOOO.....
SO, NOT JUST HUMANS BUT WOLVES LIVE HERE TOO. HEH HEH, OLD *STARJUMPER* WOULD'VE LED THE SONG TONIGHT...

 ?? EYES..!

 TIMMAIN!!

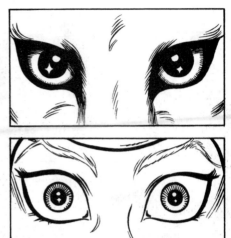

 SEEK ONE VOICE AMONG THE MANY!

 HUH??! YOU-YOU'RE SENDING!!

SEEK ONE VOICE..? YOU MEAN AMONG THE WOLVES..? OR US? OR WHAT?!

 ΞΞΞΞΞΞΞΞΞΞΞWWW!

 ≥GASP!≤

RAYEK! RAYEK'S SENT OUT THE CRY!!

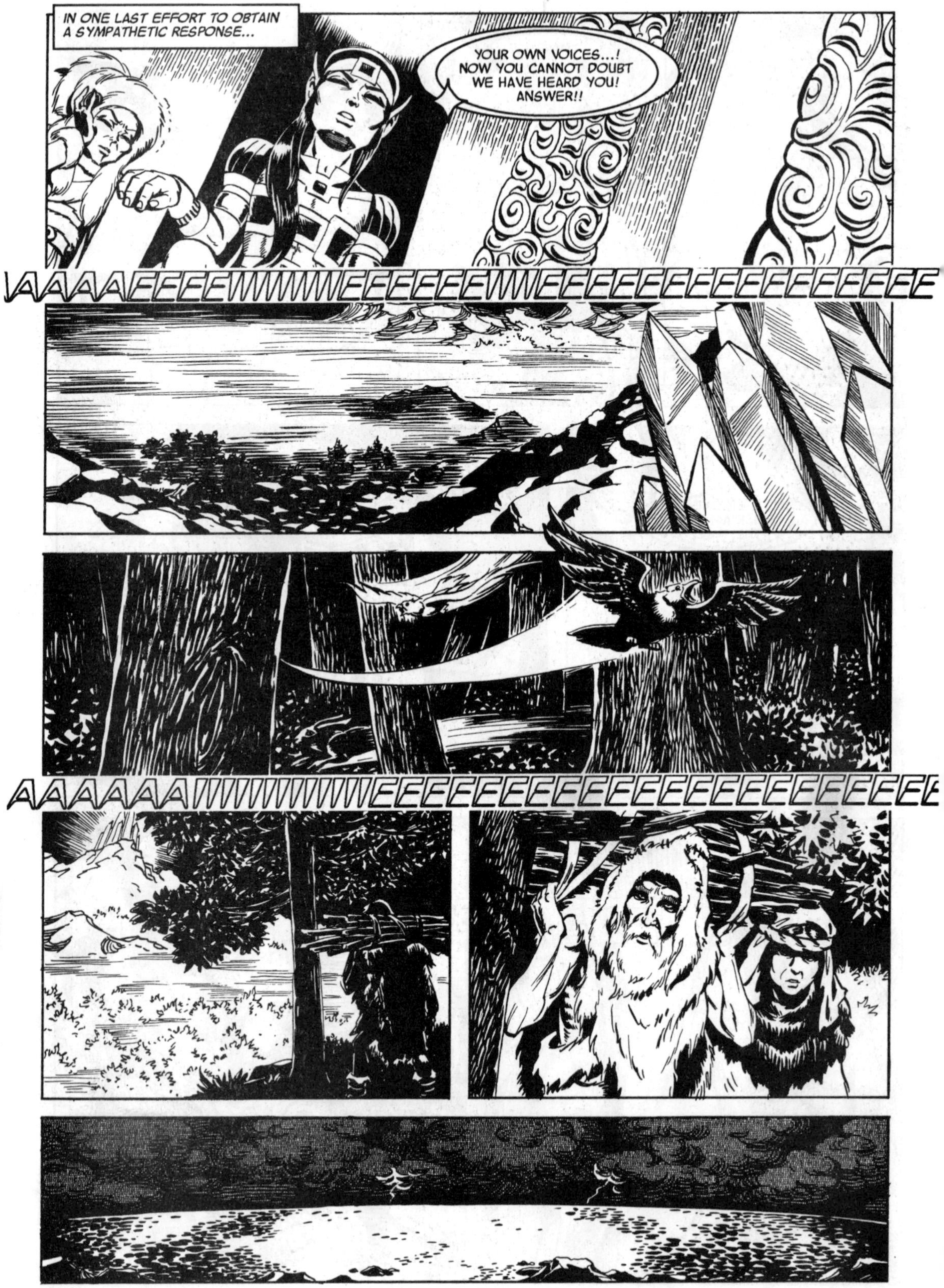
IN ONE LAST EFFORT TO OBTAIN A SYMPATHETIC RESPONSE...
YOUR OWN VOICES...! NOW YOU CANNOT DOUBT WE HAVE HEARD YOU! ANSWER!!
AAAAEEEEWWWWWEEEEEEWWEEEEEEEEEEEEEEEE
AAAAAAIIIIIIIIIIIIIIIIEEEEEEEEEEEEEEEEEEEE

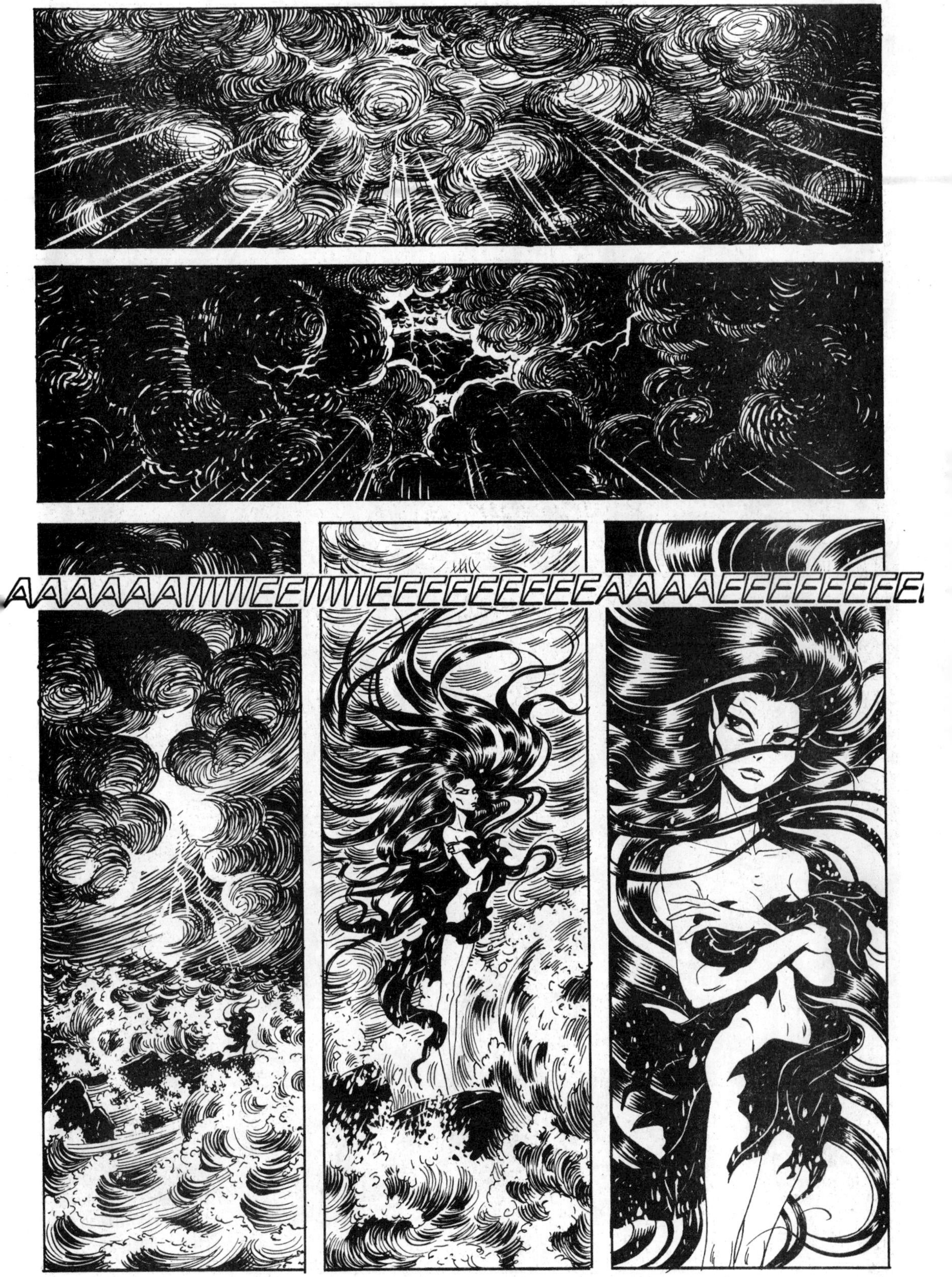
AAAAAAIIIIIEEIIIIIEEEEEEEEEEAAAAEEEEEEEEEE

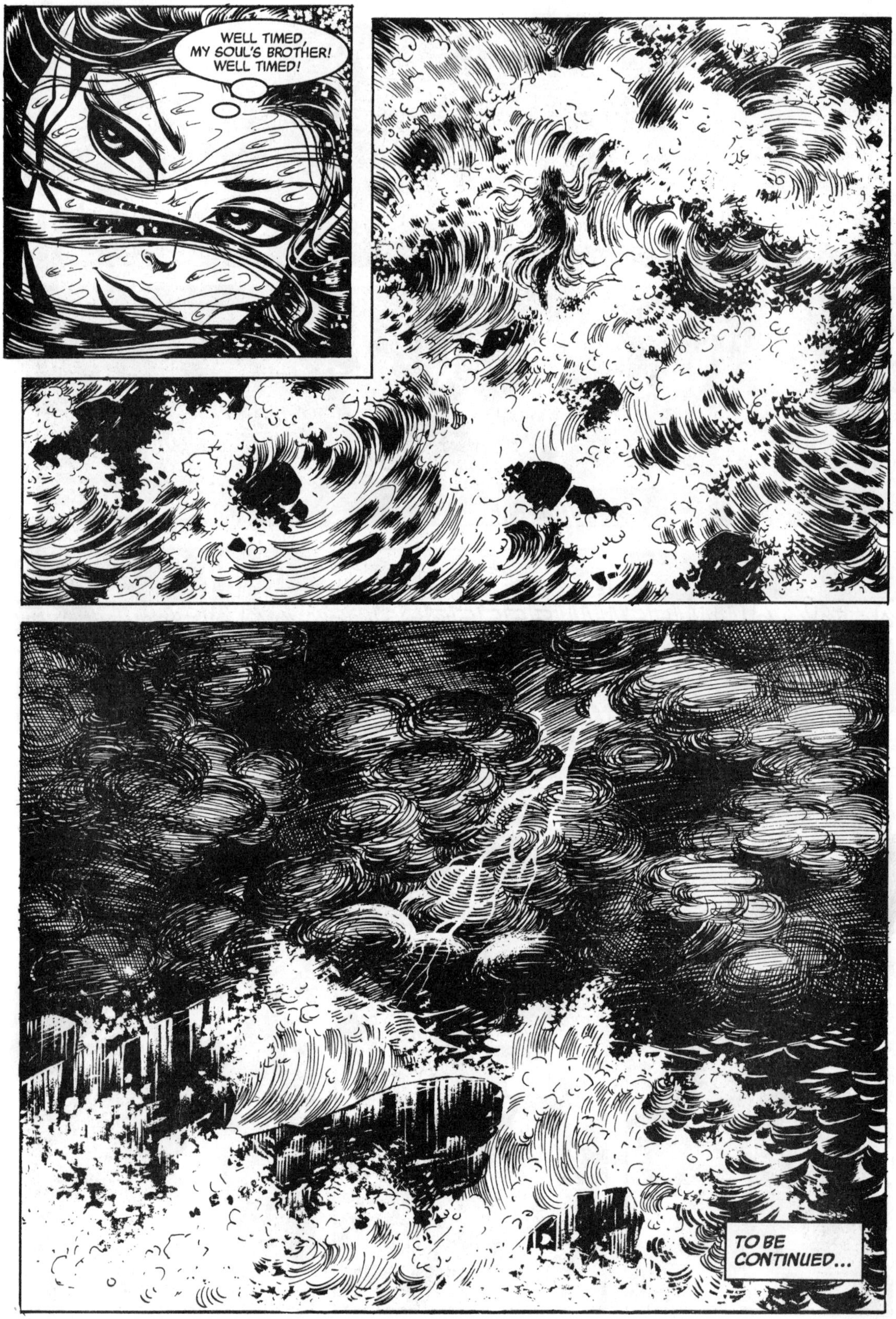
WELL TIMED, MY SOUL'S BROTHER! WELL TIMED!
TO BE CONTINUED...

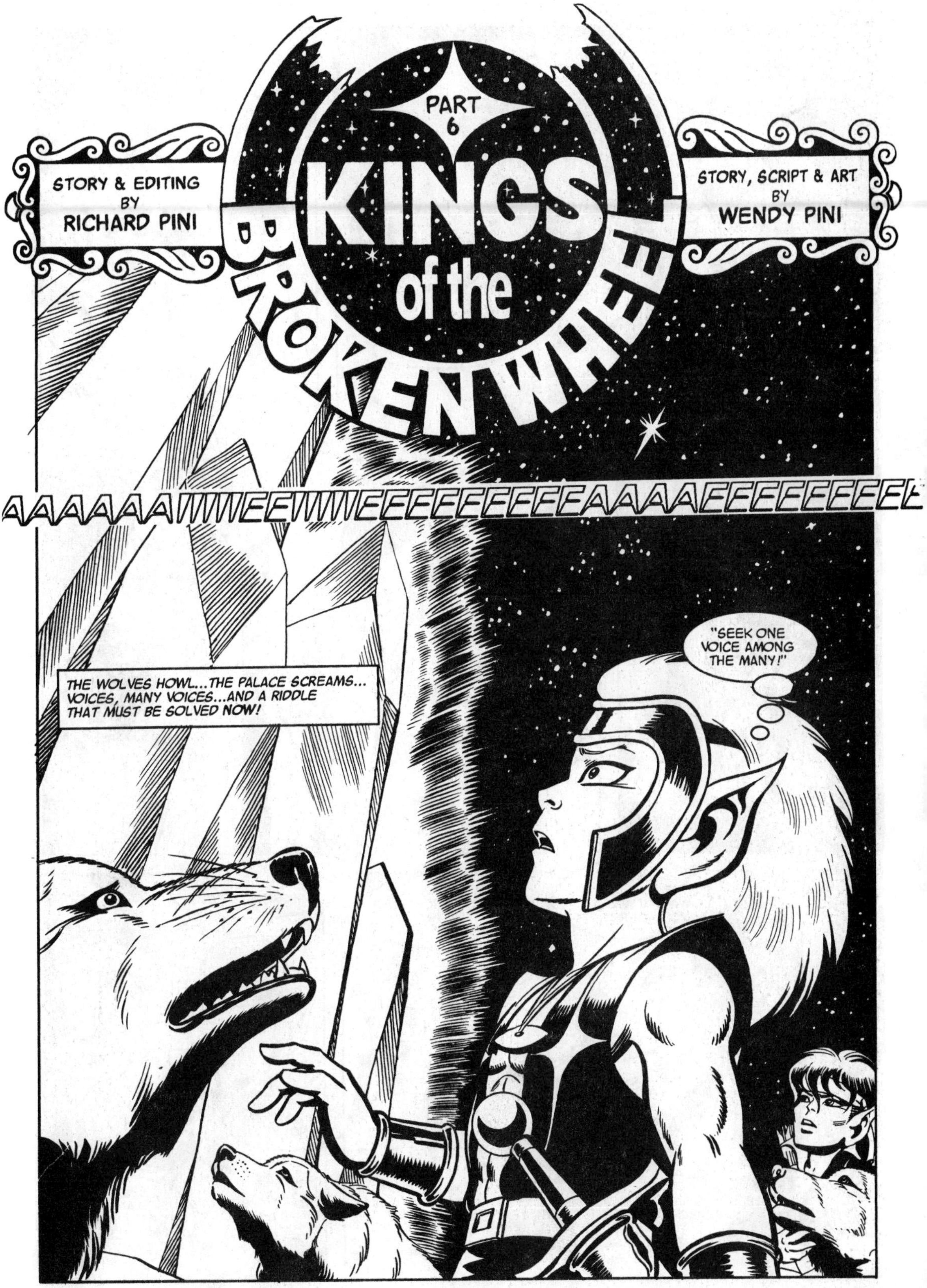
PART 6
KINGS of the BROKEN WHEEL
STORY & EDITING BY RICHARD PINI
STORY, SCRIPT & ART BY WENDY PINI
AAAAAAIIIIIEEIIIIIEEEEEEEEEEEEAAAAAEEEEEEEEEEEE
THE WOLVES HOWL...THE PALACE SCREAMS... VOICES, MANY VOICES...AND A RIDDLE THAT MUST BE SOLVED NOW!
"SEEK ONE VOICE AMONG THE MANY!"

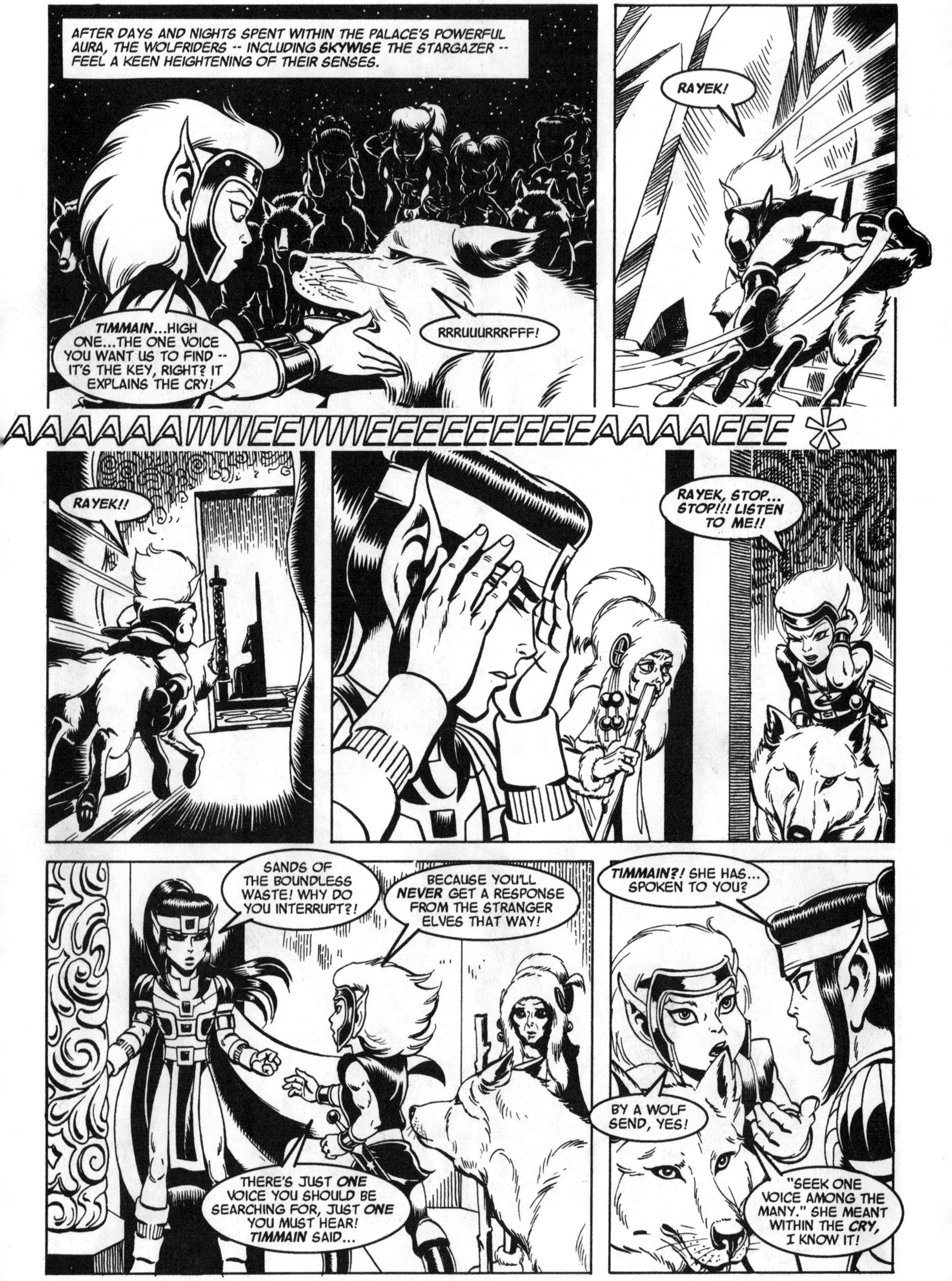

AFTER DAYS AND NIGHTS SPENT WITHIN THE PALACE'S POWERFUL AURA, THE WOLFRIDERS -- INCLUDING SKYWISE THE STARGAZER -- FEEL A KEEN HEIGHTENING OF THEIR SENSES.
TIMMAIN...HIGH ONE...THE ONE VOICE YOU WANT US TO FIND -- IT'S THE KEY, RIGHT? IT EXPLAINS THE CRY!
RRRUUURRRFFF!
RAYEK!
AAAAAAIIIIIIEEIIIIIIEEEEEEEEEEEEAAAAAEEE *
RAYEK!!
RAYEK, STOP... STOP!!! LISTEN TO ME!!
SANDS OF THE BOUNDLESS WASTE! WHY DO YOU INTERRUPT?!
BECAUSE YOU'LL NEVER GET A RESPONSE FROM THE STRANGER ELVES THAT WAY!
THERE'S JUST ONE VOICE YOU SHOULD BE SEARCHING FOR, JUST ONE YOU MUST HEAR! TIMMAIN SAID...
TIMMAIN?! SHE HAS... SPOKEN TO YOU?
BY A WOLF SEND, YES!
"SEEK ONE VOICE AMONG THE MANY." SHE MEANT WITHIN THE CRY, I KNOW IT!

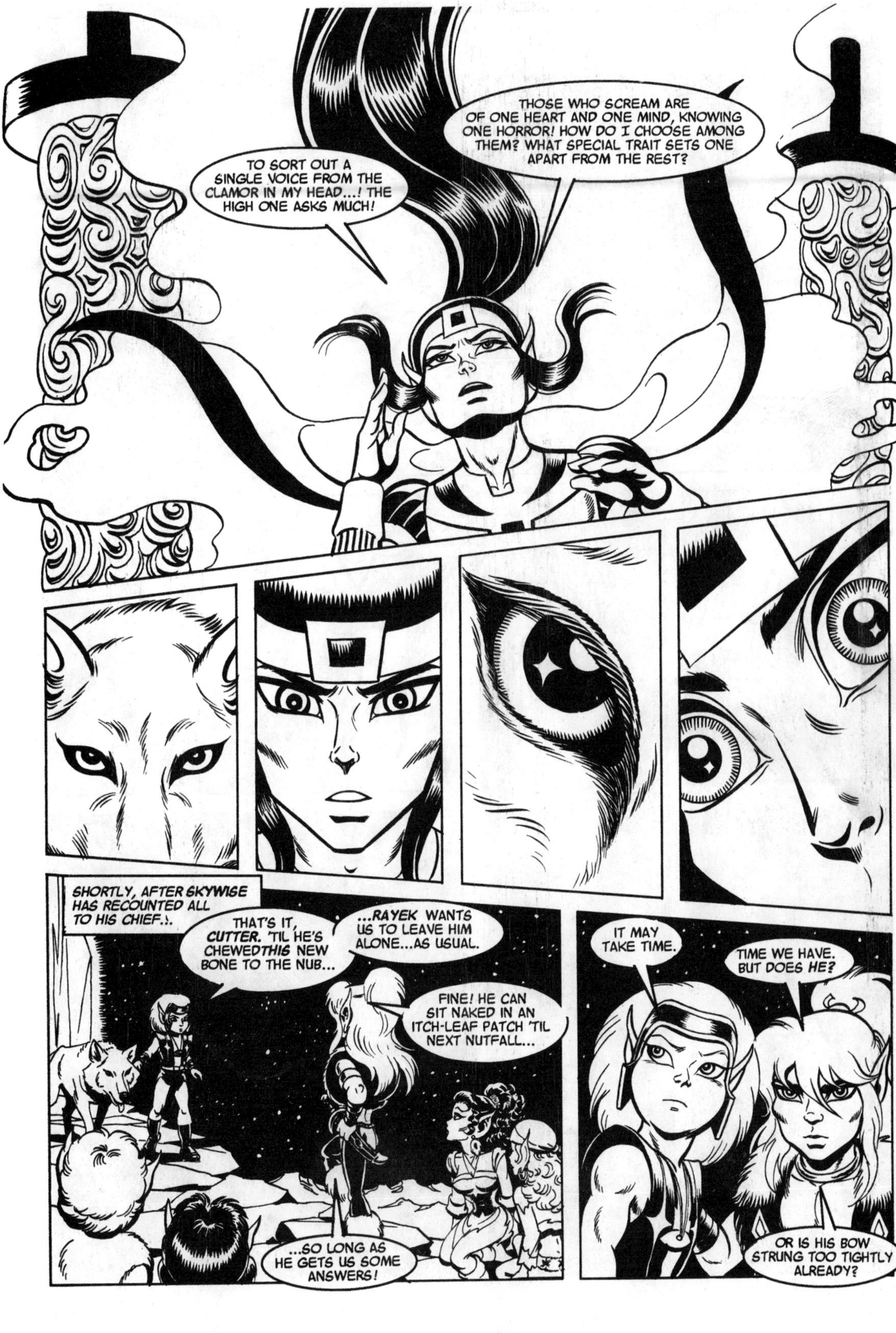
TO SORT OUT A SINGLE VOICE FROM THE CLAMOR IN MY HEAD...! THE HIGH ONE ASKS MUCH!
THOSE WHO SCREAM ARE OF ONE HEART AND ONE MIND, KNOWING ONE HORROR! HOW DO I CHOOSE AMONG THEM? WHAT SPECIAL TRAIT SETS ONE APART FROM THE REST?
SHORTLY, AFTER SKYWISE HAS RECOUNTED ALL TO HIS CHIEF...
THAT'S IT, CUTTER. 'TIL HE'S CHEWED THIS NEW BONE TO THE NUB...
...RAYEK WANTS US TO LEAVE HIM ALONE...AS USUAL.
FINE! HE CAN SIT NAKED IN AN ITCH-LEAF PATCH 'TIL NEXT NUTFALL...
...SO LONG AS HE GETS US SOME ANSWERS!
IT MAY TAKE TIME.
TIME WE HAVE. BUT DOES HE?
OR IS HIS BOW STRUNG TOO TIGHTLY ALREADY?

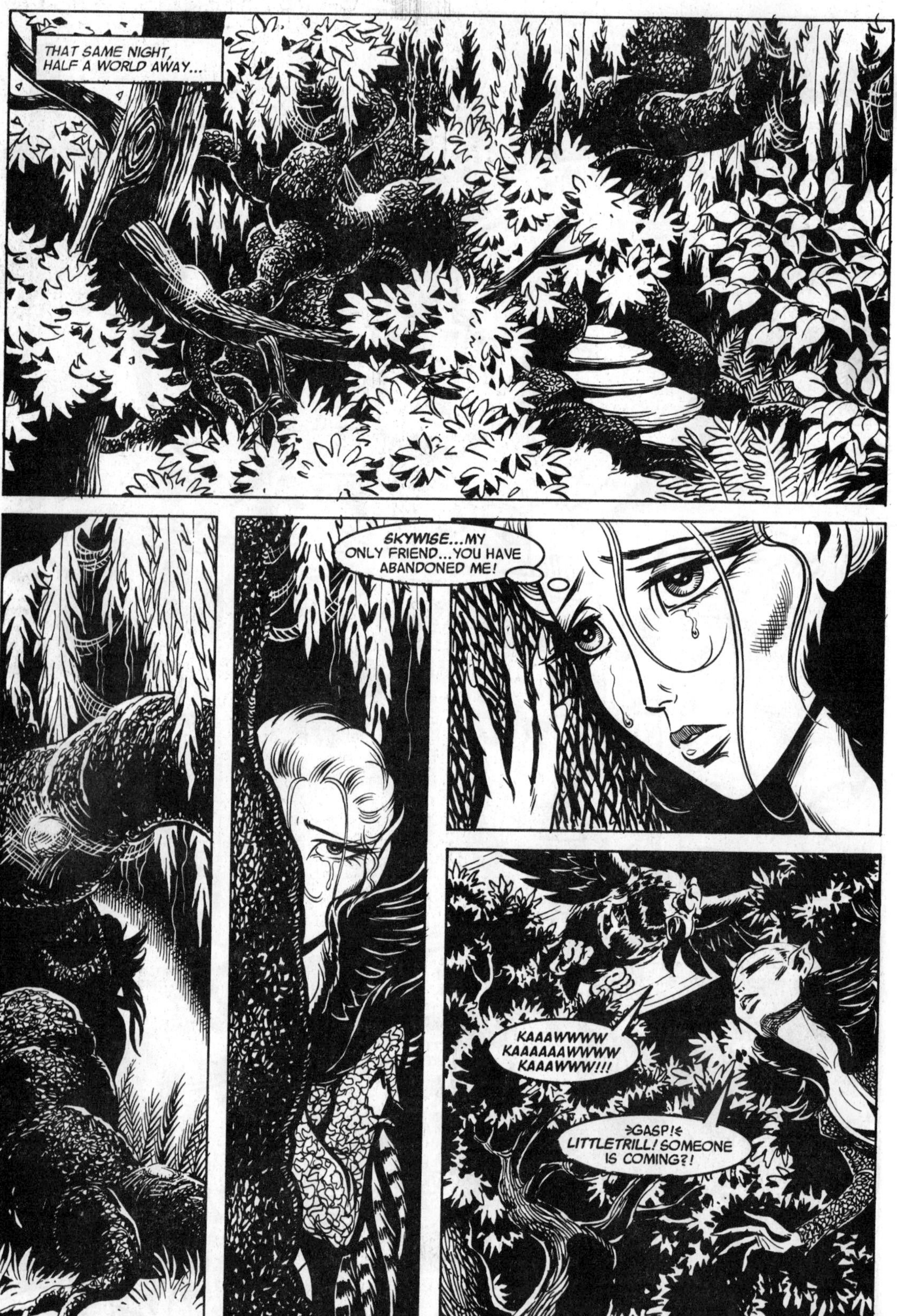
THAT SAME NIGHT, HALF A WORLD AWAY...
SKYWISE...MY ONLY FRIEND...YOU HAVE ABANDONED ME!
KAAAWWWW KAAAAAAWWWW KAAAWW!!!
GASP! LITTLETRILL! SOMEONE IS COMING?!

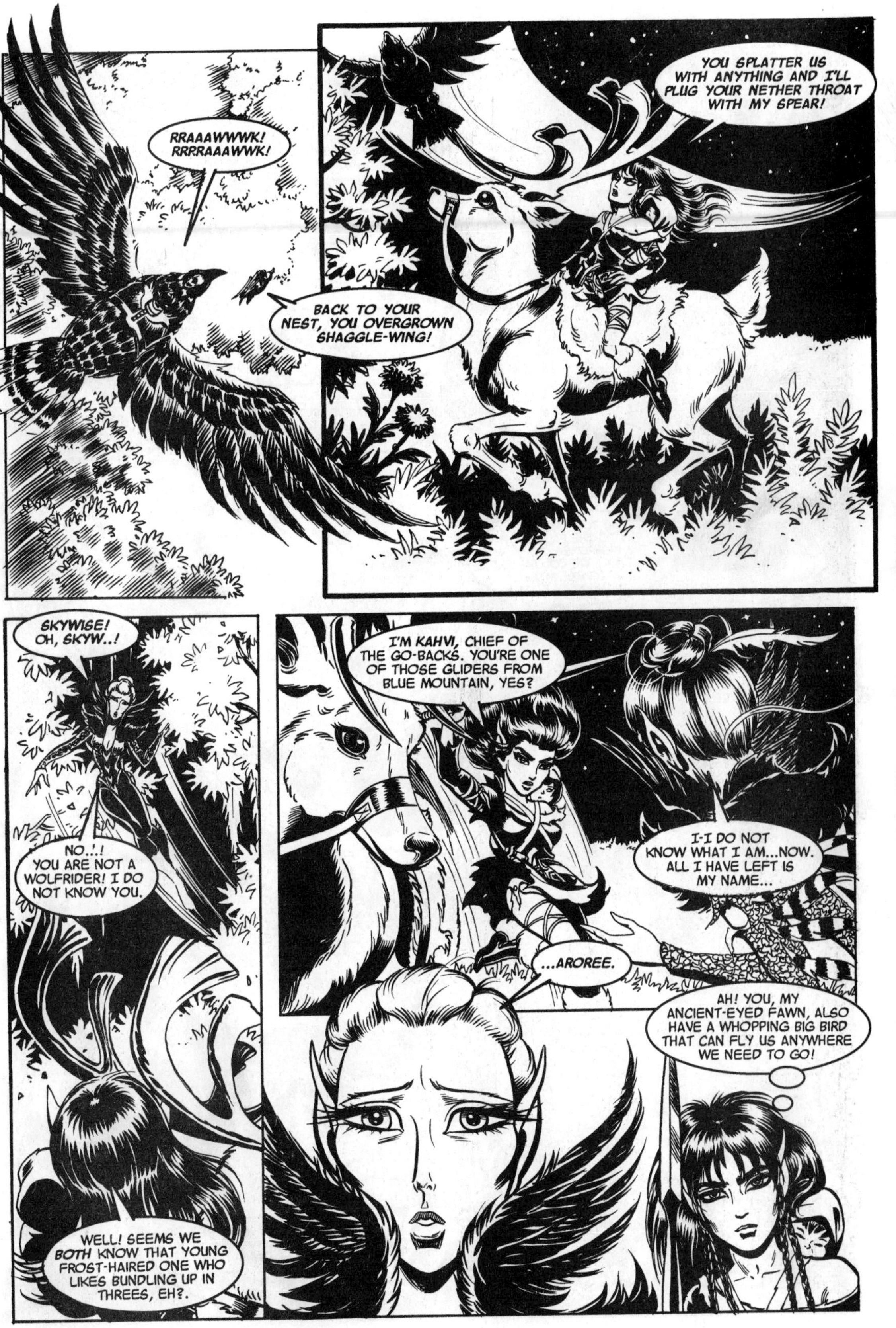
RRAAAWWWK! RRRRAAAWWK!
BACK TO YOUR NEST, YOU OVERGROWN SHAGGLE-WING!
YOU SPLATTER US WITH ANYTHING AND I'LL PLUG YOUR NETHER THROAT WITH MY SPEAR!
SKYWISE! OH, SKYW..!
NO..! YOU ARE NOT A WOLFRIDER! I DO NOT KNOW YOU.
I'M KAHVI, CHIEF OF THE GO-BACKS. YOU'RE ONE OF THOSE GLIDERS FROM BLUE MOUNTAIN, YES?
I-I DO NOT KNOW WHAT I AM...NOW. ALL I HAVE LEFT IS MY NAME...
...AROREE.
AH! YOU, MY ANCIENT-EYED FAWN, ALSO HAVE A WHOPPING BIG BIRD THAT CAN FLY US ANYWHERE WE NEED TO GO!
WELL! SEEMS WE BOTH KNOW THAT YOUNG FROST-HAIRED ONE WHO LIKES BUNDLING UP IN THREES, EH?.

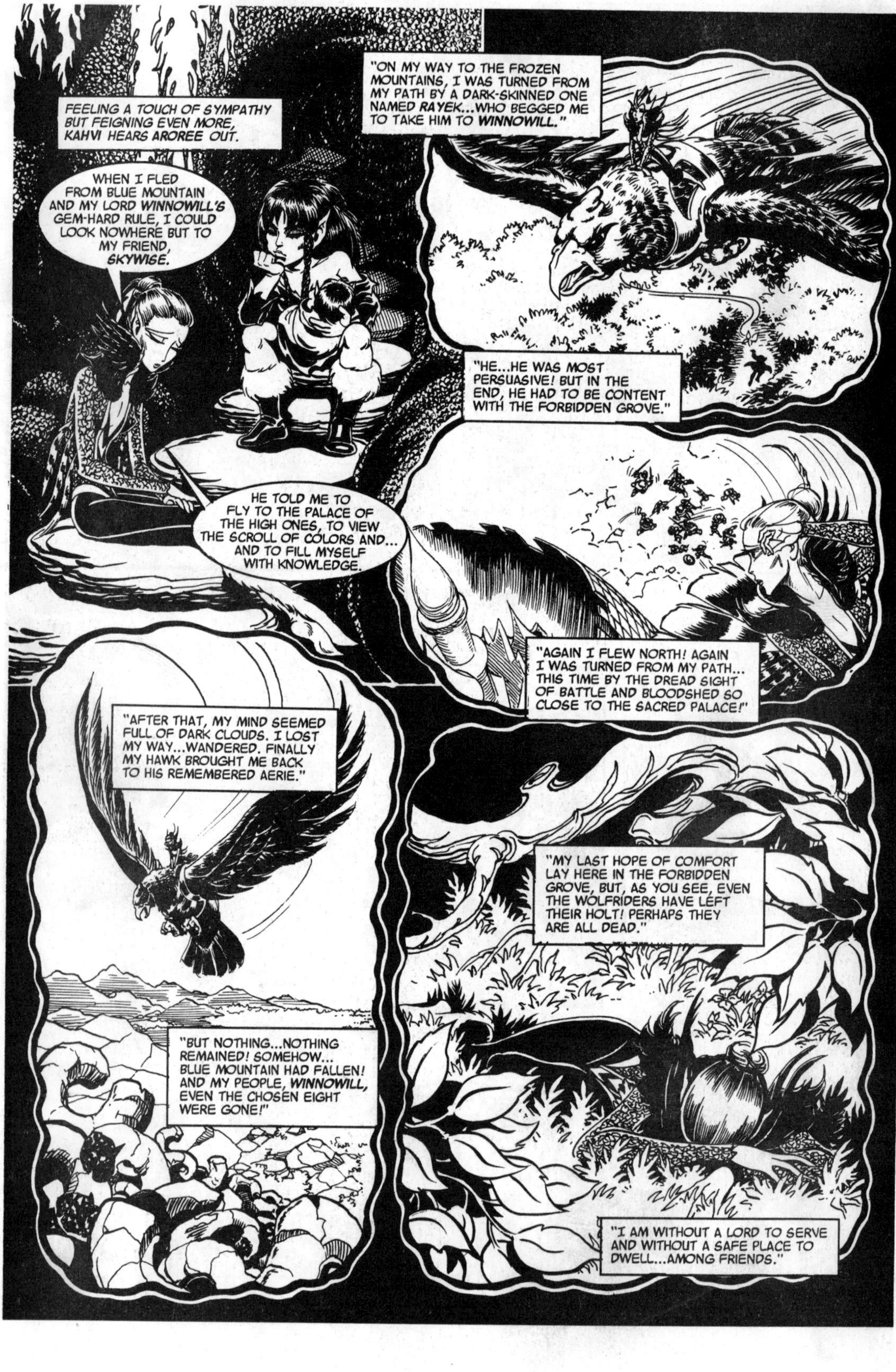
FEELING A TOUCH OF SYMPATHY BUT FEIGNING EVEN MORE, KAHVI HEARS AROREE OUT.
WHEN I FLED FROM BLUE MOUNTAIN AND MY LORD WINNOWILL'S GEM-HARD RULE, I COULD LOOK NOWHERE BUT TO MY FRIEND, SKYWISE.
HE TOLD ME TO FLY TO THE PALACE OF THE HIGH ONES, TO VIEW THE SCROLL OF COLORS AND... AND TO FILL MYSELF WITH KNOWLEDGE.
"ON MY WAY TO THE FROZEN MOUNTAINS, I WAS TURNED FROM MY PATH BY A DARK-SKINNED ONE NAMED RAYEK...WHO BEGGED ME TO TAKE HIM TO WINNOWILL."
"HE...HE WAS MOST PERSUASIVE! BUT IN THE END, HE HAD TO BE CONTENT WITH THE FORBIDDEN GROVE."
"AGAIN I FLEW NORTH! AGAIN I WAS TURNED FROM MY PATH... THIS TIME BY THE DREAD SIGHT OF BATTLE AND BLOODSHED SO CLOSE TO THE SACRED PALACE!"
"AFTER THAT, MY MIND SEEMED FULL OF DARK CLOUDS. I LOST MY WAY...WANDERED. FINALLY MY HAWK BROUGHT ME BACK TO HIS REMEMBERED AERIE."
"BUT NOTHING...NOTHING REMAINED! SOMEHOW... BLUE MOUNTAIN HAD FALLEN! AND MY PEOPLE, WINNOWILL, EVEN THE CHOSEN EIGHT WERE GONE!"
"MY LAST HOPE OF COMFORT LAY HERE IN THE FORBIDDEN GROVE, BUT, AS YOU SEE, EVEN THE WOLFRIDERS HAVE LEFT THEIR HOLT! PERHAPS THEY ARE ALL DEAD."
"I AM WITHOUT A LORD TO SERVE AND WITHOUT A SAFE PLACE TO DWELL...AMONG FRIENDS."

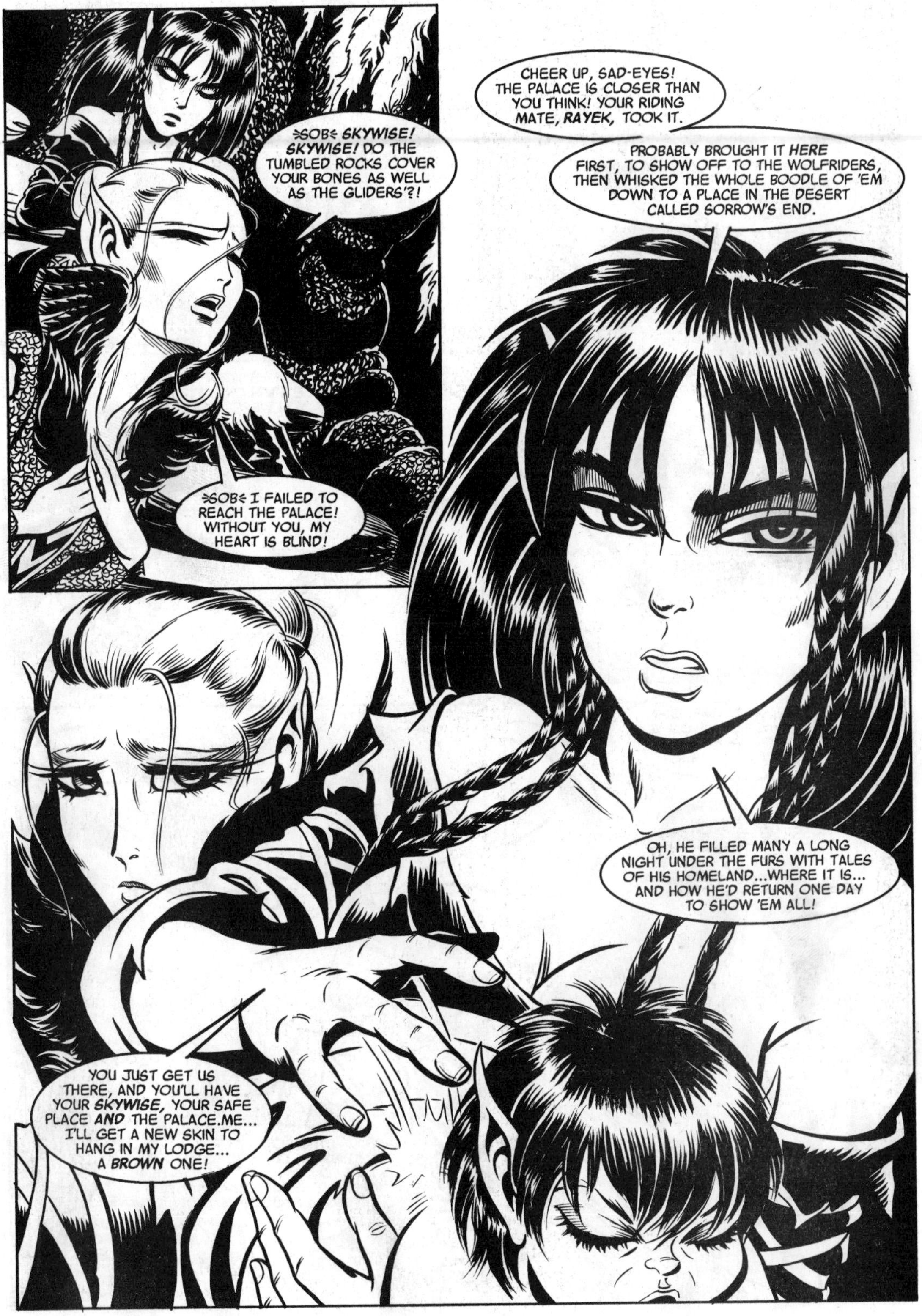
≽SOB≼ SKYWISE! SKYWISE! DO THE TUMBLED ROCKS COVER YOUR BONES AS WELL AS THE GLIDERS'?!
≽SOB≼ I FAILED TO REACH THE PALACE! WITHOUT YOU, MY HEART IS BLIND!
CHEER UP, SAD-EYES! THE PALACE IS CLOSER THAN YOU THINK! YOUR RIDING MATE, RAYEK, TOOK IT.
PROBABLY BROUGHT IT HERE FIRST, TO SHOW OFF TO THE WOLFRIDERS, THEN WHISKED THE WHOLE BOODLE OF 'EM DOWN TO A PLACE IN THE DESERT CALLED SORROW'S END.
OH, HE FILLED MANY A LONG NIGHT UNDER THE FURS WITH TALES OF HIS HOMELAND...WHERE IT IS... AND HOW HE'D RETURN ONE DAY TO SHOW 'EM ALL!
YOU JUST GET US THERE, AND YOU'LL HAVE YOUR SKYWISE, YOUR SAFE PLACE AND THE PALACE.ME... I'LL GET A NEW SKIN TO HANG IN MY LODGE... A BROWN ONE!

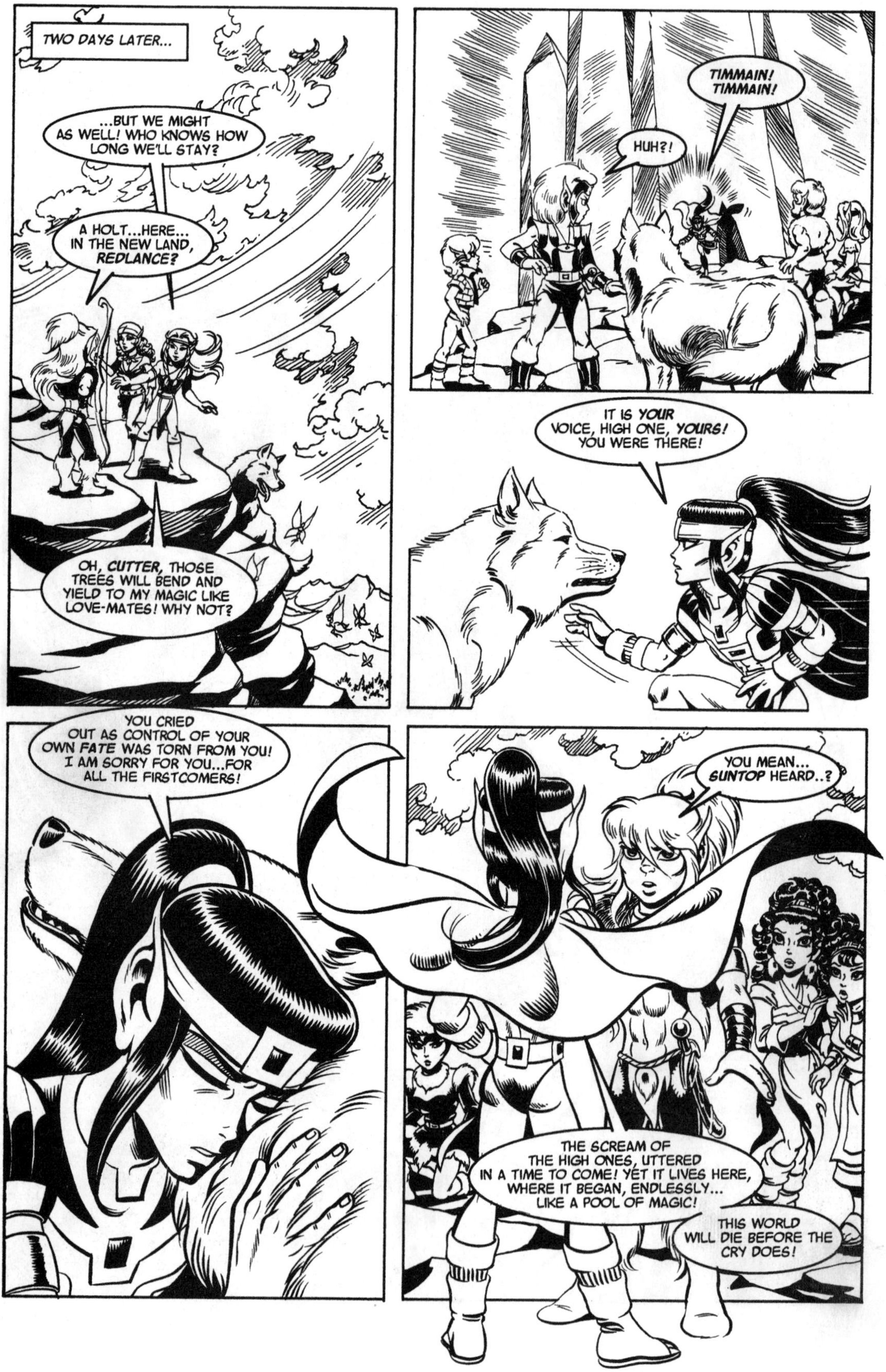

TWO DAYS LATER...
A HOLT...HERE... IN THE NEW LAND, REDLANCE?
...BUT WE MIGHT AS WELL! WHO KNOWS HOW LONG WE'LL STAY?
OH, CUTTER, THOSE TREES WILL BEND AND YIELD TO MY MAGIC LIKE LOVE-MATES! WHY NOT?
TIMMAIN! TIMMAIN!
HUH?!
IT IS YOUR VOICE, HIGH ONE, YOURS! YOU WERE THERE!
YOU CRIED OUT AS CONTROL OF YOUR OWN FATE WAS TORN FROM YOU! I AM SORRY FOR YOU...FOR ALL THE FIRSTCOMERS!
YOU MEAN... SUNTOP HEARD..?
THE SCREAM OF THE HIGH ONES, UTTERED IN A TIME TO COME! YET IT LIVES HERE, WHERE IT BEGAN, ENDLESSLY... LIKE A POOL OF MAGIC!
THIS WORLD WILL DIE BEFORE THE CRY DOES!

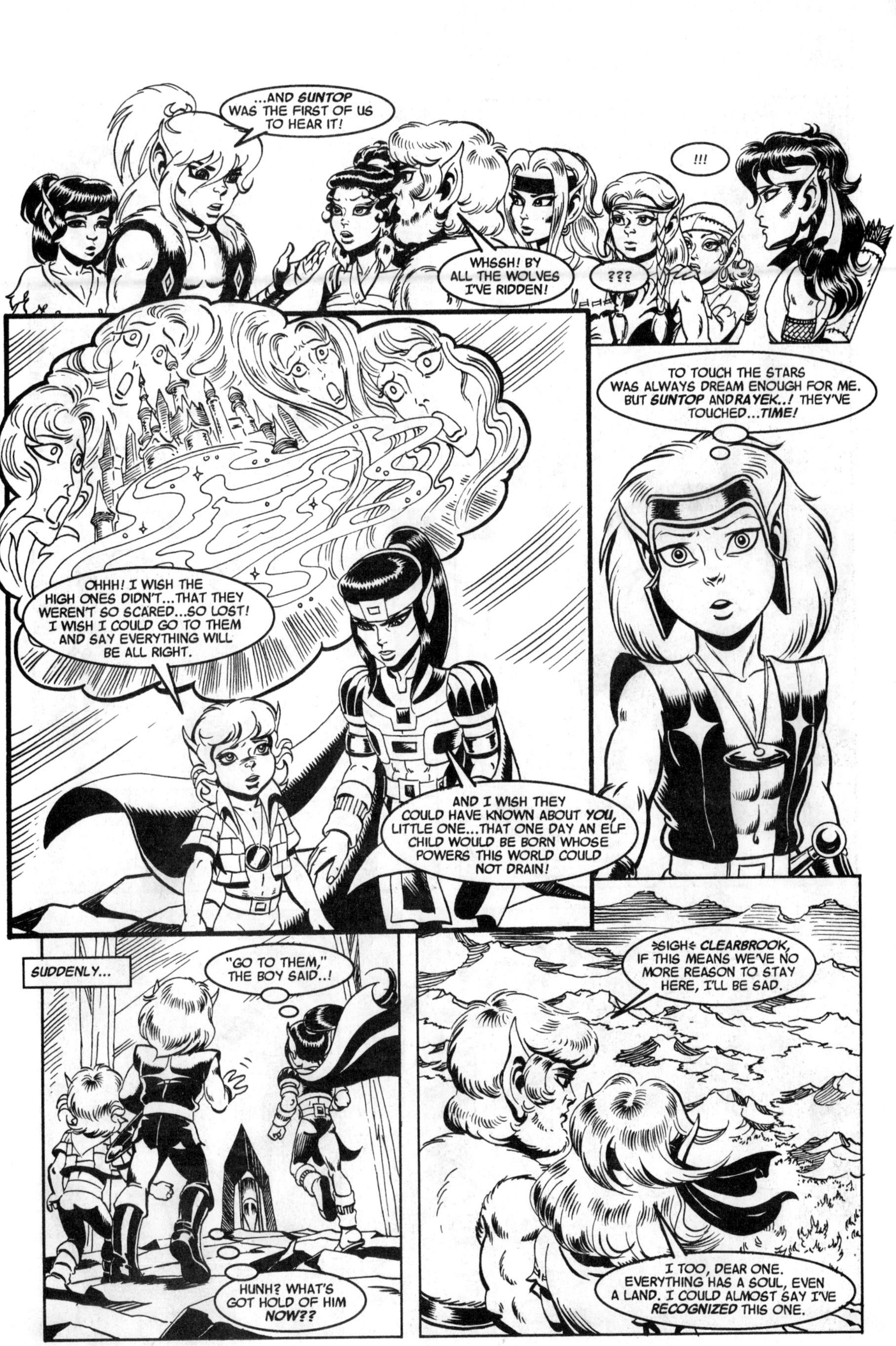
...AND SUNTOP WAS THE FIRST OF US TO HEAR IT!
WHSSH! BY ALL THE WOLVES I'VE RIDDEN!
!!!
???
OHHH! I WISH THE HIGH ONES DIDN'T...THAT THEY WEREN'T SO SCARED...SO LOST! I WISH I COULD GO TO THEM AND SAY EVERYTHING WILL BE ALL RIGHT.
AND I WISH THEY COULD HAVE KNOWN ABOUT YOU, LITTLE ONE...THAT ONE DAY AN ELF CHILD WOULD BE BORN WHOSE POWERS THIS WORLD COULD NOT DRAIN!
TO TOUCH THE STARS WAS ALWAYS DREAM ENOUGH FOR ME. BUT SUNTOP AND RAYEK..! THEY'VE TOUCHED...TIME!
SUDDENLY...
"GO TO THEM," THE BOY SAID..!
HUNH? WHAT'S GOT HOLD OF HIM NOW??
≥SIGH≤ CLEARBROOK, IF THIS MEANS WE'VE NO MORE REASON TO STAY HERE, I'LL BE SAD.
I TOO, DEAR ONE. EVERYTHING HAS A SOUL, EVEN A LAND. I COULD ALMOST SAY I'VE RECOGNIZED THIS ONE.

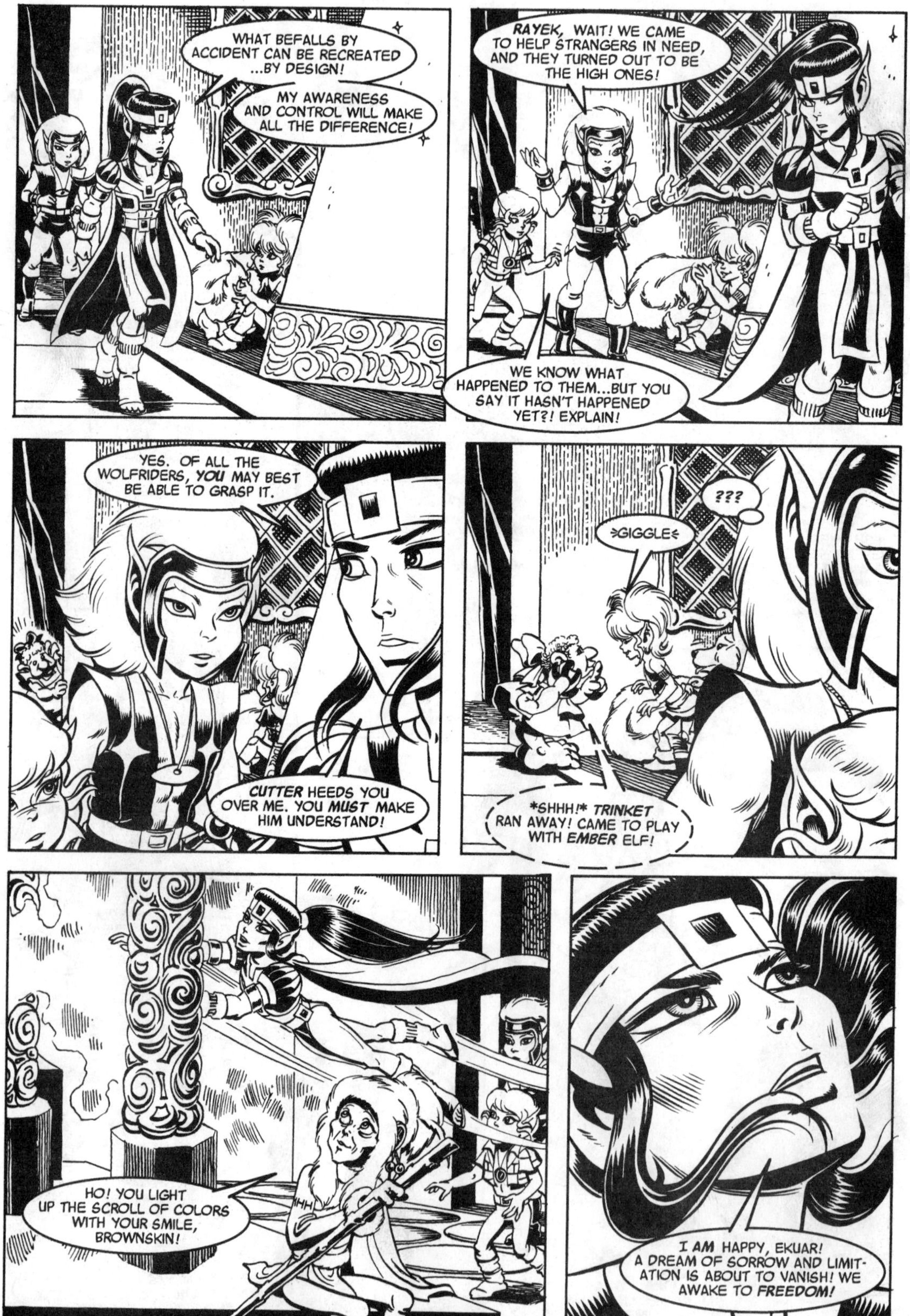
WHAT BEFALLS BY ACCIDENT CAN BE RECREATED ...BY DESIGN!
MY AWARENESS AND CONTROL WILL MAKE ALL THE DIFFERENCE!
RAYEK, WAIT! WE CAME TO HELP STRANGERS IN NEED, AND THEY TURNED OUT TO BE THE HIGH ONES!
WE KNOW WHAT HAPPENED TO THEM...BUT YOU SAY IT HASN'T HAPPENED YET?! EXPLAIN!
YES. OF ALL THE WOLFRIDERS, YOU MAY BEST BE ABLE TO GRASP IT.
CUTTER HEEDS YOU OVER ME. YOU MUST MAKE HIM UNDERSTAND!
???
GIGGLE
SHHH! TRINKET RAN AWAY! CAME TO PLAY WITH EMBER ELF!
HO! YOU LIGHT UP THE SCROLL OF COLORS WITH YOUR SMILE, BROWNSKIN!
I AM HAPPY, EKUAR! A DREAM OF SORROW AND LIMITATION IS ABOUT TO VANISH! WE AWAKE TO FREEDOM!

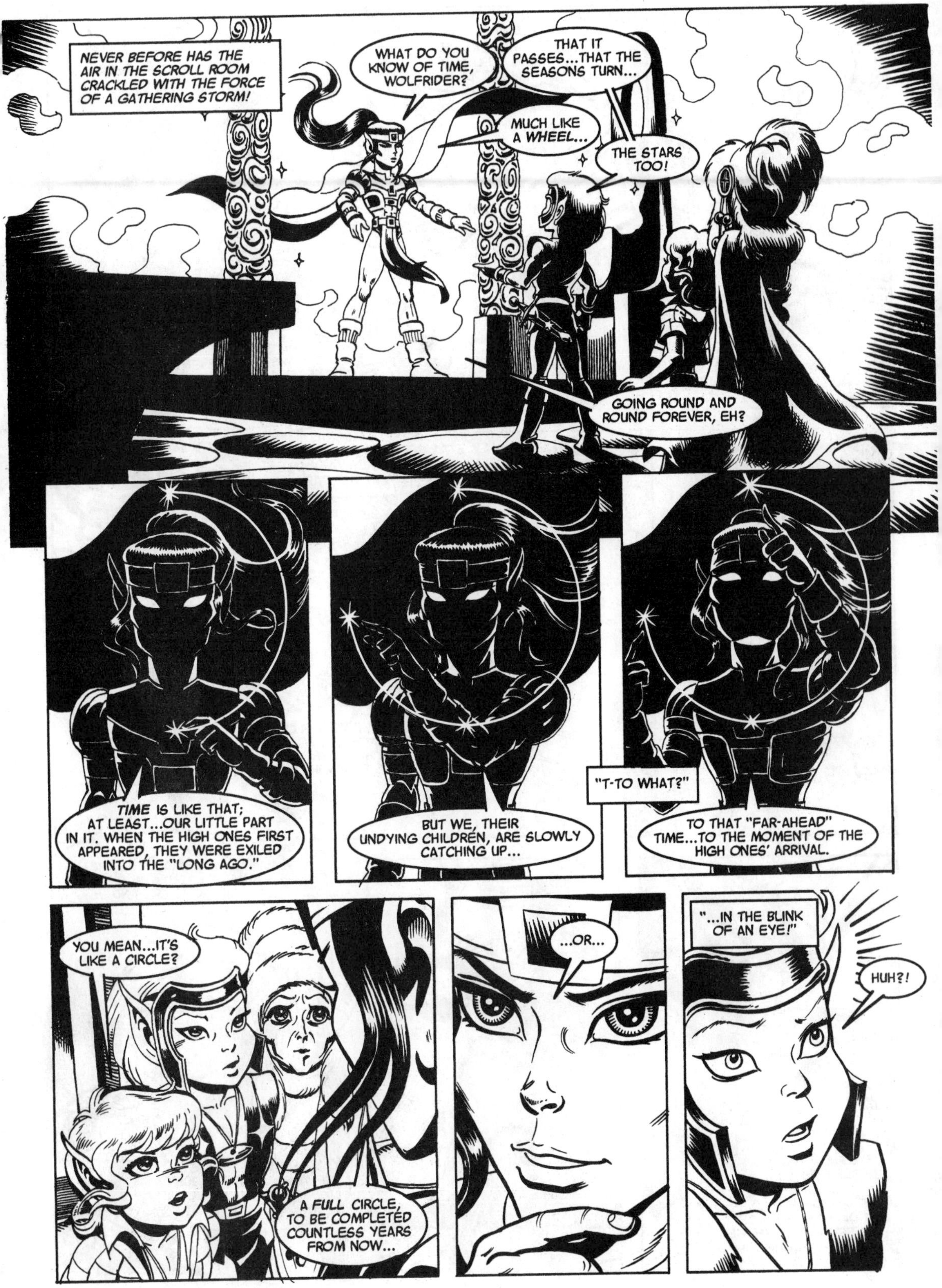

NEVER BEFORE HAS THE AIR IN THE SCROLL ROOM CRACKLED WITH THE FORCE OF A GATHERING STORM!
WHAT DO YOU KNOW OF TIME, WOLFRIDER?
THAT IT PASSES...THAT THE SEASONS TURN...
MUCH LIKE A WHEEL...
THE STARS TOO!
GOING ROUND AND ROUND FOREVER, EH?
TIME IS LIKE THAT; AT LEAST...OUR LITTLE PART IN IT. WHEN THE HIGH ONES FIRST APPEARED, THEY WERE EXILED INTO THE "LONG AGO."
BUT WE, THEIR UNDYING CHILDREN, ARE SLOWLY CATCHING UP...
"T-TO WHAT?"
TO THAT "FAR-AHEAD" TIME...TO THE MOMENT OF THE HIGH ONES' ARRIVAL.
YOU MEAN...IT'S LIKE A CIRCLE?
A FULL CIRCLE, TO BE COMPLETED COUNTLESS YEARS FROM NOW...
...OR...
"...IN THE BLINK OF AN EYE!"
HUH?!

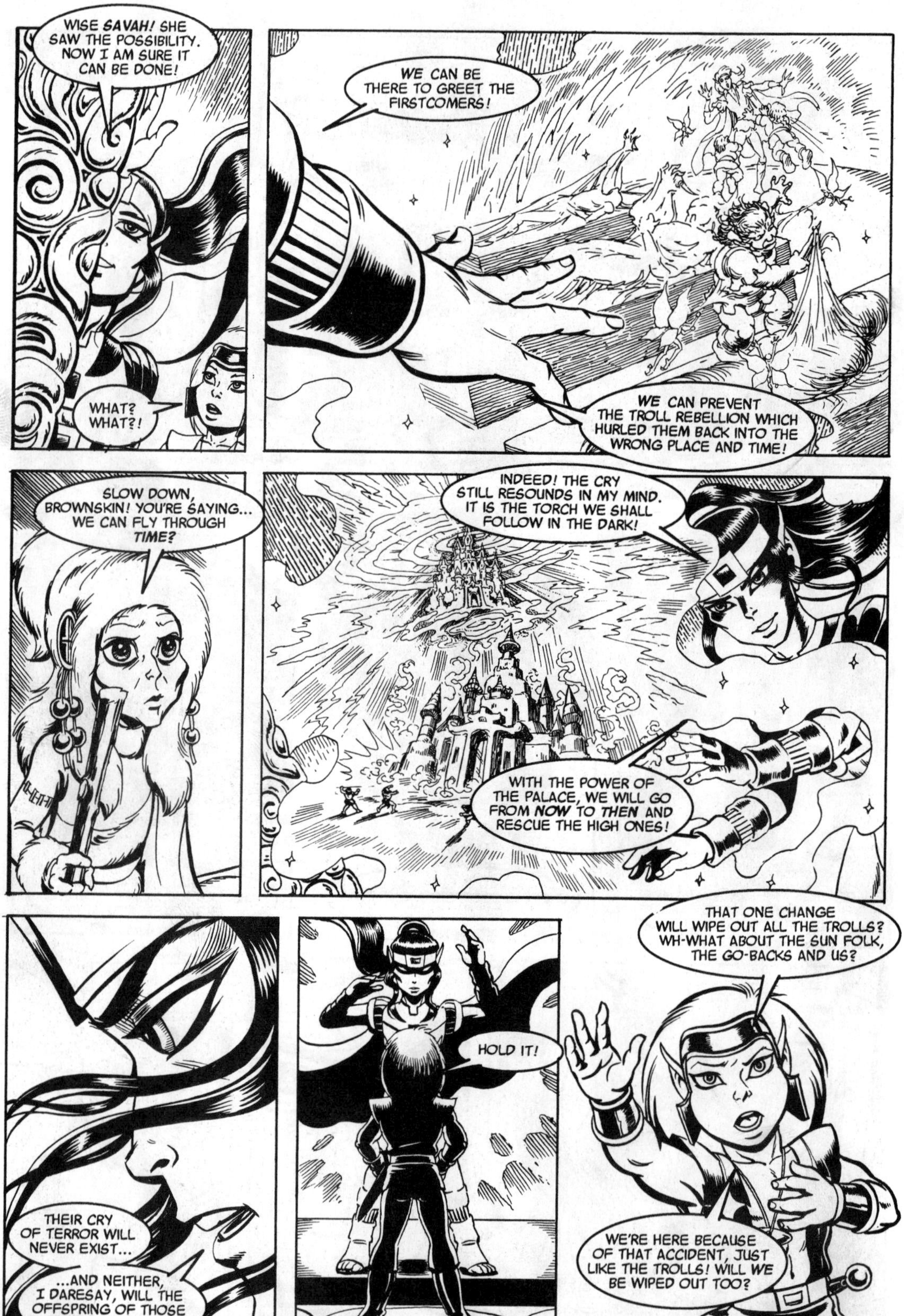
WISE SAVAH! SHE SAW THE POSSIBILITY. NOW I AM SURE IT CAN BE DONE!
WHAT? WHAT?!
WE CAN BE THERE TO GREET THE FIRSTCOMERS!
WE CAN PREVENT THE TROLL REBELLION WHICH HURLED THEM BACK INTO THE WRONG PLACE AND TIME!
SLOW DOWN, BROWNSKIN! YOU'RE SAYING... WE CAN FLY THROUGH TIME?
INDEED! THE CRY STILL RESOUNDS IN MY MIND. IT IS THE TORCH WE SHALL FOLLOW IN THE DARK!
WITH THE POWER OF THE PALACE, WE WILL GO FROM NOW TO THEN AND RESCUE THE HIGH ONES!
THEIR CRY OF TERROR WILL NEVER EXIST...
...AND NEITHER, I DARESAY, WILL THE OFFSPRING OF THOSE BETRAYING TROLLS!
HOLD IT!
THAT ONE CHANGE WILL WIPE OUT ALL THE TROLLS? WH-WHAT ABOUT THE SUN FOLK, THE GO-BACKS AND US?
WE'RE HERE BECAUSE OF THAT ACCIDENT, JUST LIKE THE TROLLS! WILL WE BE WIPED OUT TOO?

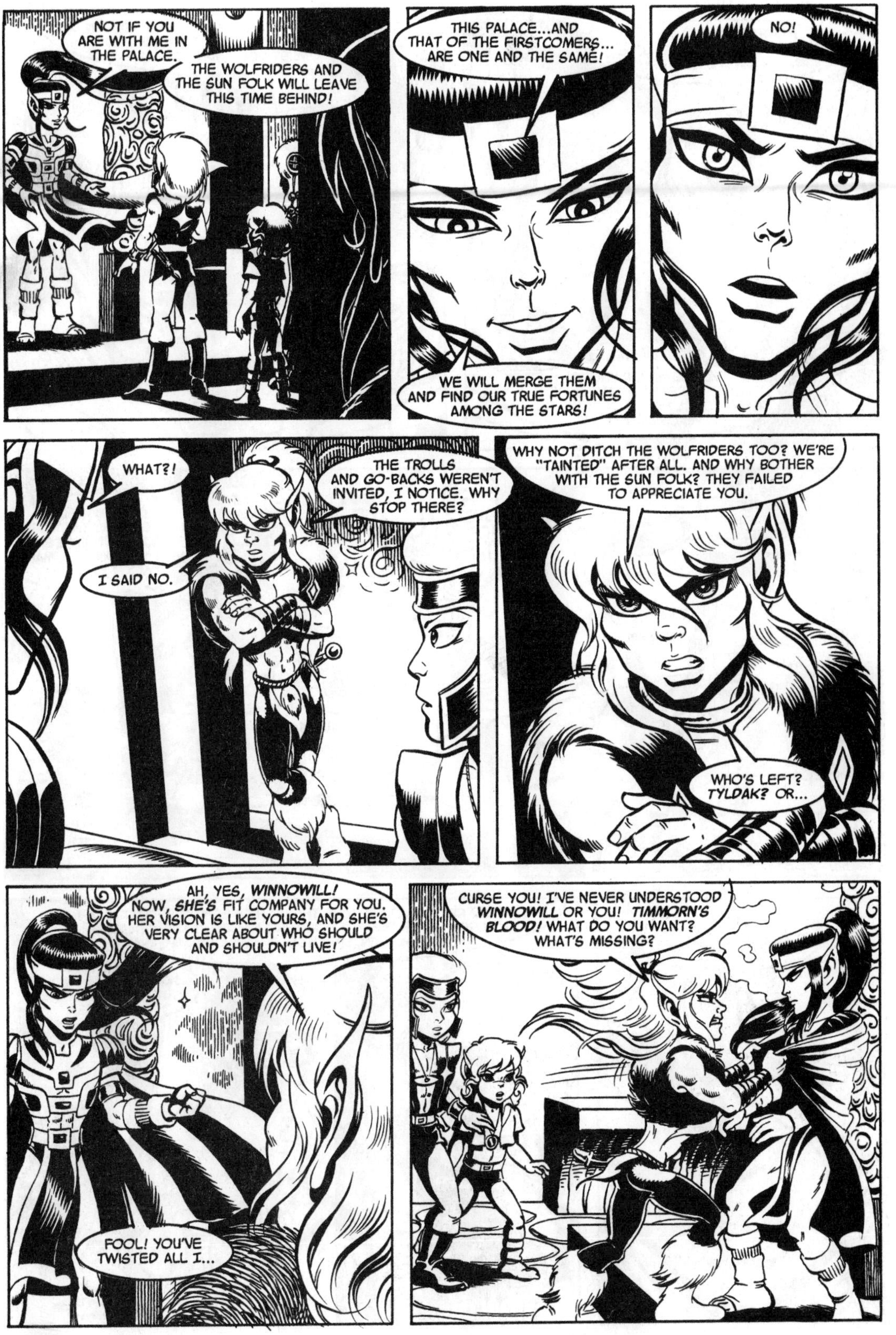
NOT IF YOU ARE WITH ME IN THE PALACE.
THE WOLFRIDERS AND THE SUN FOLK WILL LEAVE THIS TIME BEHIND!
THIS PALACE...AND THAT OF THE FIRSTCOMERS... ARE ONE AND THE SAME!
WE WILL MERGE THEM AND FIND OUR TRUE FORTUNES AMONG THE STARS!
NO!
WHAT?!
I SAID NO.
THE TROLLS AND GO-BACKS WEREN'T INVITED, I NOTICE. WHY STOP THERE?
WHY NOT DITCH THE WOLFRIDERS TOO? WE'RE "TAINTED" AFTER ALL. AND WHY BOTHER WITH THE SUN FOLK? THEY FAILED TO APPRECIATE YOU.
WHO'S LEFT? *TYLDAK?* OR...
AH, YES, *WINNOWILL!* NOW, *SHE'S* FIT COMPANY FOR YOU. HER VISION IS LIKE YOURS, AND SHE'S VERY CLEAR ABOUT WHO SHOULD AND SHOULDN'T LIVE!
FOOL! YOU'VE TWISTED ALL I...
CURSE YOU! I'VE NEVER UNDERSTOOD *WINNOWILL* OR YOU! *TIMMORN'S BLOOD!* WHAT DO YOU WANT? WHAT'S MISSING?

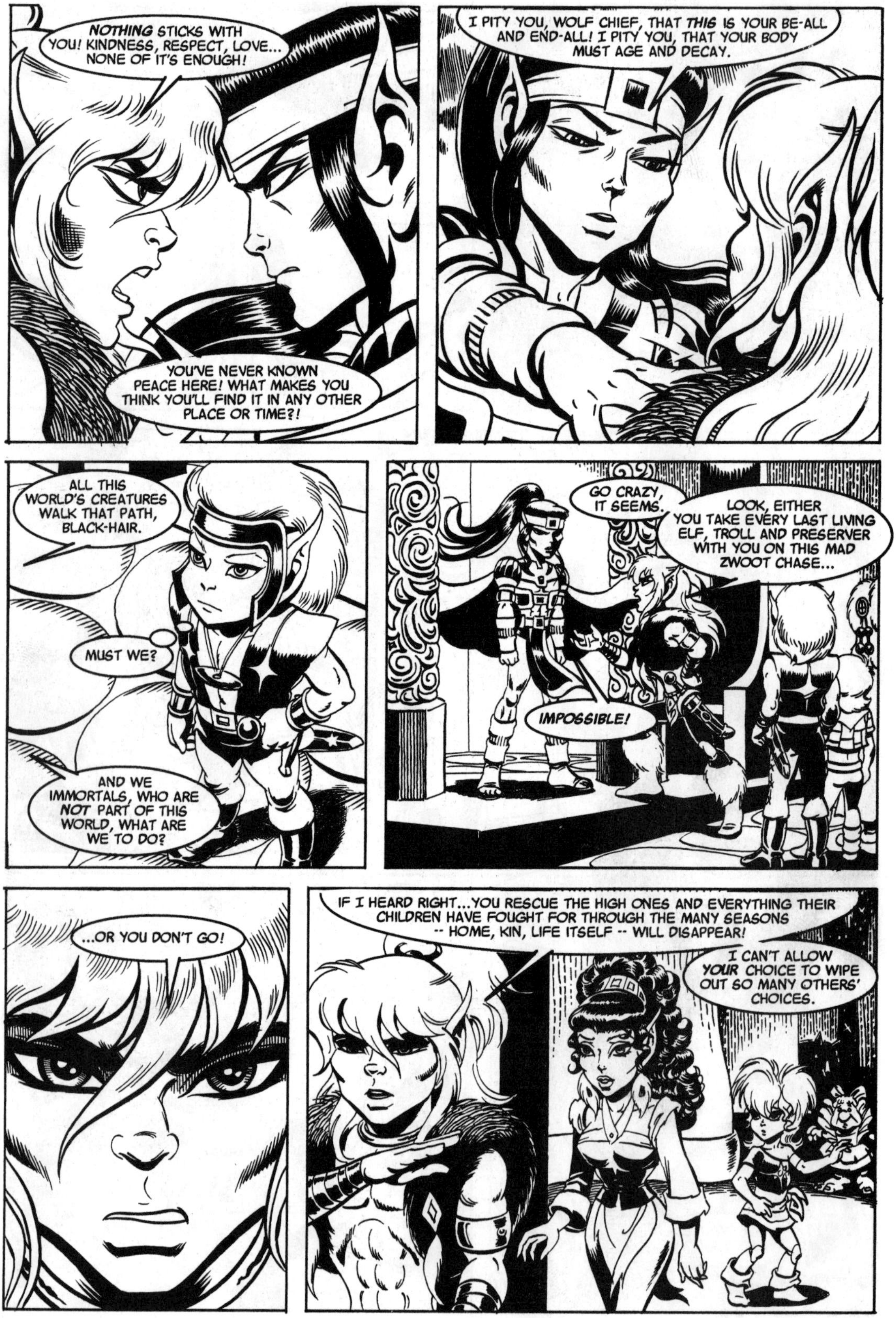
NOTHING STICKS WITH YOU! KINDNESS, RESPECT, LOVE... NONE OF IT'S ENOUGH!
YOU'VE NEVER KNOWN PEACE HERE! WHAT MAKES YOU THINK YOU'LL FIND IT IN ANY OTHER PLACE OR TIME?!
I PITY YOU, WOLF CHIEF, THAT THIS IS YOUR BE-ALL AND END-ALL! I PITY YOU, THAT YOUR BODY MUST AGE AND DECAY.
ALL THIS WORLD'S CREATURES WALK THAT PATH, BLACK-HAIR.
MUST WE?
AND WE IMMORTALS, WHO ARE NOT PART OF THIS WORLD, WHAT ARE WE TO DO?
GO CRAZY, IT SEEMS.
LOOK, EITHER YOU TAKE EVERY LAST LIVING ELF, TROLL AND PRESERVER WITH YOU ON THIS MAD ZWOOT CHASE...
IMPOSSIBLE!
...OR YOU DON'T GO!
IF I HEARD RIGHT...YOU RESCUE THE HIGH ONES AND EVERYTHING THEIR CHILDREN HAVE FOUGHT FOR THROUGH THE MANY SEASONS -- HOME, KIN, LIFE ITSELF -- WILL DISAPPEAR!
I CAN'T ALLOW YOUR CHOICE TO WIPE OUT SO MANY OTHERS' CHOICES.

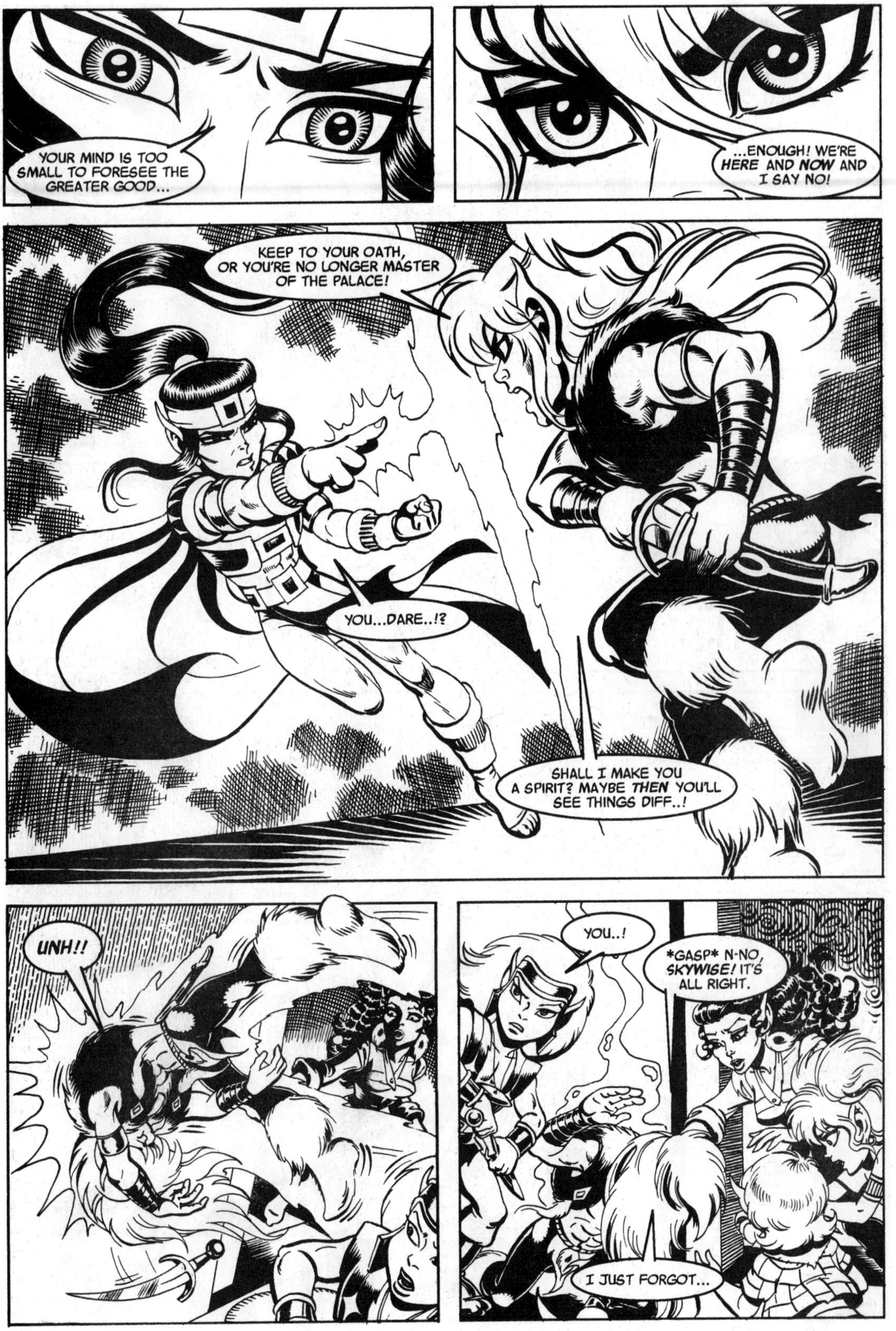
YOUR MIND IS TOO SMALL TO FORESEE THE GREATER GOOD...
...ENOUGH! WE'RE *HERE* AND *NOW* AND I SAY NO!
KEEP TO YOUR OATH, OR YOU'RE NO LONGER MASTER OF THE PALACE!
YOU...DARE..!?
SHALL I MAKE YOU A SPIRIT? MAYBE *THEN* YOU'LL SEE THINGS DIFF..!
UNH!!
YOU..!
GASP N-NO, *SKYWISE!* IT'S ALL RIGHT.
I JUST FORGOT...

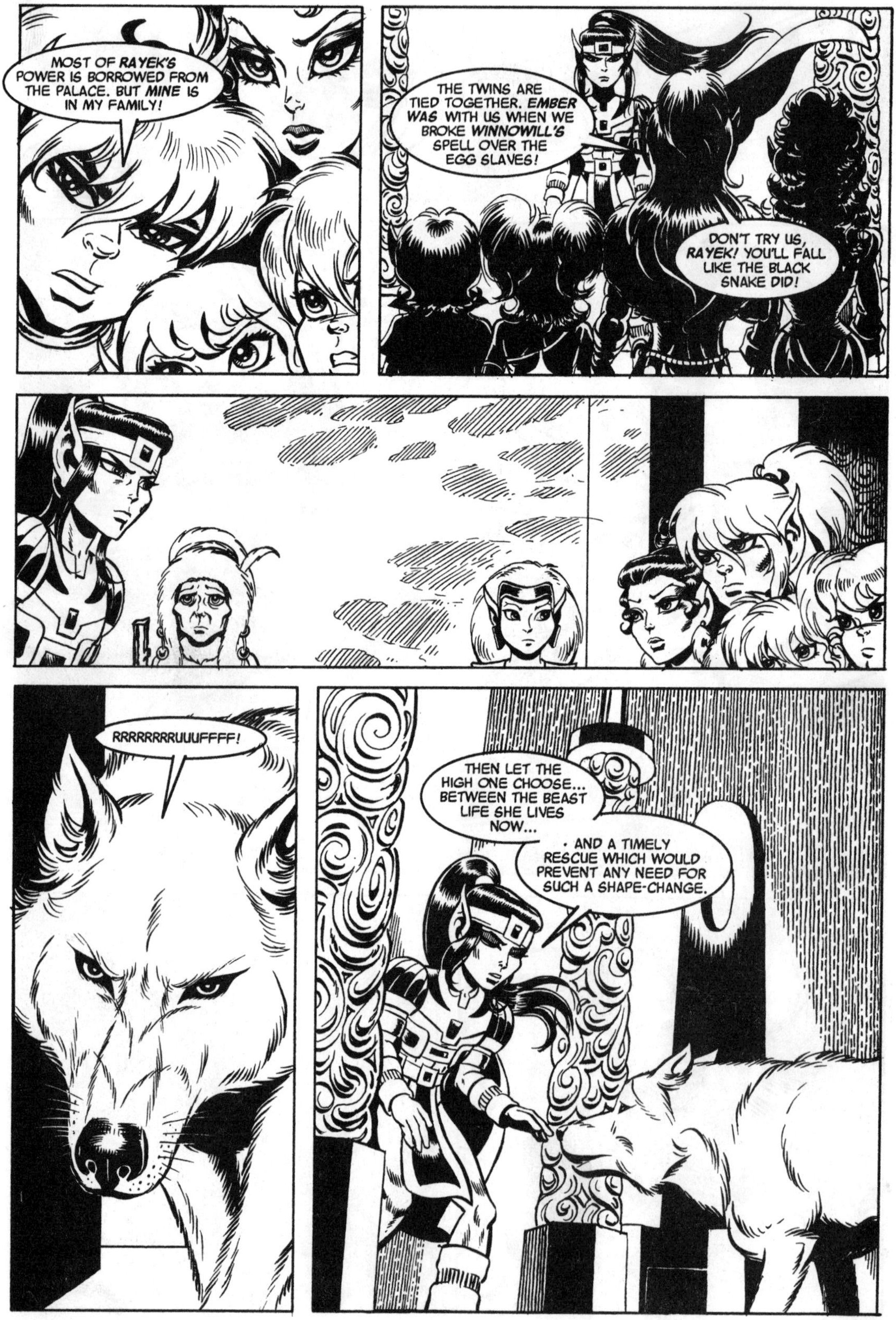
MOST OF RAYEK'S POWER IS BORROWED FROM THE PALACE. BUT MINE IS IN MY FAMILY!
THE TWINS ARE TIED TOGETHER. EMBER WAS WITH US WHEN WE BROKE WINNOWILL'S SPELL OVER THE EGG SLAVES!
DON'T TRY US, RAYEK! YOU'LL FALL LIKE THE BLACK SNAKE DID!
RRRRRRRRUUUFFFF!
THEN LET THE HIGH ONE CHOOSE... BETWEEN THE BEAST LIFE SHE LIVES NOW...
· AND A TIMELY RESCUE WHICH WOULD PREVENT ANY NEED FOR SUCH A SHAPE-CHANGE.

TIMMAIN, YOU CRIED OUT WITH THE OTHERS. THIS BANISHMENT... THIS-THIS GROUNDING CANNOT BE WHAT YOU WANTED!

IT CAN UN-HAPPEN! AND YET YOUR CHILDREN, THE WOLFRIDERS, CAN STILL BE WITH YOU. IS THAT NOT BEST?

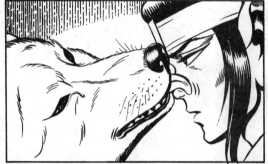

SHE WON'T TAKE SIDES. FOR GOOD OR ILL, WHAT HAPPENED TO THE HIGH ONES HAPPENED.

I SAY IT WAS FOR THE GOOD.

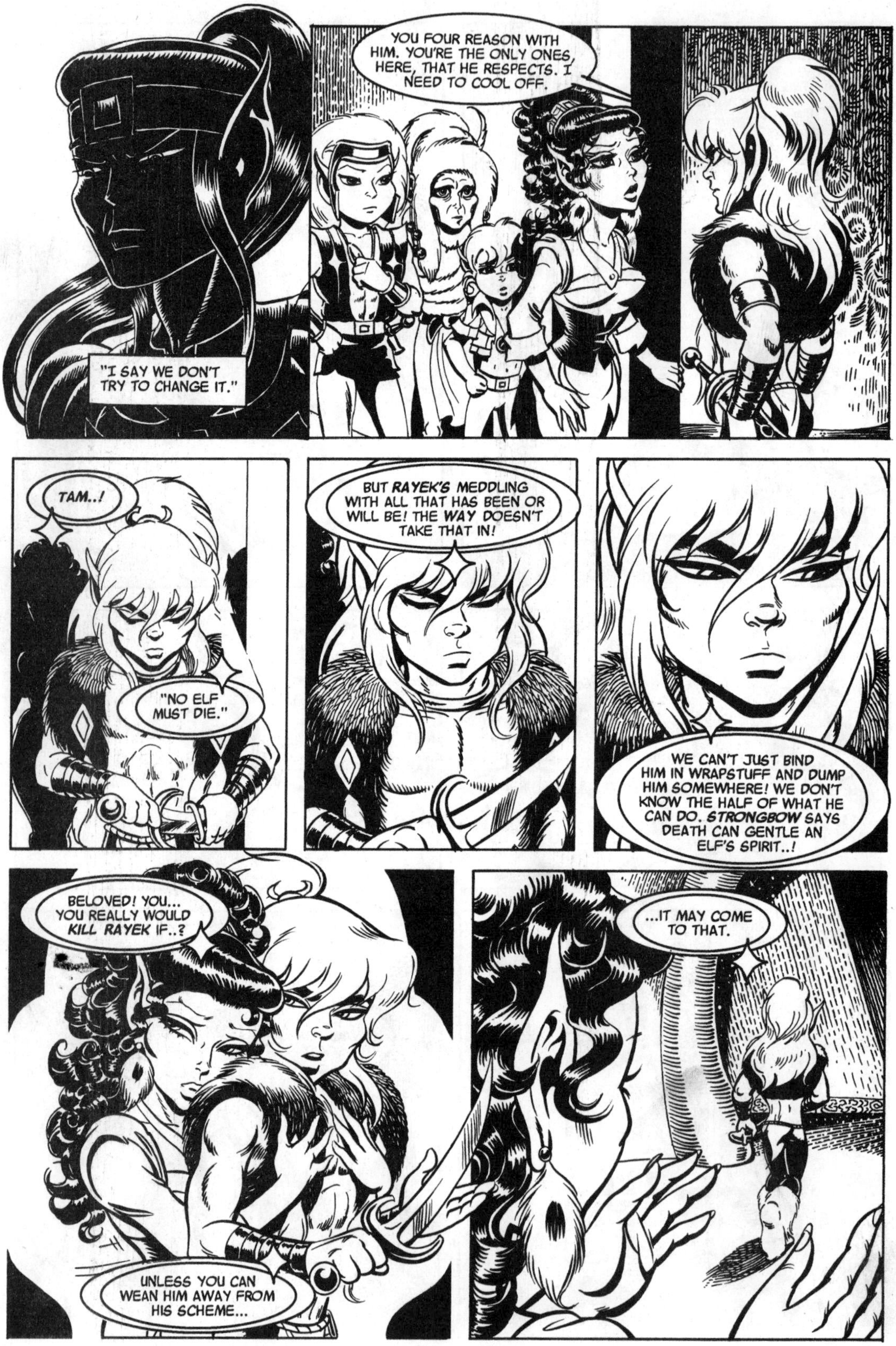
"I SAY WE DON'T TRY TO CHANGE IT."
YOU FOUR REASON WITH HIM. YOU'RE THE ONLY ONES, HERE, THAT HE RESPECTS. I NEED TO COOL OFF.
TAM..!
"NO ELF MUST DIE."
BUT RAYEK'S MEDDLING WITH ALL THAT HAS BEEN OR WILL BE! THE WAY DOESN'T TAKE THAT IN!
WE CAN'T JUST BIND HIM IN WRAPSTUFF AND DUMP HIM SOMEWHERE! WE DON'T KNOW THE HALF OF WHAT HE CAN DO. STRONGBOW SAYS DEATH CAN GENTLE AN ELF'S SPIRIT..!
BELOVED! YOU... YOU REALLY WOULD KILL RAYEK IF..?
UNLESS YOU CAN WEAN HIM AWAY FROM HIS SCHEME...
...IT MAY COME TO THAT.

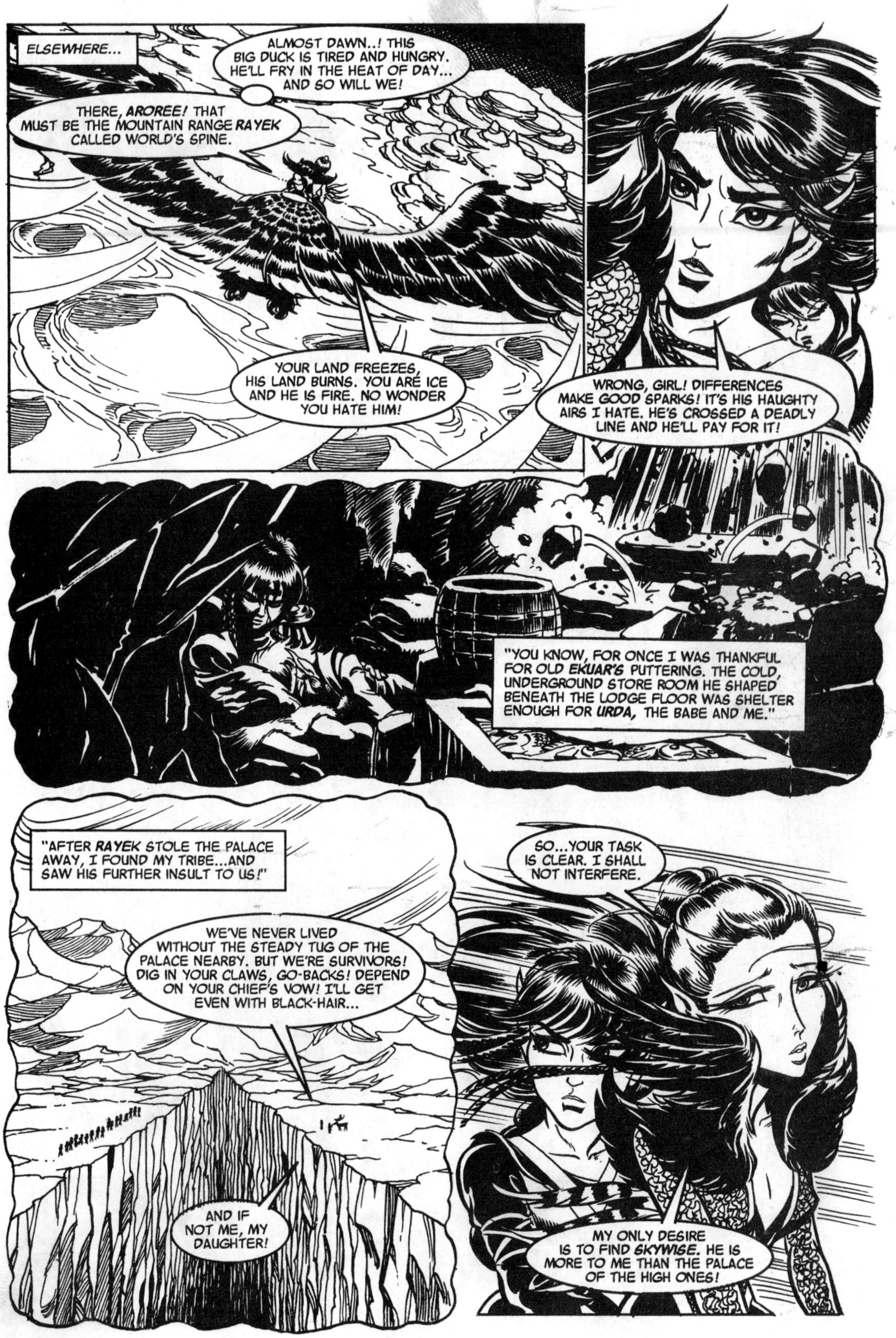
ELSEWHERE...
ALMOST DAWN..! THIS BIG DUCK IS TIRED AND HUNGRY. HE'LL FRY IN THE HEAT OF DAY... AND SO WILL WE!
THERE, AROREE! THAT MUST BE THE MOUNTAIN RANGE RAYEK CALLED WORLD'S SPINE.
YOUR LAND FREEZES, HIS LAND BURNS. YOU ARE ICE AND HE IS FIRE. NO WONDER YOU HATE HIM!
WRONG, GIRL! DIFFERENCES MAKE GOOD SPARKS! IT'S HIS HAUGHTY AIRS I HATE. HE'S CROSSED A DEADLY LINE AND HE'LL PAY FOR IT!
"YOU KNOW, FOR ONCE I WAS THANKFUL FOR OLD EKUAR'S PUTTERING. THE COLD, UNDERGROUND STORE ROOM HE SHAPED BENEATH THE LODGE FLOOR WAS SHELTER ENOUGH FOR URDA, THE BABE AND ME."
"AFTER RAYEK STOLE THE PALACE AWAY, I FOUND MY TRIBE...AND SAW HIS FURTHER INSULT TO US!"
WE'VE NEVER LIVED WITHOUT THE STEADY TUG OF THE PALACE NEARBY. BUT WE'RE SURVIVORS! DIG IN YOUR CLAWS, GO-BACKS! DEPEND ON YOUR CHIEF'S VOW! I'LL GET EVEN WITH BLACK-HAIR...
AND IF NOT ME, MY DAUGHTER!
SO...YOUR TASK IS CLEAR. I SHALL NOT INTERFERE.
MY ONLY DESIRE IS TO FIND SKYWISE. HE IS MORE TO ME THAN THE PALACE OF THE HIGH ONES!

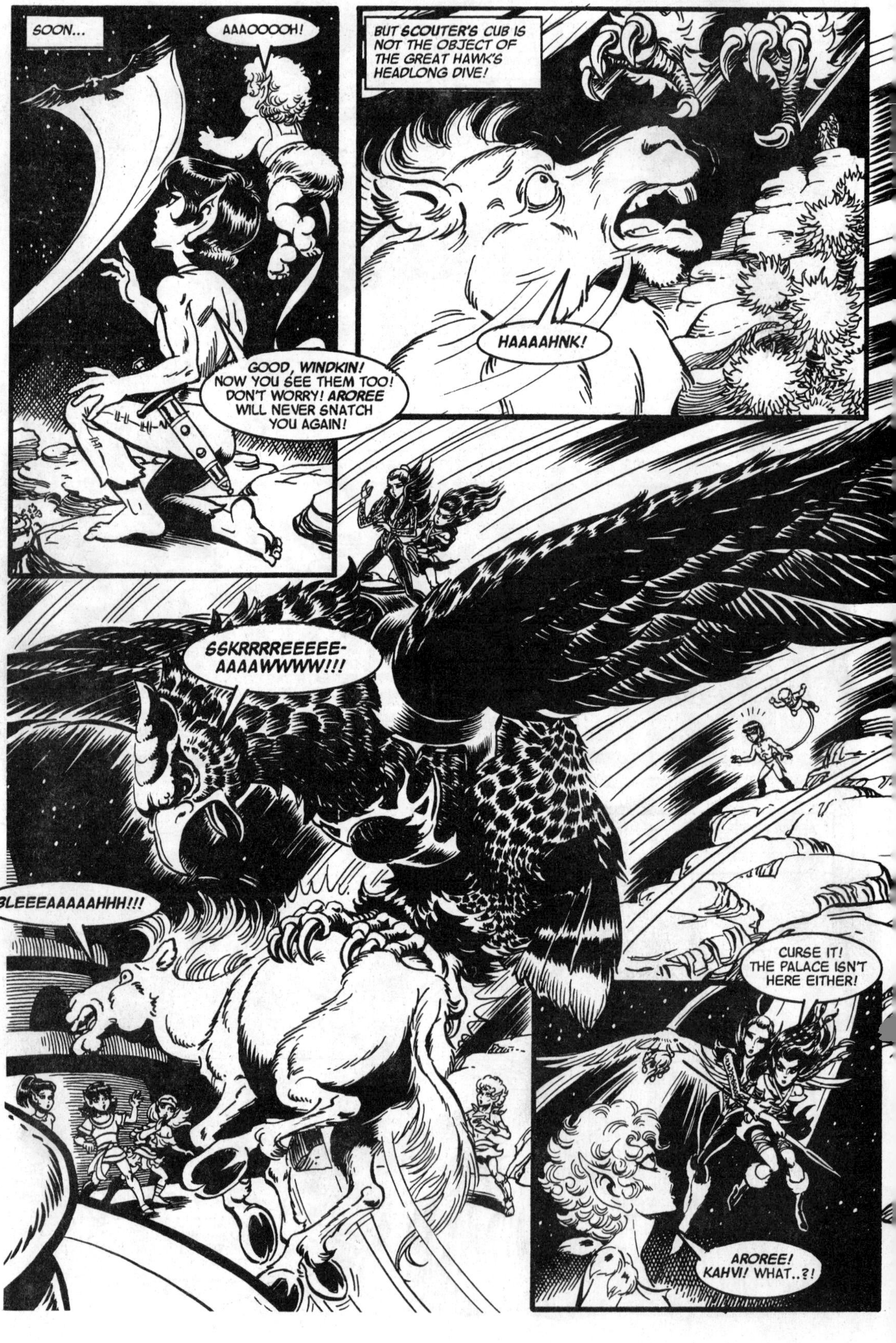
SOON...
AAAOOOOH!
GOOD, WINDKIN! NOW YOU SEE THEM TOO! DON'T WORRY! AROREE WILL NEVER SNATCH YOU AGAIN!
BUT SCOUTER'S CUB IS NOT THE OBJECT OF THE GREAT HAWK'S HEADLONG DIVE!
HAAAAHNK!
SSKRRRREEEEE-AAAAWWWW!!!
BLEEEAAAAAHHH!!!
CURSE IT! THE PALACE ISN'T HERE EITHER!
AROREE! KAHVI! WHAT..?!

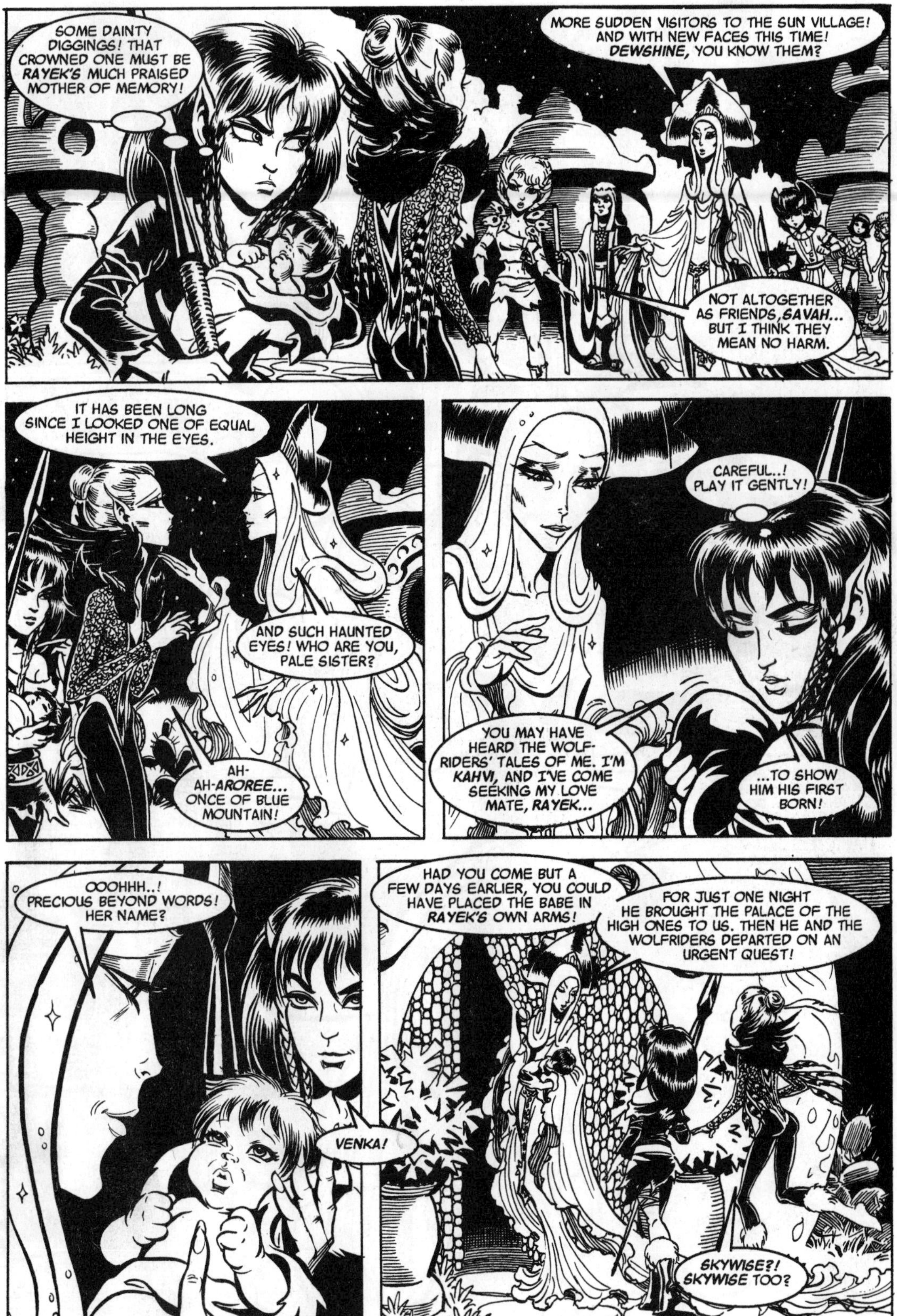
SOME DAINTY DIGGINGS! THAT CROWNED ONE MUST BE RAYEK'S MUCH PRAISED MOTHER OF MEMORY!
MORE SUDDEN VISITORS TO THE SUN VILLAGE! AND WITH NEW FACES THIS TIME! DEWSHINE, YOU KNOW THEM?
NOT ALTOGETHER AS FRIENDS, SAVAH... BUT I THINK THEY MEAN NO HARM.
IT HAS BEEN LONG SINCE I LOOKED ONE OF EQUAL HEIGHT IN THE EYES.
AND SUCH HAUNTED EYES! WHO ARE YOU, PALE SISTER?
AH-AH-AROREE... ONCE OF BLUE MOUNTAIN!
CAREFUL..! PLAY IT GENTLY!
YOU MAY HAVE HEARD THE WOLFRIDERS' TALES OF ME. I'M KAHVI, AND I'VE COME SEEKING MY LOVE MATE, RAYEK...
...TO SHOW HIM HIS FIRST BORN!
OOOHHH..! PRECIOUS BEYOND WORDS! HER NAME?
VENKA!
HAD YOU COME BUT A FEW DAYS EARLIER, YOU COULD HAVE PLACED THE BABE IN RAYEK'S OWN ARMS!
FOR JUST ONE NIGHT HE BROUGHT THE PALACE OF THE HIGH ONES TO US. THEN HE AND THE WOLFRIDERS DEPARTED ON AN URGENT QUEST!
SKYWISE?! SKYWISE TOO?

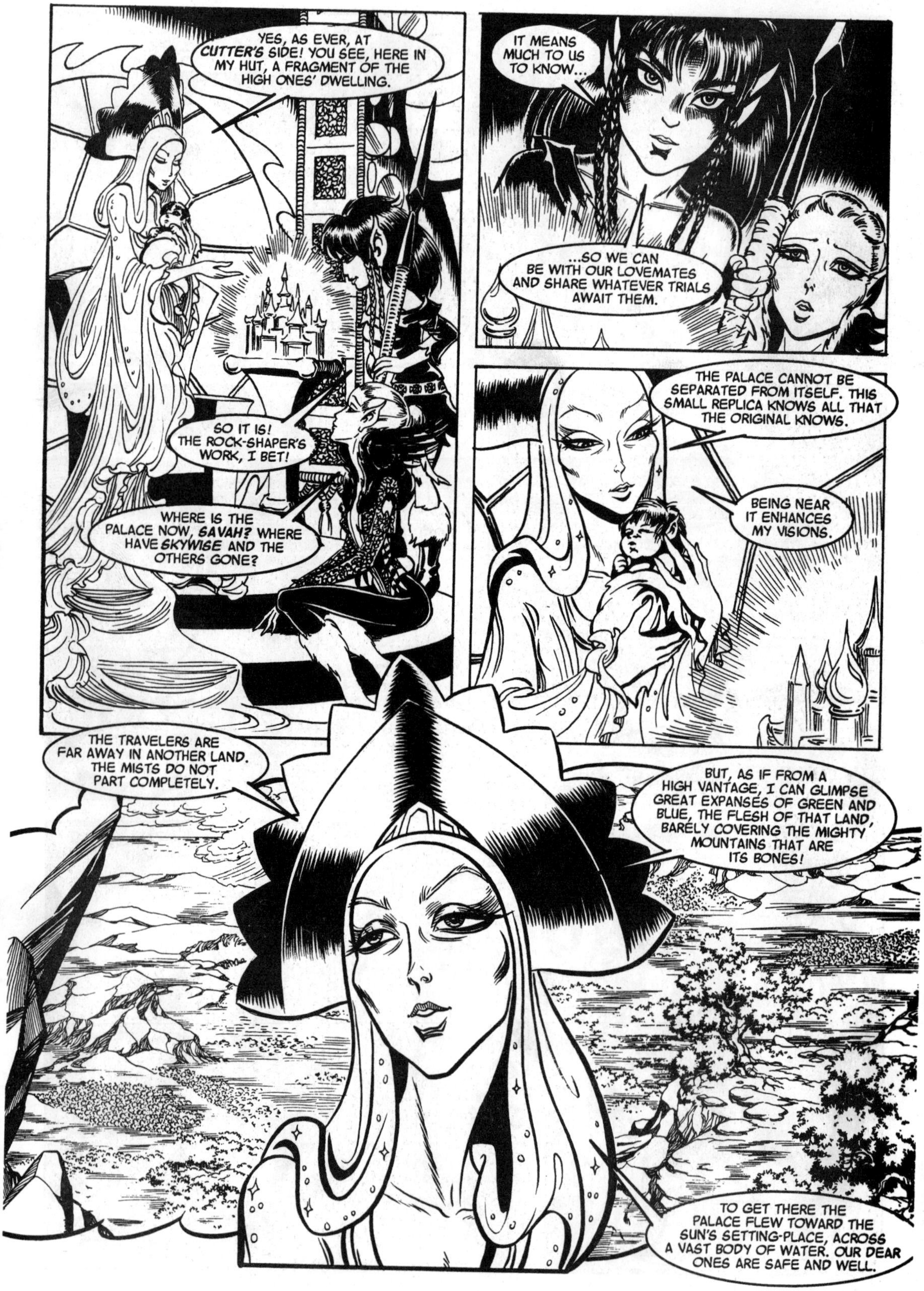
YES, AS EVER, AT CUTTER'S SIDE! YOU SEE, HERE IN MY HUT, A FRAGMENT OF THE HIGH ONES' DWELLING.
SO IT IS! THE ROCK-SHAPER'S WORK, I BET!
WHERE IS THE PALACE NOW, SAVAH? WHERE HAVE SKYWISE AND THE OTHERS GONE?
IT MEANS MUCH TO US TO KNOW...
...SO WE CAN BE WITH OUR LOVEMATES AND SHARE WHATEVER TRIALS AWAIT THEM.
THE PALACE CANNOT BE SEPARATED FROM ITSELF. THIS SMALL REPLICA KNOWS ALL THAT THE ORIGINAL KNOWS.
BEING NEAR IT ENHANCES MY VISIONS.
THE TRAVELERS ARE FAR AWAY IN ANOTHER LAND. THE MISTS DO NOT PART COMPLETELY.
BUT, AS IF FROM A HIGH VANTAGE, I CAN GLIMPSE GREAT EXPANSES OF GREEN AND BLUE, THE FLESH OF THAT LAND, BARELY COVERING THE MIGHTY MOUNTAINS THAT ARE ITS BONES!
TO GET THERE THE PALACE FLEW TOWARD THE SUN'S SETTING-PLACE, ACROSS A VAST BODY OF WATER. OUR DEAR ONES ARE SAFE AND WELL.

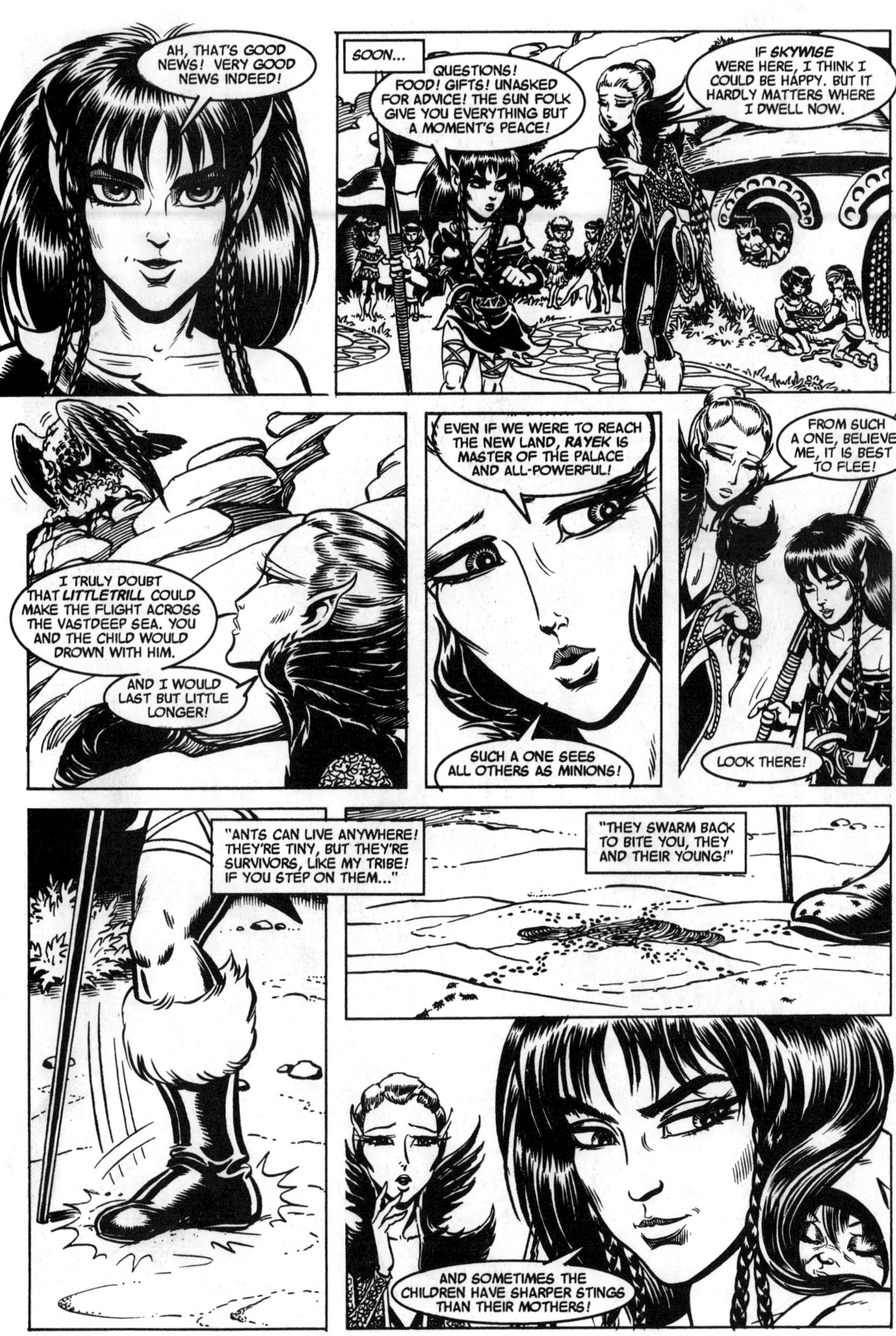
AH, THAT'S GOOD NEWS! VERY GOOD NEWS INDEED!
SOON...
QUESTIONS! FOOD! GIFTS! UNASKED FOR ADVICE! THE SUN FOLK GIVE YOU EVERYTHING BUT A MOMENT'S PEACE!
IF SKYWISE WERE HERE, I THINK I COULD BE HAPPY. BUT IT HARDLY MATTERS WHERE I DWELL NOW.
I TRULY DOUBT THAT LITTLETRILL COULD MAKE THE FLIGHT ACROSS THE VASTDEEP SEA. YOU AND THE CHILD WOULD DROWN WITH HIM.
AND I WOULD LAST BUT LITTLE LONGER!
EVEN IF WE WERE TO REACH THE NEW LAND, RAYEK IS MASTER OF THE PALACE AND ALL-POWERFUL!
SUCH A ONE SEES ALL OTHERS AS MINIONS!
FROM SUCH A ONE, BELIEVE ME, IT IS BEST TO FLEE!
LOOK THERE!
"ANTS CAN LIVE ANYWHERE! THEY'RE TINY, BUT THEY'RE SURVIVORS, LIKE MY TRIBE! IF YOU STEP ON THEM..."
"THEY SWARM BACK TO BITE YOU, THEY AND THEIR YOUNG!"
AND SOMETIMES THE CHILDREN HAVE SHARPER STINGS THAN THEIR MOTHERS!

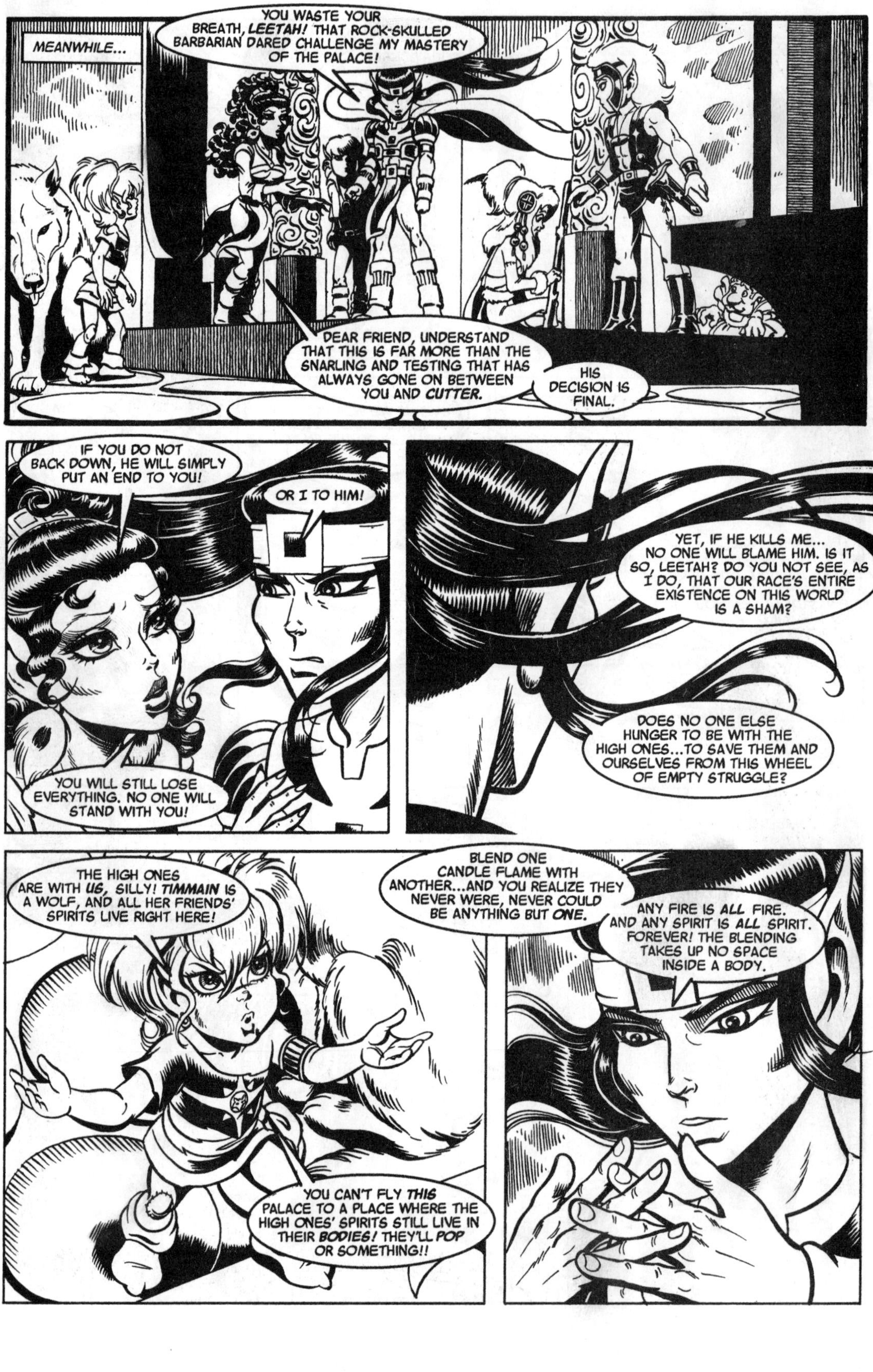
MEANWHILE...
YOU WASTE YOUR BREATH, LEETAH! THAT ROCK-SKULLED BARBARIAN DARED CHALLENGE MY MASTERY OF THE PALACE!
DEAR FRIEND, UNDERSTAND THAT THIS IS FAR MORE THAN THE SNARLING AND TESTING THAT HAS ALWAYS GONE ON BETWEEN YOU AND CUTTER.
HIS DECISION IS FINAL.
IF YOU DO NOT BACK DOWN, HE WILL SIMPLY PUT AN END TO YOU!
OR I TO HIM!
YOU WILL STILL LOSE EVERYTHING. NO ONE WILL STAND WITH YOU!
YET, IF HE KILLS ME... NO ONE WILL BLAME HIM. IS IT SO, LEETAH? DO YOU NOT SEE, AS I DO, THAT OUR RACE'S ENTIRE EXISTENCE ON THIS WORLD IS A SHAM?
DOES NO ONE ELSE HUNGER TO BE WITH THE HIGH ONES...TO SAVE THEM AND OURSELVES FROM THIS WHEEL OF EMPTY STRUGGLE?
THE HIGH ONES ARE WITH US, SILLY! TIMMAIN IS A WOLF, AND ALL HER FRIENDS' SPIRITS LIVE RIGHT HERE!
YOU CAN'T FLY THIS PALACE TO A PLACE WHERE THE HIGH ONES' SPIRITS STILL LIVE IN THEIR BODIES! THEY'LL POP OR SOMETHING!!
BLEND ONE CANDLE FLAME WITH ANOTHER...AND YOU REALIZE THEY NEVER WERE, NEVER COULD BE ANYTHING BUT ONE.
ANY FIRE IS ALL FIRE. AND ANY SPIRIT IS ALL SPIRIT. FOREVER! THE BLENDING TAKES UP NO SPACE INSIDE A BODY.

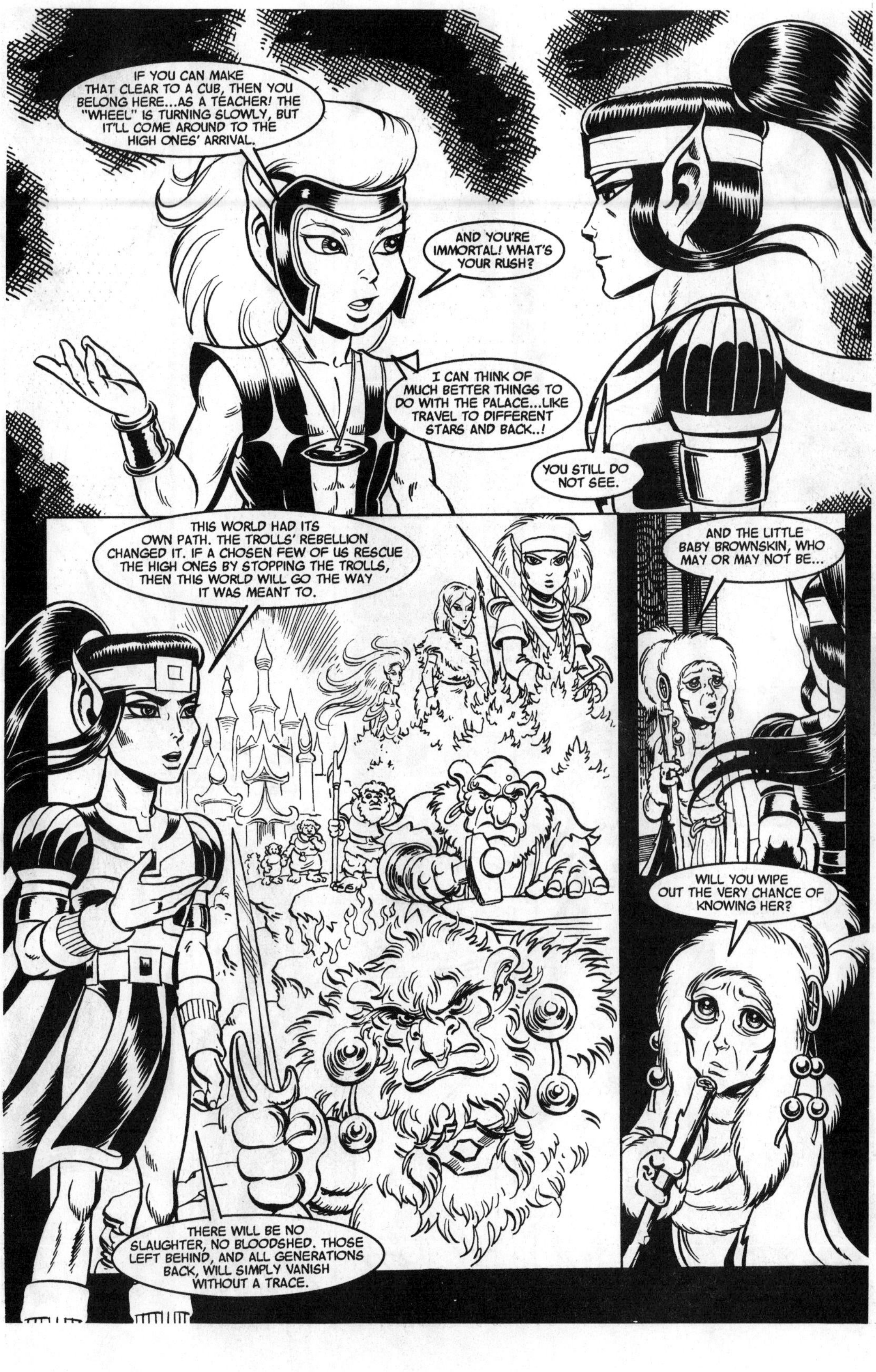

IF YOU CAN MAKE THAT CLEAR TO A CUB, THEN YOU BELONG HERE...AS A TEACHER! THE "WHEEL" IS TURNING SLOWLY, BUT IT'LL COME AROUND TO THE HIGH ONES' ARRIVAL.
AND YOU'RE IMMORTAL! WHAT'S YOUR RUSH?
I CAN THINK OF MUCH BETTER THINGS TO DO WITH THE PALACE...LIKE TRAVEL TO DIFFERENT STARS AND BACK..!
YOU STILL DO NOT SEE.
THIS WORLD HAD ITS OWN PATH. THE TROLLS' REBELLION CHANGED IT. IF A CHOSEN FEW OF US RESCUE THE HIGH ONES BY STOPPING THE TROLLS, THEN THIS WORLD WILL GO THE WAY IT WAS MEANT TO.
THERE WILL BE NO SLAUGHTER, NO BLOODSHED. THOSE LEFT BEHIND, AND ALL GENERATIONS BACK, WILL SIMPLY VANISH WITHOUT A TRACE.
AND THE LITTLE BABY BROWNSKIN, WHO MAY OR MAY NOT BE...
WILL YOU WIPE OUT THE VERY CHANCE OF KNOWING HER?

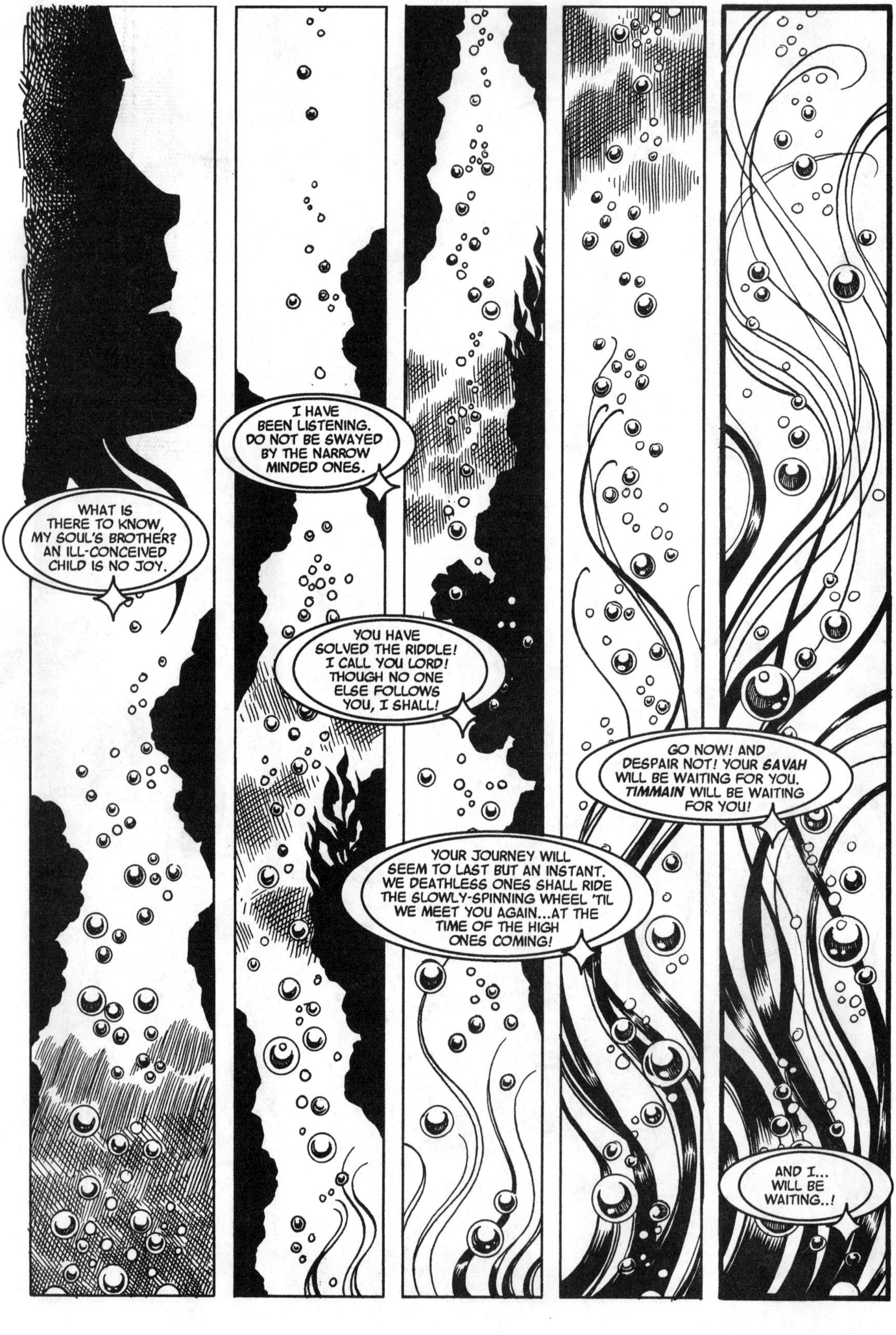
I HAVE BEEN LISTENING. DO NOT BE SWAYED BY THE NARROW MINDED ONES.
WHAT IS THERE TO KNOW, MY SOUL'S BROTHER? AN ILL-CONCEIVED CHILD IS NO JOY.
YOU HAVE SOLVED THE RIDDLE! I CALL YOU LORD! THOUGH NO ONE ELSE FOLLOWS YOU, I SHALL!
GO NOW! AND DESPAIR NOT! YOUR SAVAH WILL BE WAITING FOR YOU. TIMMAIN WILL BE WAITING FOR YOU!
YOUR JOURNEY WILL SEEM TO LAST BUT AN INSTANT. WE DEATHLESS ONES SHALL RIDE THE SLOWLY-SPINNING WHEEL 'TIL WE MEET YOU AGAIN...AT THE TIME OF THE HIGH ONES COMING!
AND I... WILL BE WAITING..!

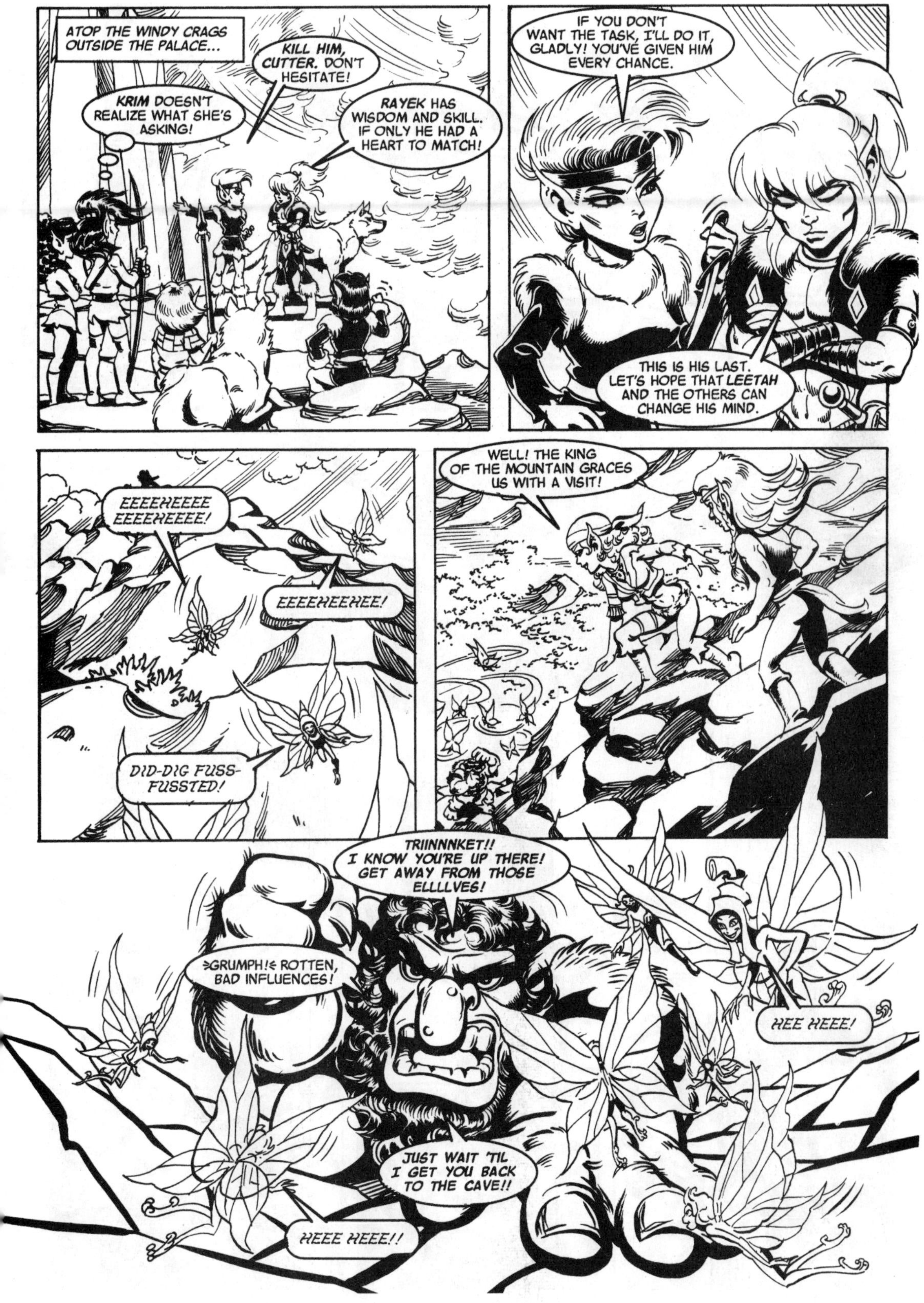
ATOP THE WINDY CRAGS OUTSIDE THE PALACE...
KILL HIM, CUTTER. DON'T HESITATE!
KRIM DOESN'T REALIZE WHAT SHE'S ASKING!
RAYEK HAS WISDOM AND SKILL. IF ONLY HE HAD A HEART TO MATCH!
IF YOU DON'T WANT THE TASK, I'LL DO IT, GLADLY! YOU'VE GIVEN HIM EVERY CHANCE.
THIS IS HIS LAST. LET'S HOPE THAT LEETAH AND THE OTHERS CAN CHANGE HIS MIND.
EEEEHEEEE EEEEHEEEE!
EEEEHEEHEE!
DID-DIG FUSS-FUSSTED!
WELL! THE KING OF THE MOUNTAIN GRACES US WITH A VISIT!
TRIINNNKET!! I KNOW YOU'RE UP THERE! GET AWAY FROM THOSE ELLLLVES!
>GRUMPH!< ROTTEN, BAD INFLUENCES!
HEE HEEE!
JUST WAIT 'TIL I GET YOU BACK TO THE CAVE!!
HEEE HEEE!!

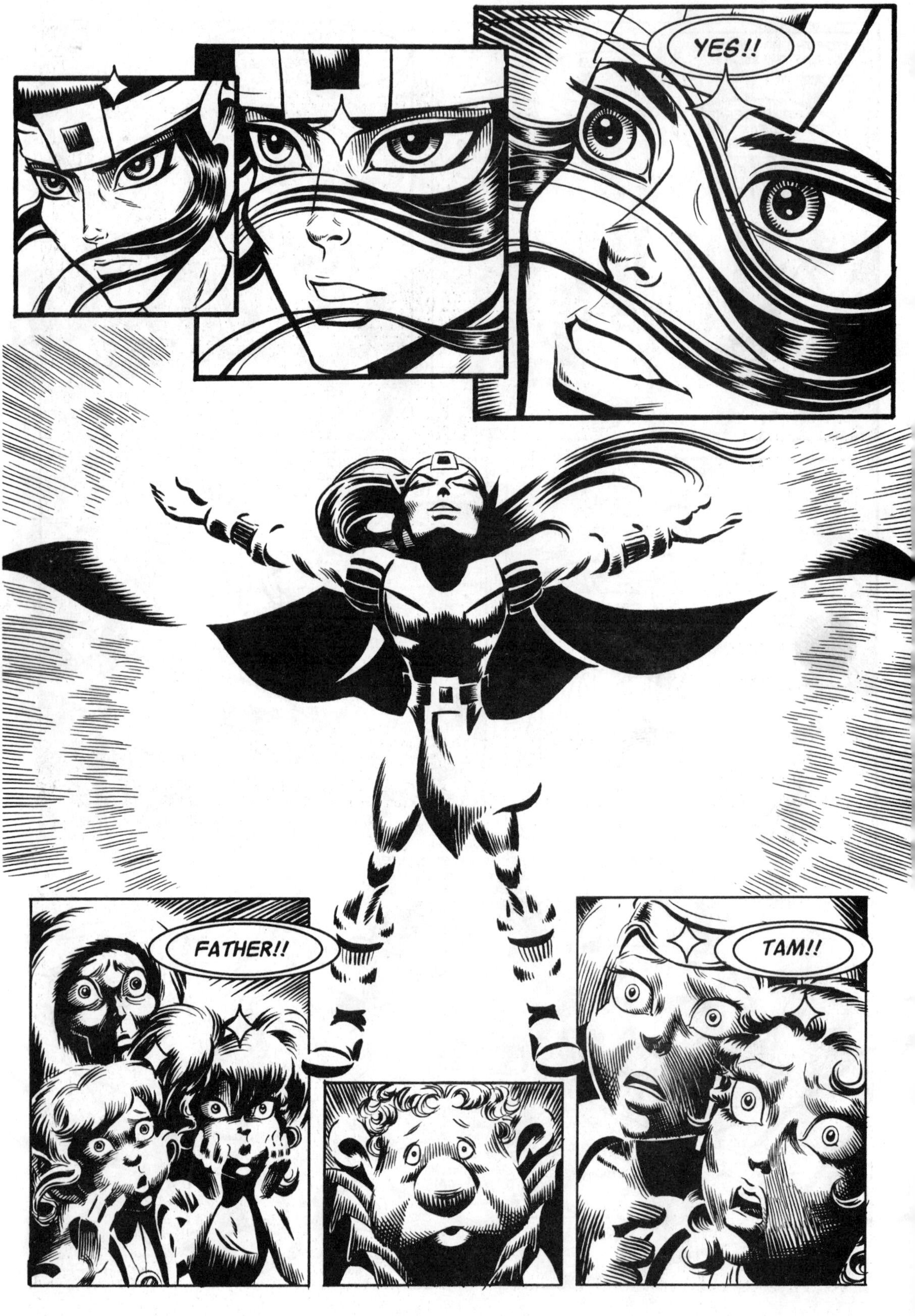
YES!!
FATHER!!
TAM!!

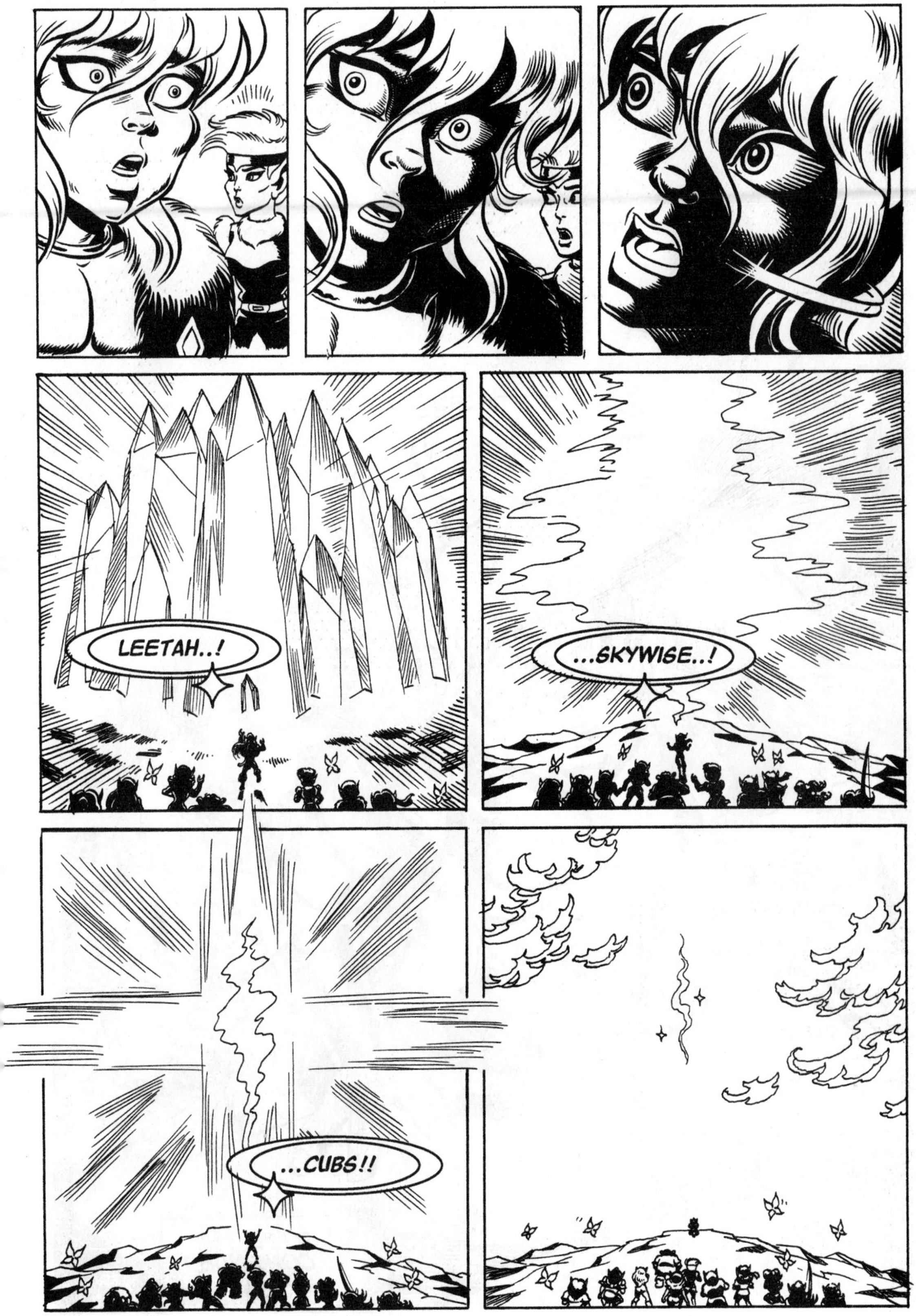
LEETAH..!
...SKYWISE..!
...CUBS!!

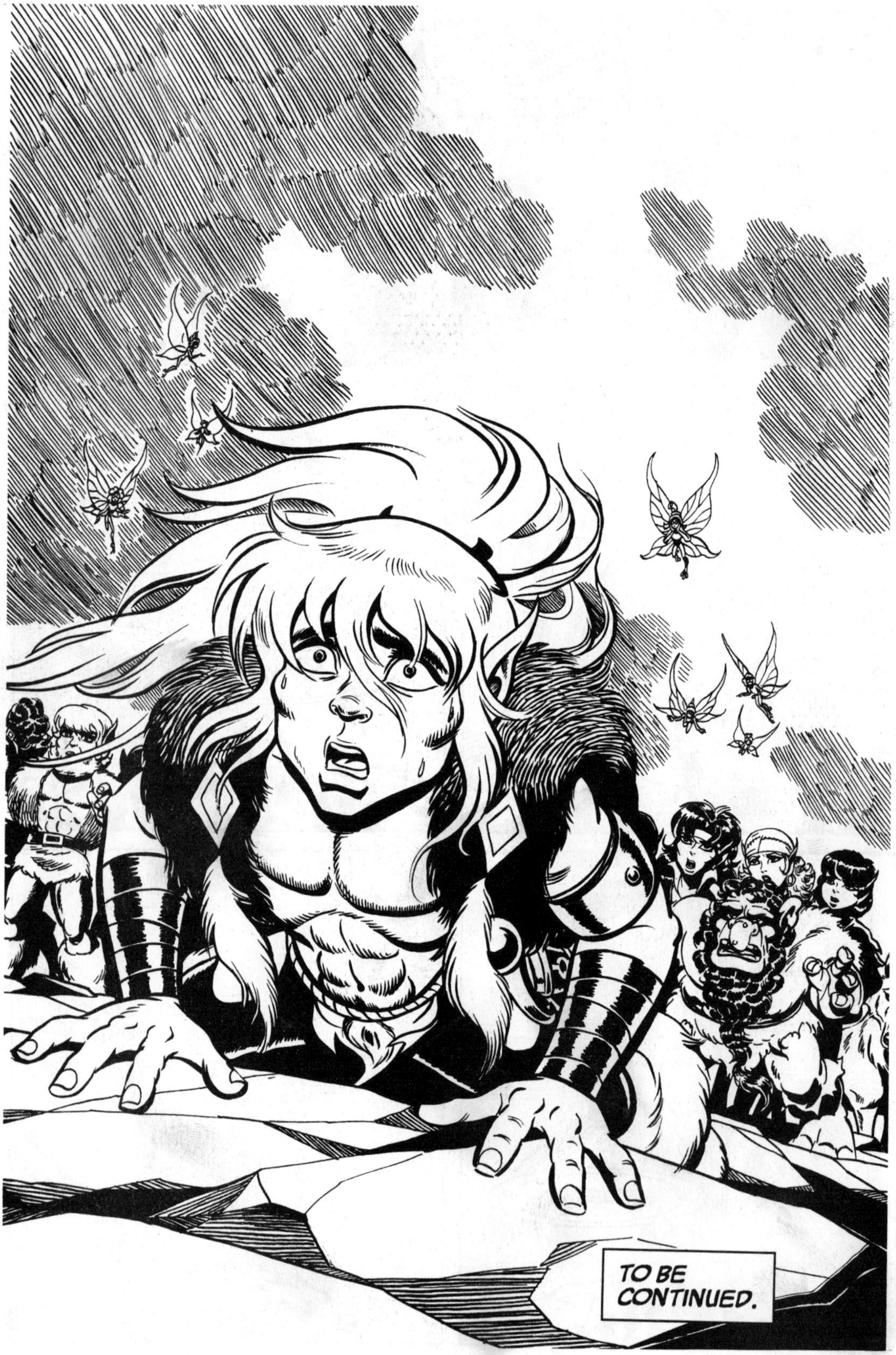
TO BE CONTINUED.

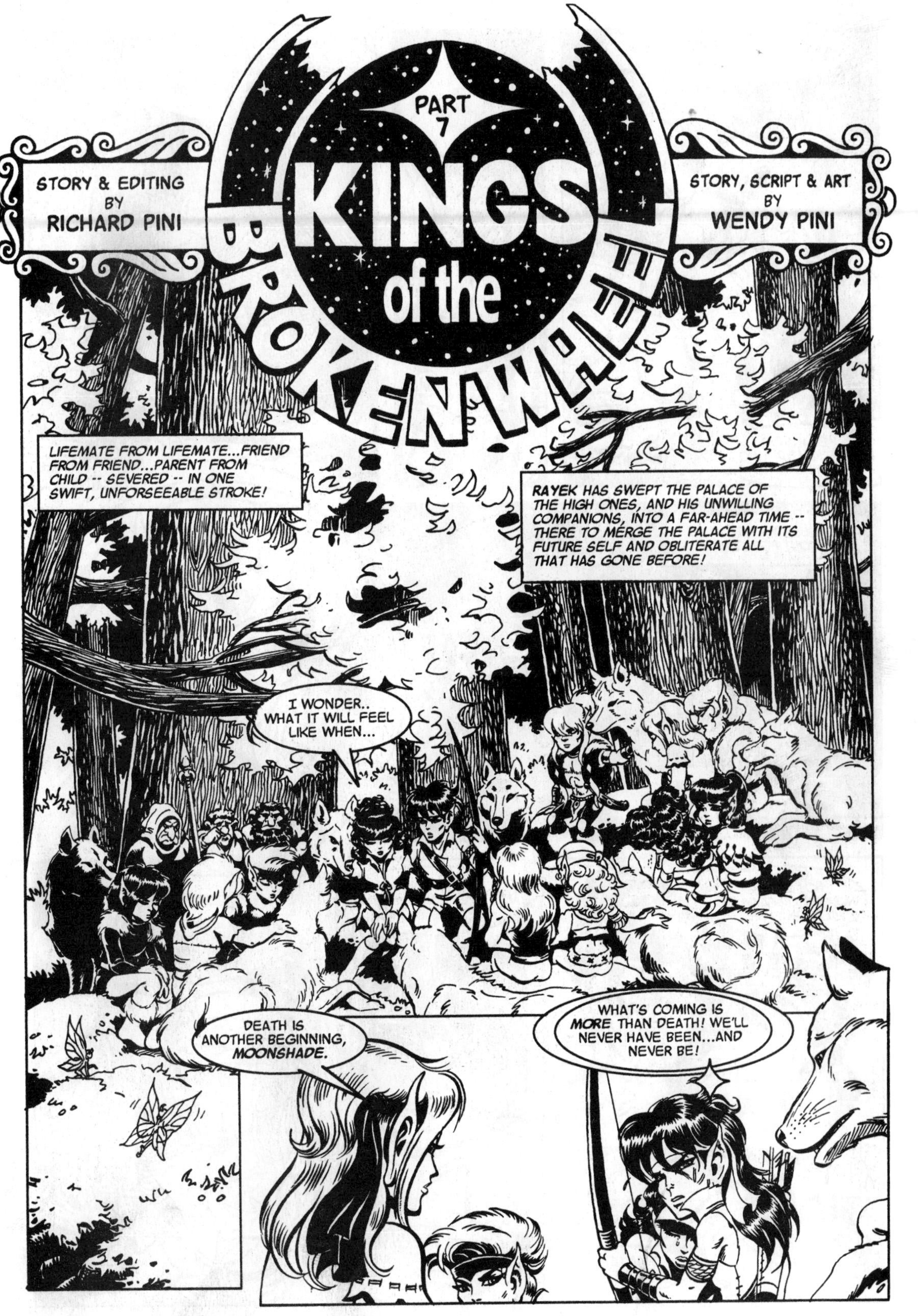

PART 7
KINGS of the BROKEN WHEEL
STORY & EDITING BY RICHARD PINI
STORY, SCRIPT & ART BY WENDY PINI
LIFEMATE FROM LIFEMATE...FRIEND FROM FRIEND...PARENT FROM CHILD -- SEVERED -- IN ONE SWIFT, UNFORSEEABLE STROKE!
RAYEK HAS SWEPT THE PALACE OF THE HIGH ONES, AND HIS UNWILLING COMPANIONS, INTO A FAR-AHEAD TIME -- THERE TO MERGE THE PALACE WITH ITS FUTURE SELF AND OBLITERATE ALL THAT HAS GONE BEFORE!
I WONDER.. WHAT IT WILL FEEL LIKE WHEN...
DEATH IS ANOTHER BEGINNING, MOONSHADE.
WHAT'S COMING IS MORE THAN DEATH! WE'LL NEVER HAVE BEEN...AND NEVER BE!

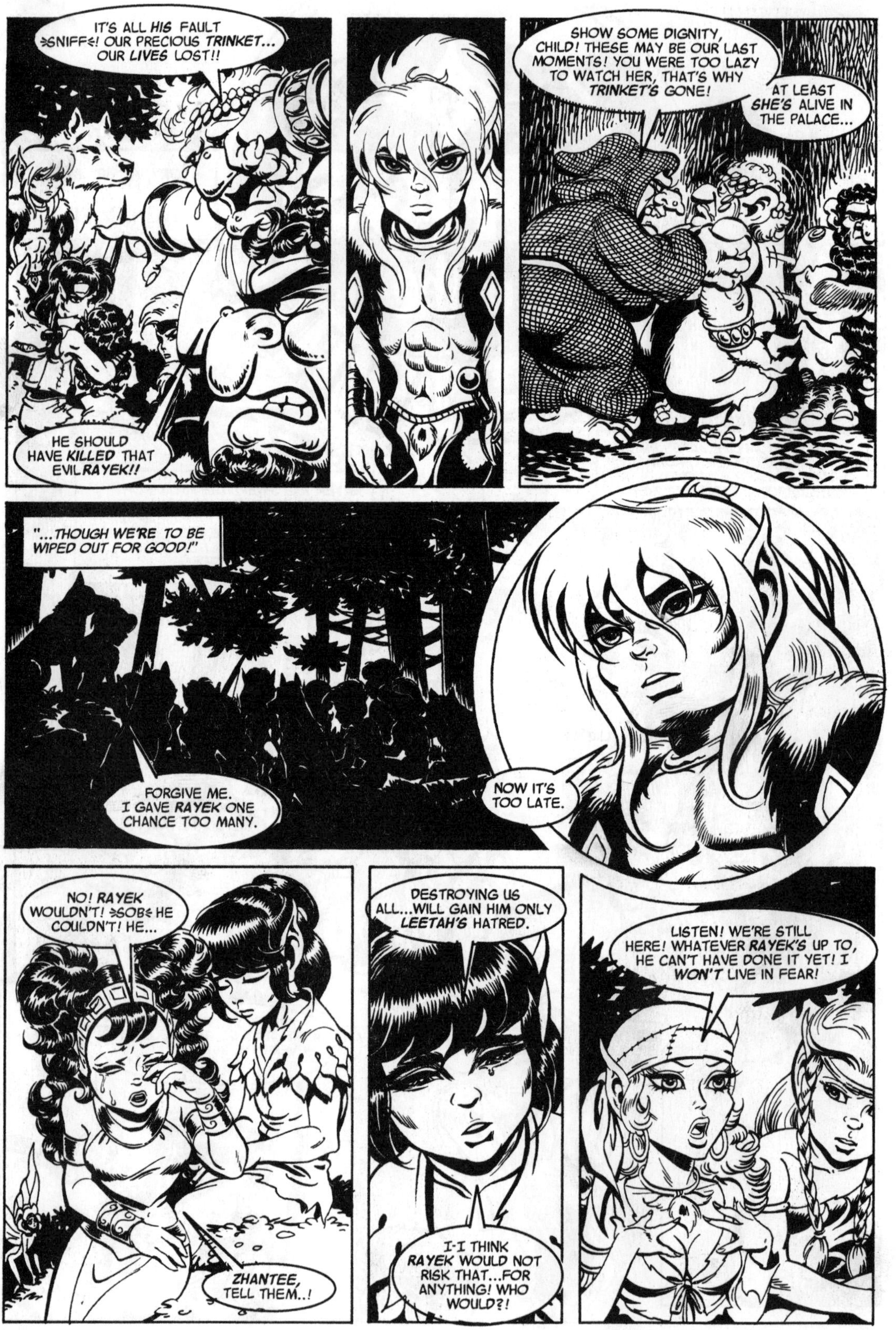
IT'S ALL HIS FAULT >SNIFF<! OUR PRECIOUS TRINKET... OUR LIVES LOST!!
HE SHOULD HAVE KILLED THAT EVIL RAYEK!!
SHOW SOME DIGNITY, CHILD! THESE MAY BE OUR LAST MOMENTS! YOU WERE TOO LAZY TO WATCH HER, THAT'S WHY TRINKET'S GONE!
AT LEAST SHE'S ALIVE IN THE PALACE...
"...THOUGH WE'RE TO BE WIPED OUT FOR GOOD!"
FORGIVE ME. I GAVE RAYEK ONE CHANCE TOO MANY.
NOW IT'S TOO LATE.
NO! RAYEK WOULDN'T! >SOB< HE COULDN'T! HE...
ZHANTEE, TELL THEM..!
DESTROYING US ALL...WILL GAIN HIM ONLY LEETAH'S HATRED.
I-I THINK RAYEK WOULD NOT RISK THAT...FOR ANYTHING! WHO WOULD?!
LISTEN! WE'RE STILL HERE! WHATEVER RAYEK'S UP TO, HE CAN'T HAVE DONE IT YET! I WON'T LIVE IN FEAR!

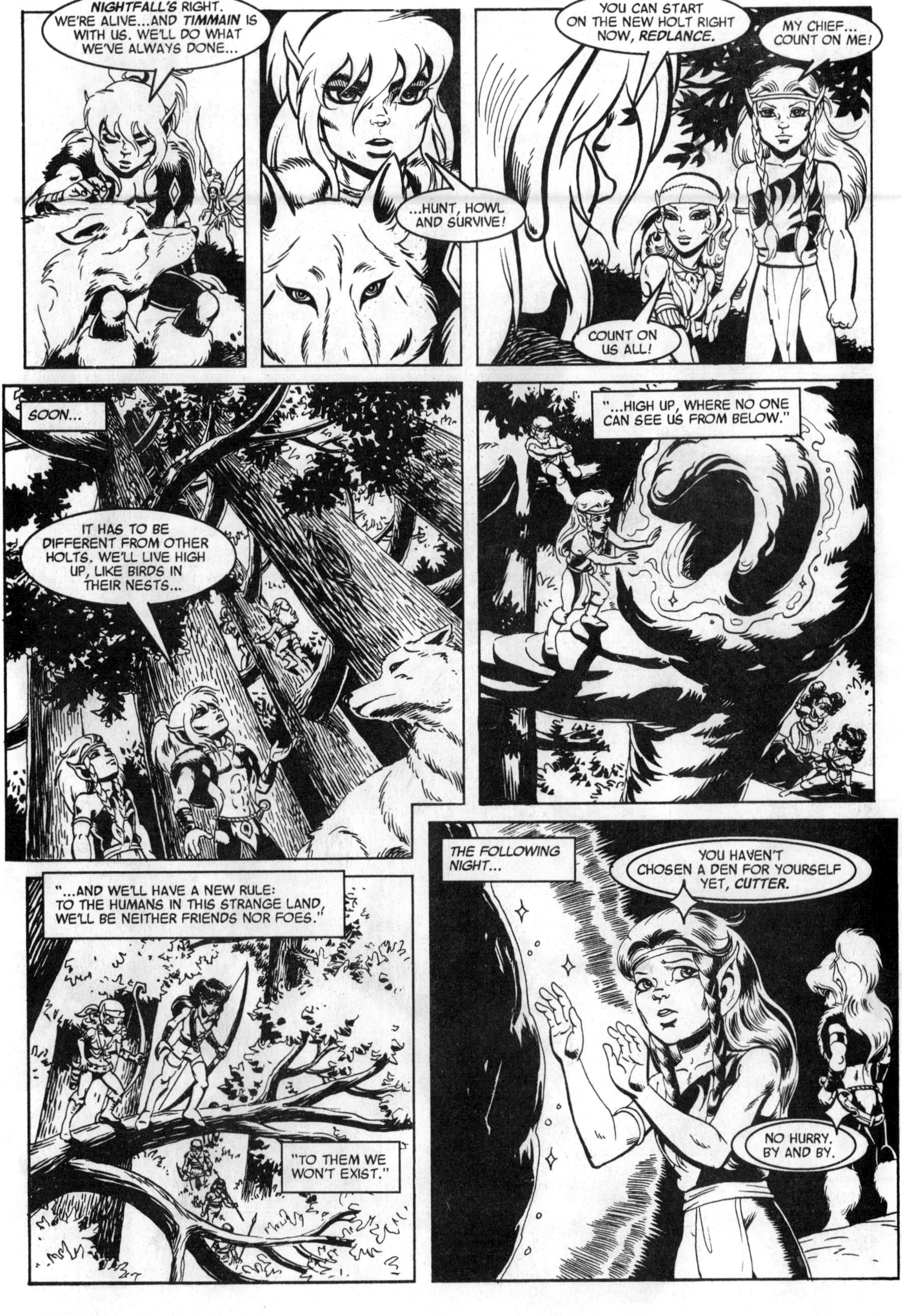
NIGHTFALL'S RIGHT. WE'RE ALIVE...AND TIMMAIN IS WITH US. WE'LL DO WHAT WE'VE ALWAYS DONE...
...HUNT, HOWL AND SURVIVE!
YOU CAN START ON THE NEW HOLT RIGHT NOW, REDLANCE.
MY CHIEF... COUNT ON ME!
COUNT ON US ALL!
SOON...
IT HAS TO BE DIFFERENT FROM OTHER HOLTS. WE'LL LIVE HIGH UP, LIKE BIRDS IN THEIR NESTS...
"...HIGH UP, WHERE NO ONE CAN SEE US FROM BELOW."
"...AND WE'LL HAVE A NEW RULE: TO THE HUMANS IN THIS STRANGE LAND, WE'LL BE NEITHER FRIENDS NOR FOES."
"TO THEM WE WON'T EXIST."
THE FOLLOWING NIGHT...
YOU HAVEN'T CHOSEN A DEN FOR YOURSELF YET, CUTTER.
NO HURRY. BY AND BY.

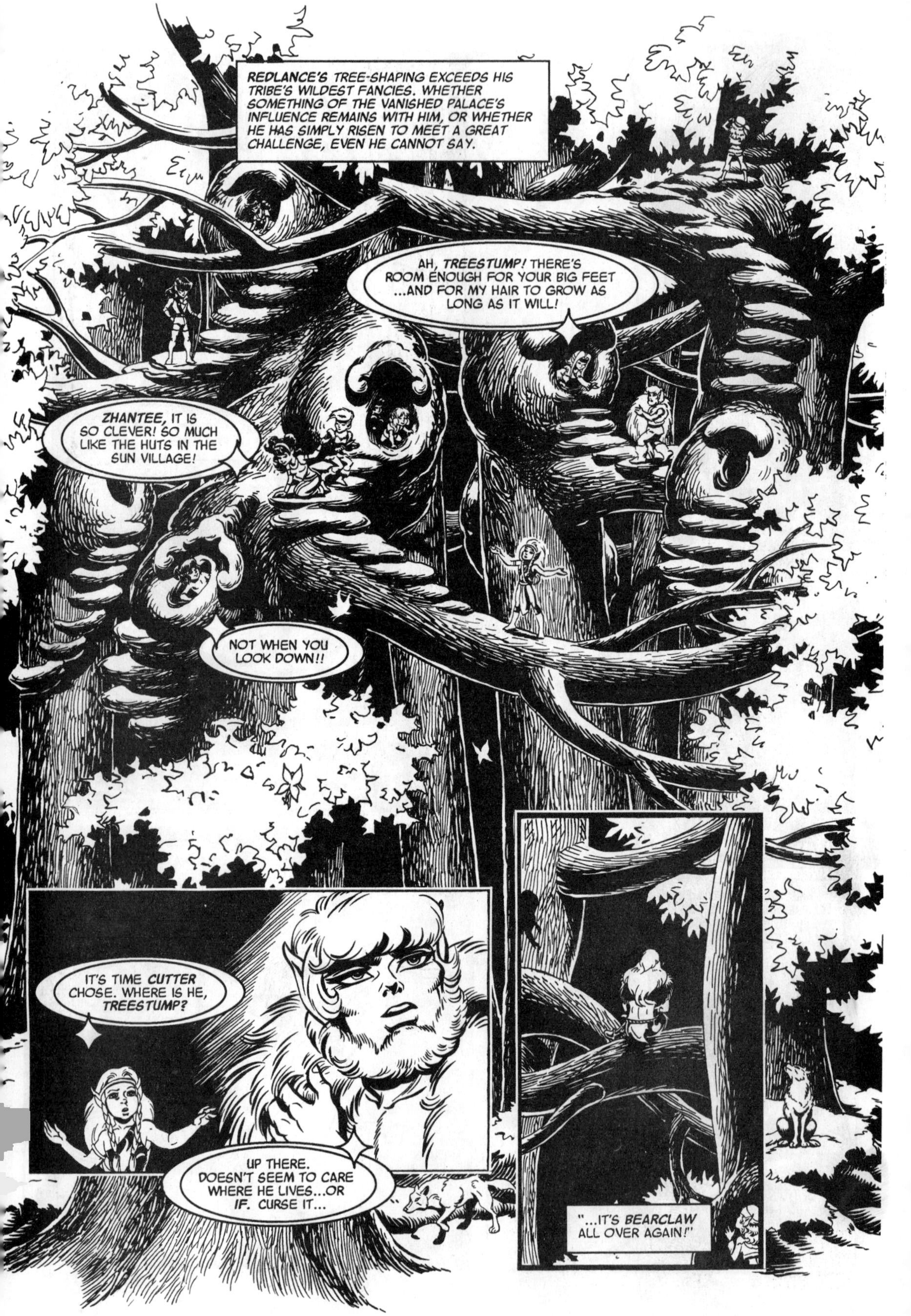
REDLANCE'S TREE-SHAPING EXCEEDS HIS TRIBE'S WILDEST FANCIES. WHETHER SOMETHING OF THE VANISHED PALACE'S INFLUENCE REMAINS WITH HIM, OR WHETHER HE HAS SIMPLY RISEN TO MEET A GREAT CHALLENGE, EVEN HE CANNOT SAY.
AH, TREESTUMP! THERE'S ROOM ENOUGH FOR YOUR BIG FEET ...AND FOR MY HAIR TO GROW AS LONG AS IT WILL!
ZHANTEE, IT IS SO CLEVER! SO MUCH LIKE THE HUTS IN THE SUN VILLAGE!
NOT WHEN YOU LOOK DOWN!!
IT'S TIME CUTTER CHOSE. WHERE IS HE, TREESTUMP?
UP THERE. DOESN'T SEEM TO CARE WHERE HE LIVES...OR IF. CURSE IT...
"...IT'S BEARCLAW ALL OVER AGAIN!"

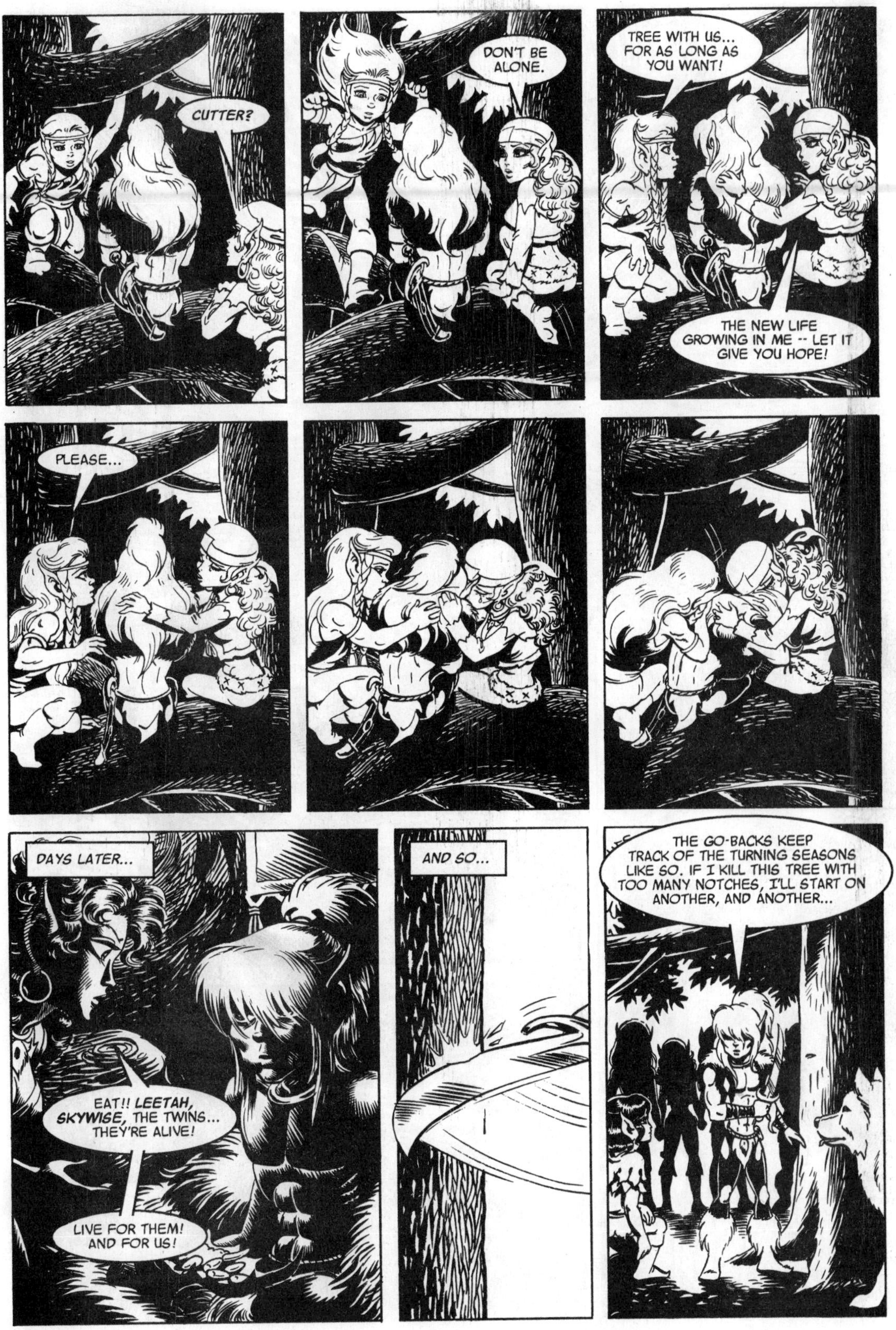
CUTTER?
DON'T BE ALONE.
TREE WITH US... FOR AS LONG AS YOU WANT!
THE NEW LIFE GROWING IN ME -- LET IT GIVE YOU HOPE!
PLEASE...
DAYS LATER...
EAT!! LEETAH, SKYWISE, THE TWINS... THEY'RE ALIVE!
LIVE FOR THEM! AND FOR US!
AND SO...
THE GO-BACKS KEEP TRACK OF THE TURNING SEASONS LIKE SO. IF I KILL THIS TREE WITH TOO MANY NOTCHES, I'LL START ON ANOTHER, AND ANOTHER...

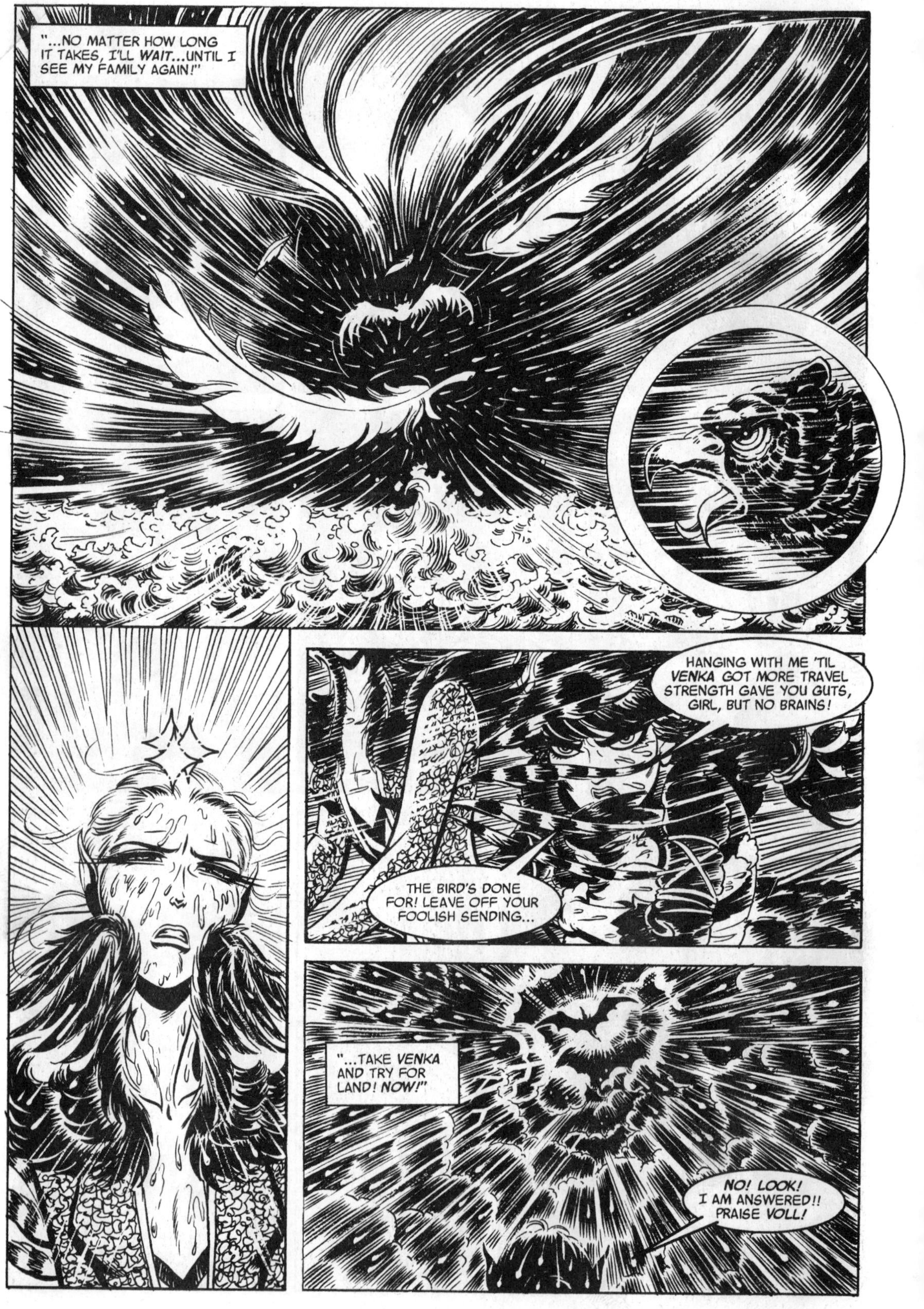
"...NO MATTER HOW LONG IT TAKES, I'LL WAIT...UNTIL I SEE MY FAMILY AGAIN!"
HANGING WITH ME 'TIL VENKA GOT MORE TRAVEL STRENGTH GAVE YOU GUTS, GIRL, BUT NO BRAINS!
THE BIRD'S DONE FOR! LEAVE OFF YOUR FOOLISH SENDING...
"...TAKE VENKA AND TRY FOR LAND! NOW!"
NO! LOOK! I AM ANSWERED!! PRAISE VOLL!

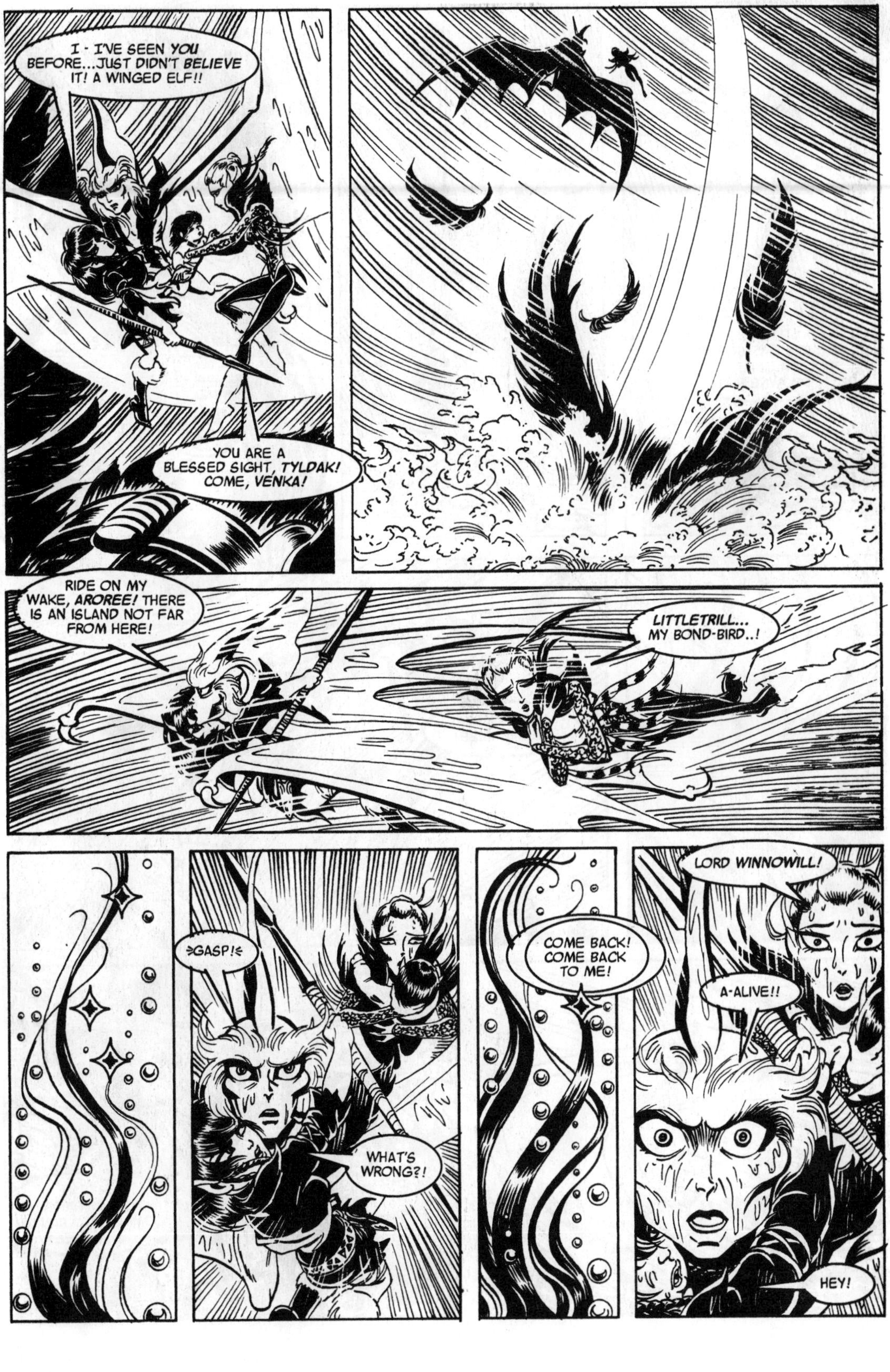
I - I'VE SEEN YOU BEFORE...JUST DIDN'T BELIEVE IT! A WINGED ELF!!
YOU ARE A BLESSED SIGHT, TYLDAK! COME, VENKA!
RIDE ON MY WAKE, AROREE! THERE IS AN ISLAND NOT FAR FROM HERE!
LITTLETRILL... MY BOND-BIRD..!
GASP!
WHAT'S WRONG?!
COME BACK! COME BACK TO ME!
LORD WINNOWILL!
A-ALIVE!!
HEY!

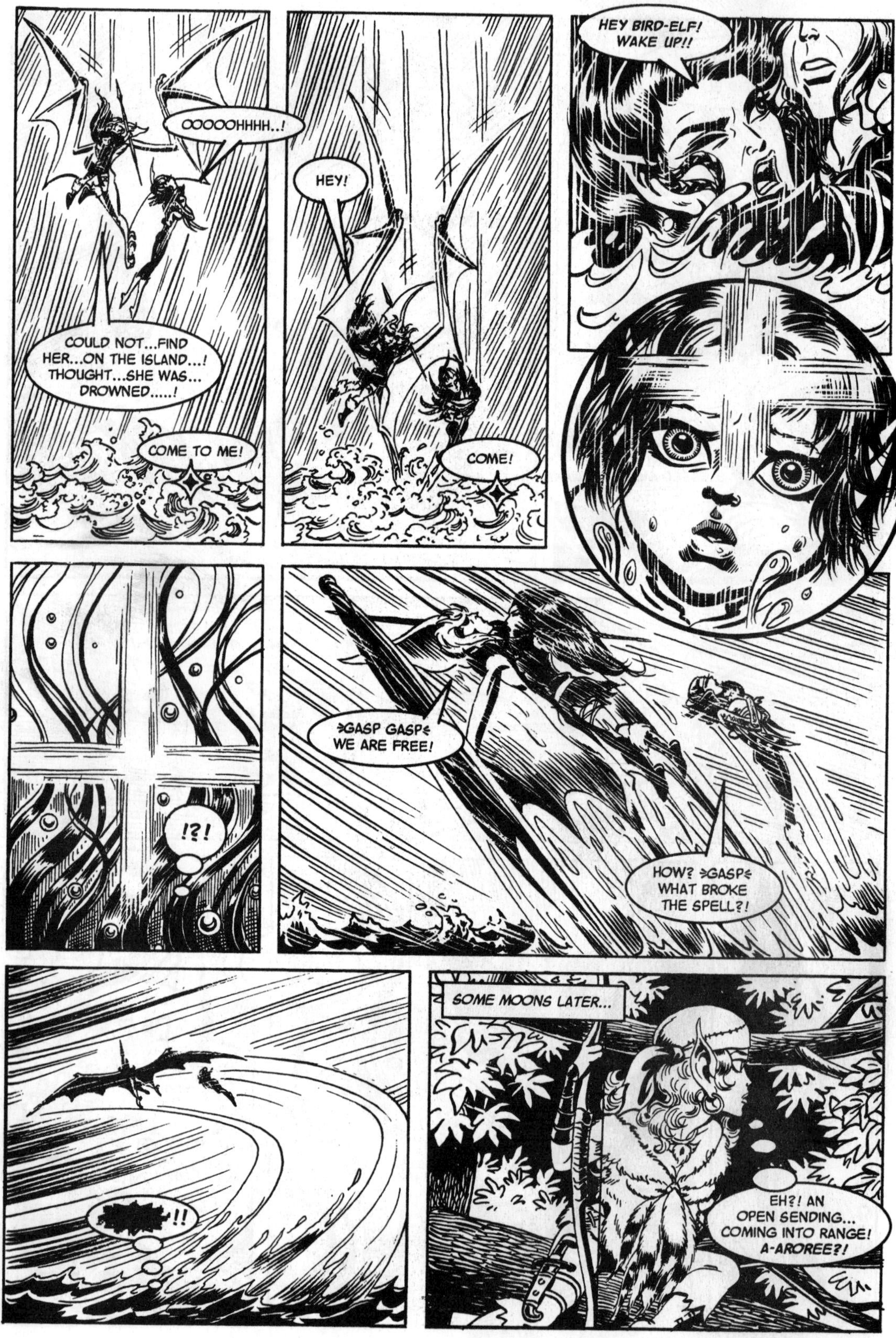
OOOOOHHHH..!
COULD NOT...FIND HER...ON THE ISLAND...! THOUGHT...SHE WAS... DROWNED.....!
COME TO ME!
HEY!
COME!
HEY BIRD-ELF! WAKE UP!!
!?!
GASP GASP WE ARE FREE!
HOW? GASP WHAT BROKE THE SPELL?!
!!
SOME MOONS LATER...
EH?! AN OPEN SENDING... COMING INTO RANGE! A-AROREE?!

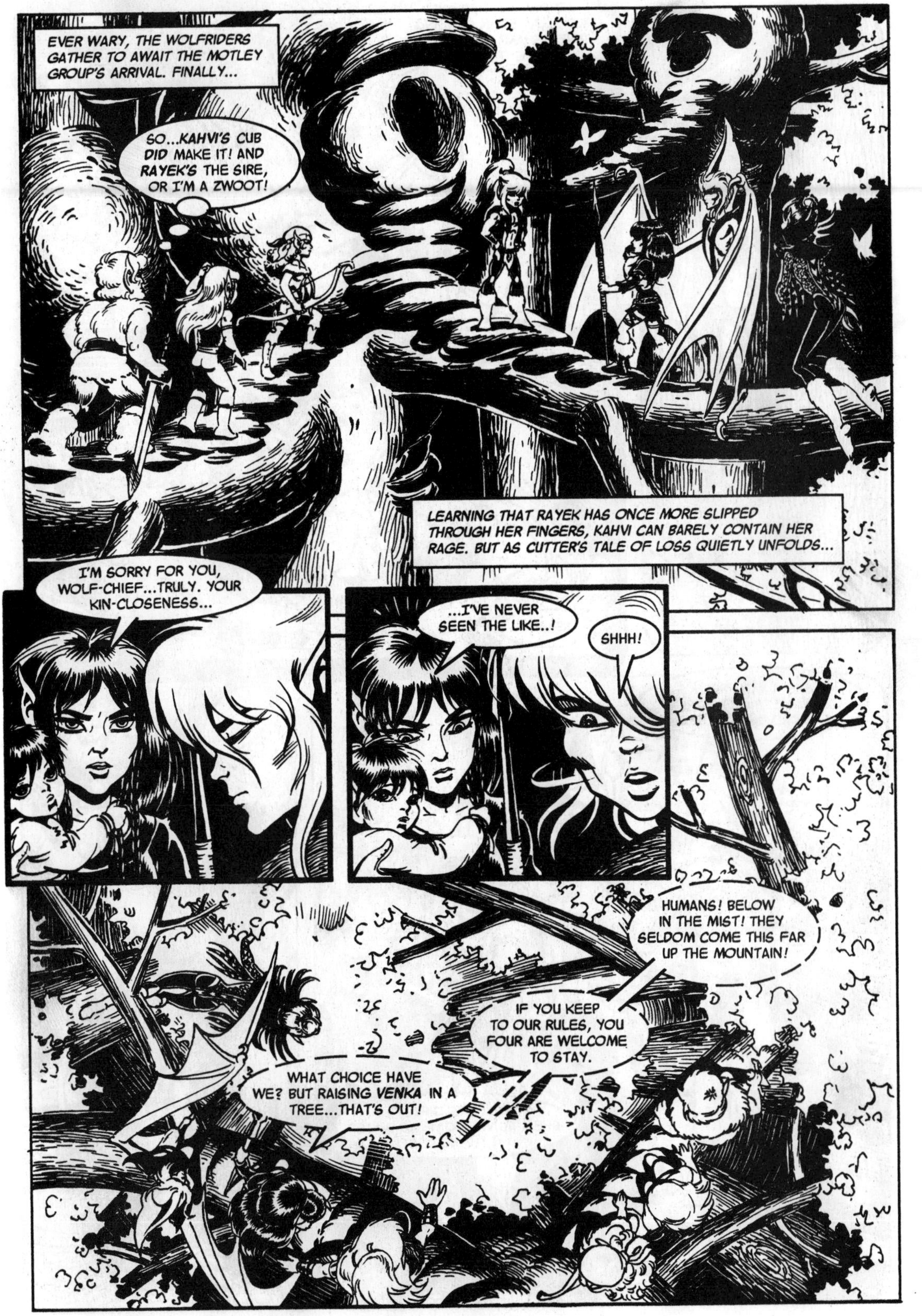
EVER WARY, THE WOLFRIDERS GATHER TO AWAIT THE MOTLEY GROUP'S ARRIVAL. FINALLY...
SO...KAHVI'S CUB DID MAKE IT! AND RAYEK'S THE SIRE, OR I'M A ZWOOT!
LEARNING THAT RAYEK HAS ONCE MORE SLIPPED THROUGH HER FINGERS, KAHVI CAN BARELY CONTAIN HER RAGE. BUT AS CUTTER'S TALE OF LOSS QUIETLY UNFOLDS...
I'M SORRY FOR YOU, WOLF-CHIEF...TRULY. YOUR KIN-CLOSENESS...
...I'VE NEVER SEEN THE LIKE..!
SHHH!
HUMANS! BELOW IN THE MIST! THEY SELDOM COME THIS FAR UP THE MOUNTAIN!
IF YOU KEEP TO OUR RULES, YOU FOUR ARE WELCOME TO STAY.
WHAT CHOICE HAVE WE? BUT RAISING VENKA IN A TREE...THAT'S OUT!

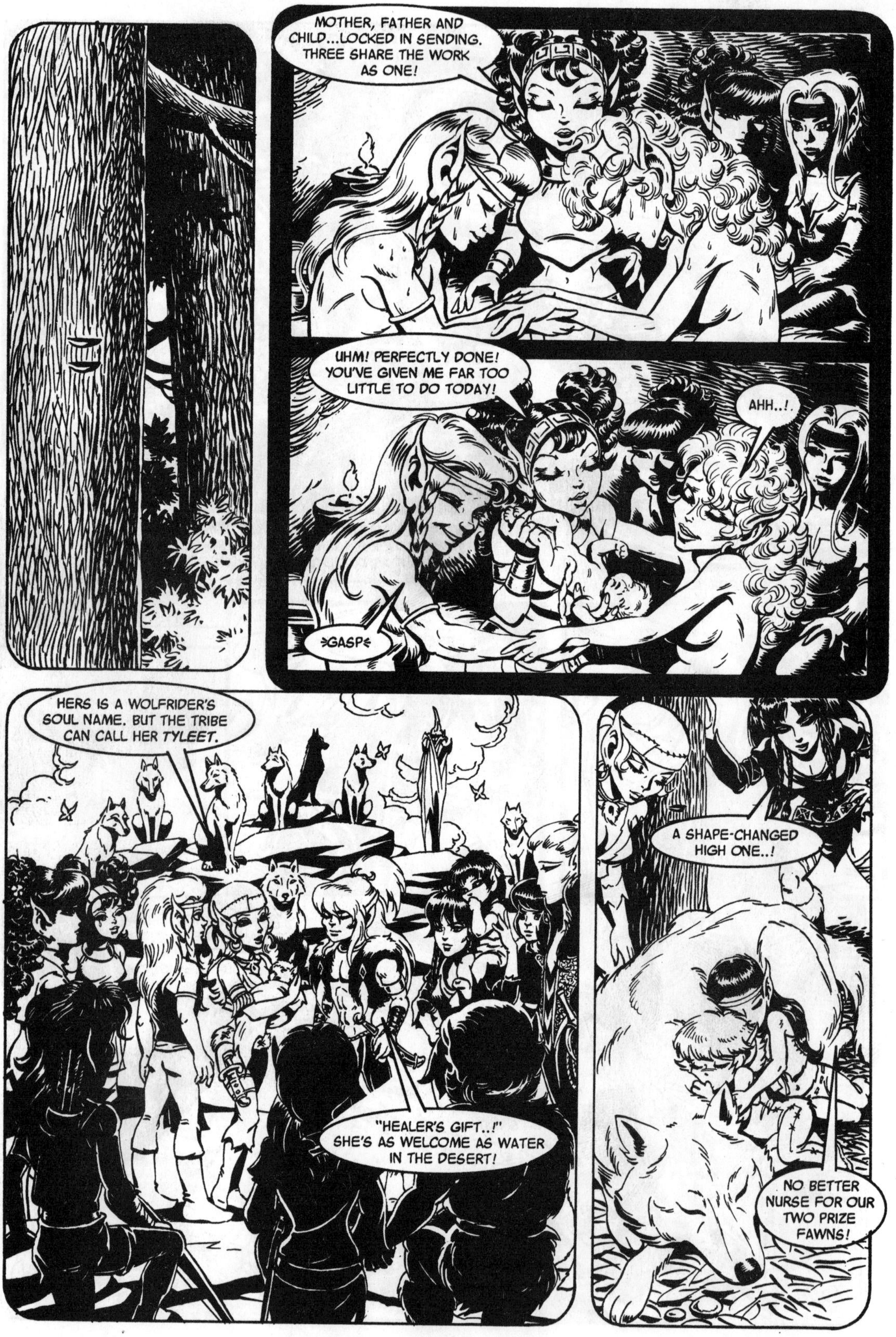
MOTHER, FATHER AND CHILD...LOCKED IN SENDING. THREE SHARE THE WORK AS ONE!
UHM! PERFECTLY DONE! YOU'VE GIVEN ME FAR TOO LITTLE TO DO TODAY!
AHH..!.
GASP
HERS IS A WOLFRIDER'S SOUL NAME. BUT THE TRIBE CAN CALL HER *TYLEET.*
"HEALER'S GIFT..!" SHE'S AS WELCOME AS WATER IN THE DESERT!
A SHAPE-CHANGED HIGH ONE..!
NO BETTER NURSE FOR OUR TWO PRIZE FAWNS!

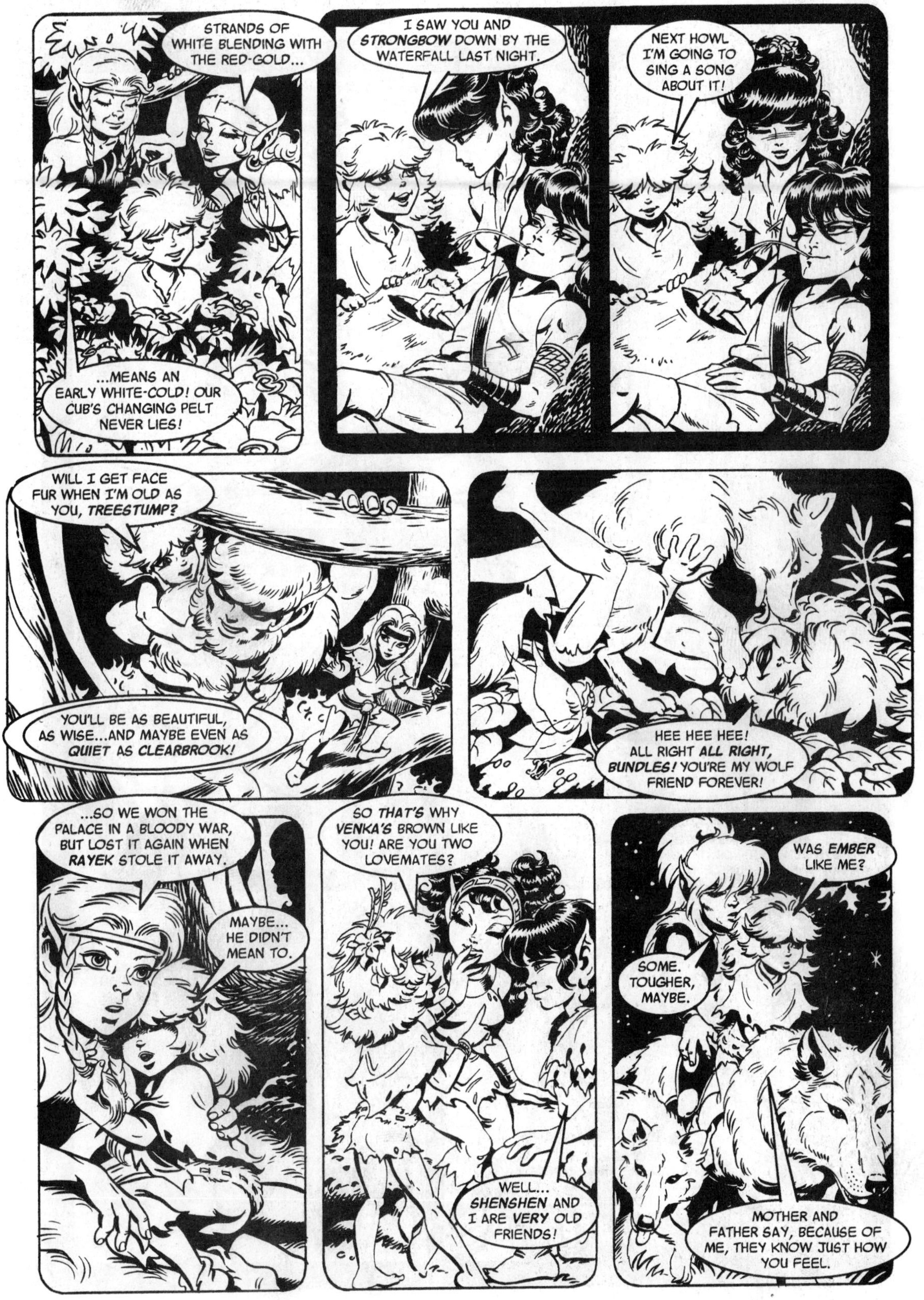
STRANDS OF WHITE BLENDING WITH THE RED-GOLD...
...MEANS AN EARLY WHITE-COLD! OUR CUB'S CHANGING PELT NEVER LIES!
I SAW YOU AND STRONGBOW DOWN BY THE WATERFALL LAST NIGHT.
NEXT HOWL I'M GOING TO SING A SONG ABOUT IT!
WILL I GET FACE FUR WHEN I'M OLD AS YOU, TREESTUMP?
YOU'LL BE AS BEAUTIFUL, AS WISE...AND MAYBE EVEN AS QUIET AS CLEARBROOK!
HEE HEE HEE! ALL RIGHT ALL RIGHT, BUNDLES! YOU'RE MY WOLF FRIEND FOREVER!
...SO WE WON THE PALACE IN A BLOODY WAR, BUT LOST IT AGAIN WHEN RAYEK STOLE IT AWAY.
MAYBE... HE DIDN'T MEAN TO.
SO THAT'S WHY VENKA'S BROWN LIKE YOU! ARE YOU TWO LOVEMATES?
WELL... SHENSHEN AND I ARE VERY OLD FRIENDS!
WAS EMBER LIKE ME?
SOME. TOUGHER, MAYBE.
MOTHER AND FATHER SAY, BECAUSE OF ME, THEY KNOW JUST HOW YOU FEEL.

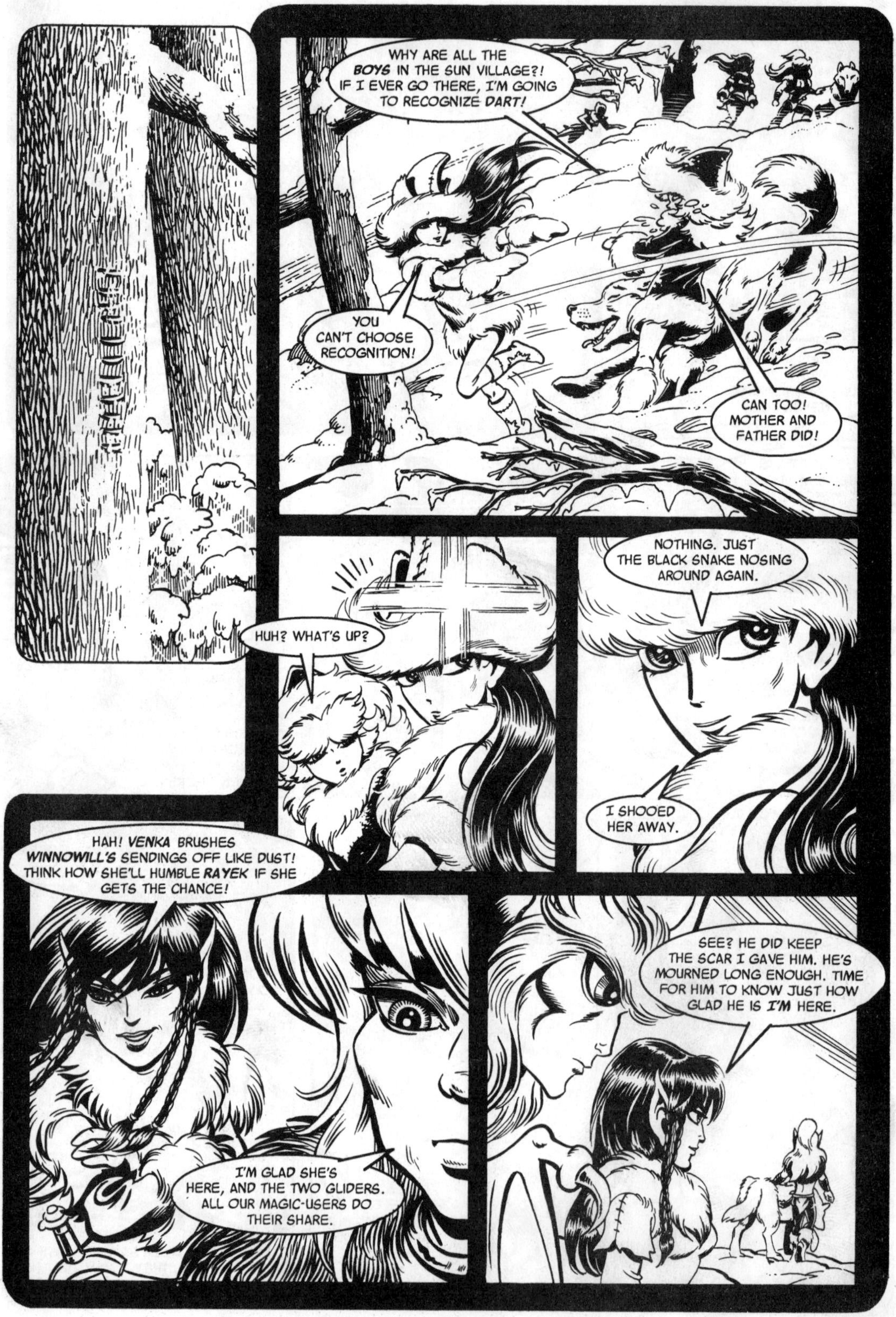

WHY ARE ALL THE BOYS IN THE SUN VILLAGE?! IF I EVER GO THERE, I'M GOING TO RECOGNIZE DART!
YOU CAN'T CHOOSE RECOGNITION!
CAN TOO! MOTHER AND FATHER DID!
HUH? WHAT'S UP?
NOTHING. JUST THE BLACK SNAKE NOSING AROUND AGAIN.
I SHOOED HER AWAY.
HAH! VENKA BRUSHES WINNOWILL'S SENDINGS OFF LIKE DUST! THINK HOW SHE'LL HUMBLE RAYEK IF SHE GETS THE CHANCE!
I'M GLAD SHE'S HERE, AND THE TWO GLIDERS. ALL OUR MAGIC-USERS DO THEIR SHARE.
SEE? HE DID KEEP THE SCAR I GAVE HIM. HE'S MOURNED LONG ENOUGH. TIME FOR HIM TO KNOW JUST HOW GLAD HE IS I'M HERE.

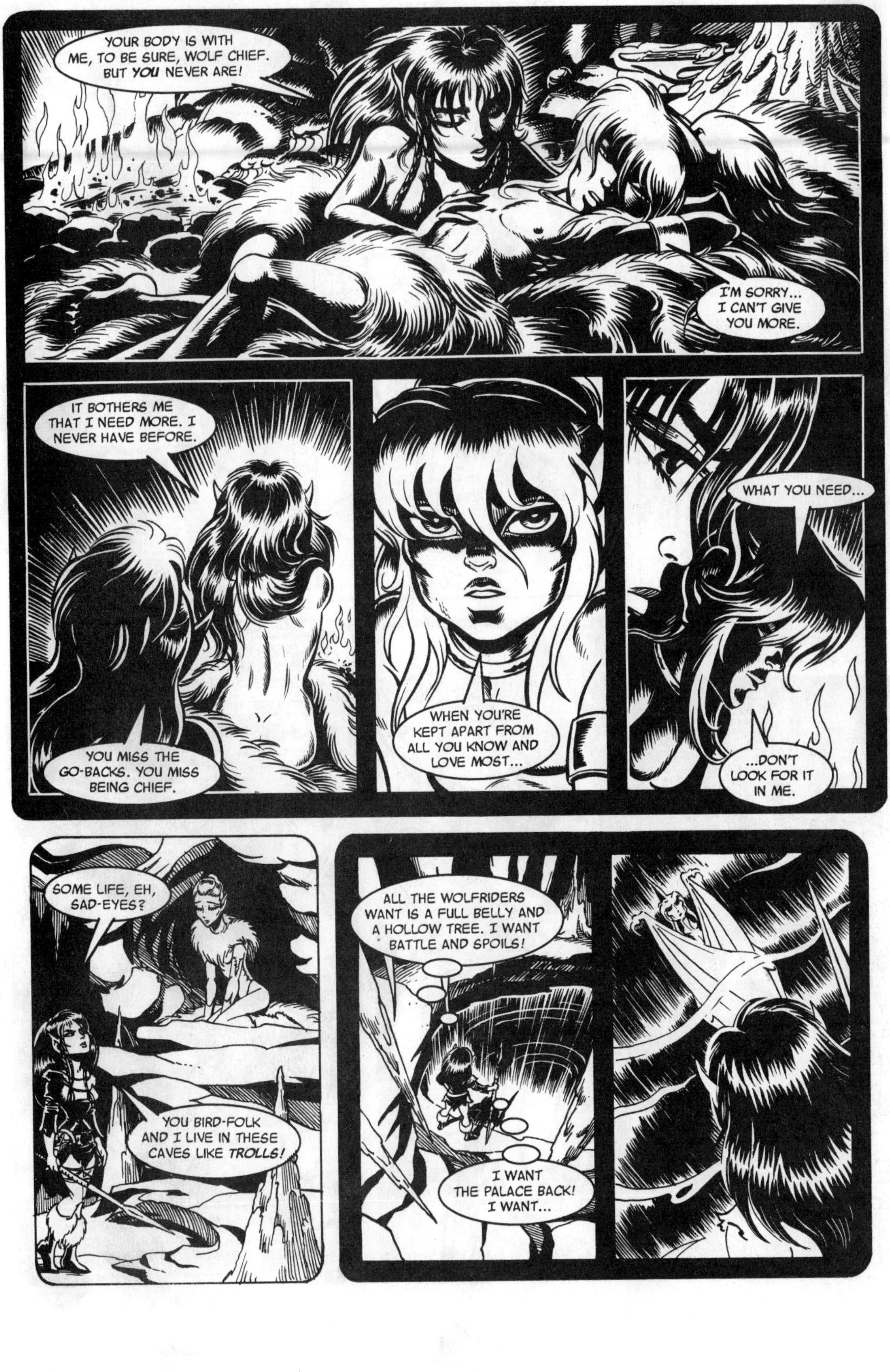
YOUR BODY IS WITH ME, TO BE SURE, WOLF CHIEF. BUT YOU NEVER ARE!
I'M SORRY... I CAN'T GIVE YOU MORE.
IT BOTHERS ME THAT I NEED MORE. I NEVER HAVE BEFORE.
YOU MISS THE GO-BACKS. YOU MISS BEING CHIEF.
WHEN YOU'RE KEPT APART FROM ALL YOU KNOW AND LOVE MOST...
WHAT YOU NEED...
...DON'T LOOK FOR IT IN ME.
SOME LIFE, EH, SAD-EYES?
YOU BIRD-FOLK AND I LIVE IN THESE CAVES LIKE TROLLS!
ALL THE WOLFRIDERS WANT IS A FULL BELLY AND A HOLLOW TREE. I WANT BATTLE AND SPOILS!
I WANT THE PALACE BACK! I WANT...

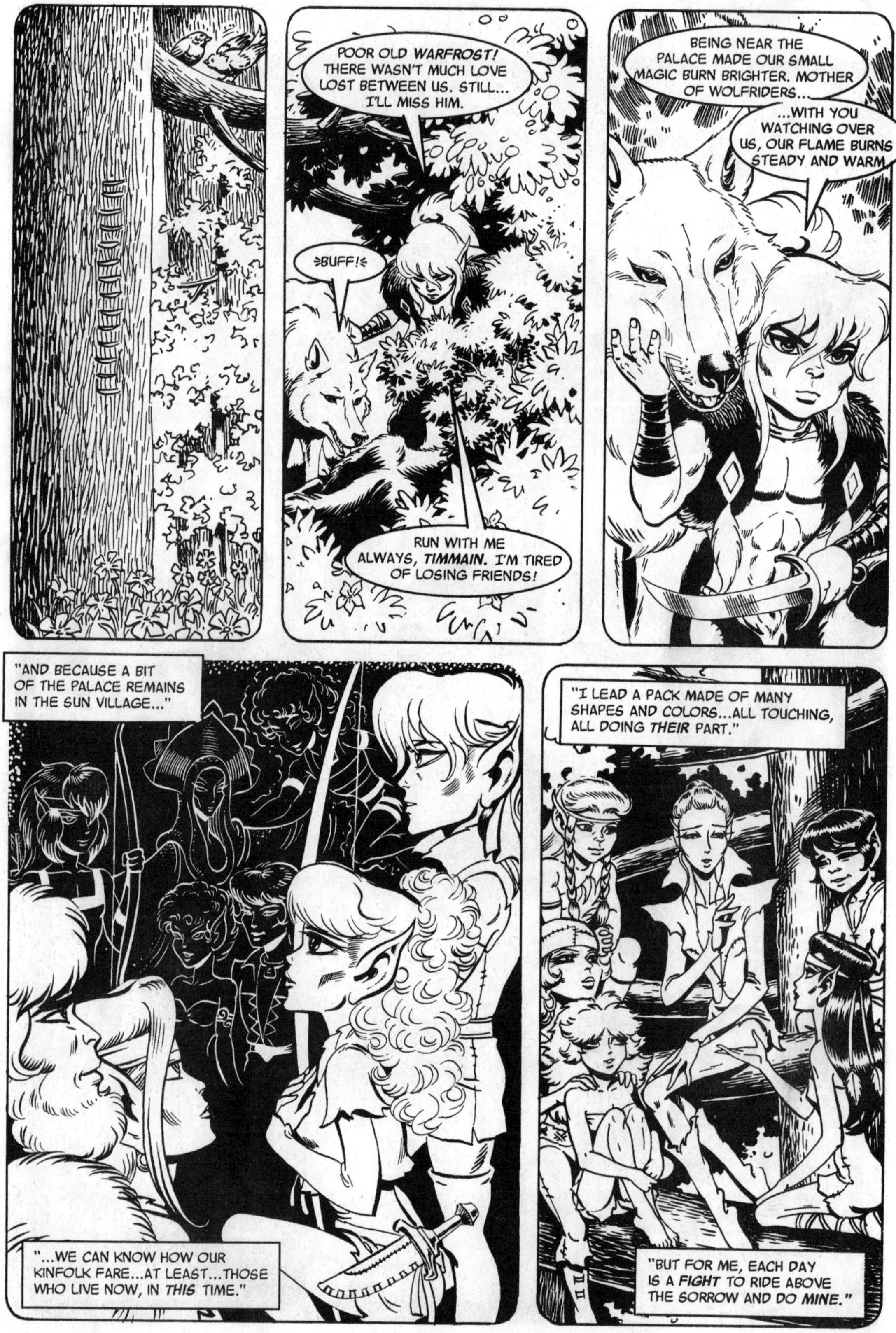
POOR OLD WARFROST! THERE WASN'T MUCH LOVE LOST BETWEEN US. STILL... I'LL MISS HIM.
≥BUFF!≤
RUN WITH ME ALWAYS, TIMMAIN. I'M TIRED OF LOSING FRIENDS!
BEING NEAR THE PALACE MADE OUR SMALL MAGIC BURN BRIGHTER. MOTHER OF WOLFRIDERS...
...WITH YOU WATCHING OVER US, OUR FLAME BURNS STEADY AND WARM
"AND BECAUSE A BIT OF THE PALACE REMAINS IN THE SUN VILLAGE..."
"...WE CAN KNOW HOW OUR KINFOLK FARE...AT LEAST...THOSE WHO LIVE NOW, IN THIS TIME."
"I LEAD A PACK MADE OF MANY SHAPES AND COLORS...ALL TOUCHING, ALL DOING THEIR PART."
"BUT FOR ME, EACH DAY IS A FIGHT TO RIDE ABOVE THE SORROW AND DO MINE."

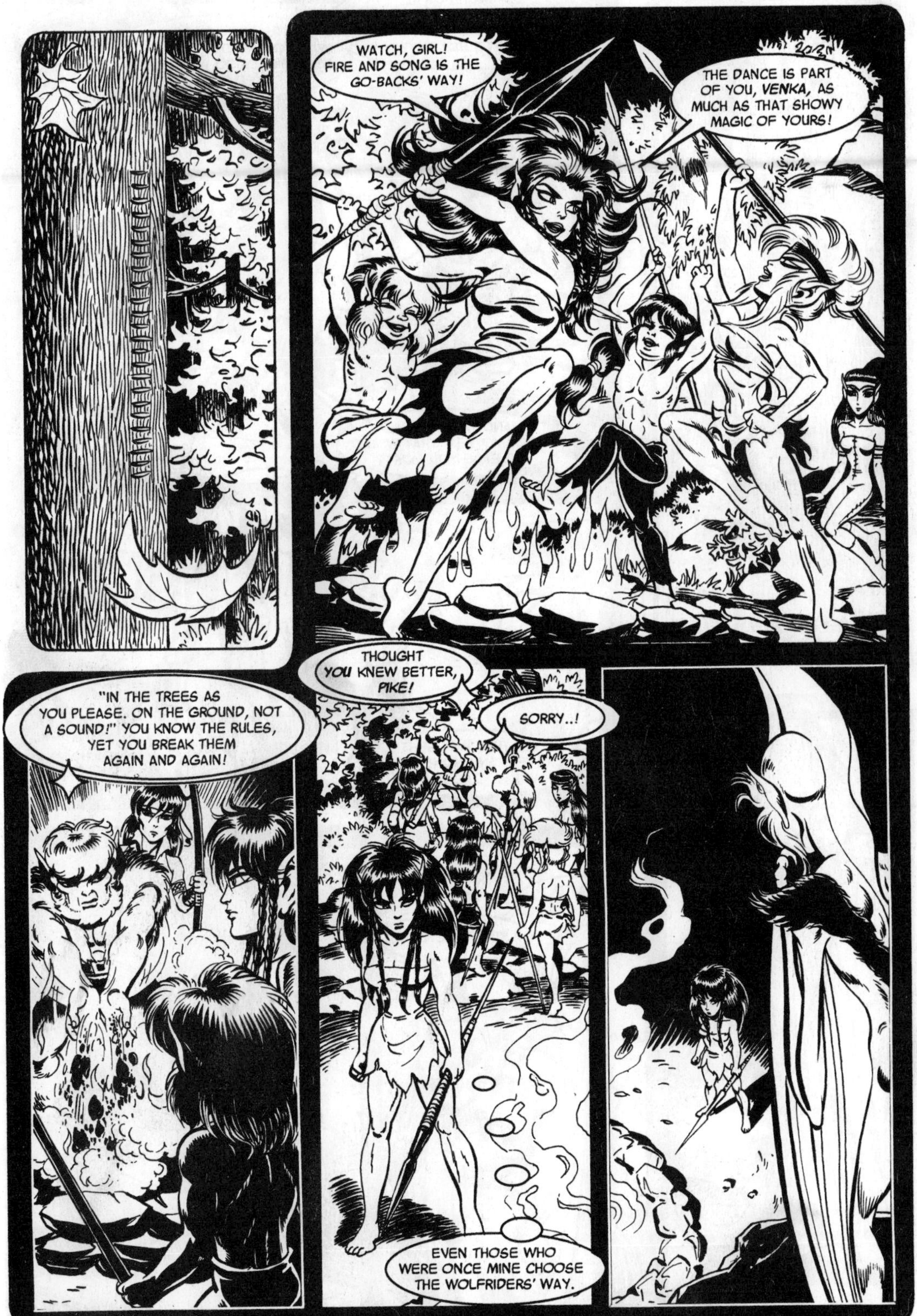
WATCH, GIRL! FIRE AND SONG IS THE GO-BACKS' WAY!
THE DANCE IS PART OF YOU, VENKA, AS MUCH AS THAT SHOWY MAGIC OF YOURS!
"IN THE TREES AS YOU PLEASE. ON THE GROUND, NOT A SOUND!" YOU KNOW THE RULES, YET YOU BREAK THEM AGAIN AND AGAIN!
THOUGHT YOU KNEW BETTER, PIKE!
SORRY..!
EVEN THOSE WHO WERE ONCE MINE CHOOSE THE WOLFRIDERS' WAY.

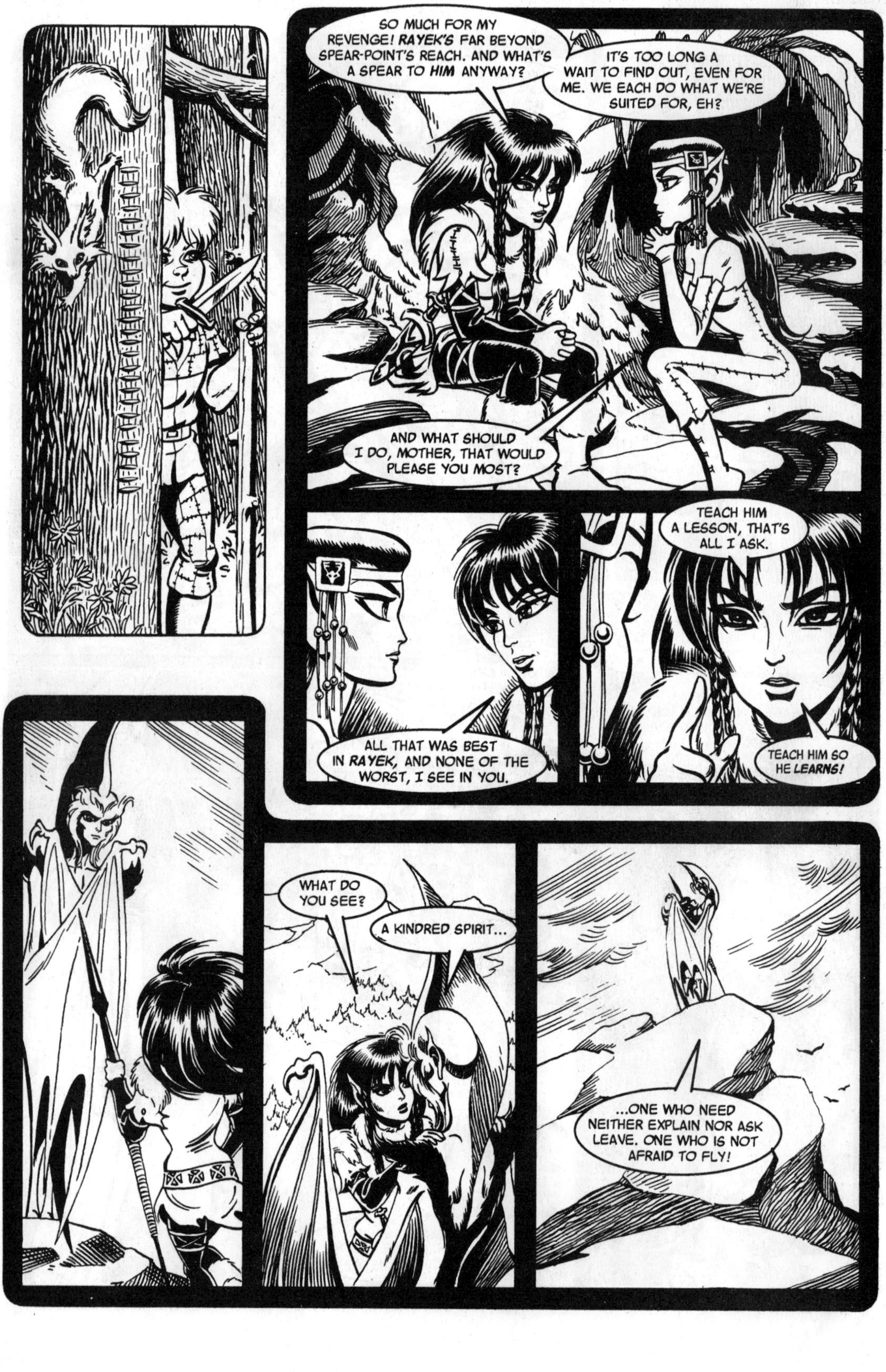
SO MUCH FOR MY REVENGE! RAYEK'S FAR BEYOND SPEAR-POINT'S REACH. AND WHAT'S A SPEAR TO HIM ANYWAY?
IT'S TOO LONG A WAIT TO FIND OUT, EVEN FOR ME. WE EACH DO WHAT WE'RE SUITED FOR, EH?
AND WHAT SHOULD I DO, MOTHER, THAT WOULD PLEASE YOU MOST?
ALL THAT WAS BEST IN RAYEK, AND NONE OF THE WORST, I SEE IN YOU.
TEACH HIM A LESSON, THAT'S ALL I ASK.
TEACH HIM SO HE LEARNS!
WHAT DO YOU SEE?
A KINDRED SPIRIT...
...ONE WHO NEED NEITHER EXPLAIN NOR ASK LEAVE. ONE WHO IS NOT AFRAID TO FLY!

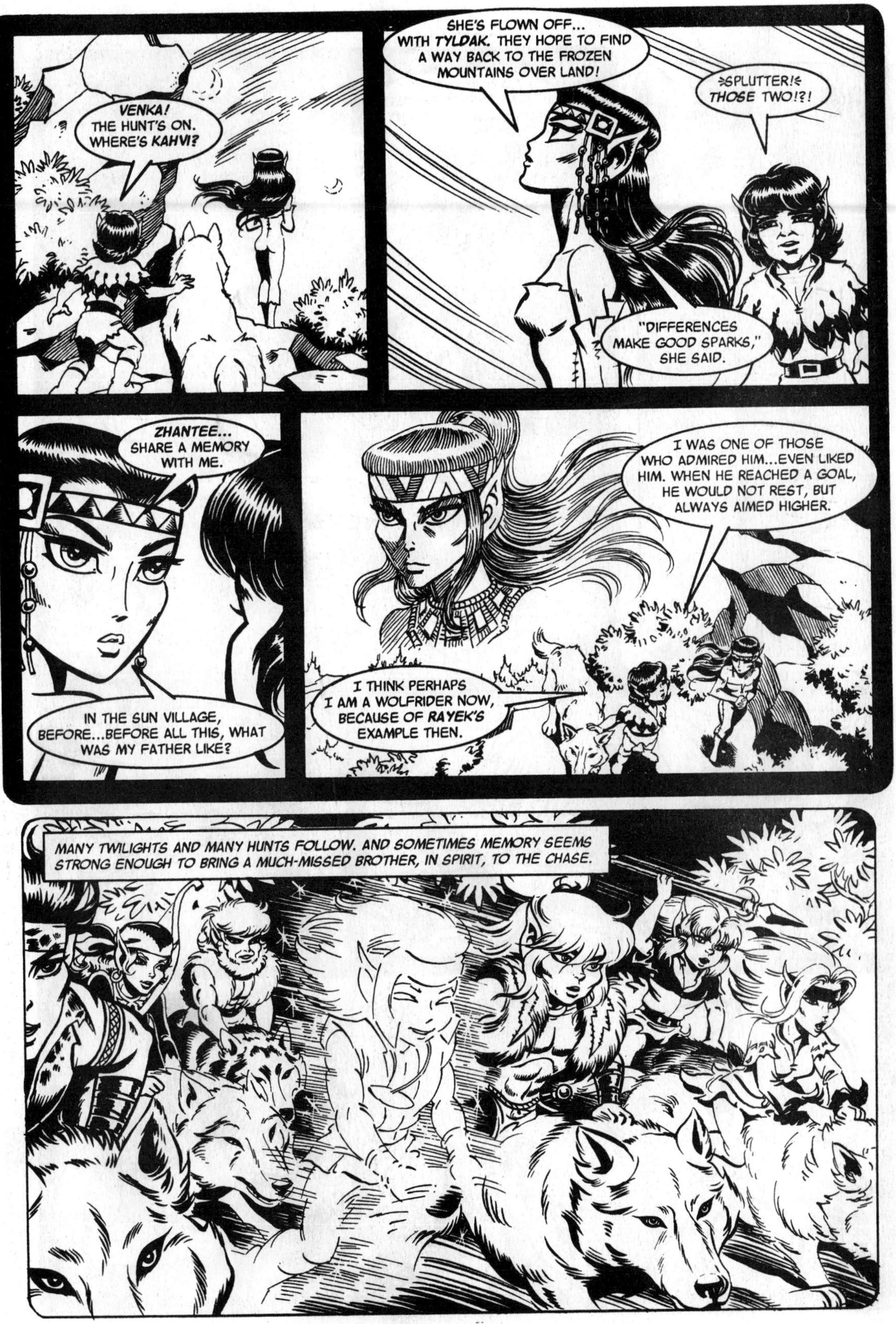
VENKA! THE HUNT'S ON. WHERE'S KAHVI?
SHE'S FLOWN OFF... WITH TYLDAK. THEY HOPE TO FIND A WAY BACK TO THE FROZEN MOUNTAINS OVER LAND!
SPLUTTER! THOSE TWO!?!
"DIFFERENCES MAKE GOOD SPARKS," SHE SAID.
ZHANTEE... SHARE A MEMORY WITH ME.
IN THE SUN VILLAGE, BEFORE...BEFORE ALL THIS, WHAT WAS MY FATHER LIKE?
I WAS ONE OF THOSE WHO ADMIRED HIM...EVEN LIKED HIM. WHEN HE REACHED A GOAL, HE WOULD NOT REST, BUT ALWAYS AIMED HIGHER.
I THINK PERHAPS I AM A WOLFRIDER NOW, BECAUSE OF RAYEK'S EXAMPLE THEN.
MANY TWILIGHTS AND MANY HUNTS FOLLOW. AND SOMETIMES MEMORY SEEMS STRONG ENOUGH TO BRING A MUCH-MISSED BROTHER, IN SPIRIT, TO THE CHASE.

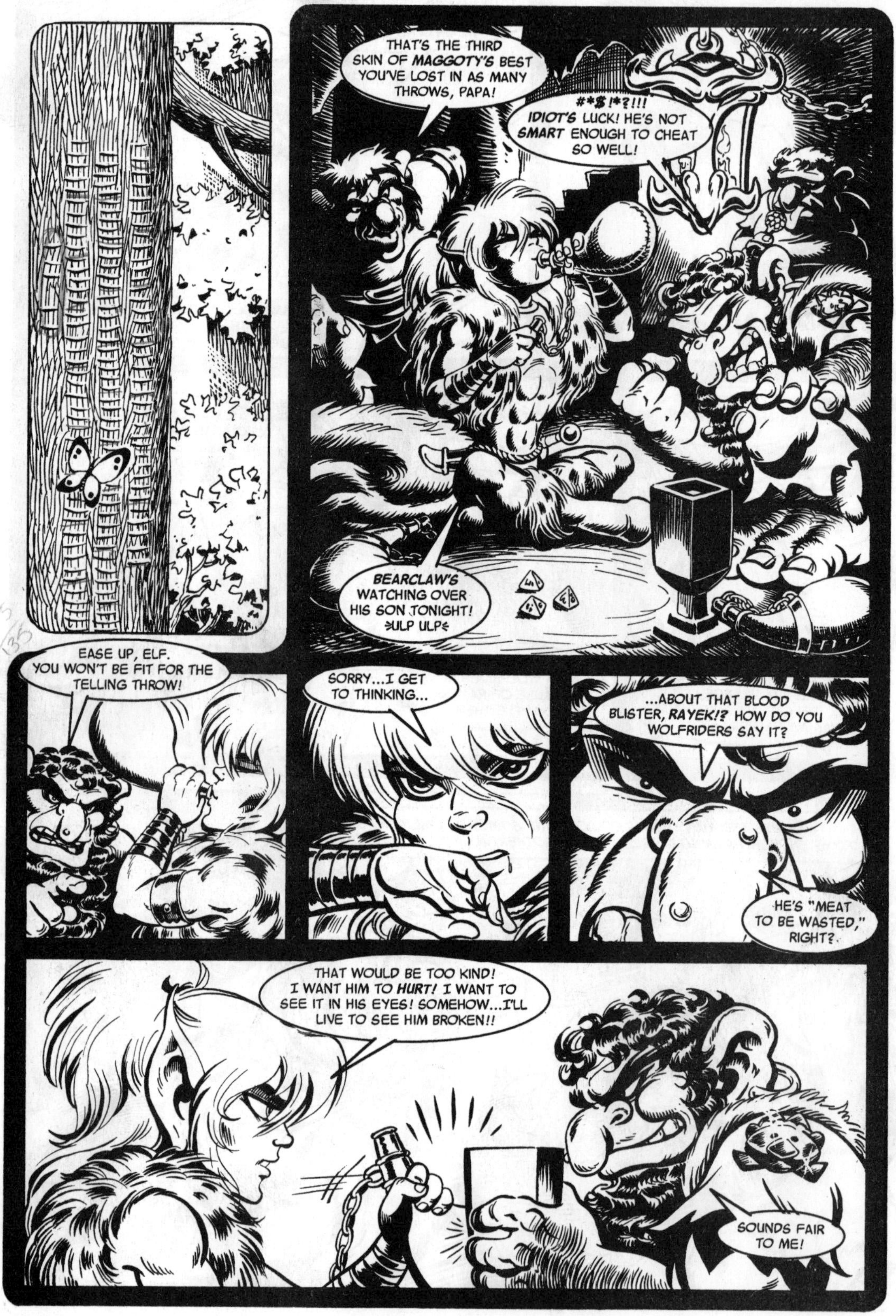
THAT'S THE THIRD SKIN OF MAGGOTY'S BEST YOU'VE LOST IN AS MANY THROWS, PAPA!
#*$!*?!!! IDIOT'S LUCK! HE'S NOT SMART ENOUGH TO CHEAT SO WELL!
BEARCLAW'S WATCHING OVER HIS SON TONIGHT! ULP ULP
EASE UP, ELF. YOU WON'T BE FIT FOR THE TELLING THROW!
SORRY...I GET TO THINKING...
...ABOUT THAT BLOOD BLISTER, RAYEK!? HOW DO YOU WOLFRIDERS SAY IT?
HE'S "MEAT TO BE WASTED," RIGHT?
THAT WOULD BE TOO KIND! I WANT HIM TO HURT! I WANT TO SEE IT IN HIS EYES! SOMEHOW...I'LL LIVE TO SEE HIM BROKEN!!
SOUNDS FAIR TO ME!

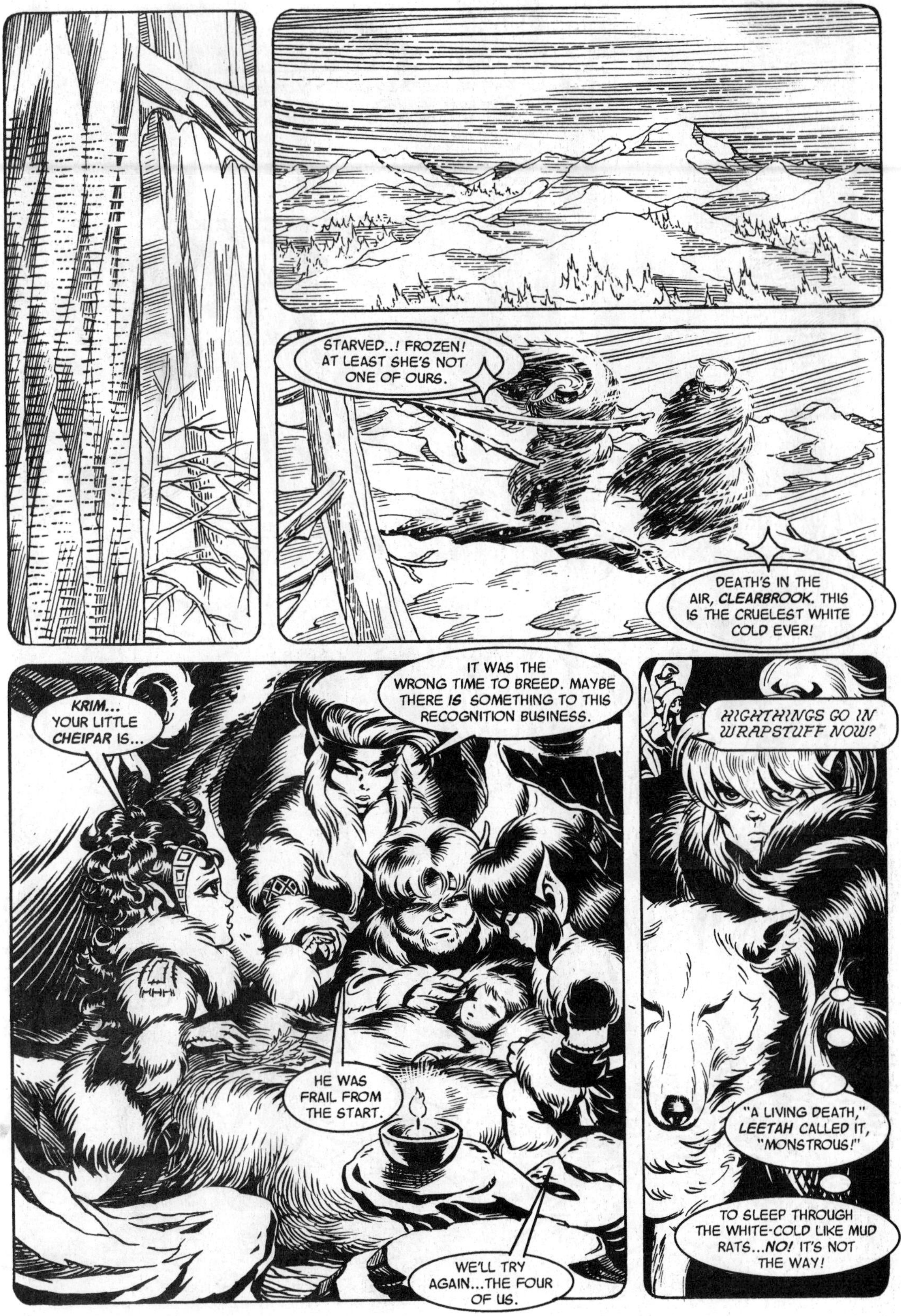
STARVED..! FROZEN! AT LEAST SHE'S NOT ONE OF OURS.
DEATH'S IN THE AIR, CLEARBROOK. THIS IS THE CRUELEST WHITE COLD EVER!
KRIM... YOUR LITTLE CHEIPAR IS...
IT WAS THE WRONG TIME TO BREED. MAYBE THERE IS SOMETHING TO THIS RECOGNITION BUSINESS.
HE WAS FRAIL FROM THE START.
WE'LL TRY AGAIN...THE FOUR OF US.
HIGHTHINGS GO IN WRAPSTUFF NOW?
"A LIVING DEATH," LEETAH CALLED IT, "MONSTROUS!"
TO SLEEP THROUGH THE WHITE-COLD LIKE MUD RATS...NO! IT'S NOT THE WAY!

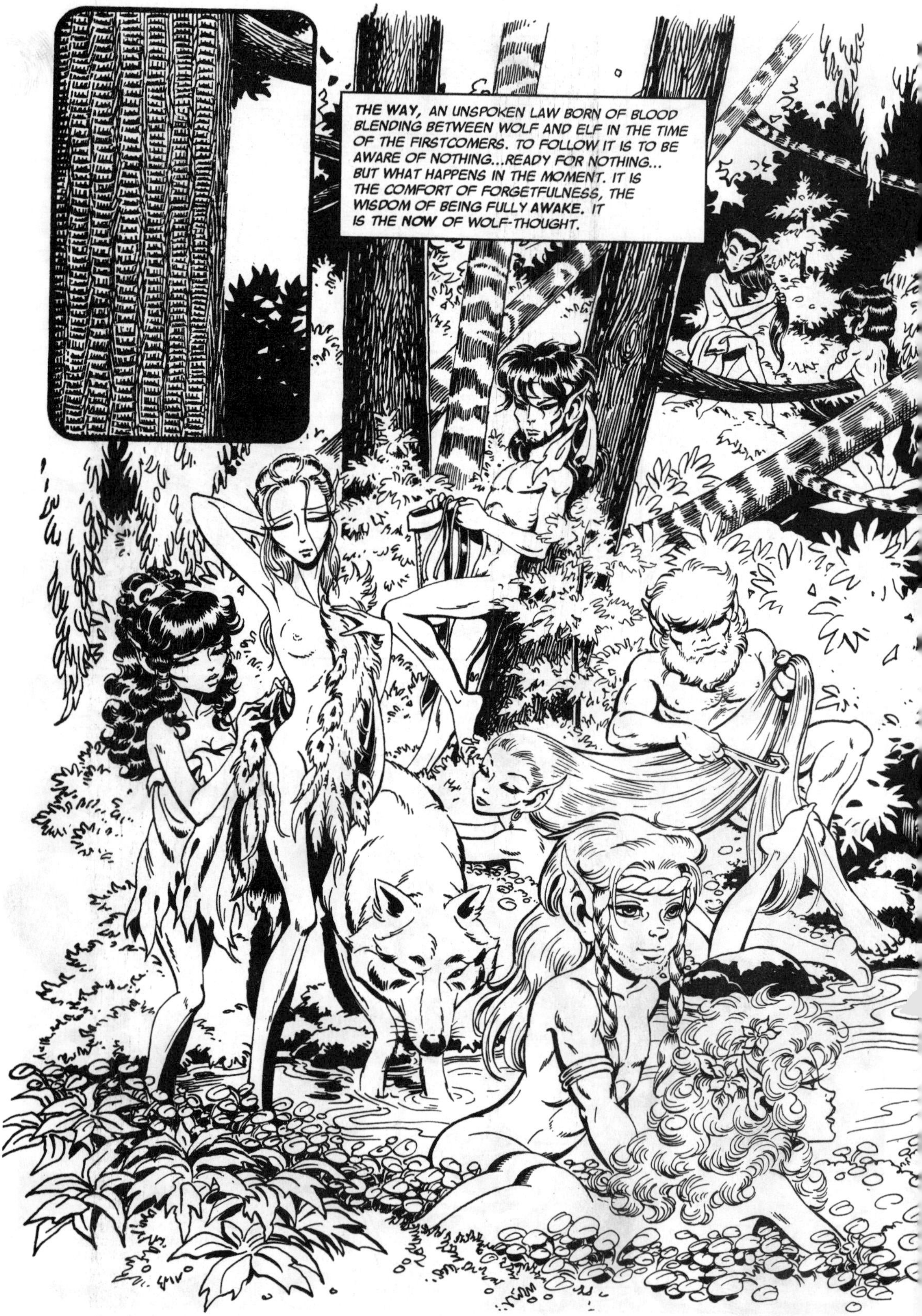
THE WAY, AN UNSPOKEN LAW BORN OF BLOOD BLENDING BETWEEN WOLF AND ELF IN THE TIME OF THE FIRSTCOMERS. TO FOLLOW IT IS TO BE AWARE OF NOTHING...READY FOR NOTHING... BUT WHAT HAPPENS IN THE MOMENT. IT IS THE COMFORT OF FORGETFULNESS, THE WISDOM OF BEING FULLY AWAKE. IT IS THE NOW OF WOLF-THOUGHT.

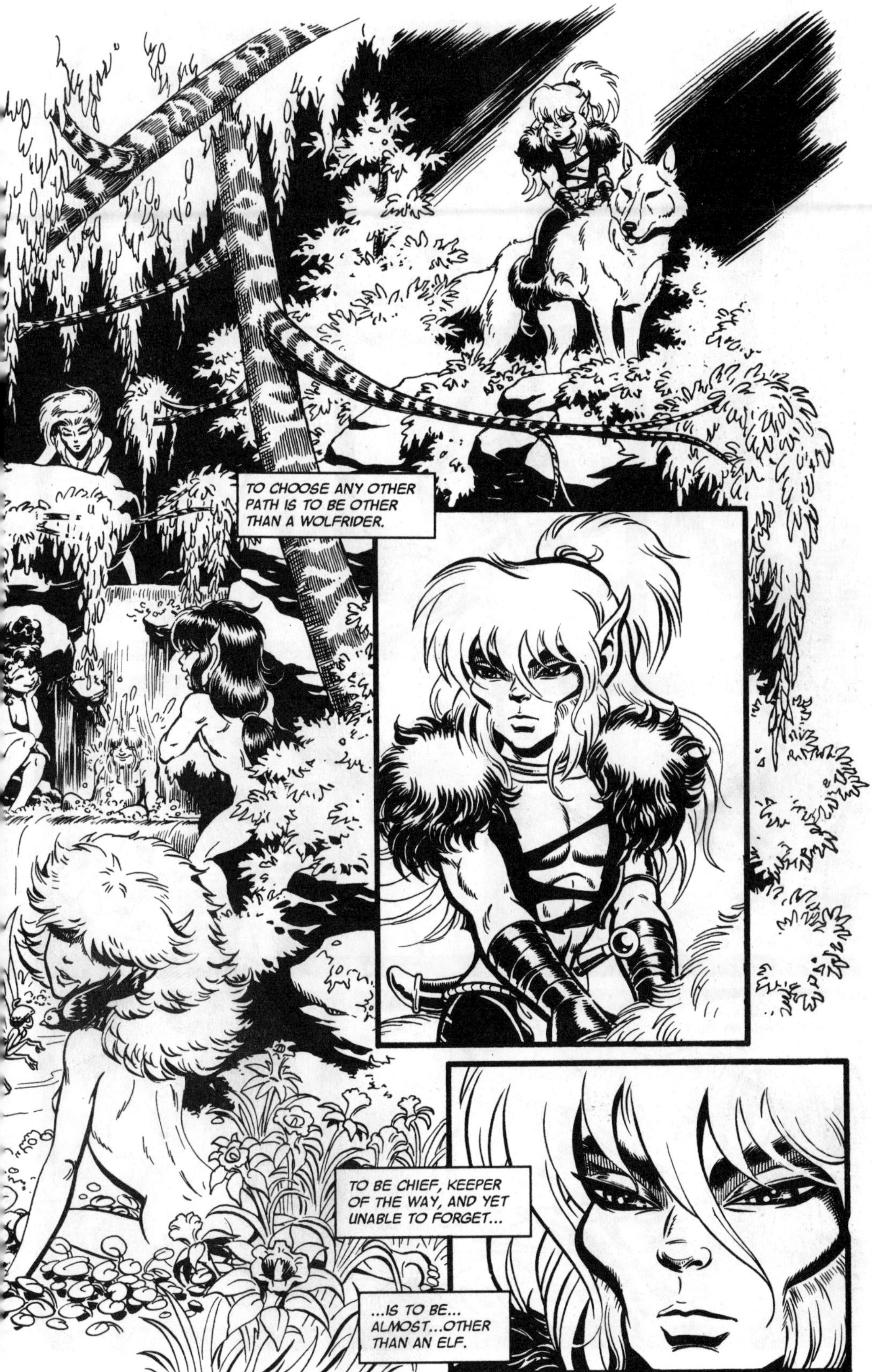
TO CHOOSE ANY OTHER PATH IS TO BE OTHER THAN A WOLFRIDER.
TO BE CHIEF, KEEPER OF THE WAY, AND YET UNABLE TO FORGET...
...IS TO BE... ALMOST...OTHER THAN AN ELF.

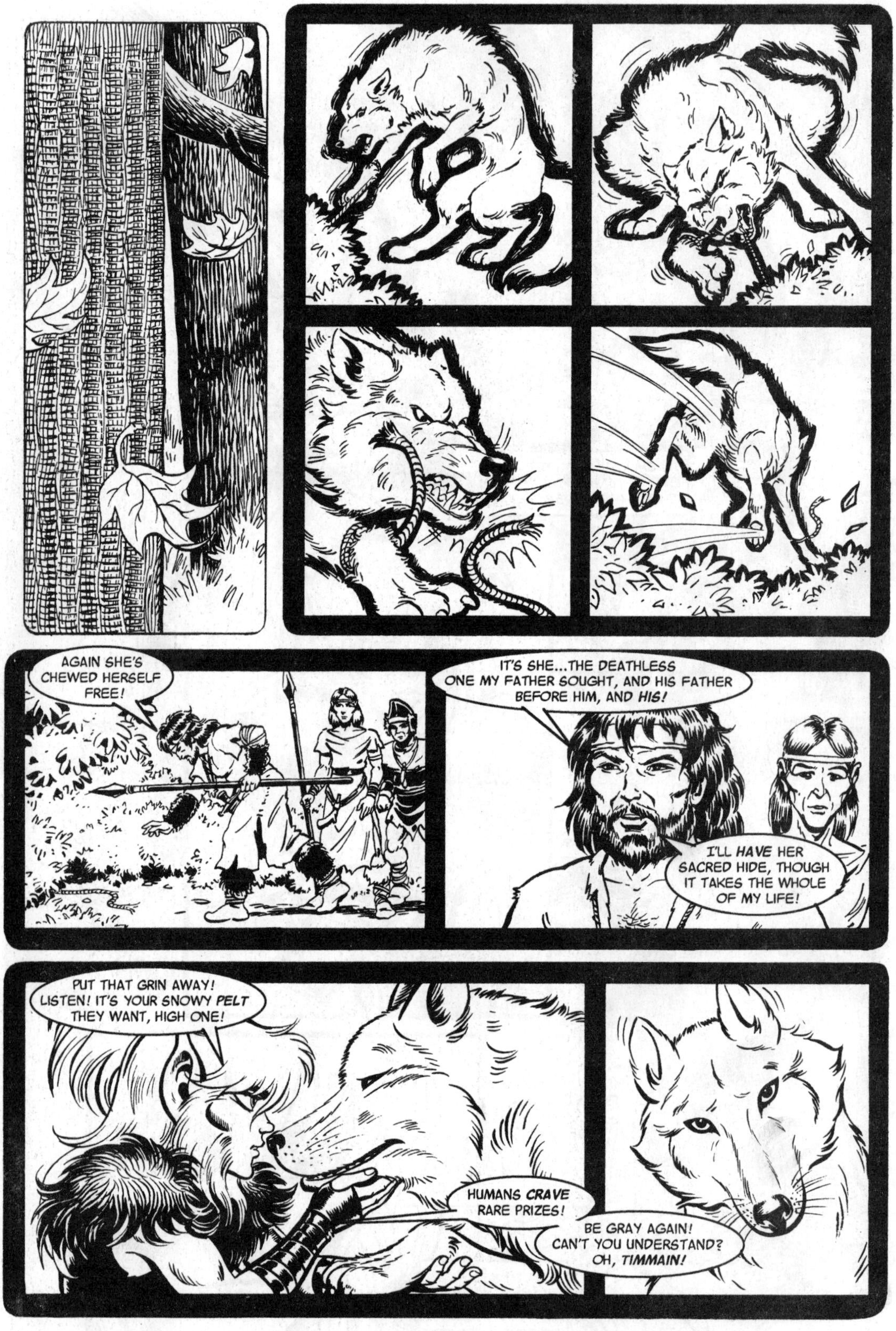
AGAIN SHE'S CHEWED HERSELF FREE!
IT'S SHE...THE DEATHLESS ONE MY FATHER SOUGHT, AND HIS FATHER BEFORE HIM, AND HIS!
I'LL HAVE HER SACRED HIDE, THOUGH IT TAKES THE WHOLE OF MY LIFE!
PUT THAT GRIN AWAY! LISTEN! IT'S YOUR SNOWY PELT THEY WANT, HIGH ONE!
HUMANS CRAVE RARE PRIZES!
BE GRAY AGAIN! CAN'T YOU UNDERSTAND? OH, TIMMAIN!

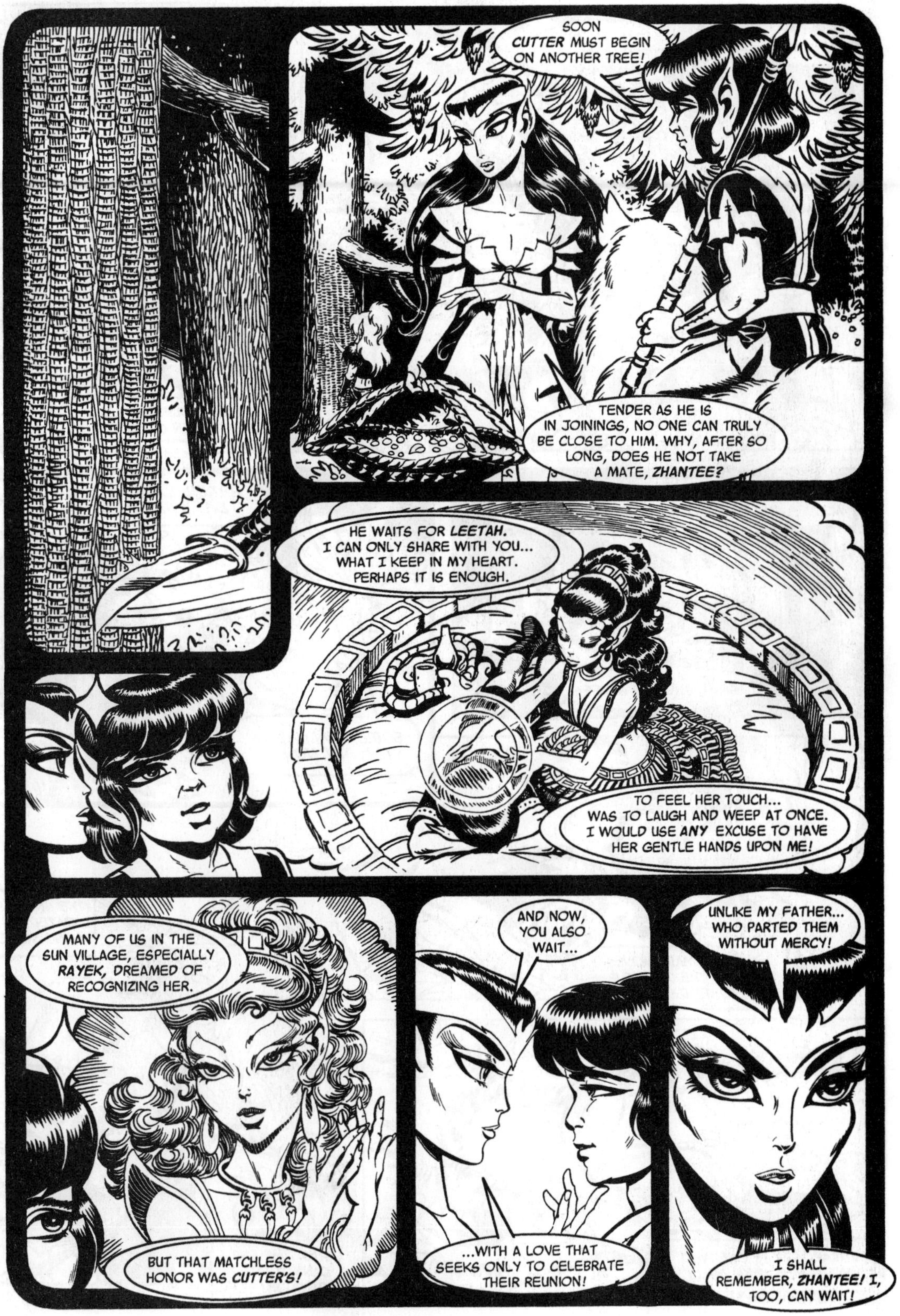
SOON CUTTER MUST BEGIN ON ANOTHER TREE!
TENDER AS HE IS IN JOININGS, NO ONE CAN TRULY BE CLOSE TO HIM. WHY, AFTER SO LONG, DOES HE NOT TAKE A MATE, ZHANTEE?
HE WAITS FOR LEETAH. I CAN ONLY SHARE WITH YOU... WHAT I KEEP IN MY HEART. PERHAPS IT IS ENOUGH.
TO FEEL HER TOUCH... WAS TO LAUGH AND WEEP AT ONCE. I WOULD USE ANY EXCUSE TO HAVE HER GENTLE HANDS UPON ME!
MANY OF US IN THE SUN VILLAGE, ESPECIALLY RAYEK, DREAMED OF RECOGNIZING HER.
BUT THAT MATCHLESS HONOR WAS CUTTER'S!
AND NOW, YOU ALSO WAIT...
...WITH A LOVE THAT SEEKS ONLY TO CELEBRATE THEIR REUNION!
UNLIKE MY FATHER... WHO PARTED THEM WITHOUT MERCY!
I SHALL REMEMBER, ZHANTEE! I, TOO, CAN WAIT!

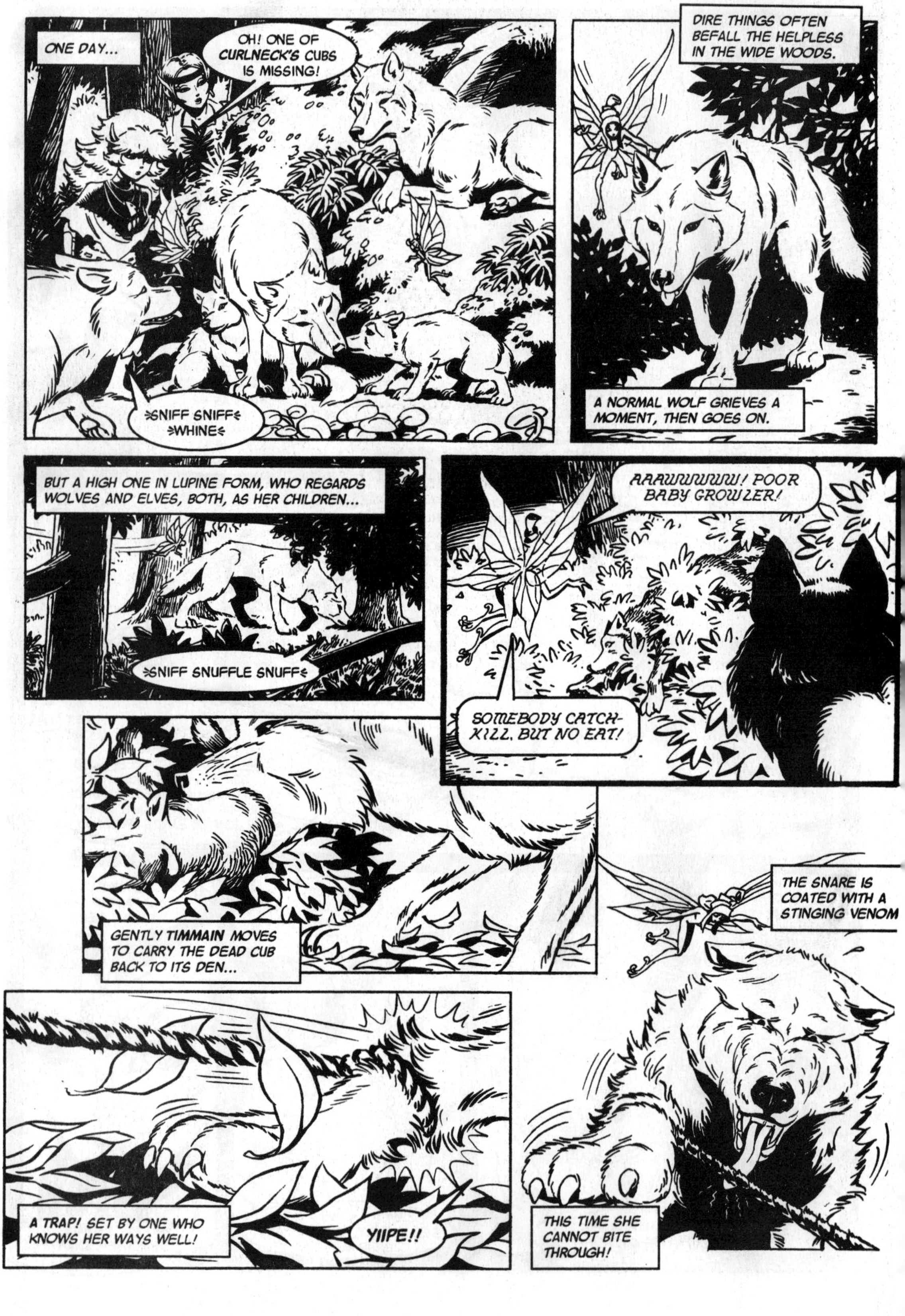
ONE DAY...
OH! ONE OF CURLNECK'S CUBS IS MISSING!
SNIFF SNIFF WHINE
DIRE THINGS OFTEN BEFALL THE HELPLESS IN THE WIDE WOODS.
A NORMAL WOLF GRIEVES A MOMENT, THEN GOES ON.
BUT A HIGH ONE IN LUPINE FORM, WHO REGARDS WOLVES AND ELVES, BOTH, AS HER CHILDREN...
SNIFF SNUFFLE SNUFF
AAAWWWWWW! POOR BABY GROWLER!
SOMEBODY CATCH-KILL, BUT NO EAT!
GENTLY TIMMAIN MOVES TO CARRY THE DEAD CUB BACK TO ITS DEN...
THE SNARE IS COATED WITH A STINGING VENOM
A TRAP! SET BY ONE WHO KNOWS HER WAYS WELL!
YIIPE!!
THIS TIME SHE CANNOT BITE THROUGH!

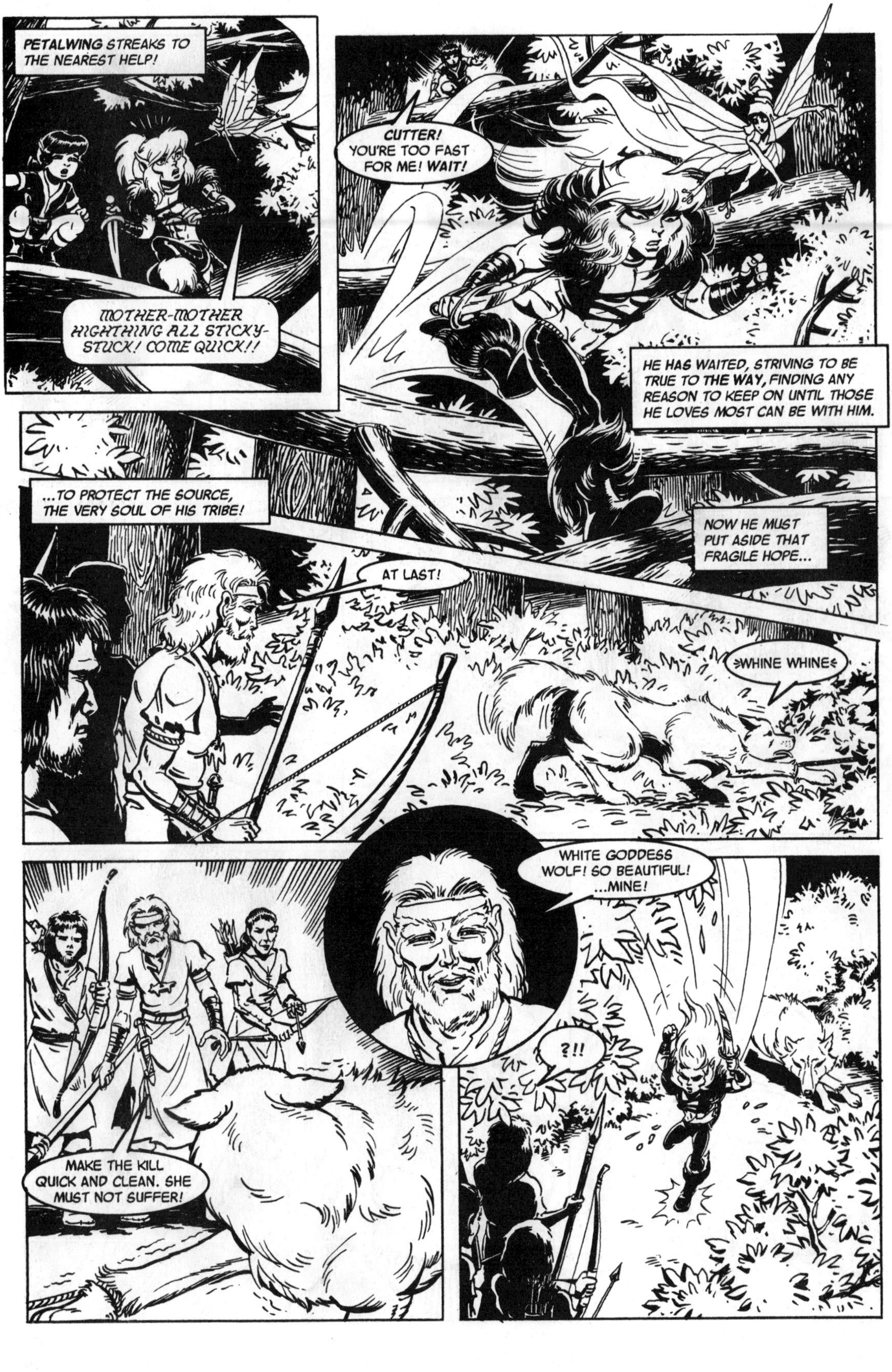
PETALWING STREAKS TO THE NEAREST HELP!
MOTHER-MOTHER HIGHTHING ALL STICKY-STUCK! COME QUICK!!
CUTTER! YOU'RE TOO FAST FOR ME! WAIT!
HE HAS WAITED, STRIVING TO BE TRUE TO THE WAY, FINDING ANY REASON TO KEEP ON UNTIL THOSE HE LOVES MOST CAN BE WITH HIM.
NOW HE MUST PUT ASIDE THAT FRAGILE HOPE...
...TO PROTECT THE SOURCE, THE VERY SOUL OF HIS TRIBE!
AT LAST!
WHINE WHINE
WHITE GODDESS WOLF! SO BEAUTIFUL! ...MINE!
MAKE THE KILL QUICK AND CLEAN. SHE MUST NOT SUFFER!
?!!

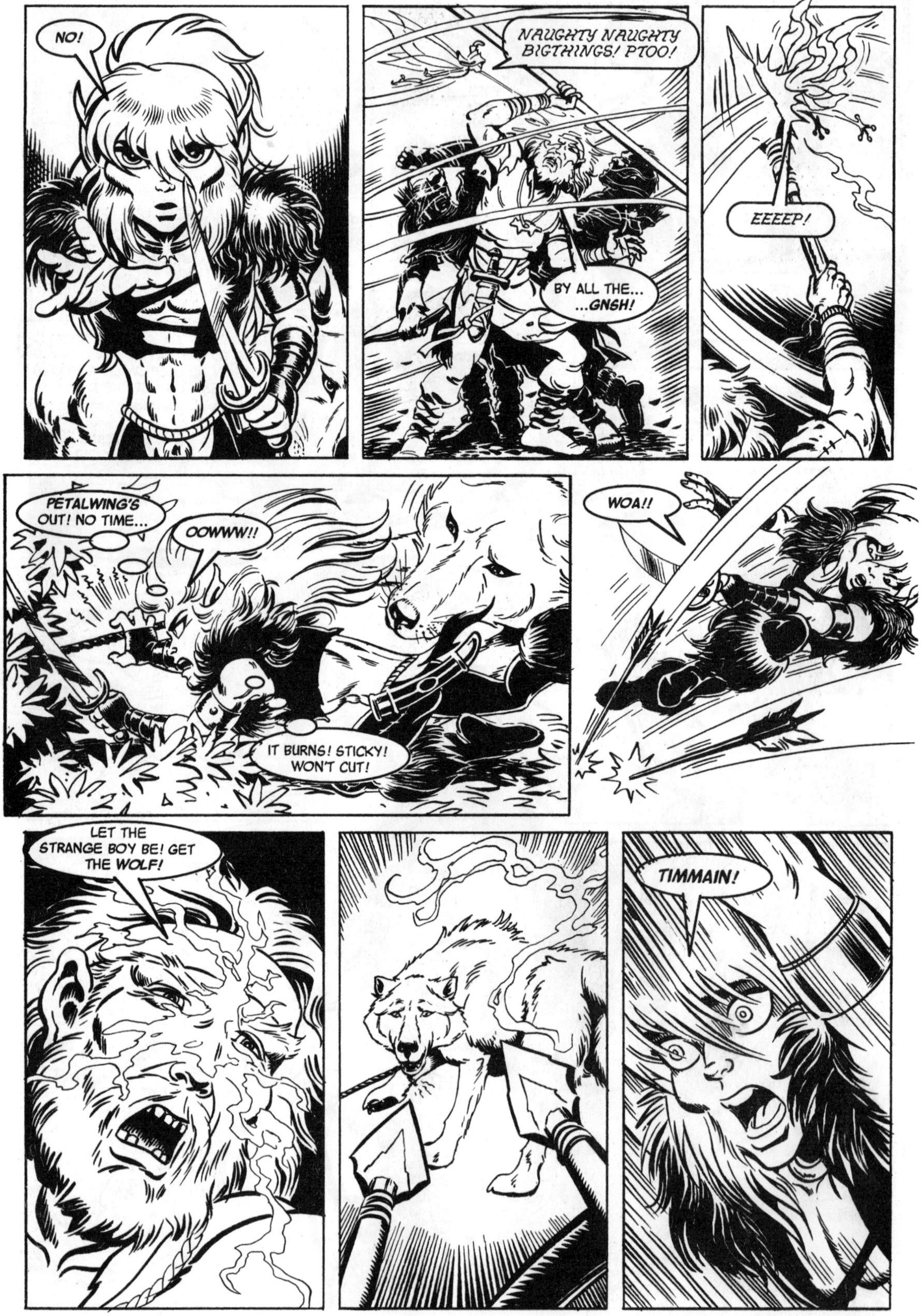
NO!
NAUGHTY NAUGHTY BIGTHINGS! PTOO!
BY ALL THE... ...GNSH!
EEEEP!
PETALWING'S OUT! NO TIME...
OOWWW!!
IT BURNS! STICKY! WON'T CUT!
WOA!!
LET THE STRANGE BOY BE! GET THE WOLF!
TIMMAIN!

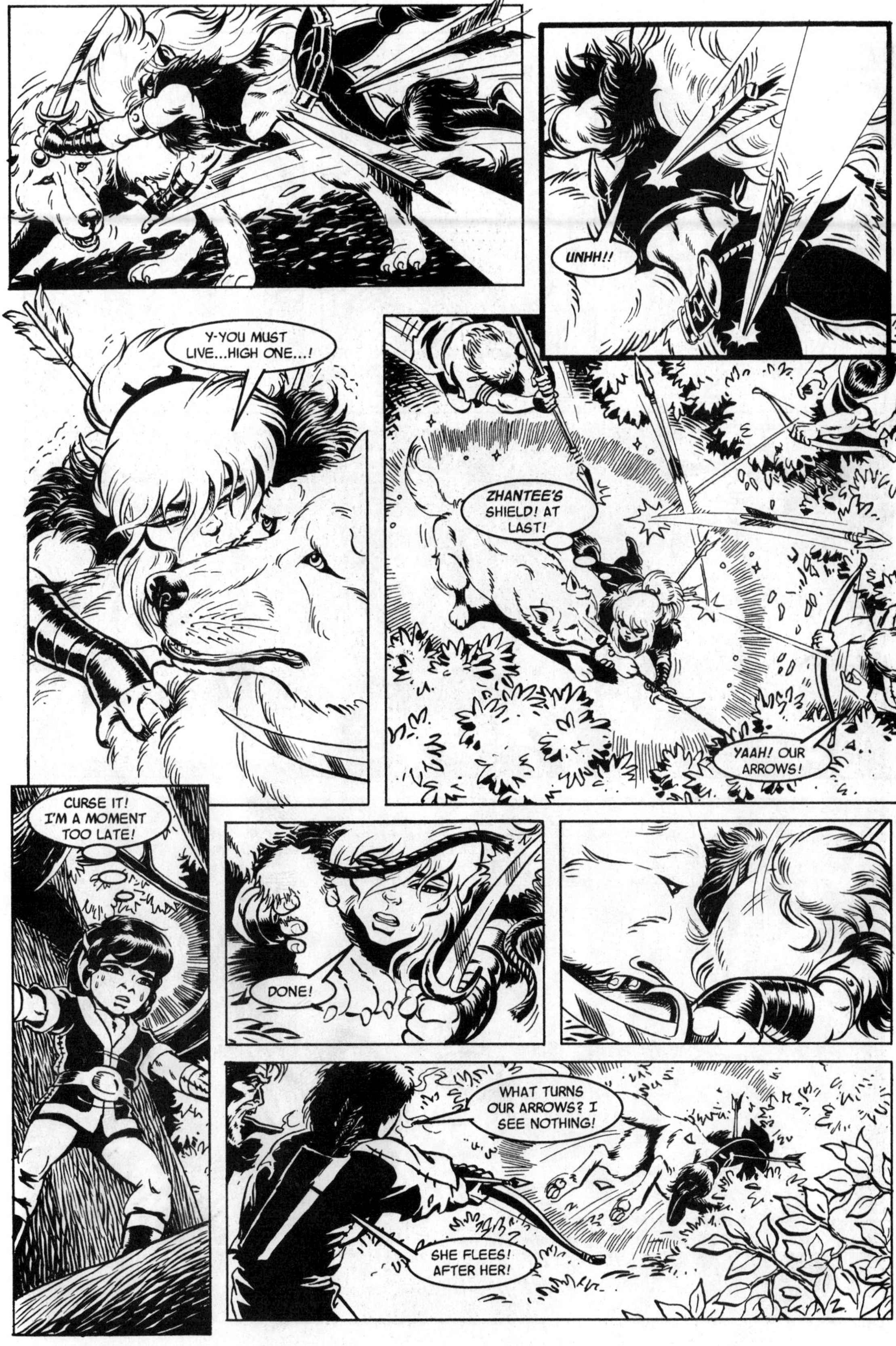
UNHH!!
Y-YOU MUST LIVE...HIGH ONE...!
ZHANTEE'S SHIELD! AT LAST!
YAAH! OUR ARROWS!
CURSE IT! I'M A MOMENT TOO LATE!
DONE!
WHAT TURNS OUR ARROWS? I SEE NOTHING!
SHE FLEES! AFTER HER!

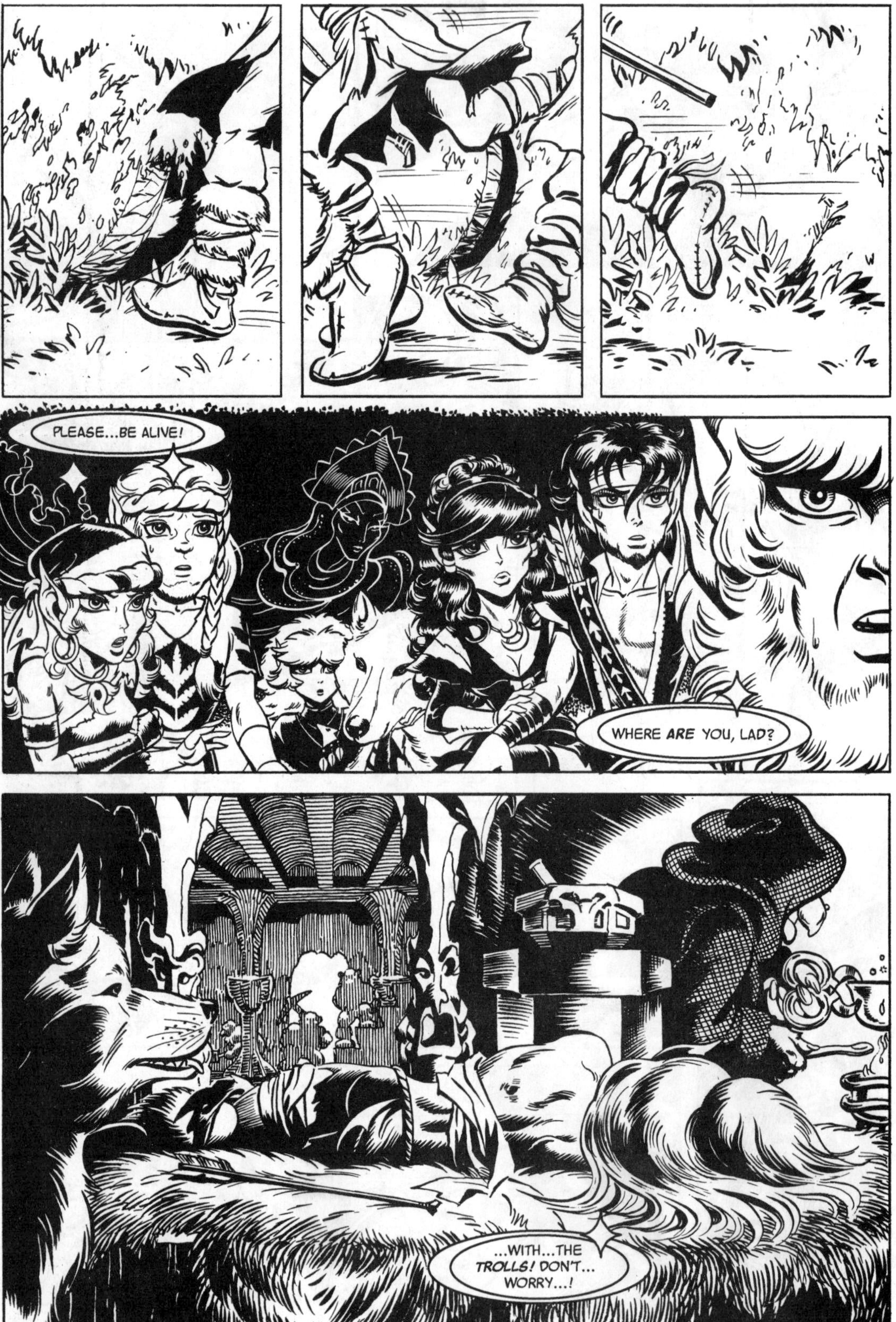
PLEASE...BE ALIVE!
WHERE ARE YOU, LAD?
...WITH...THE TROLLS! DON'T... WORRY...!

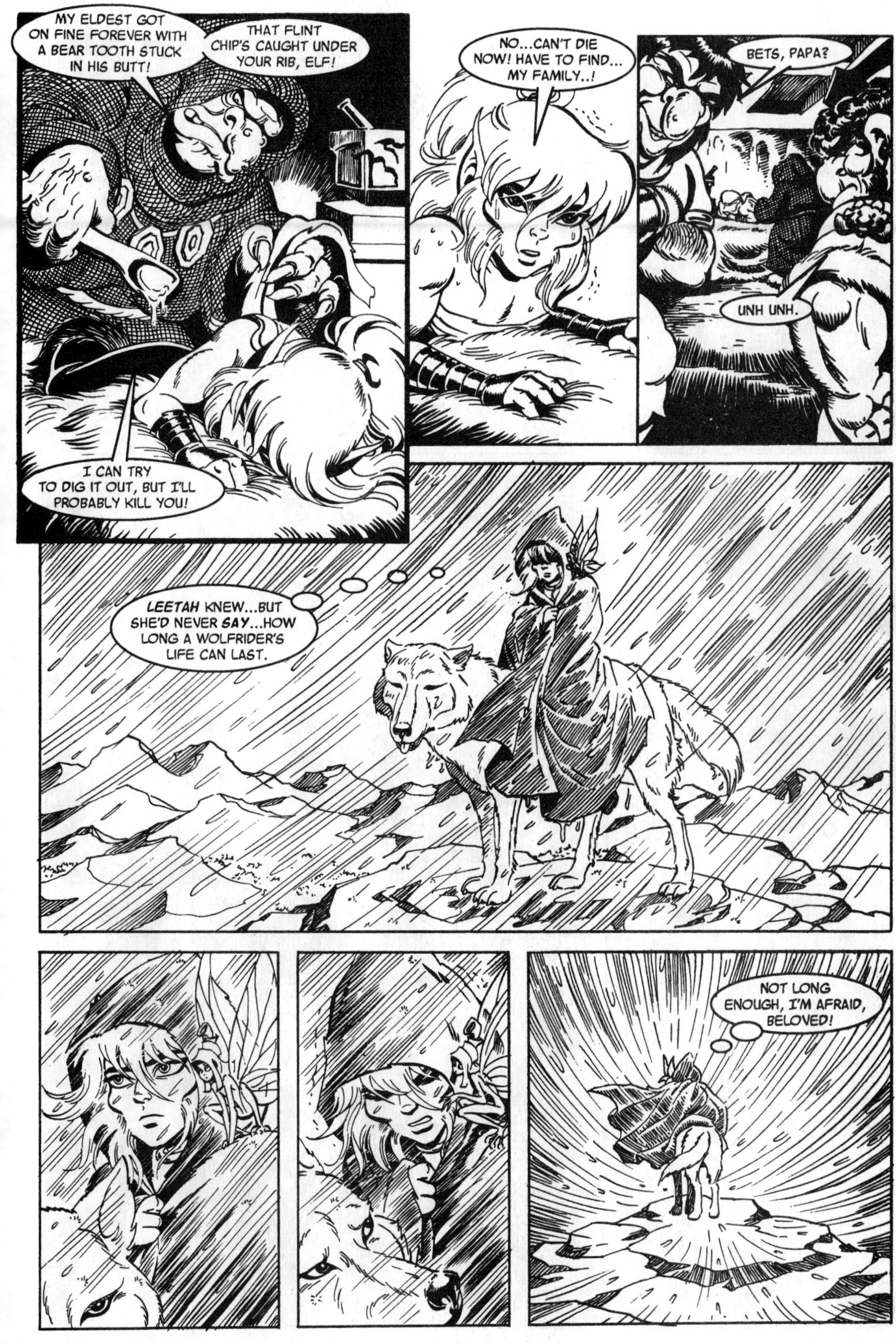
MY ELDEST GOT ON FINE FOREVER WITH A BEAR TOOTH STUCK IN HIS BUTT!
THAT FLINT CHIP'S CAUGHT UNDER YOUR RIB, ELF!
I CAN TRY TO DIG IT OUT, BUT I'LL PROBABLY KILL YOU!
NO...CAN'T DIE NOW! HAVE TO FIND... MY FAMILY..!
BETS, PAPA?
UNH UNH.
LEETAH KNEW...BUT SHE'D NEVER SAY...HOW LONG A WOLFRIDER'S LIFE CAN LAST.
NOT LONG ENOUGH, I'M AFRAID, BELOVED!

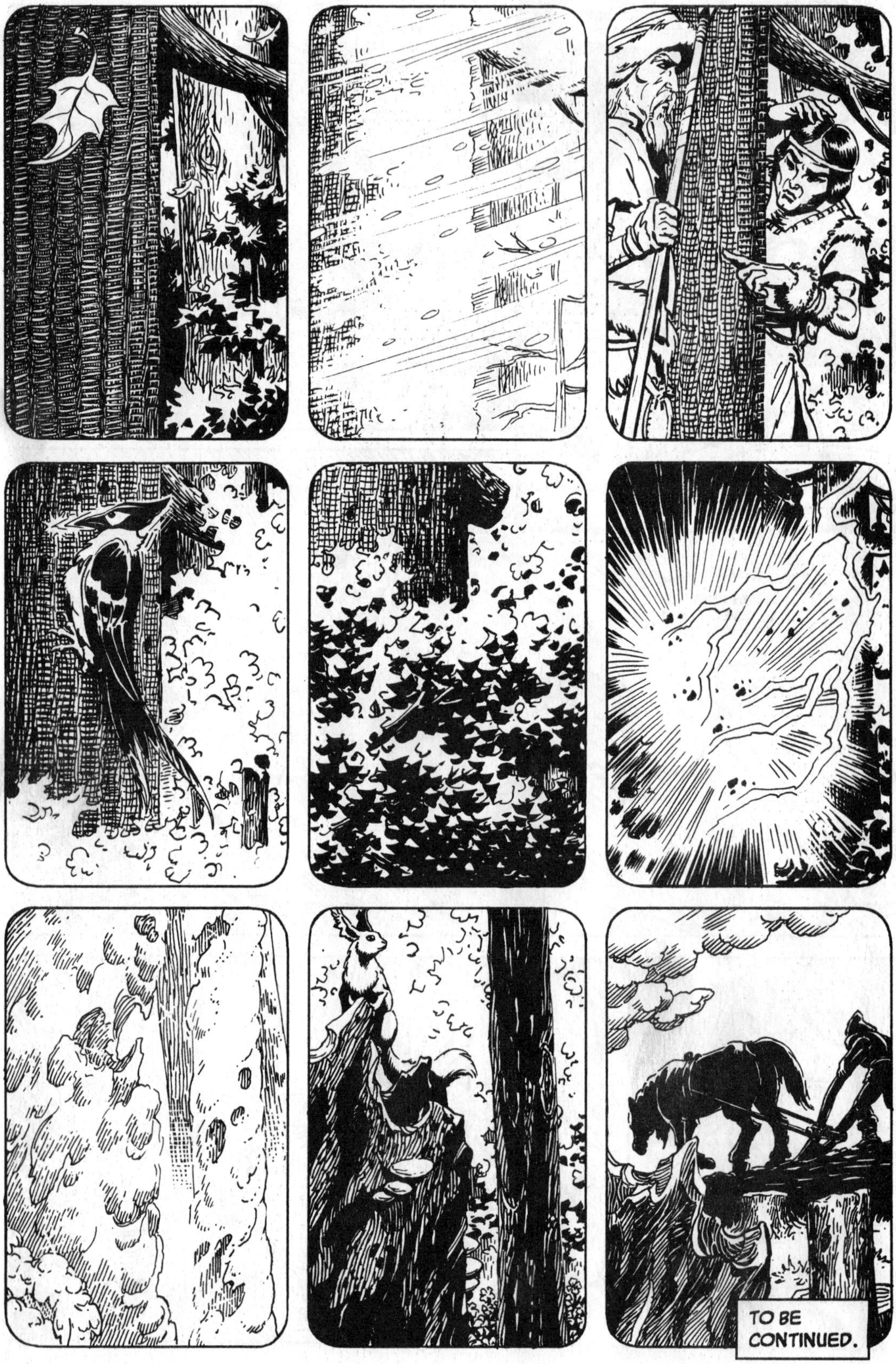
TO BE CONTINUED.

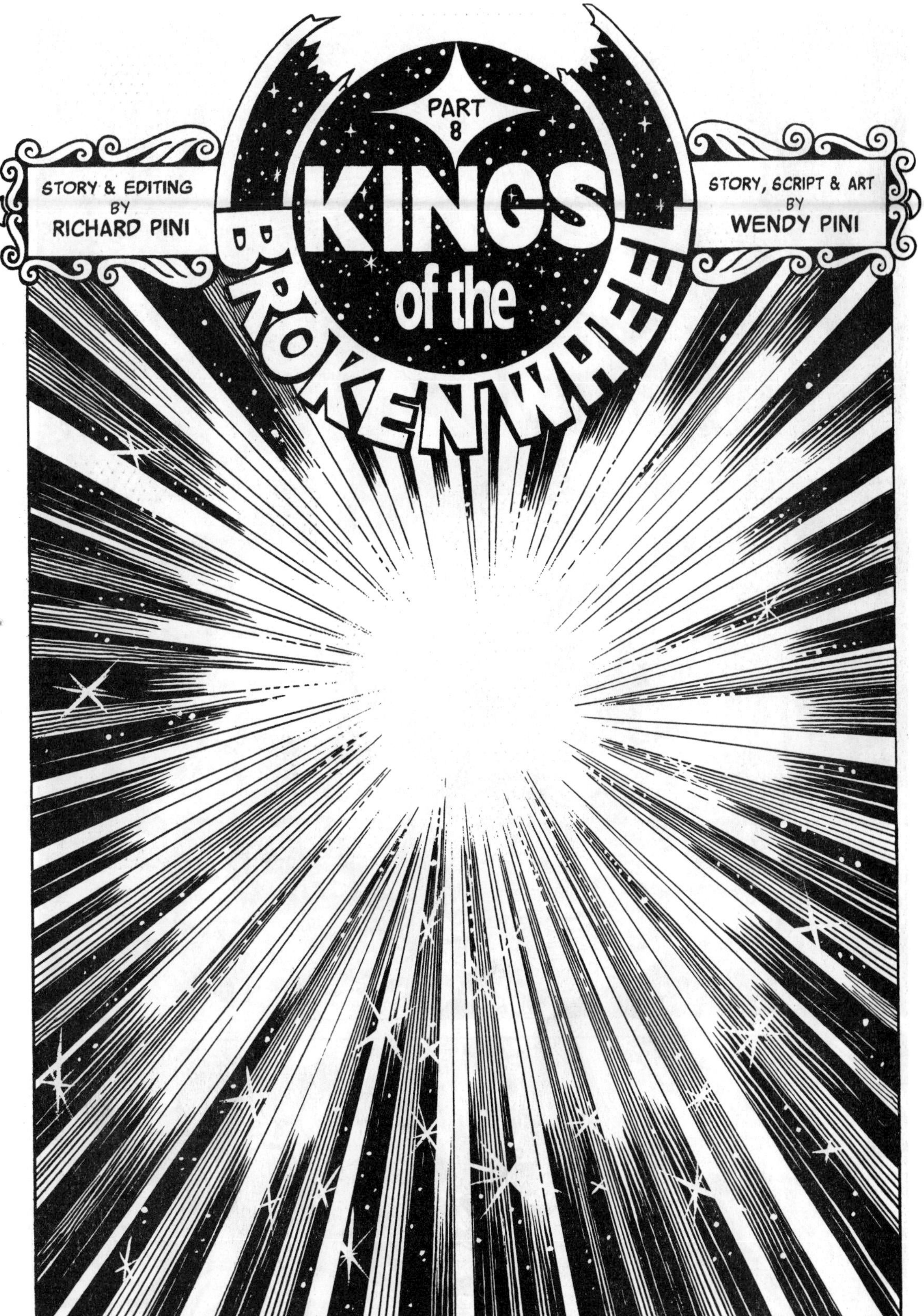
STORY & EDITING
BY
RICHARD PINI
PART
8
KINGS
of the
BROKEN WHEEL
STORY, SCRIPT & ART
BY
WENDY PINI

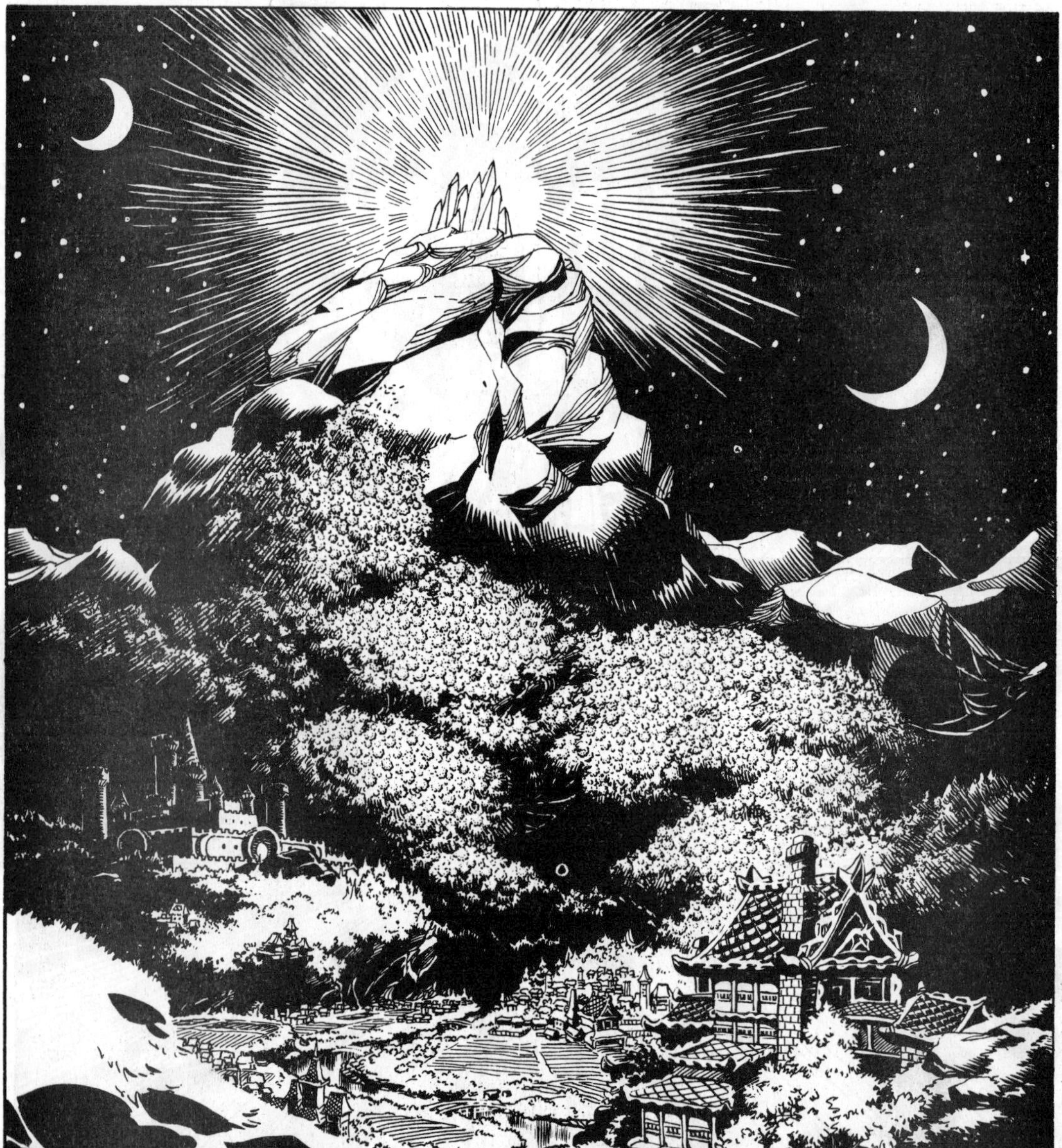

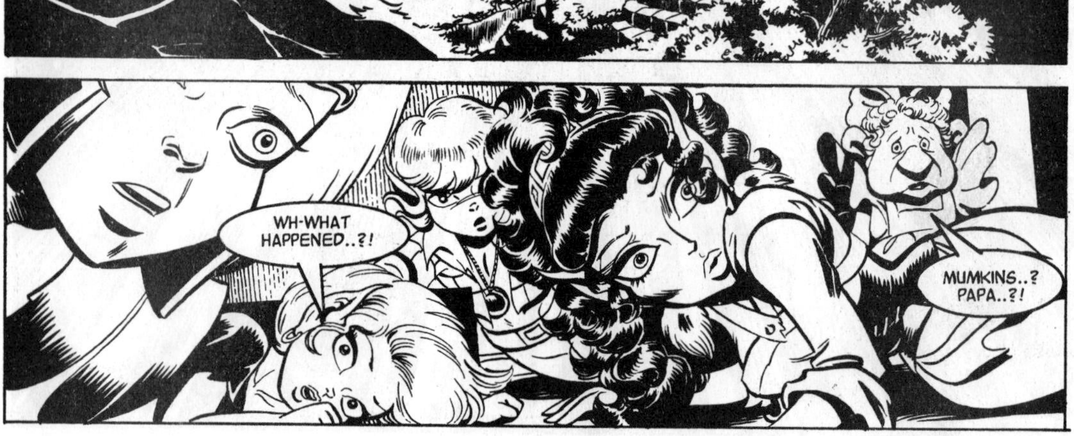
WH-WHAT HAPPENED..?!
MUMKINS..? PAPA..?!

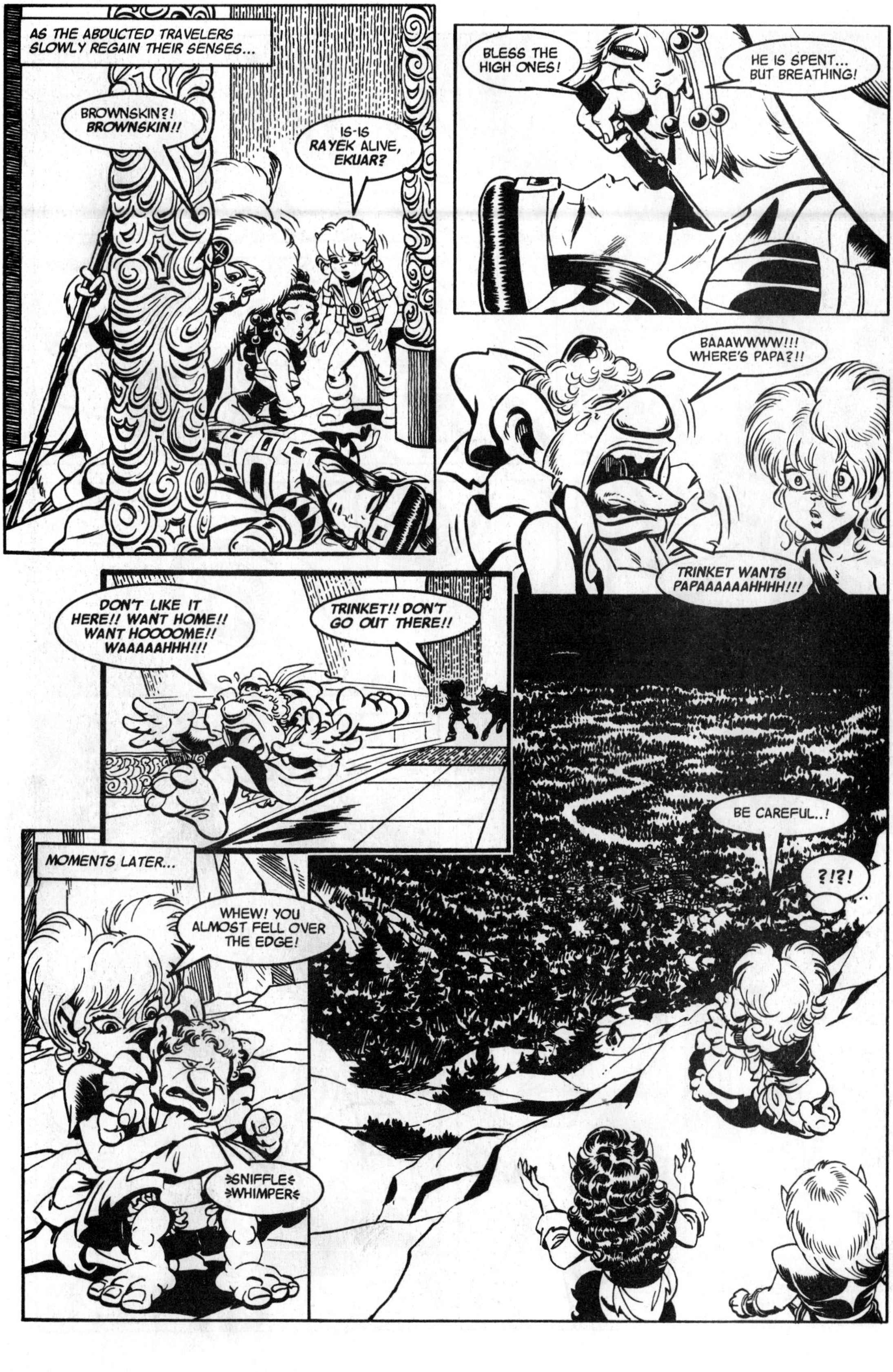
AS THE ABDUCTED TRAVELERS SLOWLY REGAIN THEIR SENSES...
BROWNSKIN?! BROWNSKIN!!
IS-IS RAYEK ALIVE, EKUAR?
BLESS THE HIGH ONES!
HE IS SPENT... BUT BREATHING!
BAAAWWW!!! WHERE'S PAPA?!!
TRINKET WANTS PAPAAAAAAHHHH!!!
DON'T LIKE IT HERE!! WANT HOME!! WANT HOOOOME!! WAAAAAHHH!!!
TRINKET!! DON'T GO OUT THERE!!
BE CAREFUL..!
?!?!
MOMENTS LATER...
WHEW! YOU ALMOST FELL OVER THE EDGE!
SNIFFLE
WHIMPER

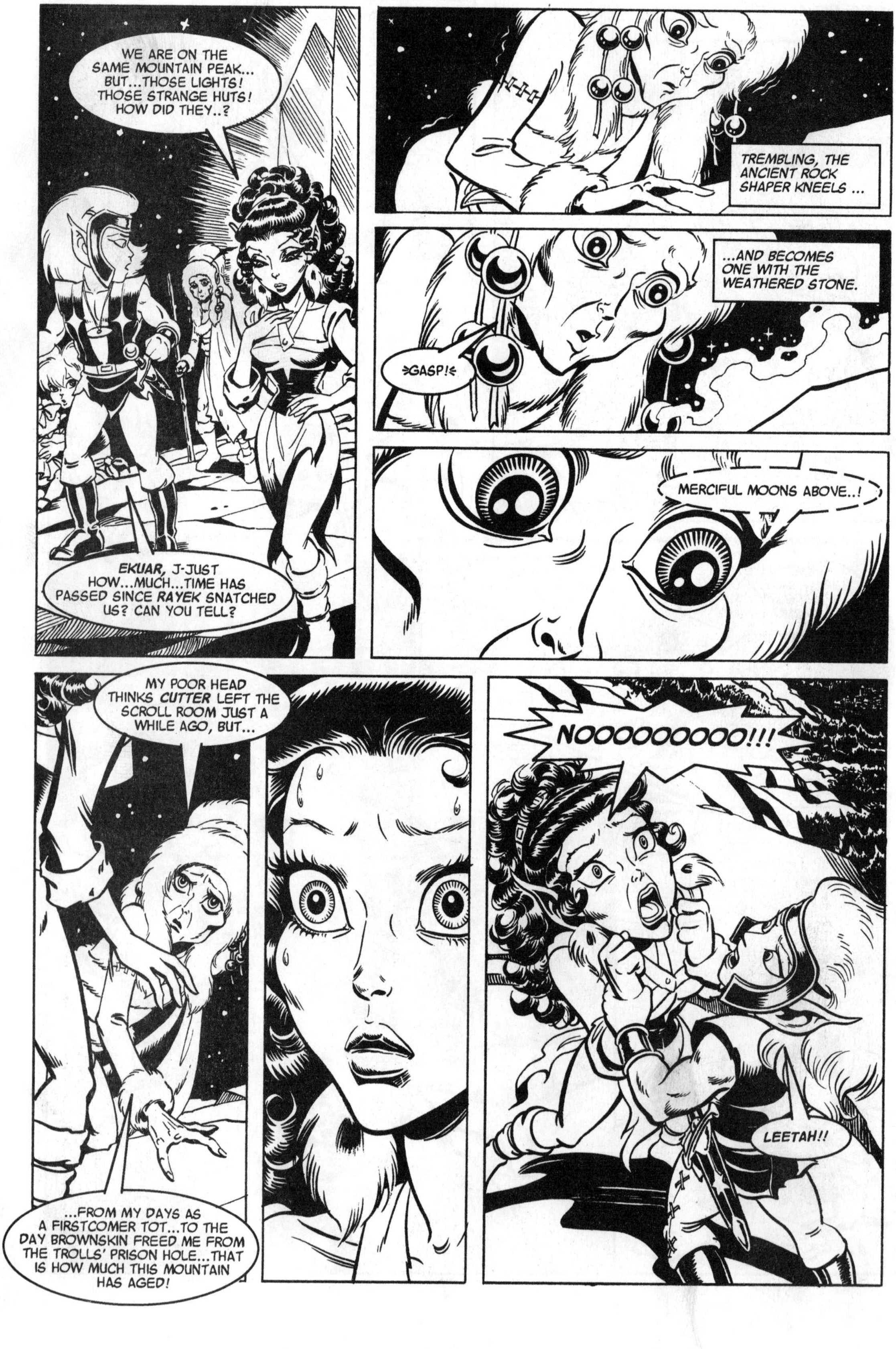
WE ARE ON THE SAME MOUNTAIN PEAK... BUT...THOSE LIGHTS! THOSE STRANGE HUTS! HOW DID THEY..?
EKUAR, J-JUST HOW...MUCH...TIME HAS PASSED SINCE RAYEK SNATCHED US? CAN YOU TELL?
TREMBLING, THE ANCIENT ROCK SHAPER KNEELS ...
...AND BECOMES ONE WITH THE WEATHERED STONE.
GASP!
MERCIFUL MOONS ABOVE..!
MY POOR HEAD THINKS CUTTER LEFT THE SCROLL ROOM JUST A WHILE AGO, BUT...
...FROM MY DAYS AS A FIRSTCOMER TOT...TO THE DAY BROWNSKIN FREED ME FROM THE TROLLS' PRISON HOLE...THAT IS HOW MUCH THIS MOUNTAIN HAS AGED!
NOOOOOOOOO!!!
LEETAH!!

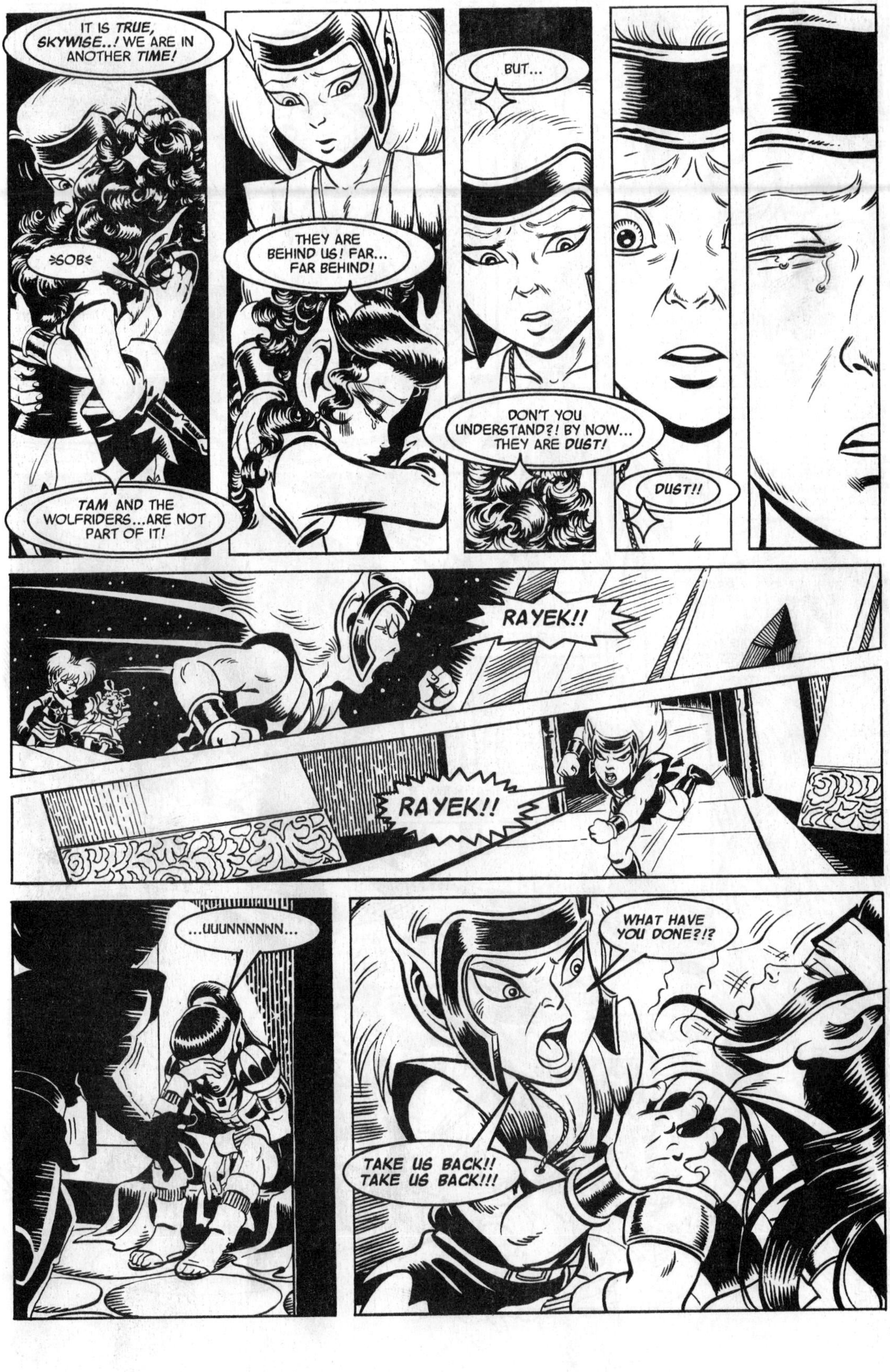
IT IS TRUE, SKYWISE..! WE ARE IN ANOTHER TIME!
≥SOB≤
TAM AND THE WOLFRIDERS...ARE NOT PART OF IT!
THEY ARE BEHIND US! FAR... FAR BEHIND!
BUT...
DON'T YOU UNDERSTAND?! BY NOW... THEY ARE DUST!
DUST!!
RAYEK!!
RAYEK!!
...UUUNNNNNN...
WHAT HAVE YOU DONE?!?
TAKE US BACK!! TAKE US BACK!!!

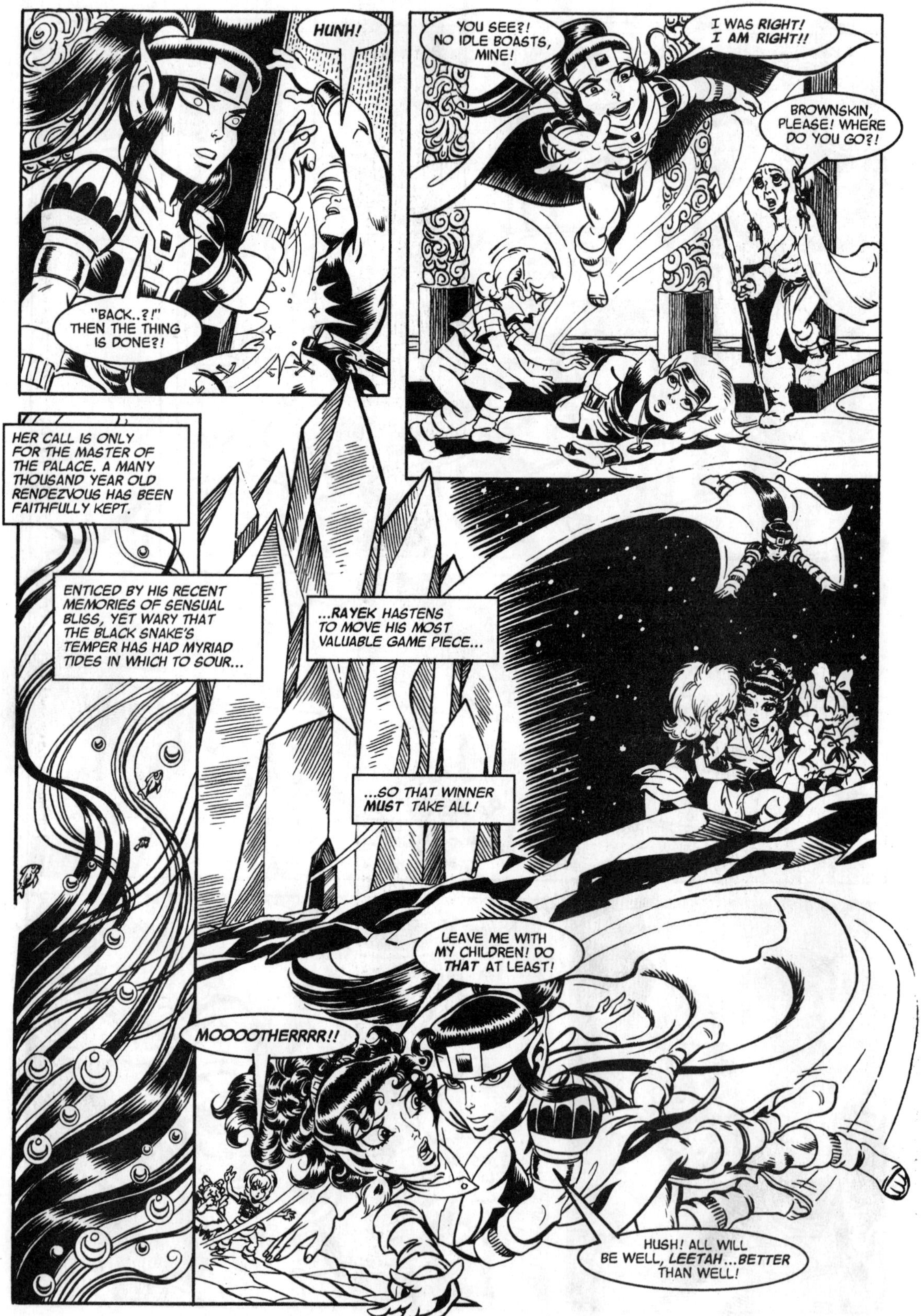
HUNH!
"BACK..?!" THEN THE THING IS DONE?!
YOU SEE?! NO IDLE BOASTS, MINE!
I WAS RIGHT! I AM RIGHT!!
BROWNSKIN, PLEASE! WHERE DO YOU GO?!
HER CALL IS ONLY FOR THE MASTER OF THE PALACE. A MANY THOUSAND YEAR OLD RENDEZVOUS HAS BEEN FAITHFULLY KEPT.
ENTICED BY HIS RECENT MEMORIES OF SENSUAL BLISS, YET WARY THAT THE BLACK SNAKE'S TEMPER HAS HAD MYRIAD TIDES IN WHICH TO SOUR...
...RAYEK HASTENS TO MOVE HIS MOST VALUABLE GAME PIECE...
...SO THAT WINNER MUST TAKE ALL!
LEAVE ME WITH MY CHILDREN! DO THAT AT LEAST!
MOOOOTHERRRR!!
HUSH! ALL WILL BE WELL, LEETAH...BETTER THAN WELL!

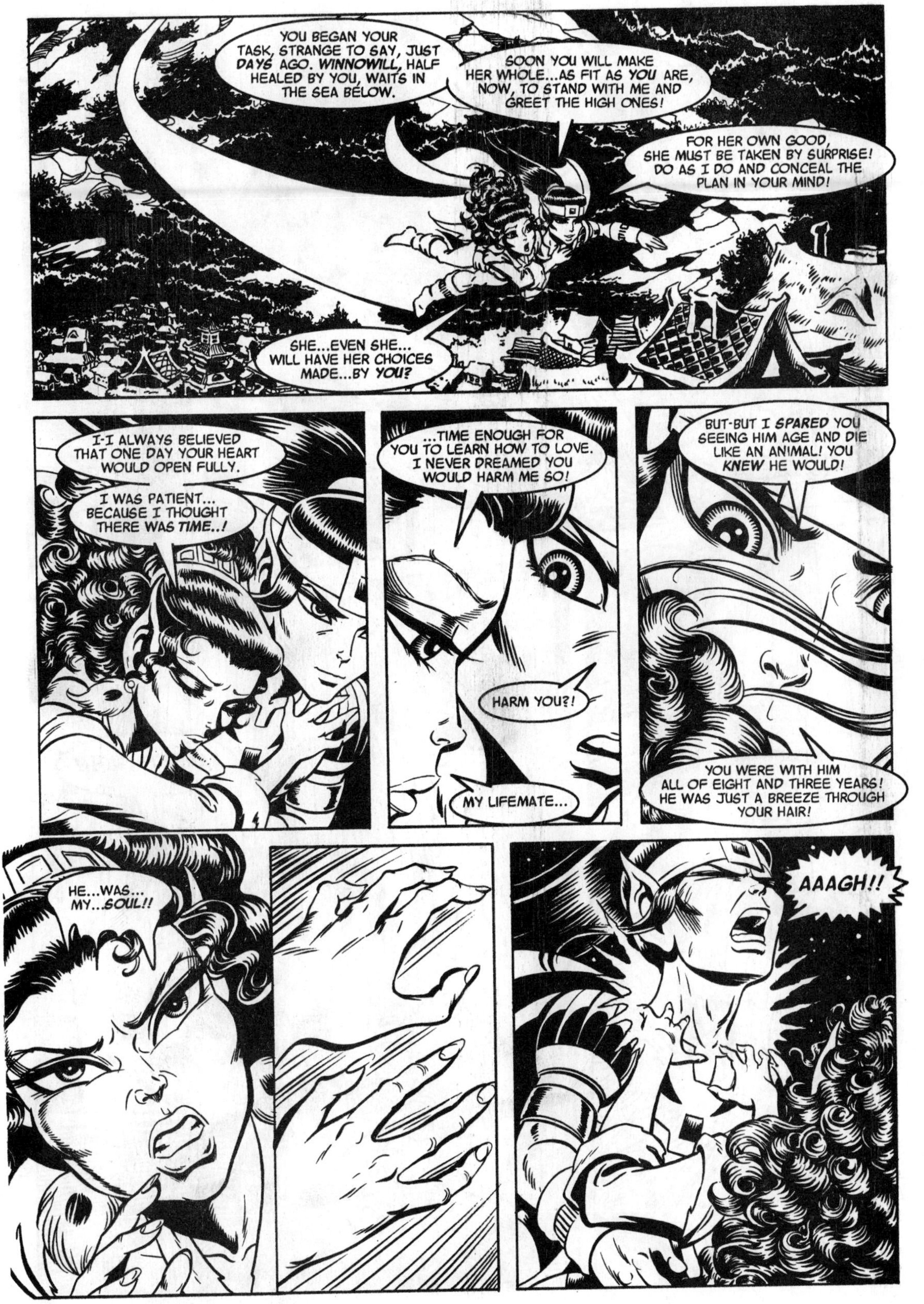
YOU BEGAN YOUR TASK, STRANGE TO SAY, JUST DAYS AGO. WINNOWILL, HALF HEALED BY YOU, WAITS IN THE SEA BELOW.
SOON YOU WILL MAKE HER WHOLE...AS FIT AS YOU ARE, NOW, TO STAND WITH ME AND GREET THE HIGH ONES!
FOR HER OWN GOOD, SHE MUST BE TAKEN BY SURPRISE! DO AS I DO AND CONCEAL THE PLAN IN YOUR MIND!
SHE...EVEN SHE... WILL HAVE HER CHOICES MADE...BY YOU?
I-I ALWAYS BELIEVED THAT ONE DAY YOUR HEART WOULD OPEN FULLY.
I WAS PATIENT... BECAUSE I THOUGHT THERE WAS TIME..!
...TIME ENOUGH FOR YOU TO LEARN HOW TO LOVE. I NEVER DREAMED YOU WOULD HARM ME SO!
HARM YOU?!
MY LIFEMATE...
BUT-BUT I SPARED YOU SEEING HIM AGE AND DIE LIKE AN ANIMAL! YOU KNEW HE WOULD!
YOU WERE WITH HIM ALL OF EIGHT AND THREE YEARS! HE WAS JUST A BREEZE THROUGH YOUR HAIR!
HE...WAS... MY...SOUL!!
AAAGH!!

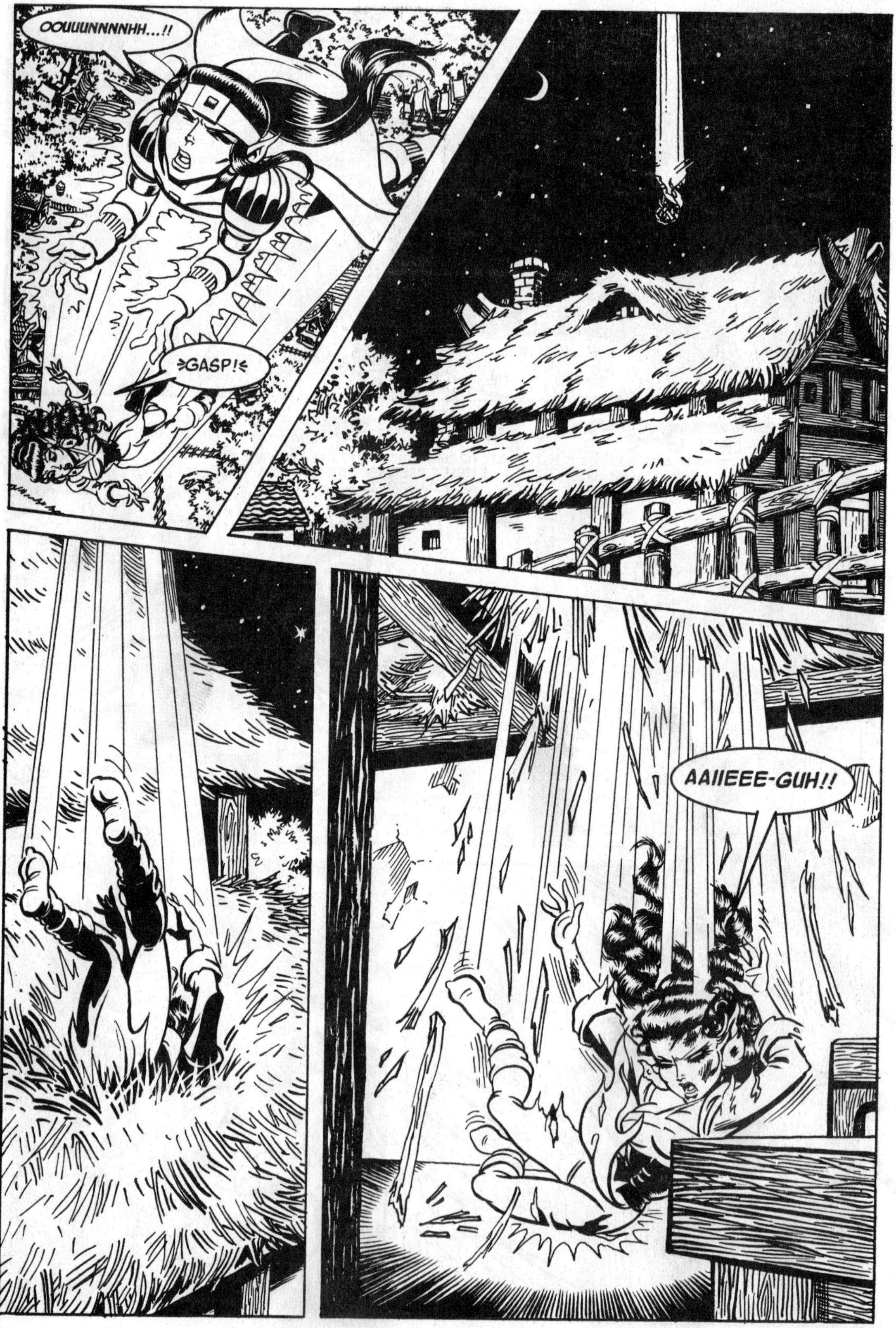
OOUUUNNNNHH...!!
GASP!
AAIIEEE-GUH!!

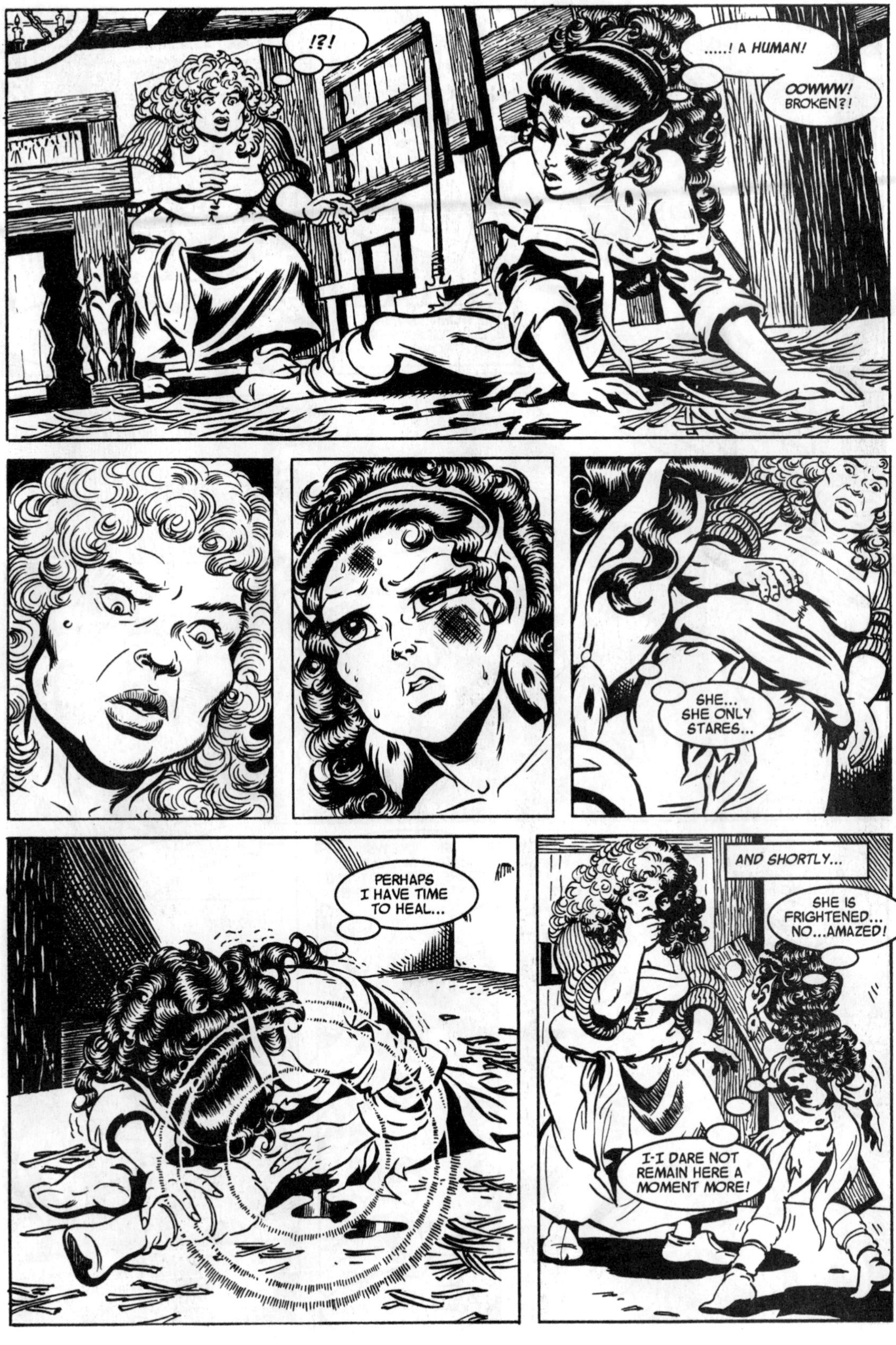
!?!
.....! A HUMAN!
OOWWW! BROKEN?!
SHE... SHE ONLY STARES...
PERHAPS I HAVE TIME TO HEAL...
AND SHORTLY...
SHE IS FRIGHTENED... NO...AMAZED!
I-I DARE NOT REMAIN HERE A MOMENT MORE!

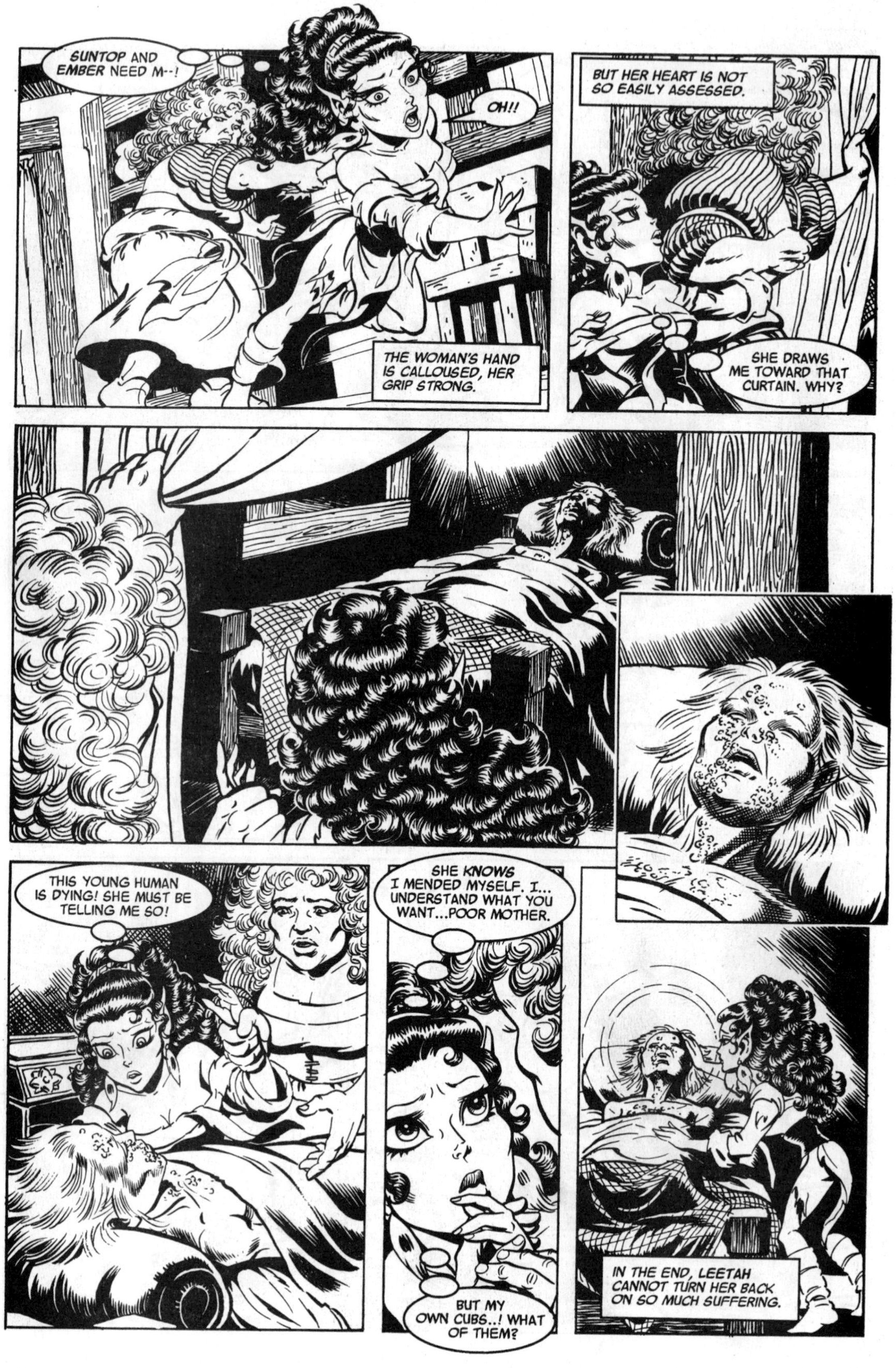

SUNTOP AND EMBER NEED M--!
OH!!
THE WOMAN'S HAND IS CALLOUSED, HER GRIP STRONG.
BUT HER HEART IS NOT SO EASILY ASSESSED.
SHE DRAWS ME TOWARD THAT CURTAIN. WHY?
THIS YOUNG HUMAN IS DYING! SHE MUST BE TELLING ME SO!
SHE KNOWS I MENDED MYSELF. I... UNDERSTAND WHAT YOU WANT...POOR MOTHER.
BUT MY OWN CUBS..! WHAT OF THEM?
IN THE END, LEETAH CANNOT TURN HER BACK ON SO MUCH SUFFERING.

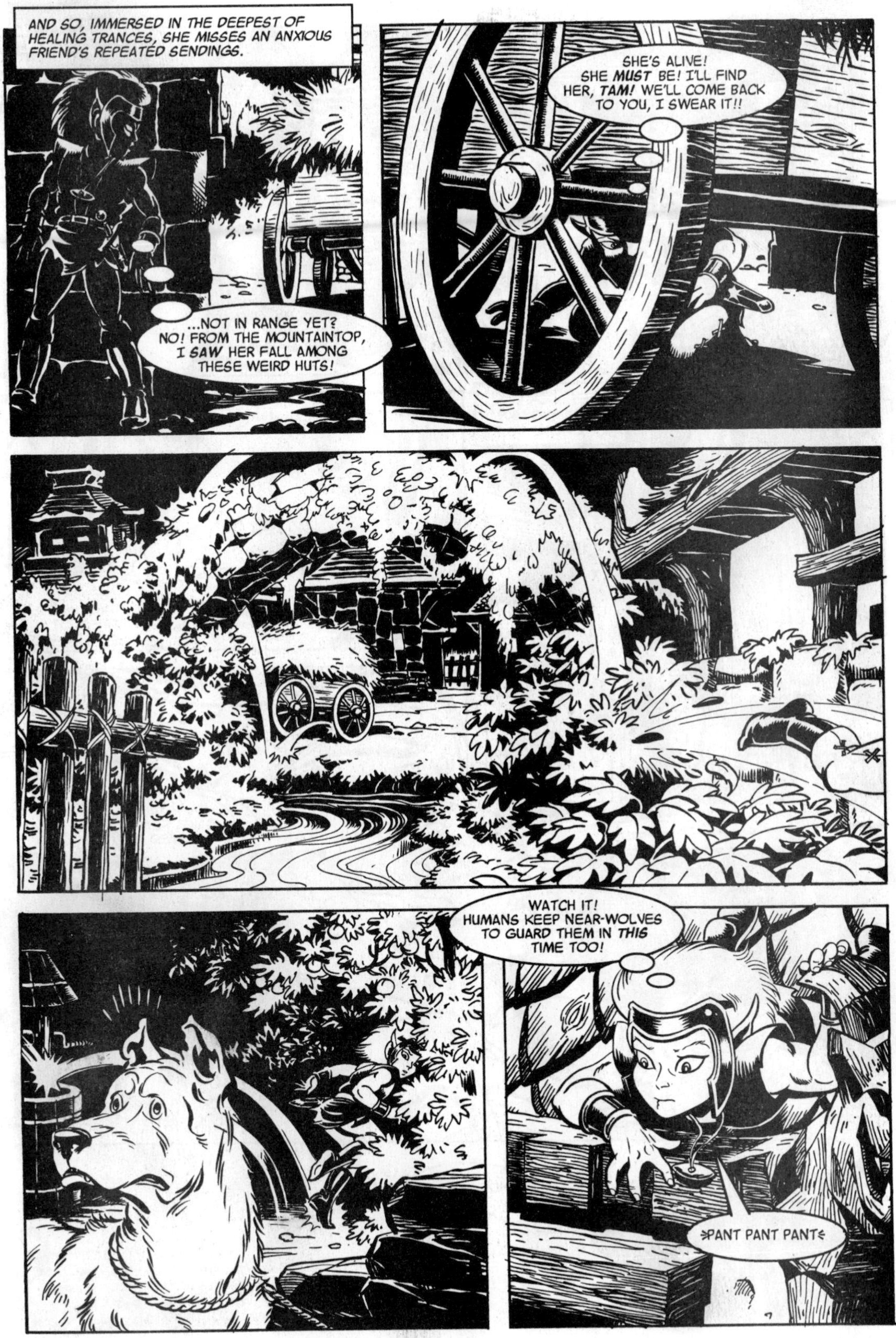
AND SO, IMMERSED IN THE DEEPEST OF HEALING TRANCES, SHE MISSES AN ANXIOUS FRIEND'S REPEATED SENDINGS.
...NOT IN RANGE YET? NO! FROM THE MOUNTAINTOP, I SAW HER FALL AMONG THESE WEIRD HUTS!
SHE'S ALIVE! SHE MUST BE! I'LL FIND HER, TAM! WE'LL COME BACK TO YOU, I SWEAR IT!!
WATCH IT! HUMANS KEEP NEAR-WOLVES TO GUARD THEM IN THIS TIME TOO!
PANT PANT PANT

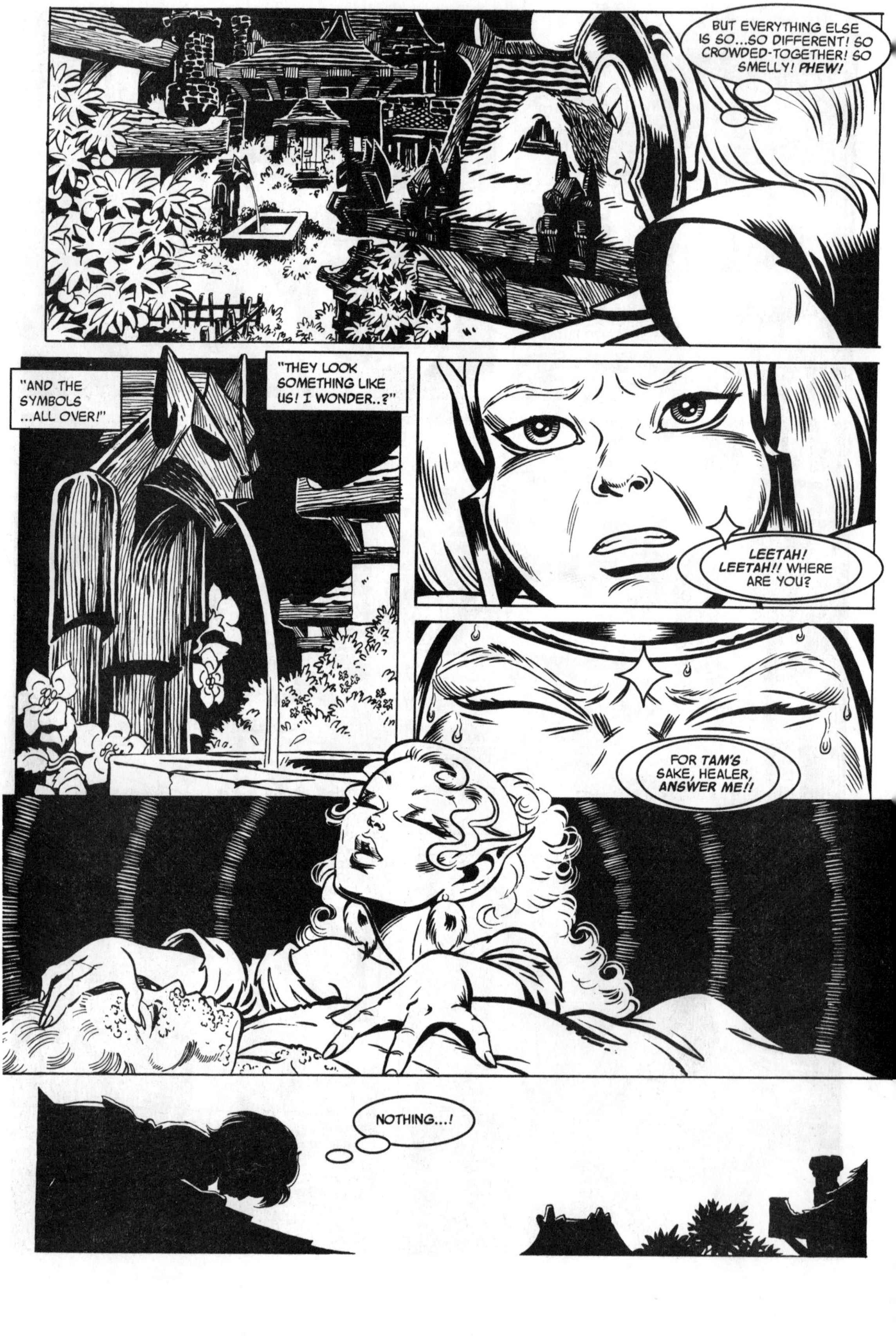
BUT EVERYTHING ELSE IS SO...SO DIFFERENT! SO CROWDED-TOGETHER! SO SMELLY! PHEW!
"AND THE SYMBOLS ...ALL OVER!"
"THEY LOOK SOMETHING LIKE US! I WONDER..?"
LEETAH! LEETAH!! WHERE ARE YOU?
FOR TAM'S SAKE, HEALER, ANSWER ME!!
NOTHING...!

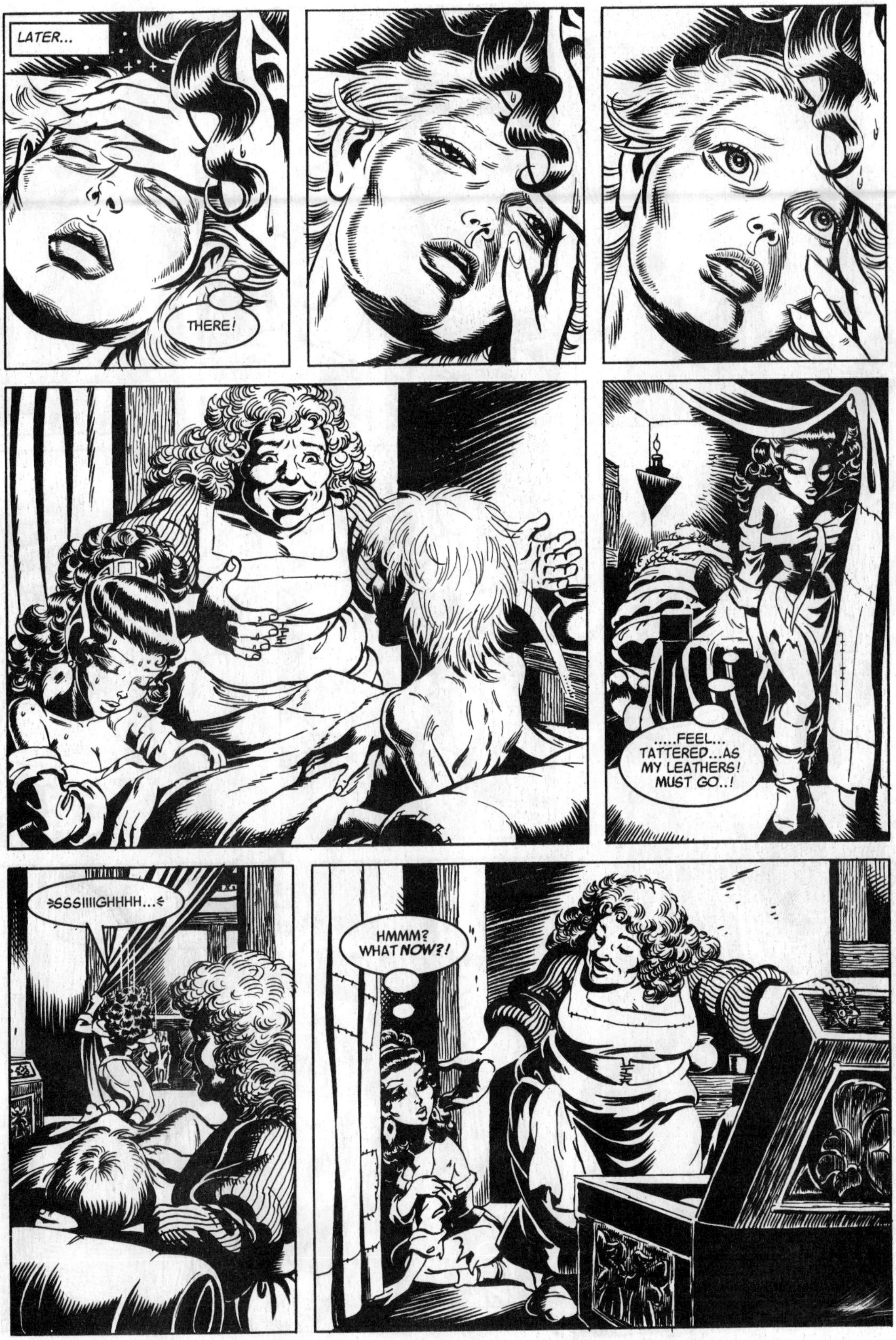
LATER...
THERE!
.....FEEL...
TATTERED...AS
MY LEATHERS!
MUST GO..!
SSSIIIIGHHHH...
HMMM?
WHAT NOW?!

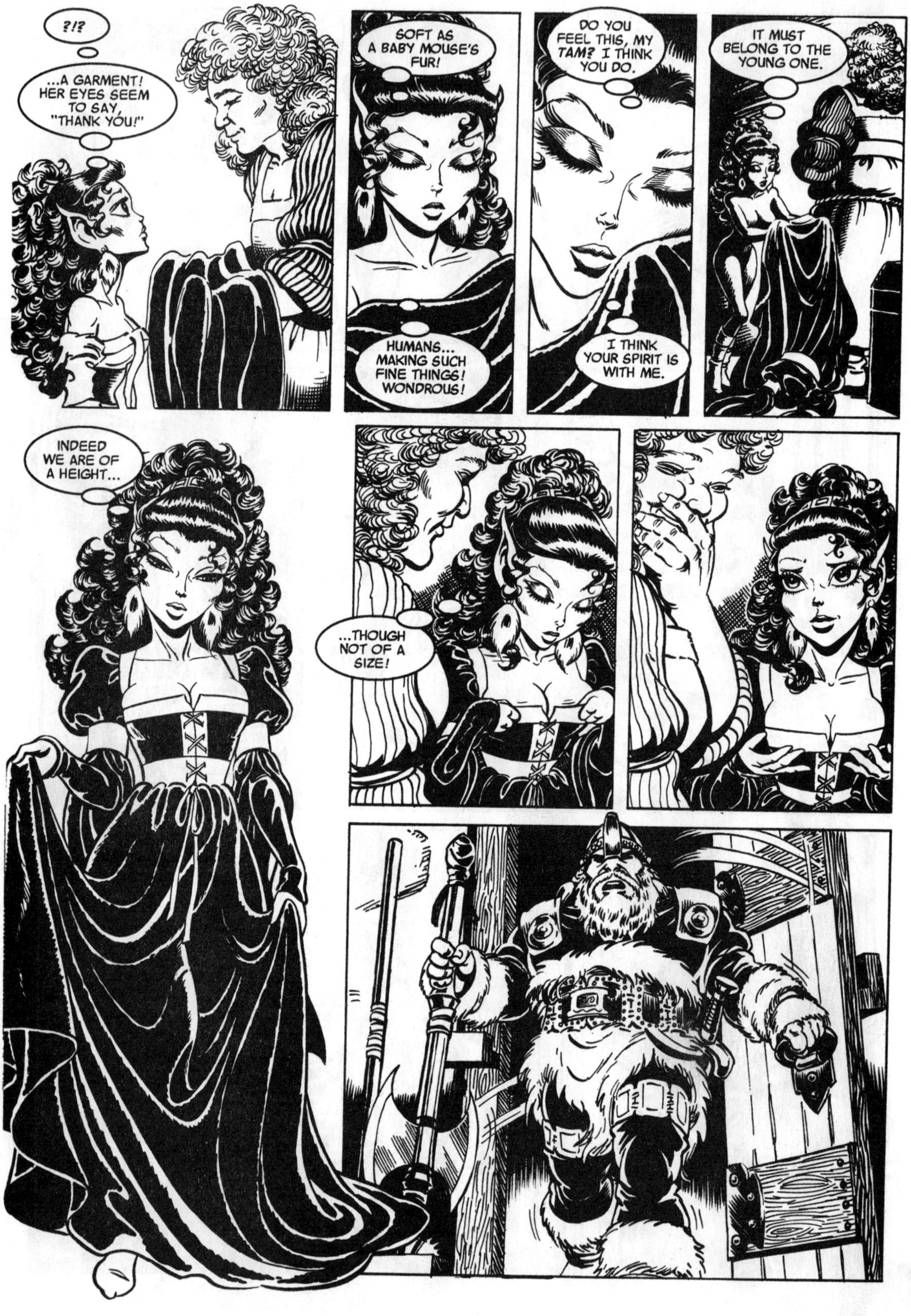
?!?
...A GARMENT! HER EYES SEEM TO SAY, "THANK YOU!"
SOFT AS A BABY MOUSE'S FUR!
HUMANS... MAKING SUCH FINE THINGS! WONDROUS!
DO YOU FEEL THIS, MY TAM? I THINK YOU DO.
I THINK YOUR SPIRIT IS WITH ME.
IT MUST BELONG TO THE YOUNG ONE.
INDEED WE ARE OF A HEIGHT...
...THOUGH NOT OF A SIZE!

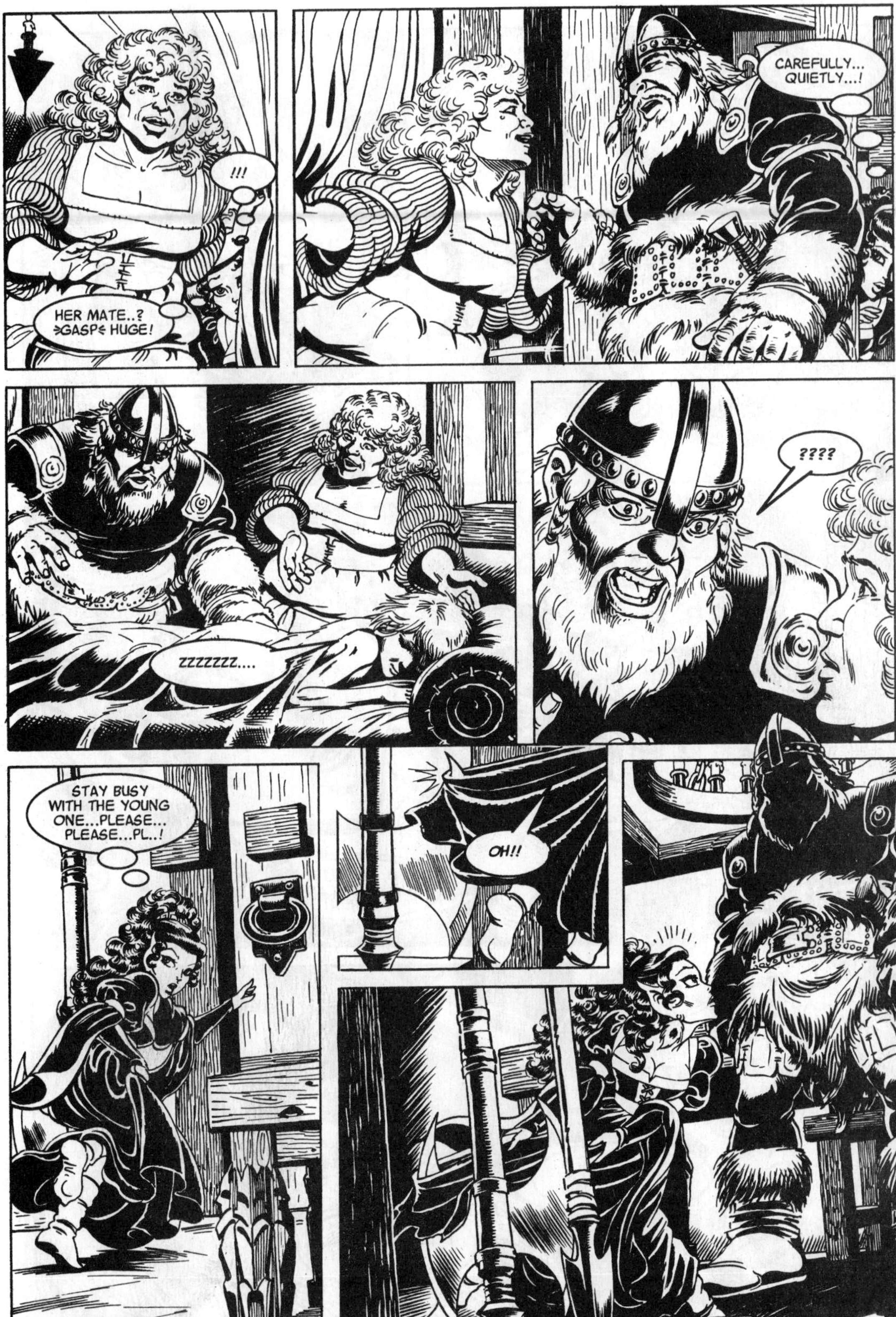
!!!
HER MATE..? ≥GASP≤ HUGE!
CAREFULLY... QUIETLY...!
ZZZZZZZ....
????
STAY BUSY WITH THE YOUNG ONE...PLEASE... PLEASE...PL...!
OH!!

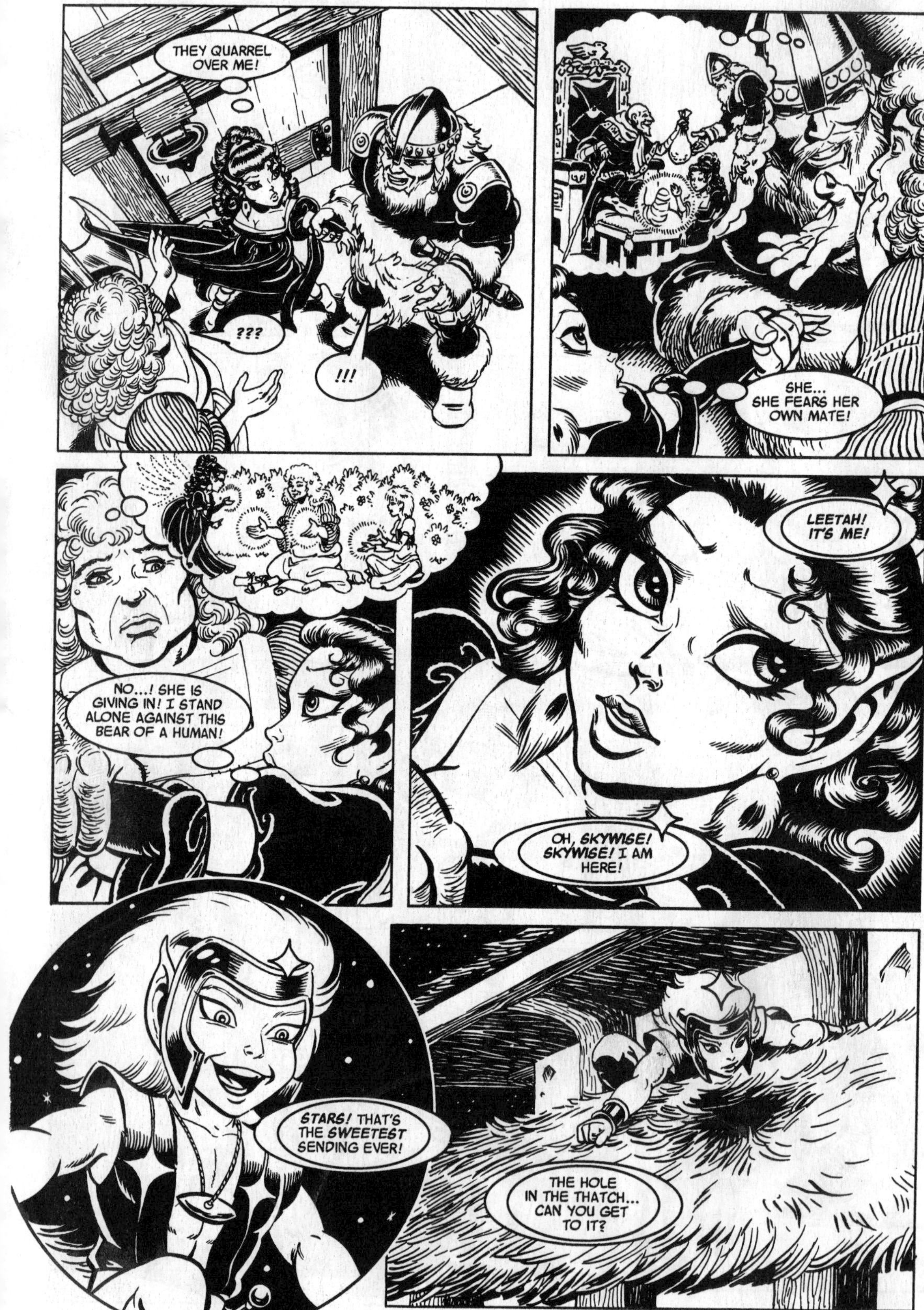
THEY QUARREL OVER ME!
???
!!!
SHE... SHE FEARS HER OWN MATE!
NO...! SHE IS GIVING IN! I STAND ALONE AGAINST THIS BEAR OF A HUMAN!
LEETAH! IT'S ME!
OH, SKYWISE! SKYWISE! I AM HERE!
STARS! THAT'S THE SWEETEST SENDING EVER!
THE HOLE IN THE THATCH... CAN YOU GET TO IT?

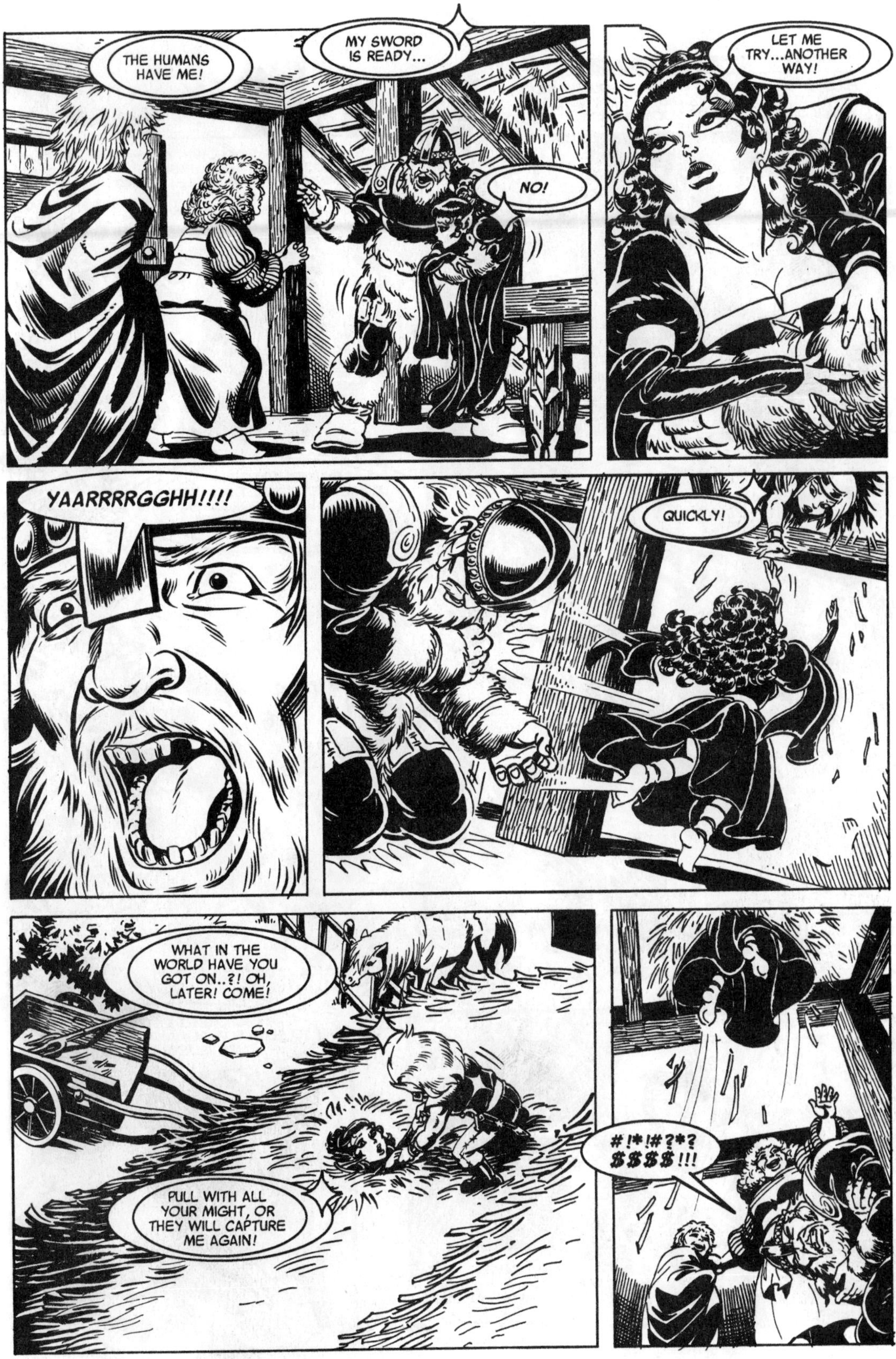
THE HUMANS HAVE ME!
MY SWORD IS READY...
NO!
LET ME TRY...ANOTHER WAY!
YAARRRRGGHH!!!!
QUICKLY!
WHAT IN THE WORLD HAVE YOU GOT ON..?! OH, LATER! COME!
PULL WITH ALL YOUR MIGHT, OR THEY WILL CAPTURE ME AGAIN!
#!*!#?*? $$$$!!!

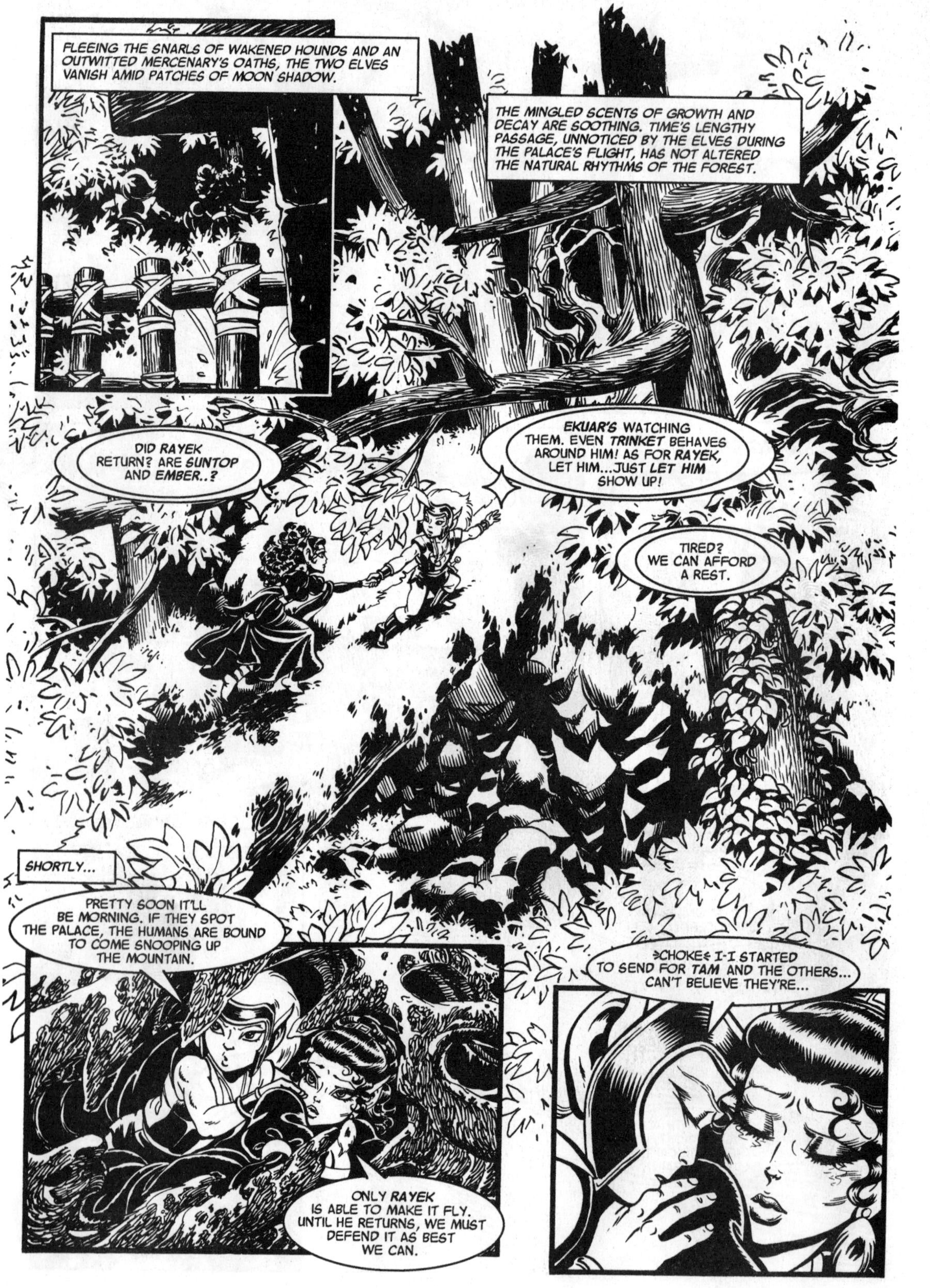
FLEEING THE SNARLS OF WAKENED HOUNDS AND AN OUTWITTED MERCENARY'S OATHS, THE TWO ELVES VANISH AMID PATCHES OF MOON SHADOW.
THE MINGLED SCENTS OF GROWTH AND DECAY ARE SOOTHING. TIME'S LENGTHY PASSAGE, UNNOTICED BY THE ELVES DURING THE PALACE'S FLIGHT, HAS NOT ALTERED THE NATURAL RHYTHMS OF THE FOREST.
DID RAYEK RETURN? ARE SUNTOP AND EMBER..?
EKUAR'S WATCHING THEM. EVEN TRINKET BEHAVES AROUND HIM! AS FOR RAYEK, LET HIM...JUST LET HIM SHOW UP!
TIRED? WE CAN AFFORD A REST.
SHORTLY...
PRETTY SOON IT'LL BE MORNING. IF THEY SPOT THE PALACE, THE HUMANS ARE BOUND TO COME SNOOPING UP THE MOUNTAIN.
ONLY RAYEK IS ABLE TO MAKE IT FLY. UNTIL HE RETURNS, WE MUST DEFEND IT AS BEST WE CAN.
≯CHOKE≮ I-I STARTED TO SEND FOR TAM AND THE OTHERS... CAN'T BELIEVE THEY'RE...

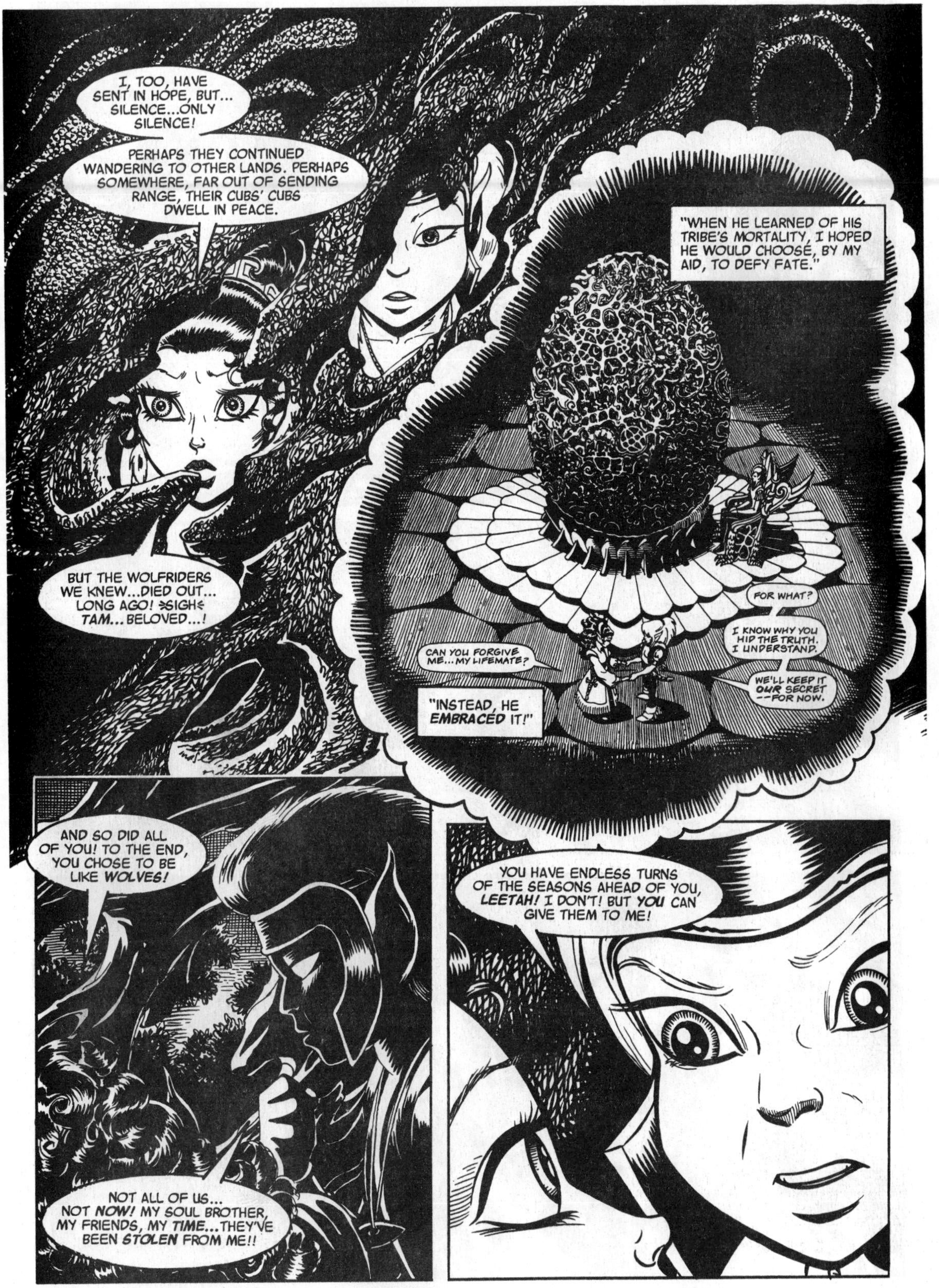
I, TOO, HAVE SENT IN HOPE, BUT... SILENCE...ONLY SILENCE!
PERHAPS THEY CONTINUED WANDERING TO OTHER LANDS. PERHAPS SOMEWHERE, FAR OUT OF SENDING RANGE, THEIR CUBS' CUBS DWELL IN PEACE.
BUT THE WOLFRIDERS WE KNEW...DIED OUT... LONG AGO! *SIGH* TAM... BELOVED...!
"WHEN HE LEARNED OF HIS TRIBE'S MORTALITY, I HOPED HE WOULD CHOOSE, BY MY AID, TO DEFY FATE."
CAN YOU FORGIVE ME... MY LIFEMATE?
FOR WHAT?
I KNOW WHY YOU HID THE TRUTH. I UNDERSTAND.
WE'LL KEEP IT OUR SECRET --FOR NOW.
"INSTEAD, HE EMBRACED IT!"
AND SO DID ALL OF YOU! TO THE END, YOU CHOSE TO BE LIKE WOLVES!
NOT ALL OF US... NOT NOW! MY SOUL BROTHER, MY FRIENDS, MY TIME... THEY'VE BEEN STOLEN FROM ME!!
YOU HAVE ENDLESS TURNS OF THE SEASONS AHEAD OF YOU, LEETAH! I DON'T! BUT YOU CAN GIVE THEM TO ME!

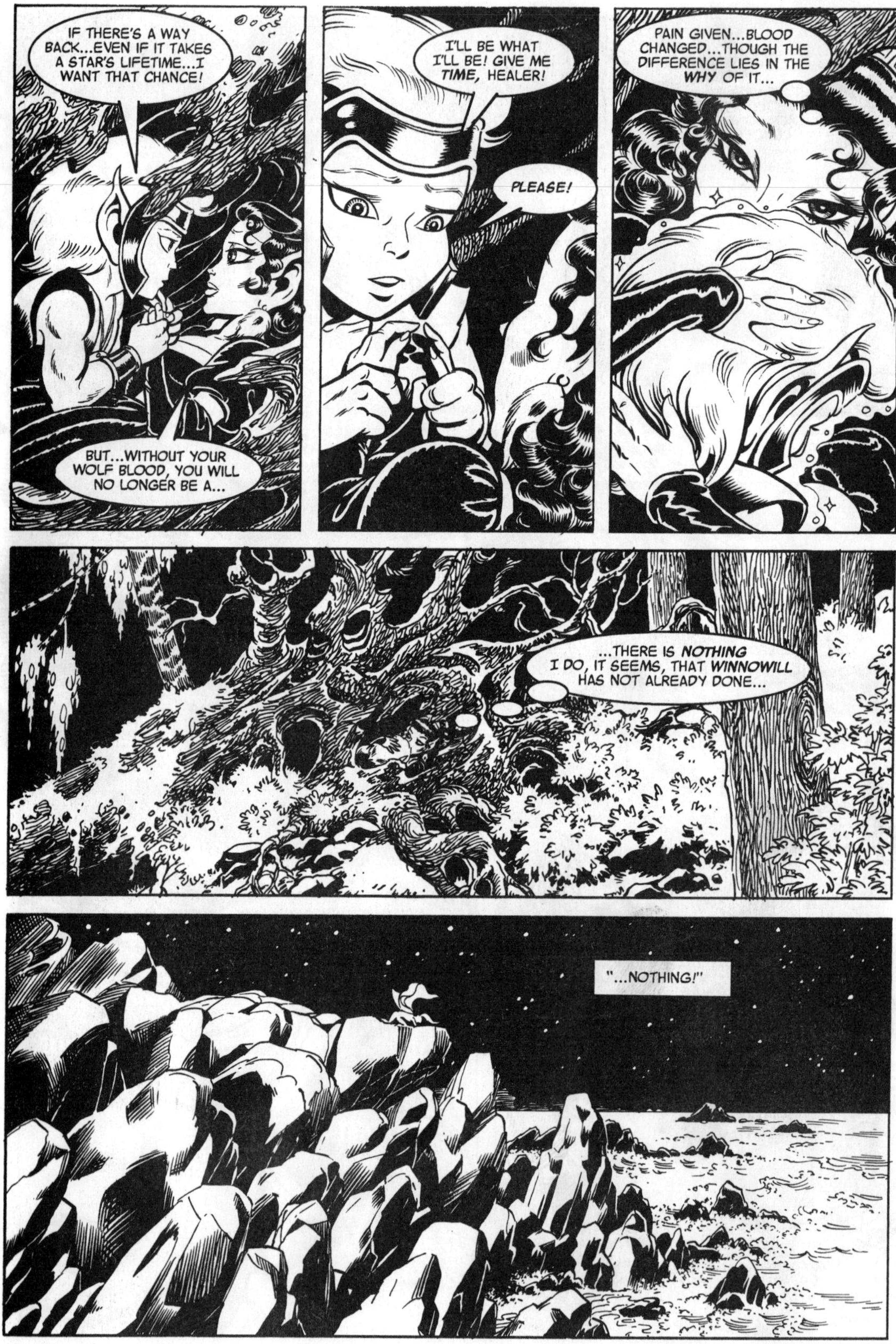
IF THERE'S A WAY BACK...EVEN IF IT TAKES A STAR'S LIFETIME...I WANT THAT CHANCE!
BUT...WITHOUT YOUR WOLF BLOOD, YOU WILL NO LONGER BE A...
I'LL BE WHAT I'LL BE! GIVE ME TIME, HEALER!
PLEASE!
PAIN GIVEN...BLOOD CHANGED...THOUGH THE DIFFERENCE LIES IN THE WHY OF IT...
...THERE IS NOTHING I DO, IT SEEMS, THAT WINNOWILL HAS NOT ALREADY DONE...
"...NOTHING!"

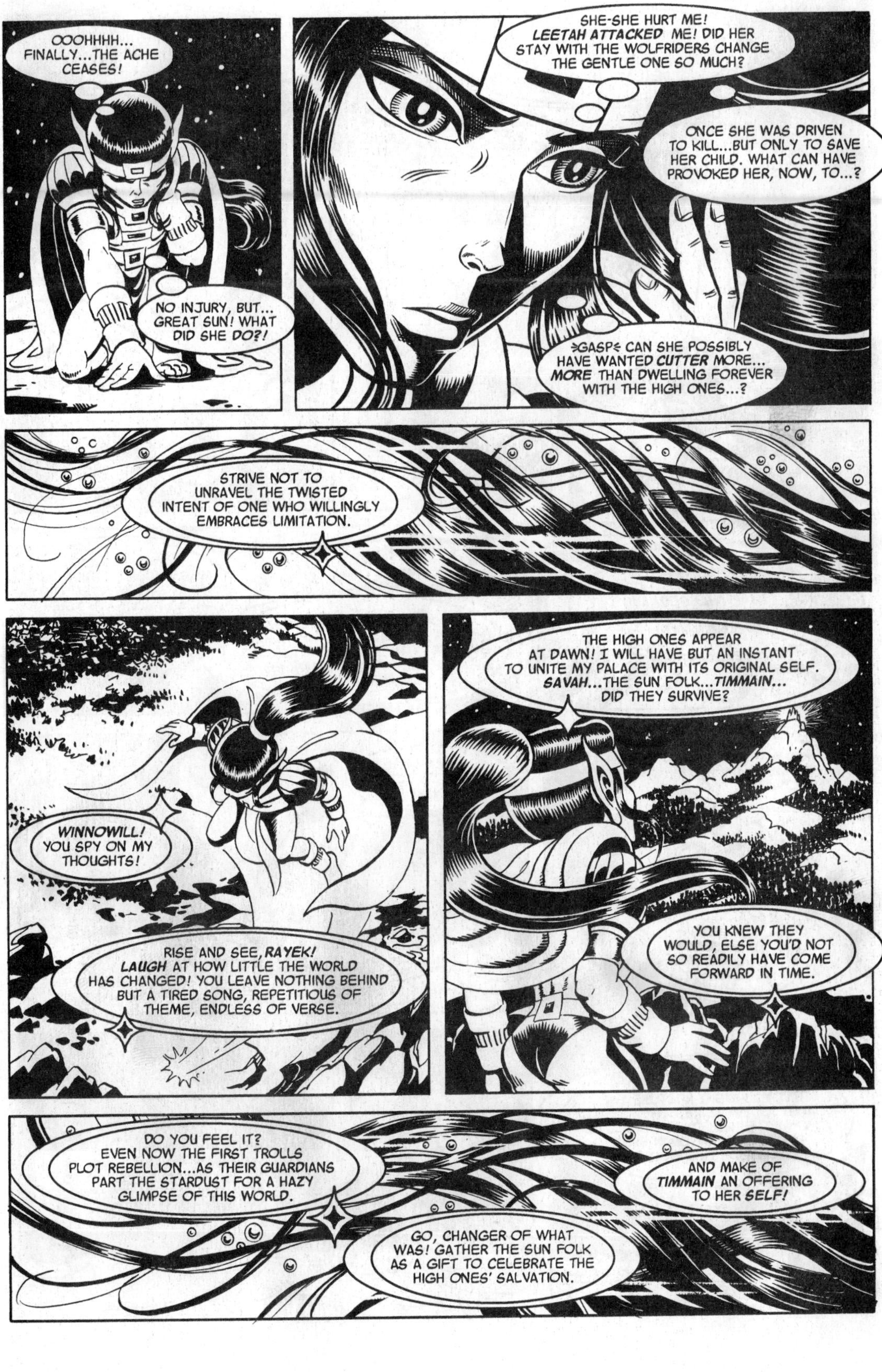
OOOHHHH... FINALLY...THE ACHE CEASES!
NO INJURY, BUT... GREAT SUN! WHAT DID SHE DO?!
SHE-SHE HURT ME! LEETAH ATTACKED ME! DID HER STAY WITH THE WOLFRIDERS CHANGE THE GENTLE ONE SO MUCH?
ONCE SHE WAS DRIVEN TO KILL...BUT ONLY TO SAVE HER CHILD. WHAT CAN HAVE PROVOKED HER, NOW, TO...?
⋟GASP⋞ CAN SHE POSSIBLY HAVE WANTED CUTTER MORE... MORE THAN DWELLING FOREVER WITH THE HIGH ONES...?
STRIVE NOT TO UNRAVEL THE TWISTED INTENT OF ONE WHO WILLINGLY EMBRACES LIMITATION.
WINNOWILL! YOU SPY ON MY THOUGHTS!
RISE AND SEE, RAYEK! LAUGH AT HOW LITTLE THE WORLD HAS CHANGED! YOU LEAVE NOTHING BEHIND BUT A TIRED SONG, REPETITIOUS OF THEME, ENDLESS OF VERSE.
THE HIGH ONES APPEAR AT DAWN! I WILL HAVE BUT AN INSTANT TO UNITE MY PALACE WITH ITS ORIGINAL SELF. SAVAH...THE SUN FOLK...TIMMAIN... DID THEY SURVIVE?
YOU KNEW THEY WOULD, ELSE YOU'D NOT SO READILY HAVE COME FORWARD IN TIME.
DO YOU FEEL IT? EVEN NOW THE FIRST TROLLS PLOT REBELLION...AS THEIR GUARDIANS PART THE STARDUST FOR A HAZY GLIMPSE OF THIS WORLD.
GO, CHANGER OF WHAT WAS! GATHER THE SUN FOLK AS A GIFT TO CELEBRATE THE HIGH ONES' SALVATION.
AND MAKE OF TIMMAIN AN OFFERING TO HER SELF!

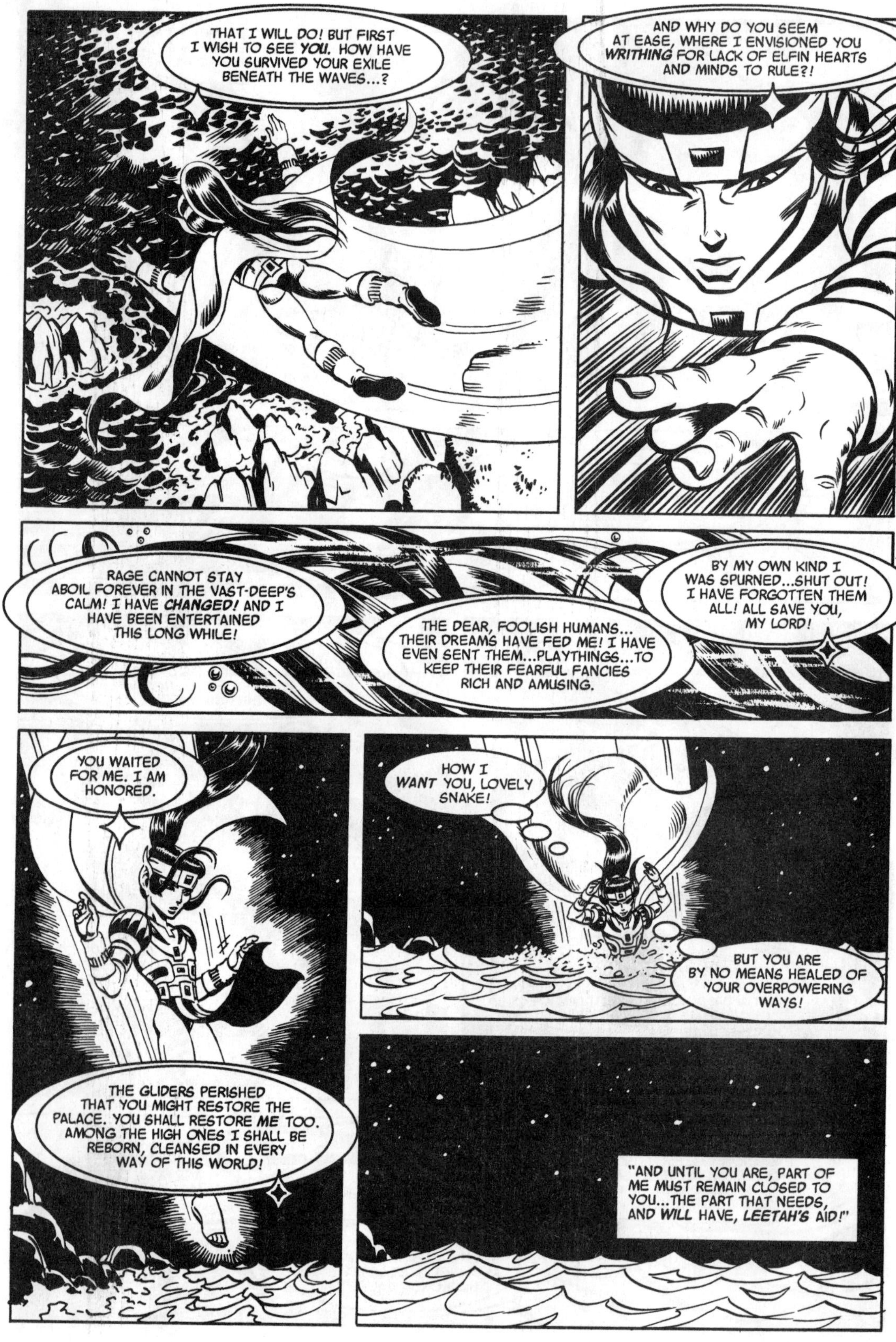
THAT I WILL DO! BUT FIRST I WISH TO SEE YOU. HOW HAVE YOU SURVIVED YOUR EXILE BENEATH THE WAVES...?
AND WHY DO YOU SEEM AT EASE, WHERE I ENVISIONED YOU WRITHING FOR LACK OF ELFIN HEARTS AND MINDS TO RULE?!
RAGE CANNOT STAY ABOIL FOREVER IN THE VAST-DEEP'S CALM! I HAVE CHANGED! AND I HAVE BEEN ENTERTAINED THIS LONG WHILE!
THE DEAR, FOOLISH HUMANS... THEIR DREAMS HAVE FED ME! I HAVE EVEN SENT THEM...PLAYTHINGS...TO KEEP THEIR FEARFUL FANCIES RICH AND AMUSING.
BY MY OWN KIND I WAS SPURNED...SHUT OUT! I HAVE FORGOTTEN THEM ALL! ALL SAVE YOU, MY LORD!
YOU WAITED FOR ME. I AM HONORED.
THE GLIDERS PERISHED THAT YOU MIGHT RESTORE THE PALACE. YOU SHALL RESTORE ME TOO. AMONG THE HIGH ONES I SHALL BE REBORN, CLEANSED IN EVERY WAY OF THIS WORLD!
HOW I WANT YOU, LOVELY SNAKE!
BUT YOU ARE BY NO MEANS HEALED OF YOUR OVERPOWERING WAYS!
"AND UNTIL YOU ARE, PART OF ME MUST REMAIN CLOSED TO YOU...THE PART THAT NEEDS, AND WILL HAVE, LEETAH'S AID!"

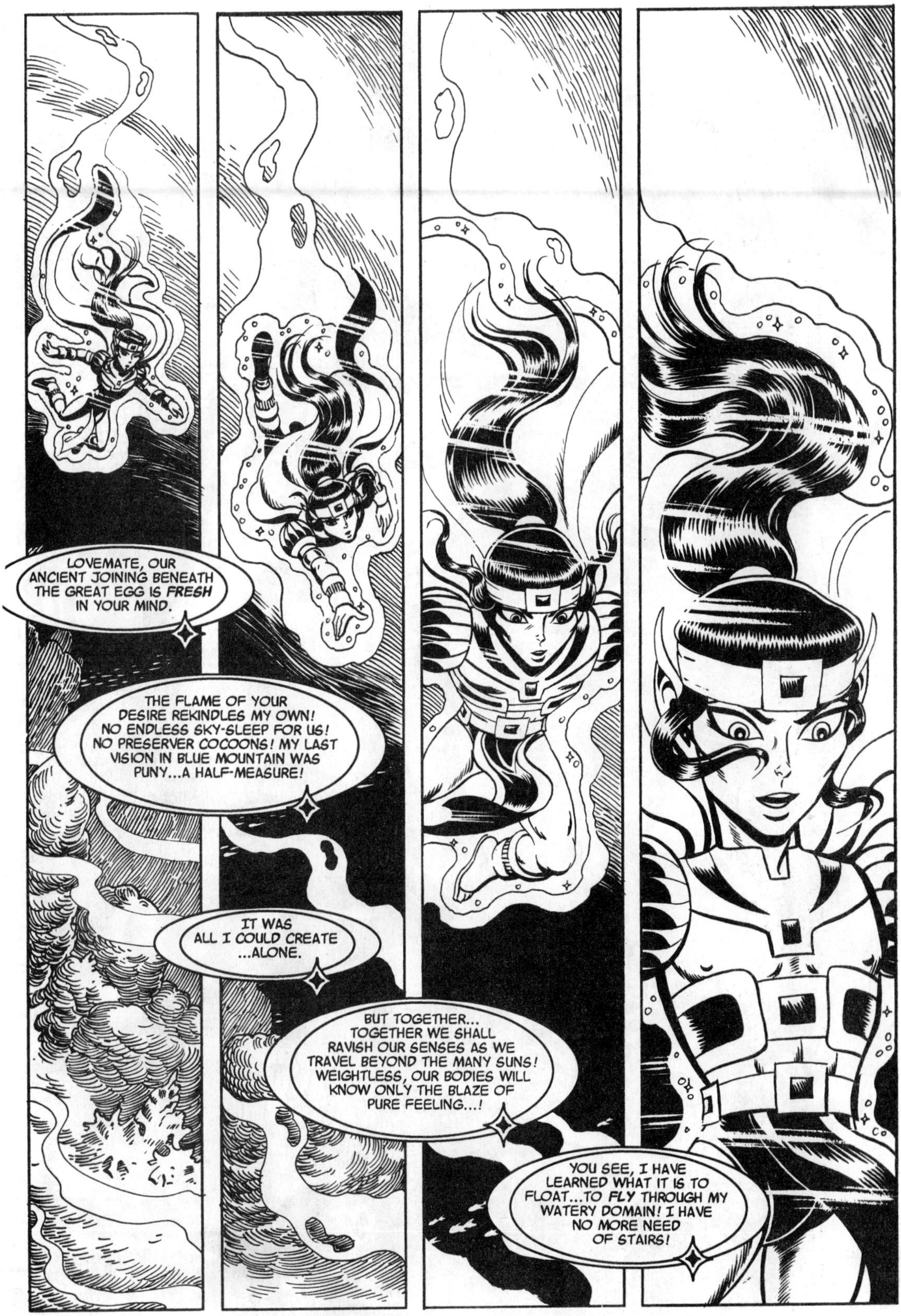
LOVEMATE, OUR ANCIENT JOINING BENEATH THE GREAT EGG IS *FRESH* IN YOUR MIND.
THE FLAME OF YOUR DESIRE REKINDLES MY OWN! NO ENDLESS SKY-SLEEP FOR US! NO PRESERVER COCOONS! MY LAST VISION IN BLUE MOUNTAIN WAS PUNY...A HALF-MEASURE!
IT WAS ALL I COULD CREATE ...ALONE.
BUT TOGETHER... TOGETHER WE SHALL RAVISH OUR SENSES AS WE TRAVEL BEYOND THE MANY SUNS! WEIGHTLESS, OUR BODIES WILL KNOW ONLY THE BLAZE OF PURE FEELING...!
YOU SEE, I HAVE LEARNED WHAT IT IS TO FLOAT...TO *FLY* THROUGH MY WATERY DOMAIN! I HAVE NO MORE NEED OF STAIRS!

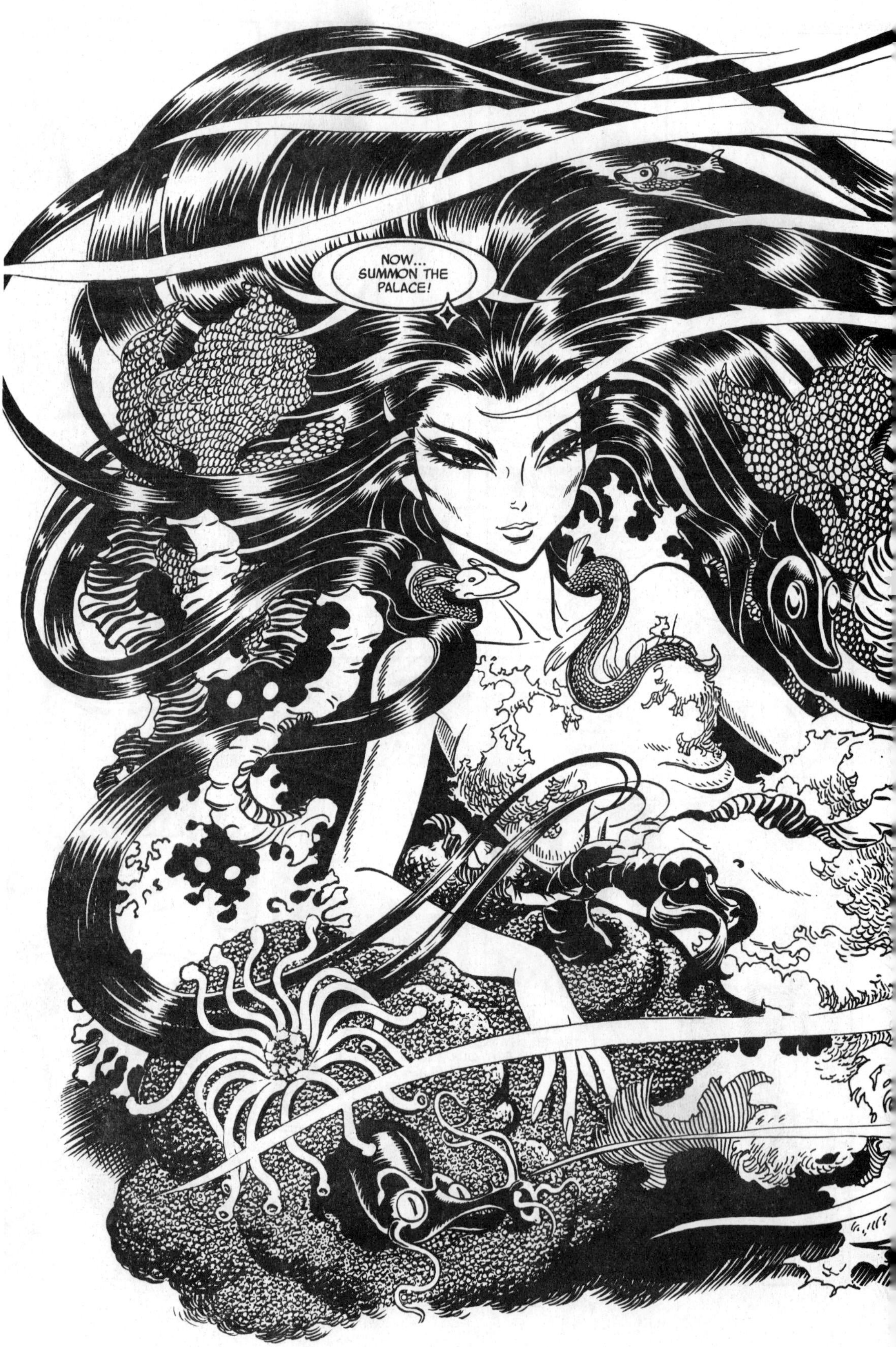
NOW... SUMMON THE PALACE!

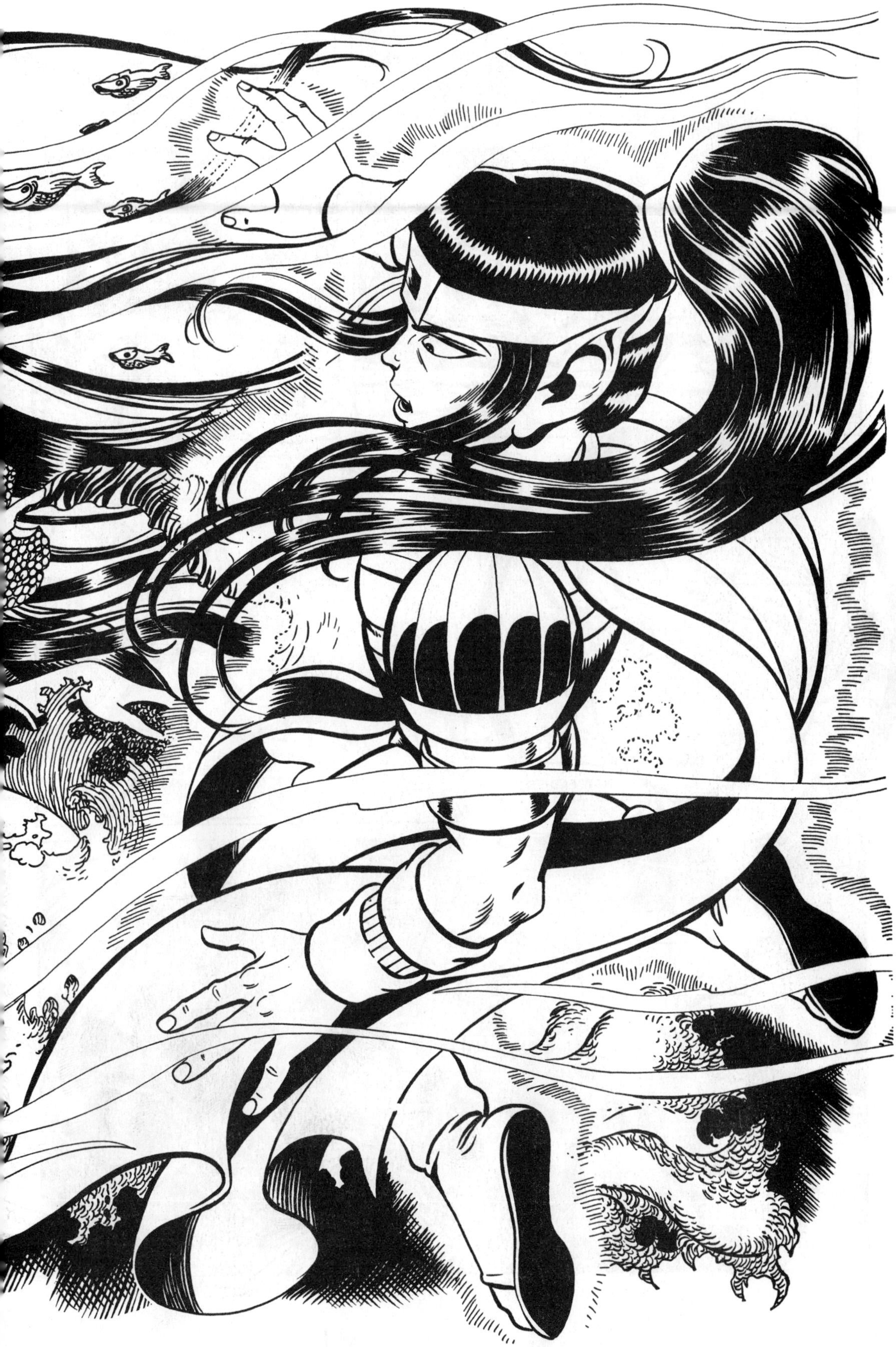

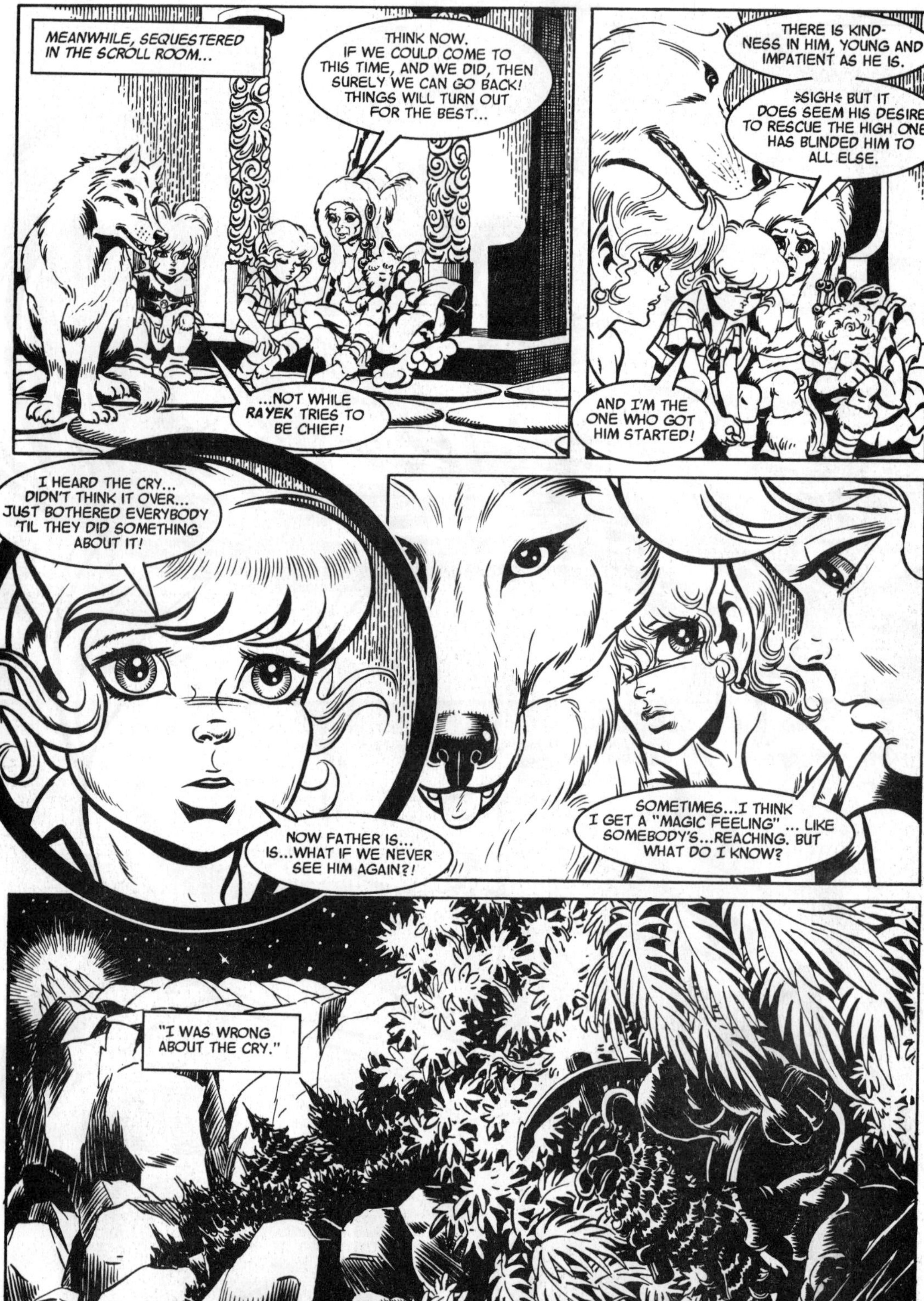
MEANWHILE, SEQUESTERED IN THE SCROLL ROOM...
THINK NOW. IF WE COULD COME TO THIS TIME, AND WE DID, THEN SURELY WE CAN GO BACK! THINGS WILL TURN OUT FOR THE BEST...
...NOT WHILE RAYEK TRIES TO BE CHIEF!
THERE IS KINDNESS IN HIM, YOUNG AND IMPATIENT AS HE IS.
>SIGH< BUT IT DOES SEEM HIS DESIRE TO RESCUE THE HIGH ONES HAS BLINDED HIM TO ALL ELSE.
AND I'M THE ONE WHO GOT HIM STARTED!
I HEARD THE CRY... DIDN'T THINK IT OVER... JUST BOTHERED EVERYBODY 'TIL THEY DID SOMETHING ABOUT IT!
NOW FATHER IS... IS...WHAT IF WE NEVER SEE HIM AGAIN?!
SOMETIMES...I THINK I GET A "MAGIC FEELING" ... LIKE SOMEBODY'S...REACHING. BUT WHAT DO I KNOW?
"I WAS WRONG ABOUT THE CRY."

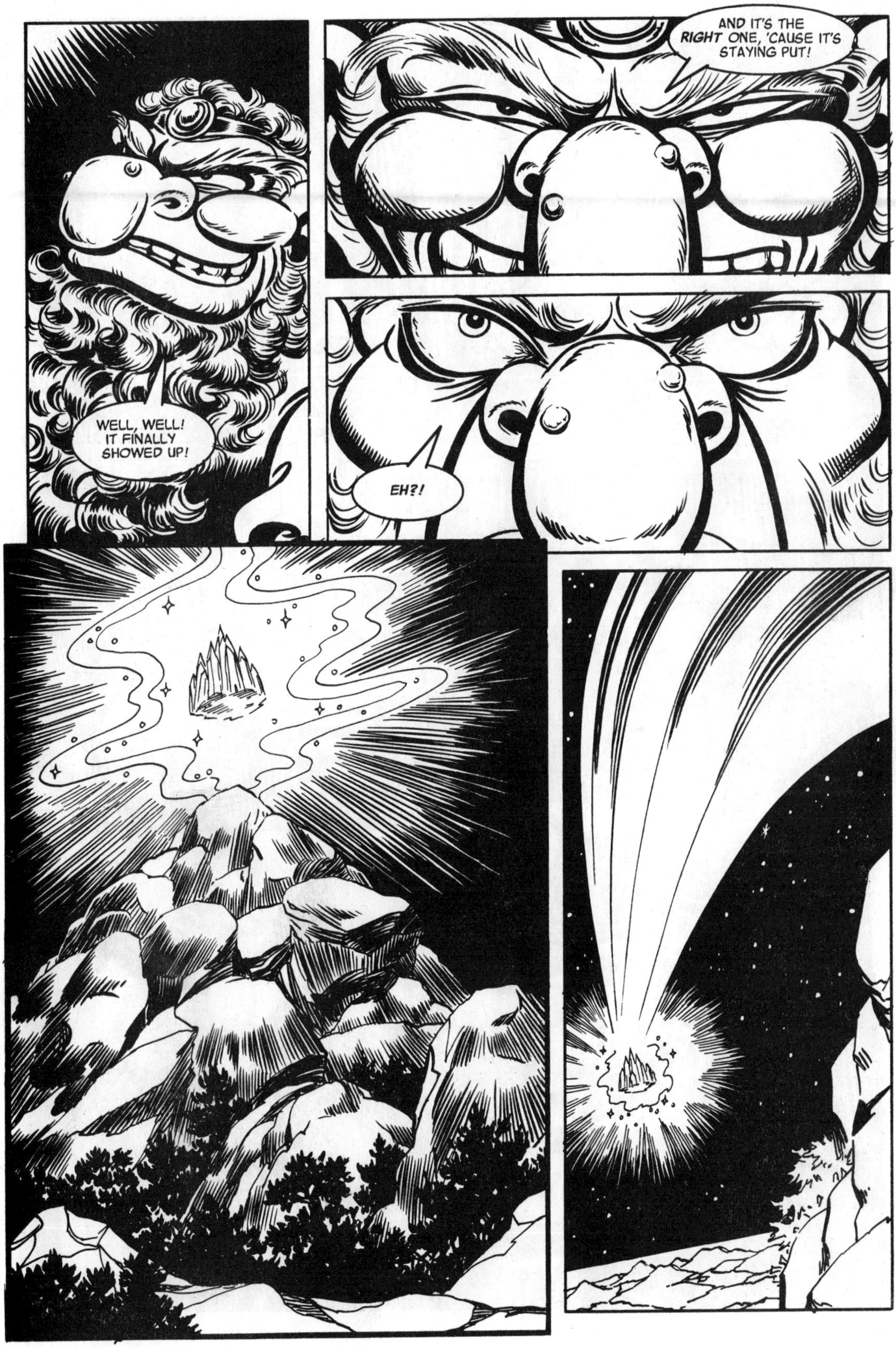
WELL, WELL! IT FINALLY SHOWED UP!
AND IT'S THE **RIGHT** ONE, 'CAUSE IT'S STAYING PUT!
EH?!

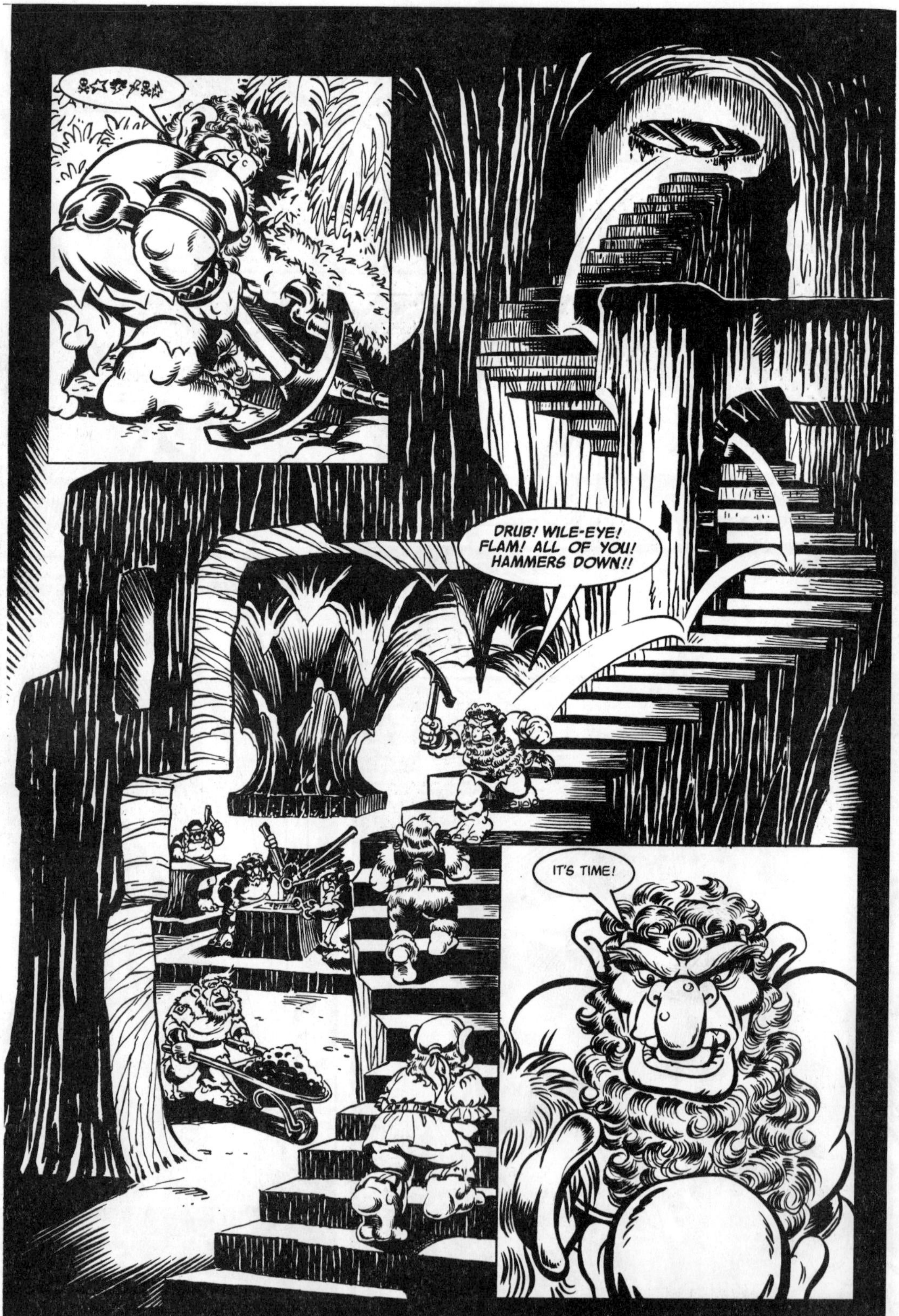
DRUB! WILE-EYE! FLAM! ALL OF YOU! HAMMERS DOWN!!
IT'S TIME!

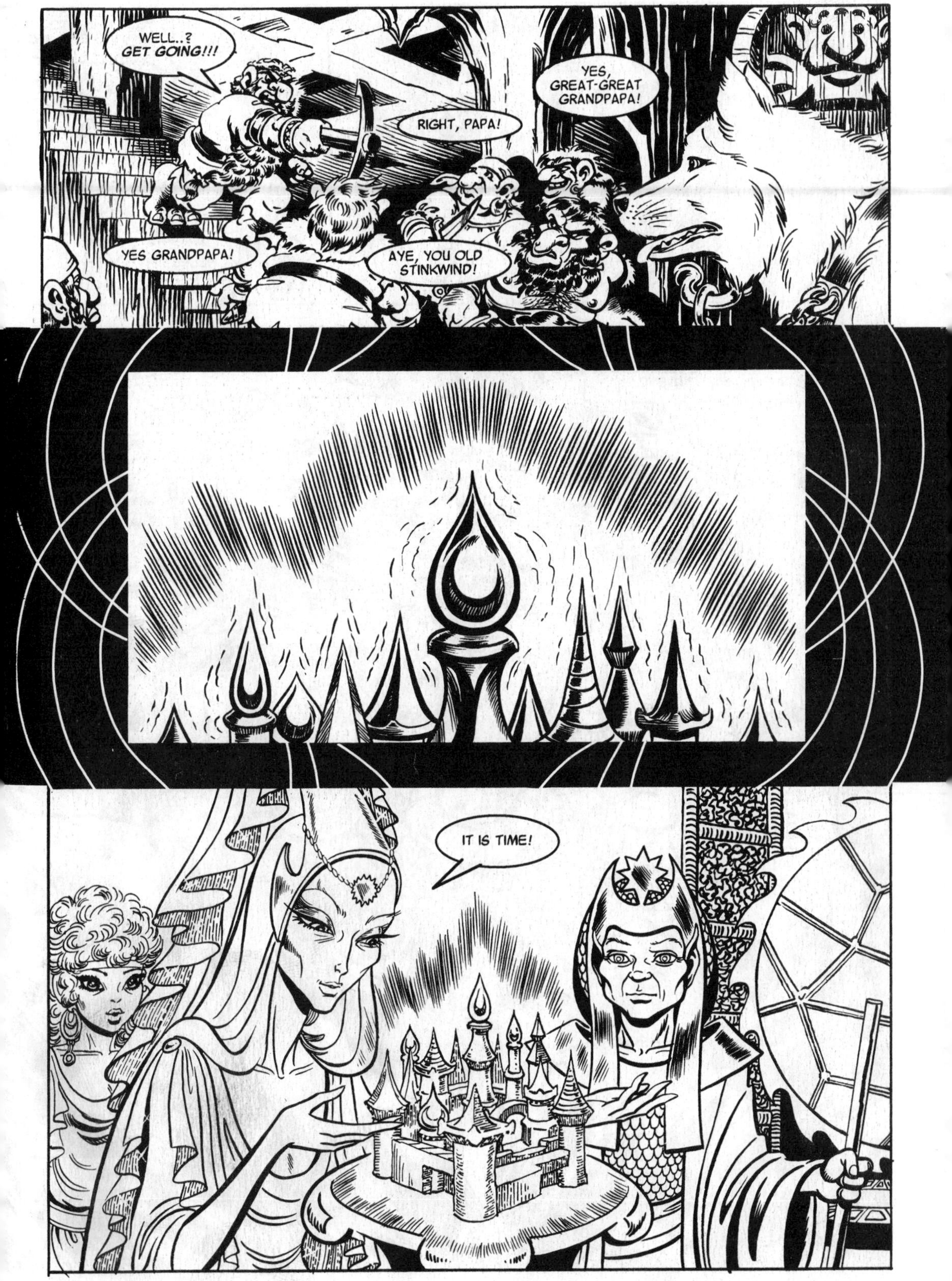
WELL..? GET GOING!!!
YES GRANDPAPA!
AYE, YOU OLD STINKWIND!
RIGHT, PAPA!
YES, GREAT-GREAT GRANDPAPA!
IT IS TIME!

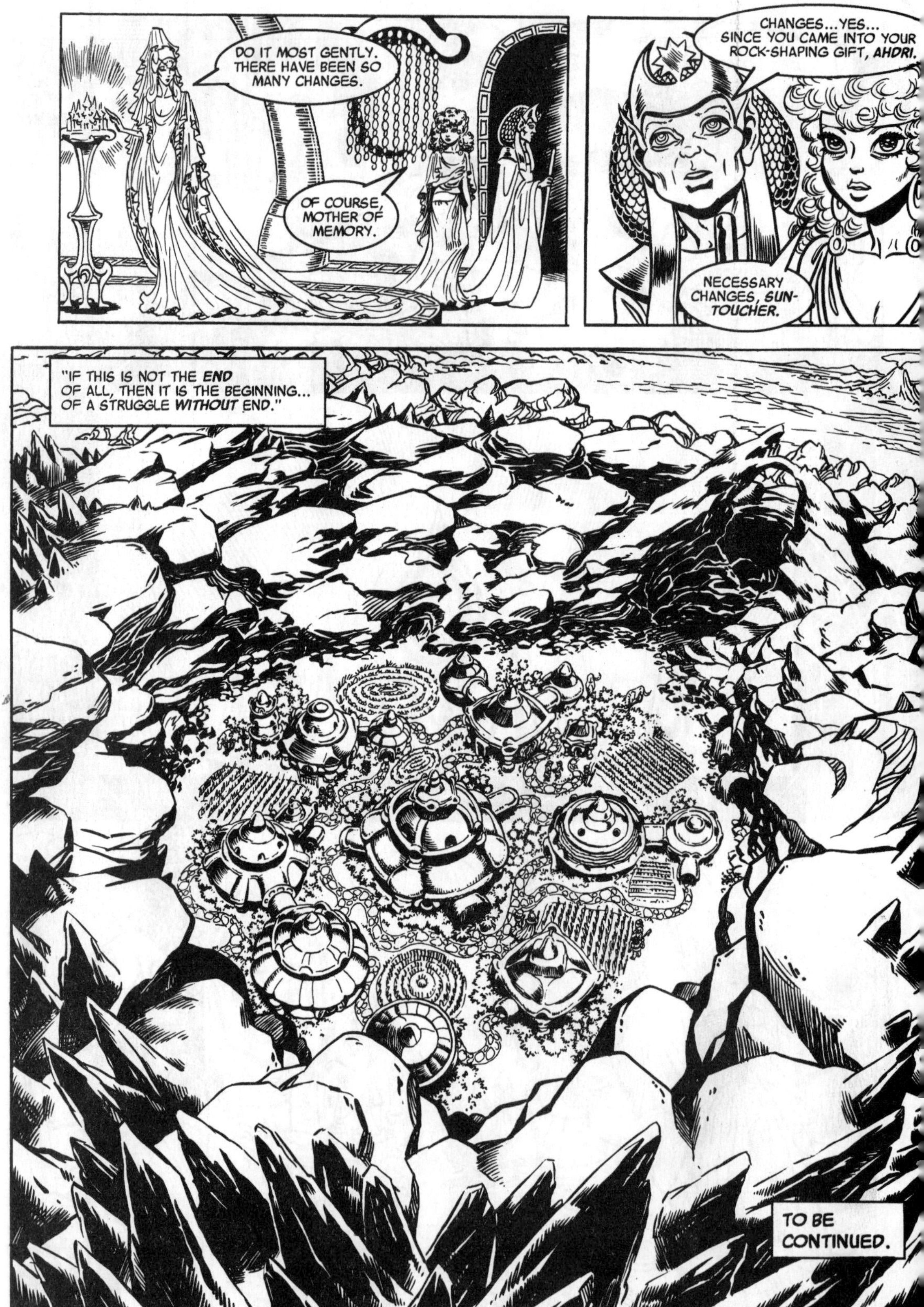
DO IT MOST GENTLY. THERE HAVE BEEN SO MANY CHANGES.
OF COURSE, MOTHER OF MEMORY.
CHANGES...YES... SINCE YOU CAME INTO YOUR ROCK-SHAPING GIFT, AHDRI.
NECESSARY CHANGES, SUN-TOUCHER.
"IF THIS IS NOT THE END OF ALL, THEN IT IS THE BEGINNING... OF A STRUGGLE WITHOUT END."
TO BE CONTINUED.

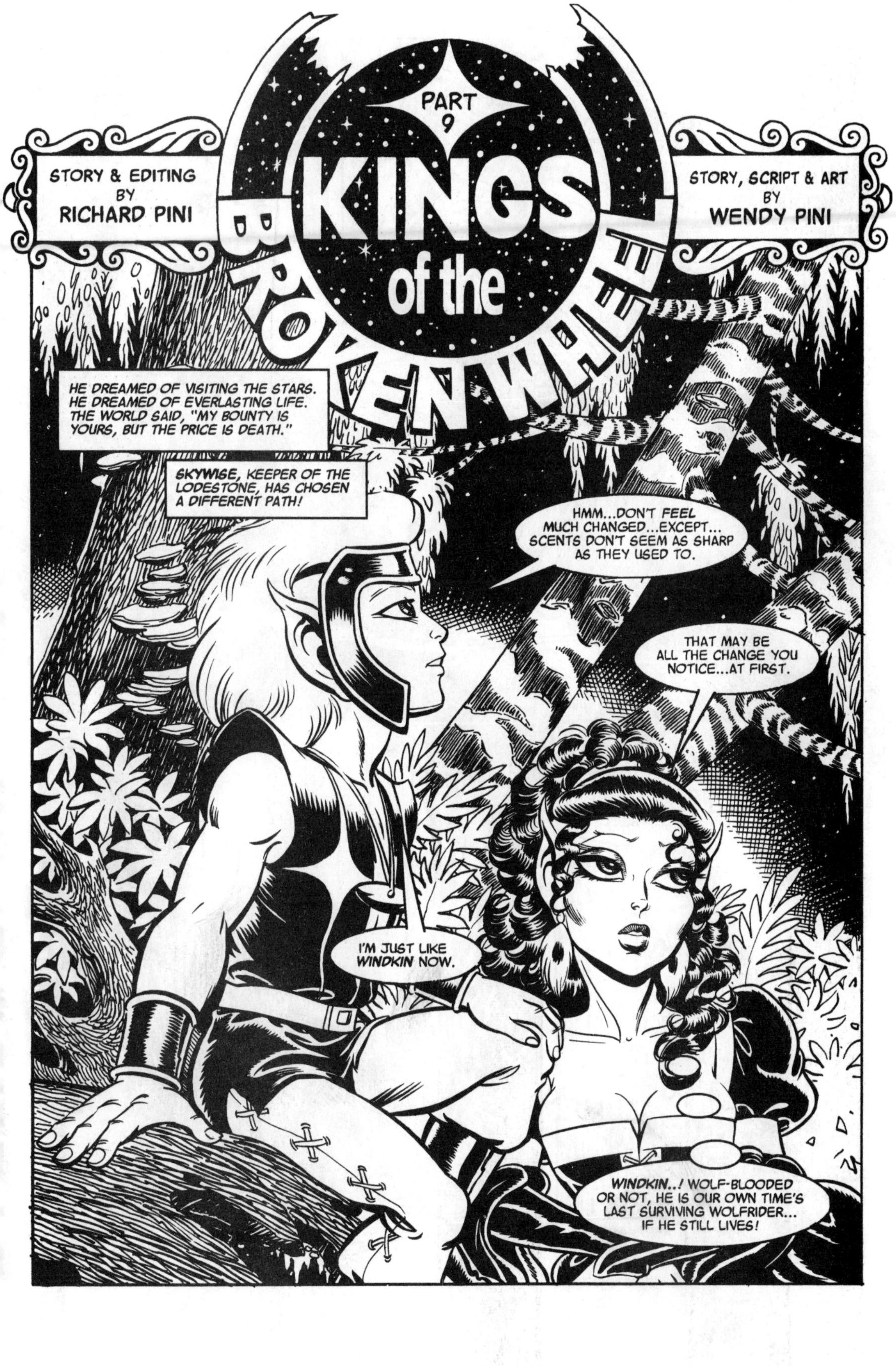

PART 9
KINGS of the BROKEN WHEEL
STORY & EDITING BY RICHARD PINI
STORY, SCRIPT & ART BY WENDY PINI
HE DREAMED OF VISITING THE STARS. HE DREAMED OF EVERLASTING LIFE. THE WORLD SAID, "MY BOUNTY IS YOURS, BUT THE PRICE IS DEATH."
SKYWISE, KEEPER OF THE LODESTONE, HAS CHOSEN A DIFFERENT PATH!
HMM...DON'T FEEL MUCH CHANGED...EXCEPT... SCENTS DON'T SEEM AS SHARP AS THEY USED TO.
THAT MAY BE ALL THE CHANGE YOU NOTICE...AT FIRST.
I'M JUST LIKE WINDKIN NOW.
WINDKIN..! WOLF-BLOODED OR NOT, HE IS OUR OWN TIME'S LAST SURVIVING WOLFRIDER... IF HE STILL LIVES!

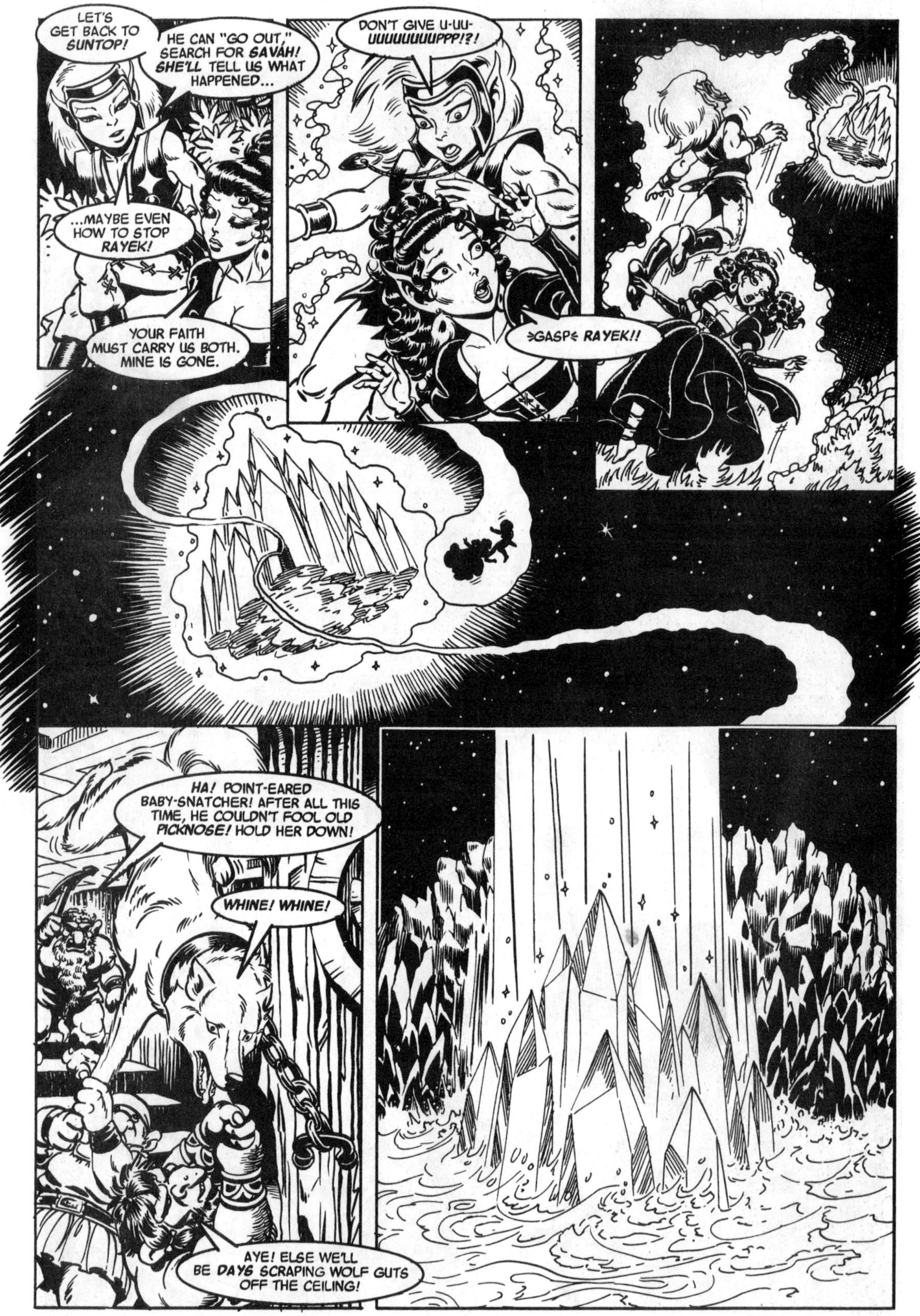
LET'S GET BACK TO SUNTOP!
HE CAN "GO OUT," SEARCH FOR SAVAH! SHE'LL TELL US WHAT HAPPENED...
...MAYBE EVEN HOW TO STOP RAYEK!
YOUR FAITH MUST CARRY US BOTH. MINE IS GONE.
DON'T GIVE U-UU-UUUUUUUUPPP!?!
≥GASP≤ RAYEK!!
HA! POINT-EARED BABY-SNATCHER! AFTER ALL THIS TIME, HE COULDN'T FOOL OLD PICKNOSE! HOLD HER DOWN!
WHINE! WHINE!
AYE! ELSE WE'LL BE DAYS SCRAPING WOLF GUTS OFF THE CEILING!

WOOOAAAAA!

AAAYOOOOAHHH!

MOTHER! SKYWISE! YOU'RE BACK! YOU'RE BACK!!

WHAT'RE YOU WEARING, MOTHER..? YOU SMELL ALL OVER LIKE *HUMANS!!* CHOPLICKER, HE'S HE WENT OUTSIDE...JUST FOR A BIT! THE PALACE FLEW AWAY SO FAST, WE LEFT HIM BEHIND ON THE MOUNTAINTOP!

HE IS A STRONG AND CRAFTY WOLF, KITLING. HE CAN PROTECT HIMSELF.

FEELS LIKE THE PALACE HAS SETTLED!

"OOOHH! MY EARS... ALL PLUGGED UP!"

"MINE TOO, EMBER! WHERE IN *FREEFOOT'S* NAME ARE WE NOW..?!"

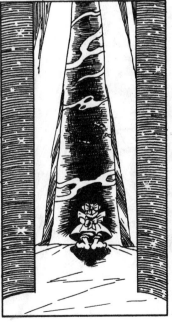

BWAAAAAAHHH!!! DON'T LIKE IT!!!

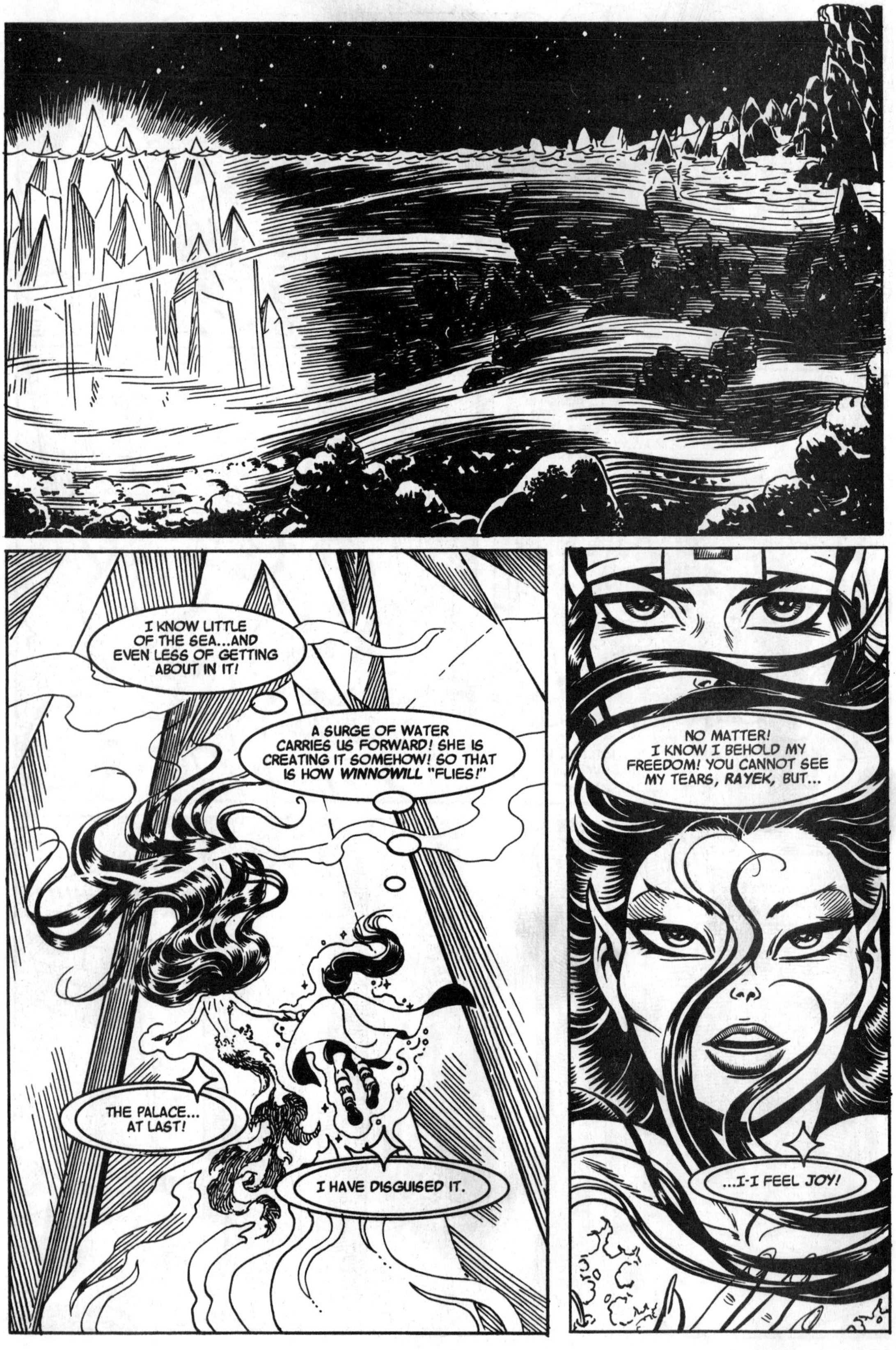
I KNOW LITTLE OF THE SEA...AND EVEN LESS OF GETTING ABOUT IN IT!
A SURGE OF WATER CARRIES US FORWARD! SHE IS CREATING IT SOMEHOW! SO THAT IS HOW *WINNOWILL* "FLIES!"
THE PALACE... AT LAST!
I HAVE DISGUISED IT.
NO MATTER! I KNOW I BEHOLD MY FREEDOM! YOU CANNOT SEE MY TEARS, *RAYEK,* BUT...
...I-I FEEL *JOY!*

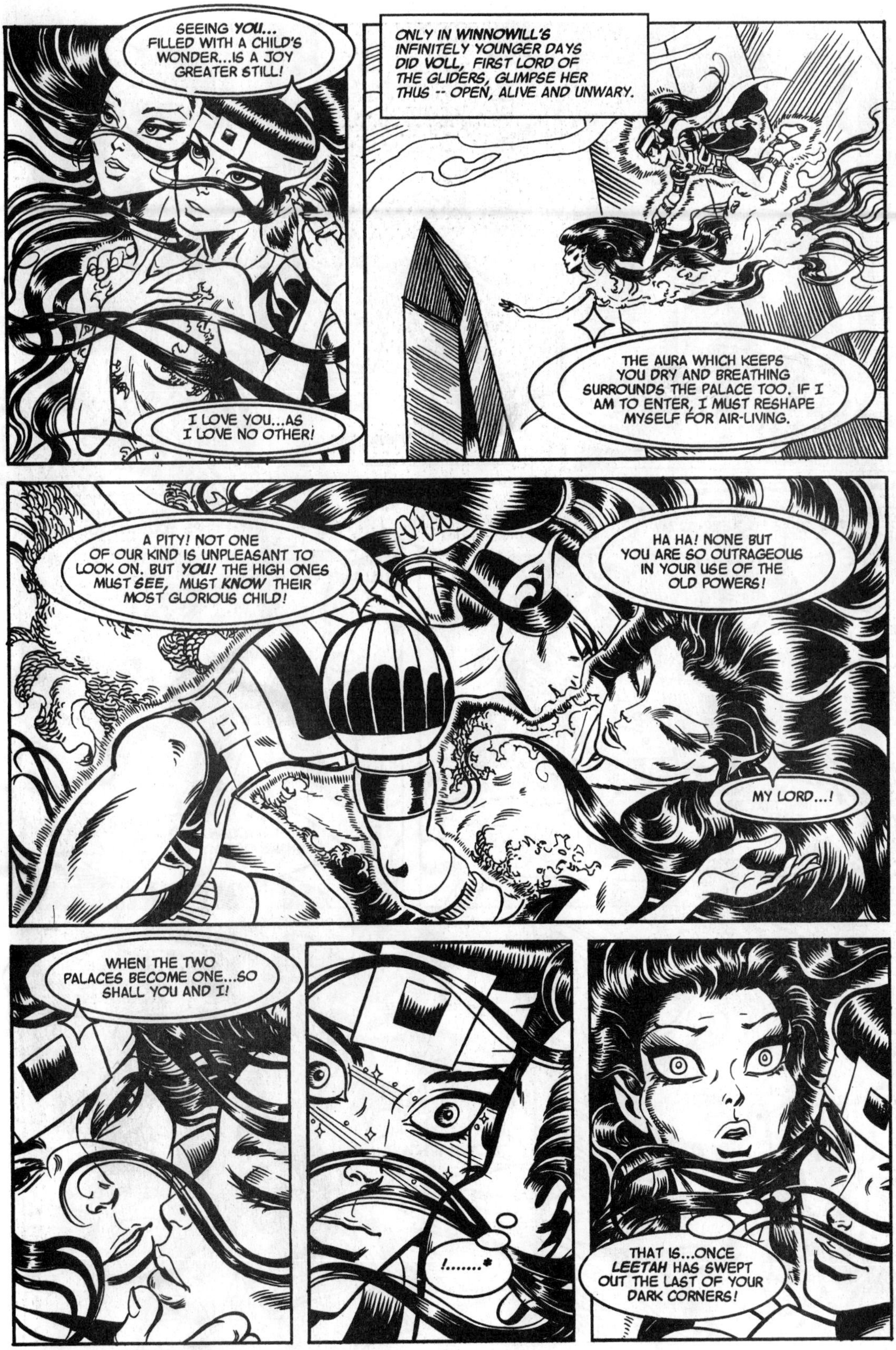
SEEING YOU... FILLED WITH A CHILD'S WONDER...IS A JOY GREATER STILL!
I LOVE YOU...AS I LOVE NO OTHER!
ONLY IN WINNOWILL'S INFINITELY YOUNGER DAYS DID VOLL, FIRST LORD OF THE GLIDERS, GLIMPSE HER THUS -- OPEN, ALIVE AND UNWARY.
THE AURA WHICH KEEPS YOU DRY AND BREATHING SURROUNDS THE PALACE TOO. IF I AM TO ENTER, I MUST RESHAPE MYSELF FOR AIR-LIVING.
A PITY! NOT ONE OF OUR KIND IS UNPLEASANT TO LOOK ON. BUT YOU! THE HIGH ONES MUST SEE, MUST KNOW THEIR MOST GLORIOUS CHILD!
HA HA! NONE BUT YOU ARE SO OUTRAGEOUS IN YOUR USE OF THE OLD POWERS!
MY LORD...!
WHEN THE TWO PALACES BECOME ONE...SO SHALL YOU AND I!
!.......*
THAT IS...ONCE LEETAH HAS SWEPT OUT THE LAST OF YOUR DARK CORNERS!

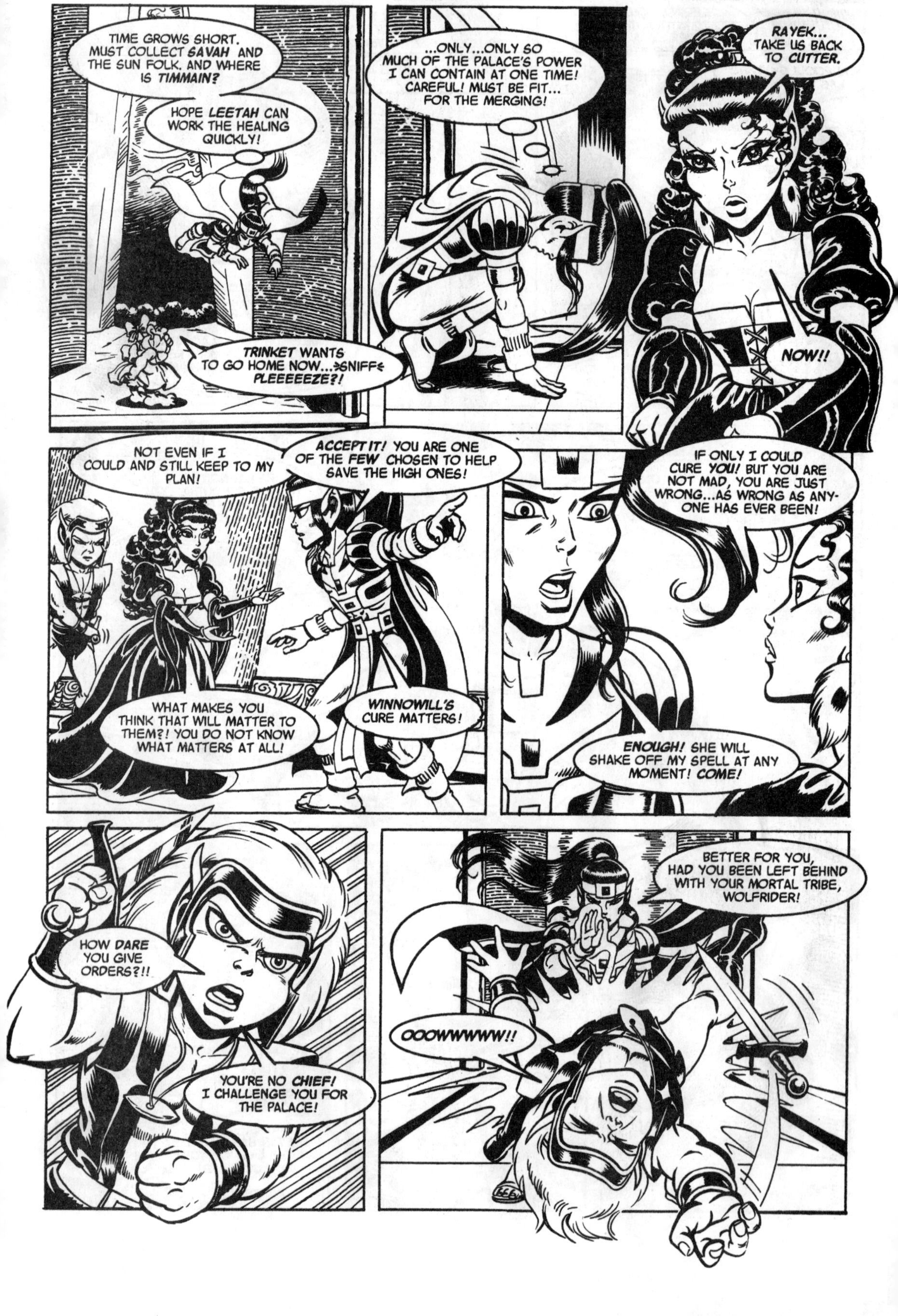
TIME GROWS SHORT. MUST COLLECT SAVAH AND THE SUN FOLK, AND WHERE IS TIMMAIN?
HOPE LEETAH CAN WORK THE HEALING QUICKLY!
TRINKET WANTS TO GO HOME NOW...>SNIFF< PLEEEEEZE?!
...ONLY...ONLY SO MUCH OF THE PALACE'S POWER I CAN CONTAIN AT ONE TIME! CAREFUL! MUST BE FIT... FOR THE MERGING!
RAYEK... TAKE US BACK TO CUTTER.
NOW!!
NOT EVEN IF I COULD AND STILL KEEP TO MY PLAN!
ACCEPT IT! YOU ARE ONE OF THE FEW CHOSEN TO HELP SAVE THE HIGH ONES!
WHAT MAKES YOU THINK THAT WILL MATTER TO THEM?! YOU DO NOT KNOW WHAT MATTERS AT ALL!
WINNOWILL'S CURE MATTERS!
IF ONLY I COULD CURE YOU! BUT YOU ARE NOT MAD, YOU ARE JUST WRONG...AS WRONG AS ANYONE HAS EVER BEEN!
ENOUGH! SHE WILL SHAKE OFF MY SPELL AT ANY MOMENT! COME!
HOW DARE YOU GIVE ORDERS?!!
YOU'RE NO CHIEF! I CHALLENGE YOU FOR THE PALACE!
BETTER FOR YOU, HAD YOU BEEN LEFT BEHIND WITH YOUR MORTAL TRIBE, WOLFRIDER!
OOOWWWWW!!

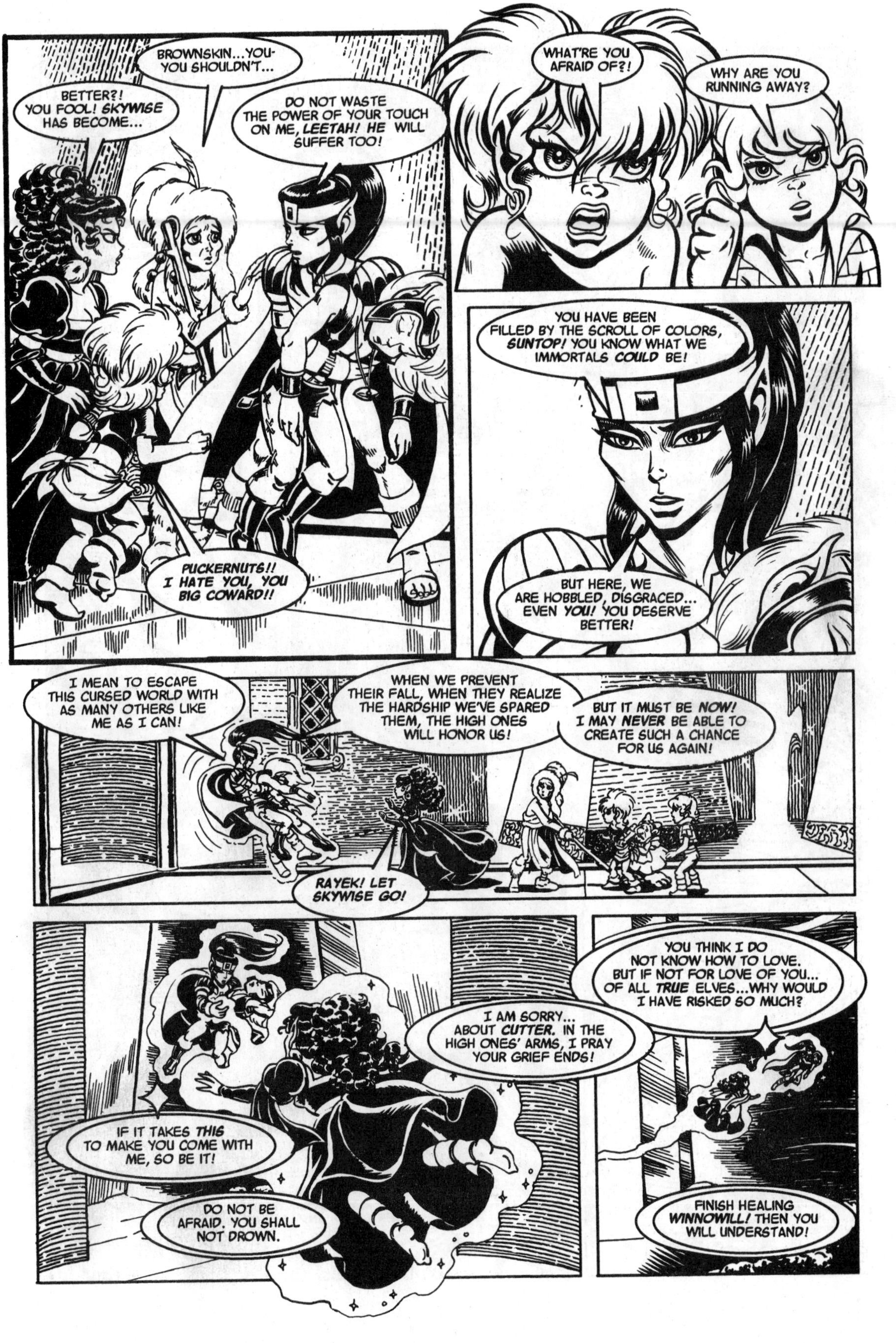
BROWNSKIN...YOU-YOU SHOULDN'T...
BETTER?! YOU FOOL! SKYWISE HAS BECOME...
DO NOT WASTE THE POWER OF YOUR TOUCH ON ME, LEETAH! HE WILL SUFFER TOO!
PUCKERNUTS!! I HATE YOU, YOU BIG COWARD!!
WHAT'RE YOU AFRAID OF?!
WHY ARE YOU RUNNING AWAY?
YOU HAVE BEEN FILLED BY THE SCROLL OF COLORS, SUNTOP! YOU KNOW WHAT WE IMMORTALS COULD BE!
BUT HERE, WE ARE HOBBLED, DISGRACED... EVEN YOU! YOU DESERVE BETTER!
I MEAN TO ESCAPE THIS CURSED WORLD WITH AS MANY OTHERS LIKE ME AS I CAN!
WHEN WE PREVENT THEIR FALL, WHEN THEY REALIZE THE HARDSHIP WE'VE SPARED THEM, THE HIGH ONES WILL HONOR US!
BUT IT MUST BE NOW! I MAY NEVER BE ABLE TO CREATE SUCH A CHANCE FOR US AGAIN!
RAYEK! LET SKYWISE GO!
I AM SORRY... ABOUT CUTTER. IN THE HIGH ONES' ARMS, I PRAY YOUR GRIEF ENDS!
IF IT TAKES THIS TO MAKE YOU COME WITH ME, SO BE IT!
DO NOT BE AFRAID. YOU SHALL NOT DROWN.
YOU THINK I DO NOT KNOW HOW TO LOVE. BUT IF NOT FOR LOVE OF YOU... OF ALL TRUE ELVES...WHY WOULD I HAVE RISKED SO MUCH?
FINISH HEALING WINNOWILL! THEN YOU WILL UNDERSTAND!

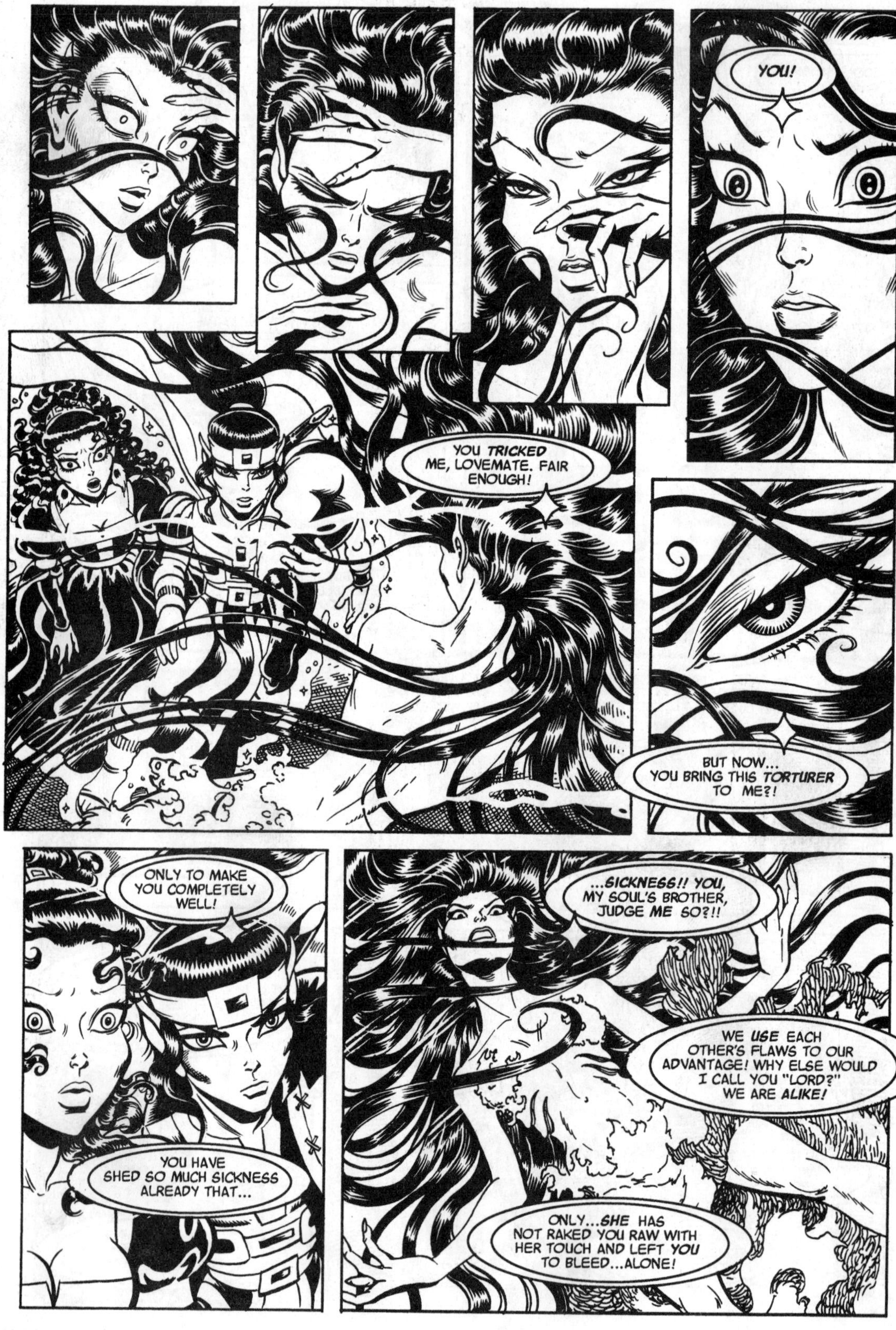
YOU!
YOU TRICKED ME, LOVEMATE. FAIR ENOUGH!
BUT NOW... YOU BRING THIS TORTURER TO ME?!
ONLY TO MAKE YOU COMPLETELY WELL!
YOU HAVE SHED SO MUCH SICKNESS ALREADY THAT...
...SICKNESS!! YOU, MY SOUL'S BROTHER, JUDGE ME SO?!!
WE USE EACH OTHER'S FLAWS TO OUR ADVANTAGE! WHY ELSE WOULD I CALL YOU "LORD?" WE ARE ALIKE!
ONLY...SHE HAS NOT RAKED YOU RAW WITH HER TOUCH AND LEFT YOU TO BLEED...ALONE!

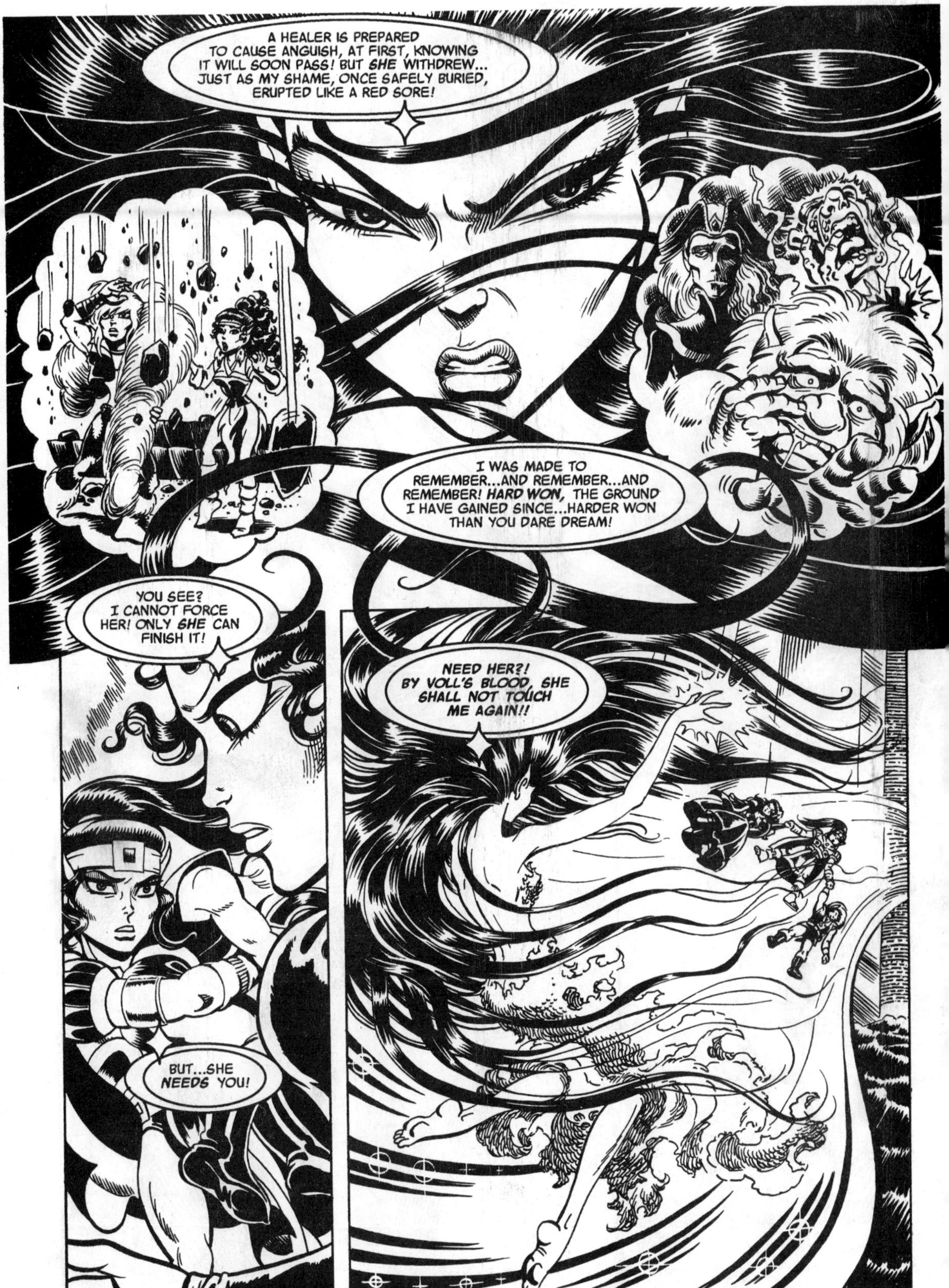
A HEALER IS PREPARED TO CAUSE ANGUISH, AT FIRST, KNOWING IT WILL SOON PASS! BUT SHE WITHDREW... JUST AS MY SHAME, ONCE SAFELY BURIED, ERUPTED LIKE A RED SORE!
I WAS MADE TO REMEMBER...AND REMEMBER...AND REMEMBER! HARD WON, THE GROUND I HAVE GAINED SINCE...HARDER WON THAN YOU DARE DREAM!
YOU SEE? I CANNOT FORCE HER! ONLY SHE CAN FINISH IT!
BUT...SHE NEEDS YOU!
NEED HER?! BY VOLL'S BLOOD, SHE SHALL NOT TOUCH ME AGAIN!!

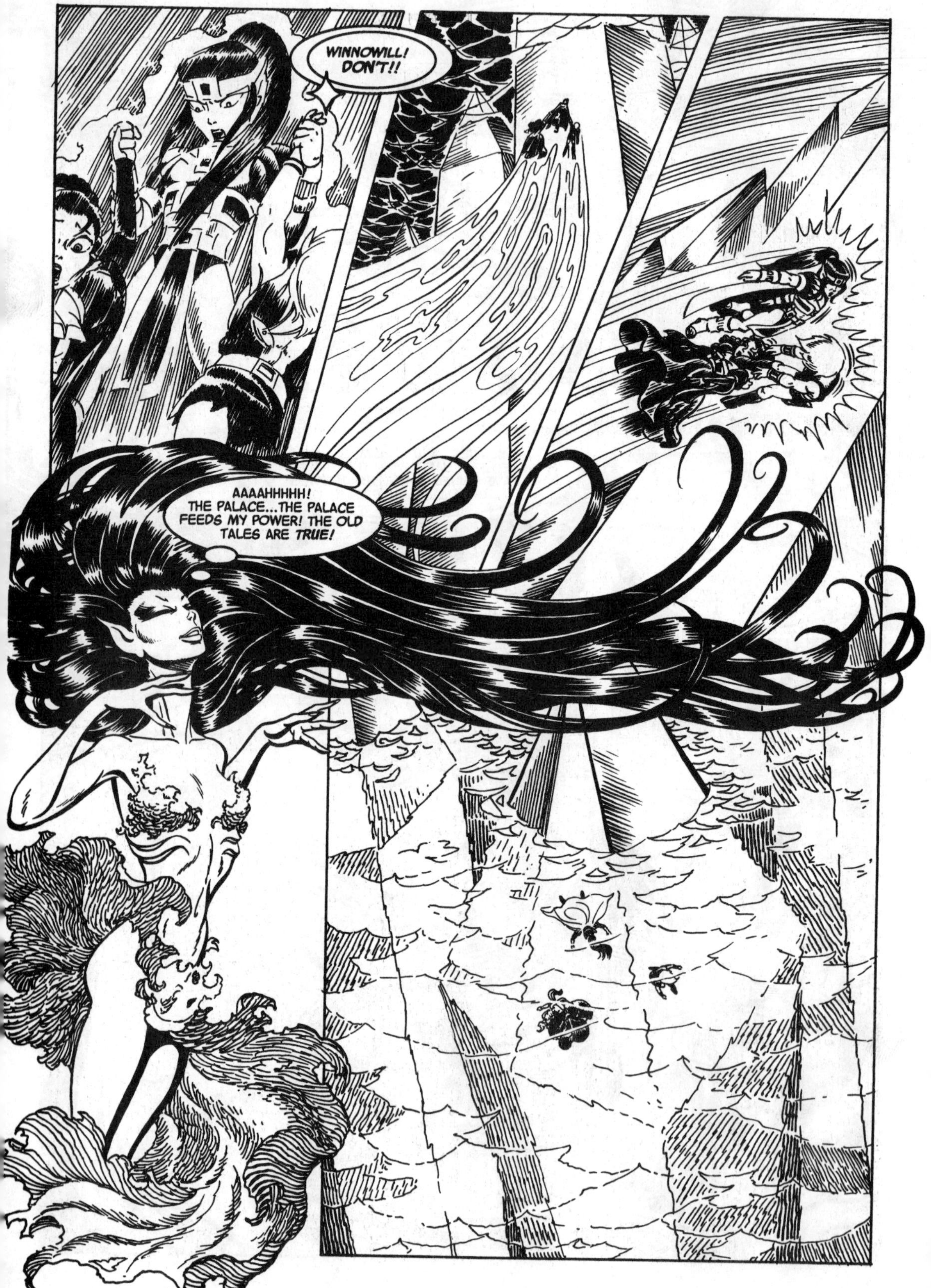
WINNOWILL! DON'T!!
AAAAHHHHH! THE PALACE...THE PALACE FEEDS MY POWER! THE OLD TALES ARE *TRUE!*

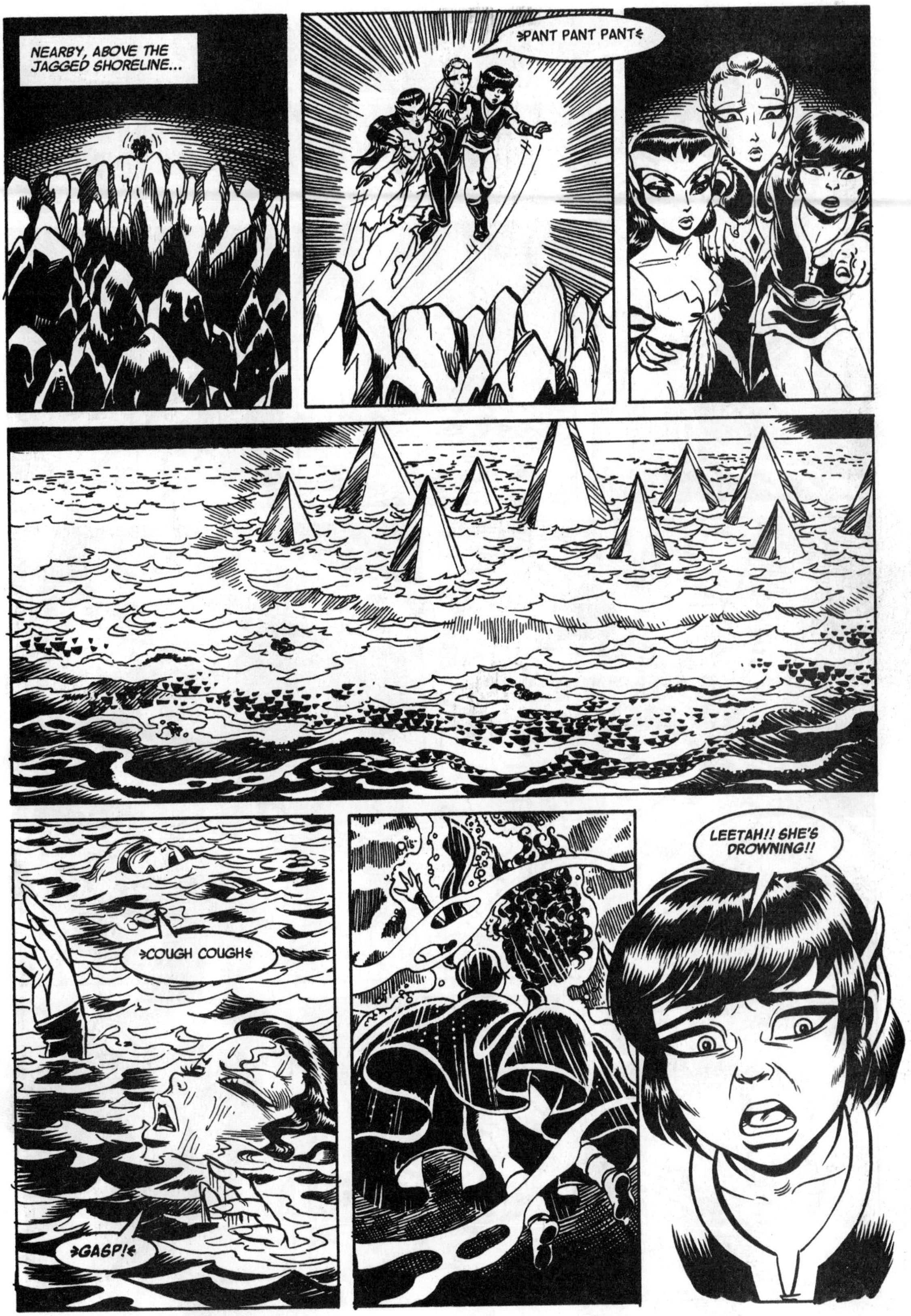
NEARBY, ABOVE THE JAGGED SHORELINE...
PANT PANT PANT
COUGH COUGH
GASP!
LEETAH!! SHE'S DROWNING!!

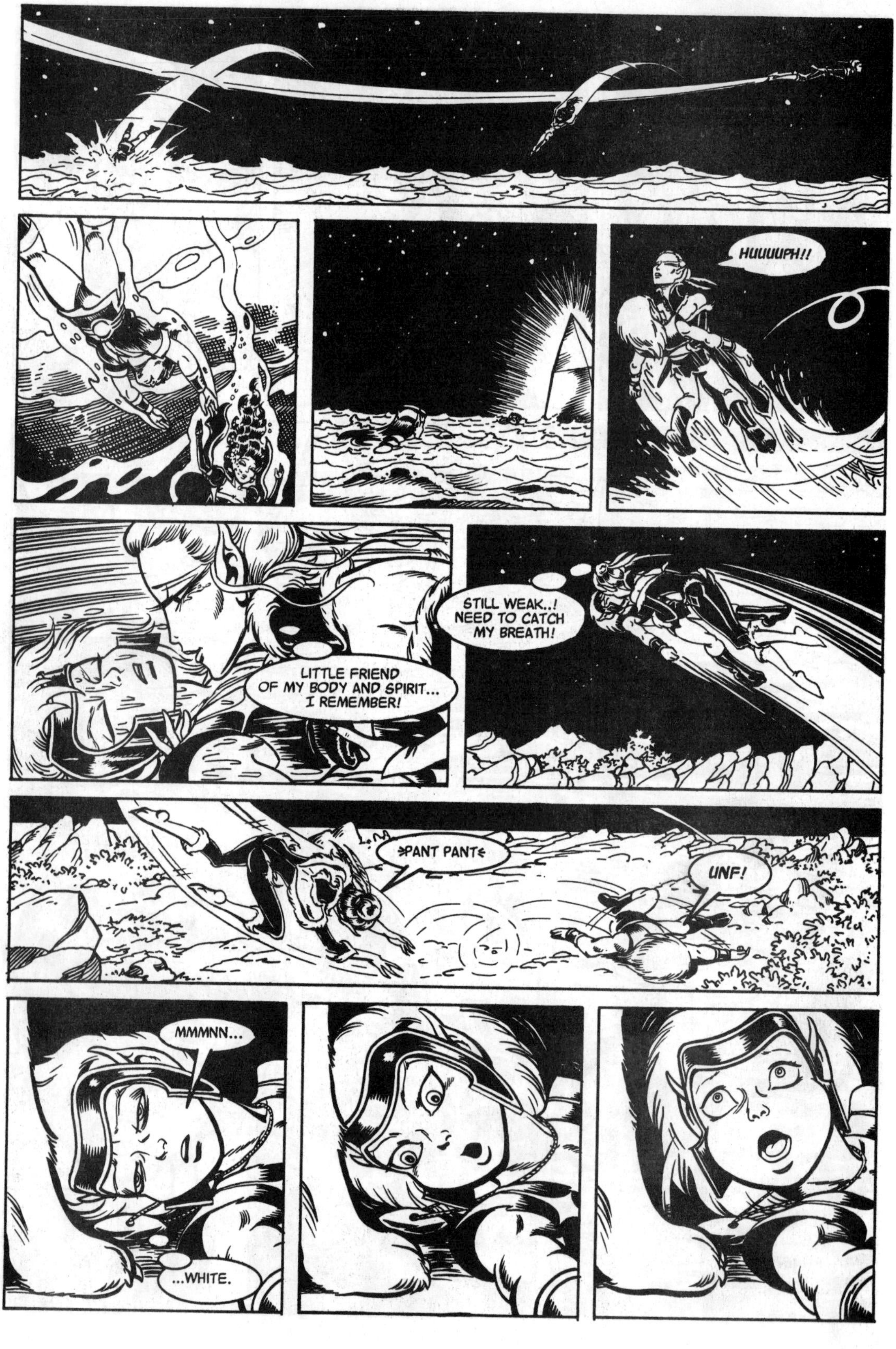
HUUUUPH!!
LITTLE FRIEND OF MY BODY AND SPIRIT... I REMEMBER!
STILL WEAK..! NEED TO CATCH MY BREATH!
≯PANT PANT≮
UNF!
MMMNN...
...WHITE.

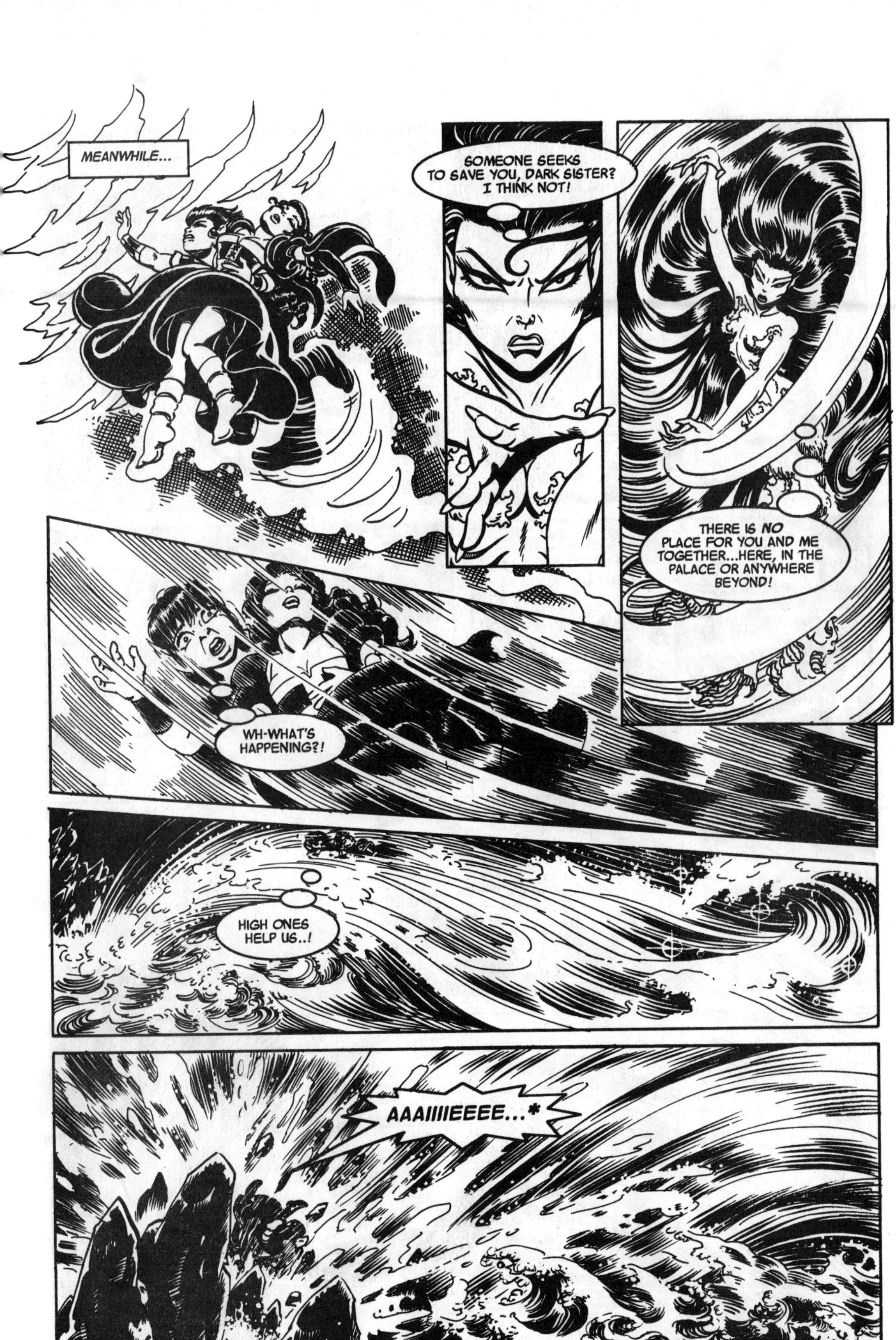
MEANWHILE...
SOMEONE SEEKS TO SAVE YOU, DARK SISTER? I THINK NOT!
THERE IS NO PLACE FOR YOU AND ME TOGETHER...HERE, IN THE PALACE OR ANYWHERE BEYOND!
WH-WHAT'S HAPPENING?!
HIGH ONES HELP US..!
AAAIIIIEEEE...*

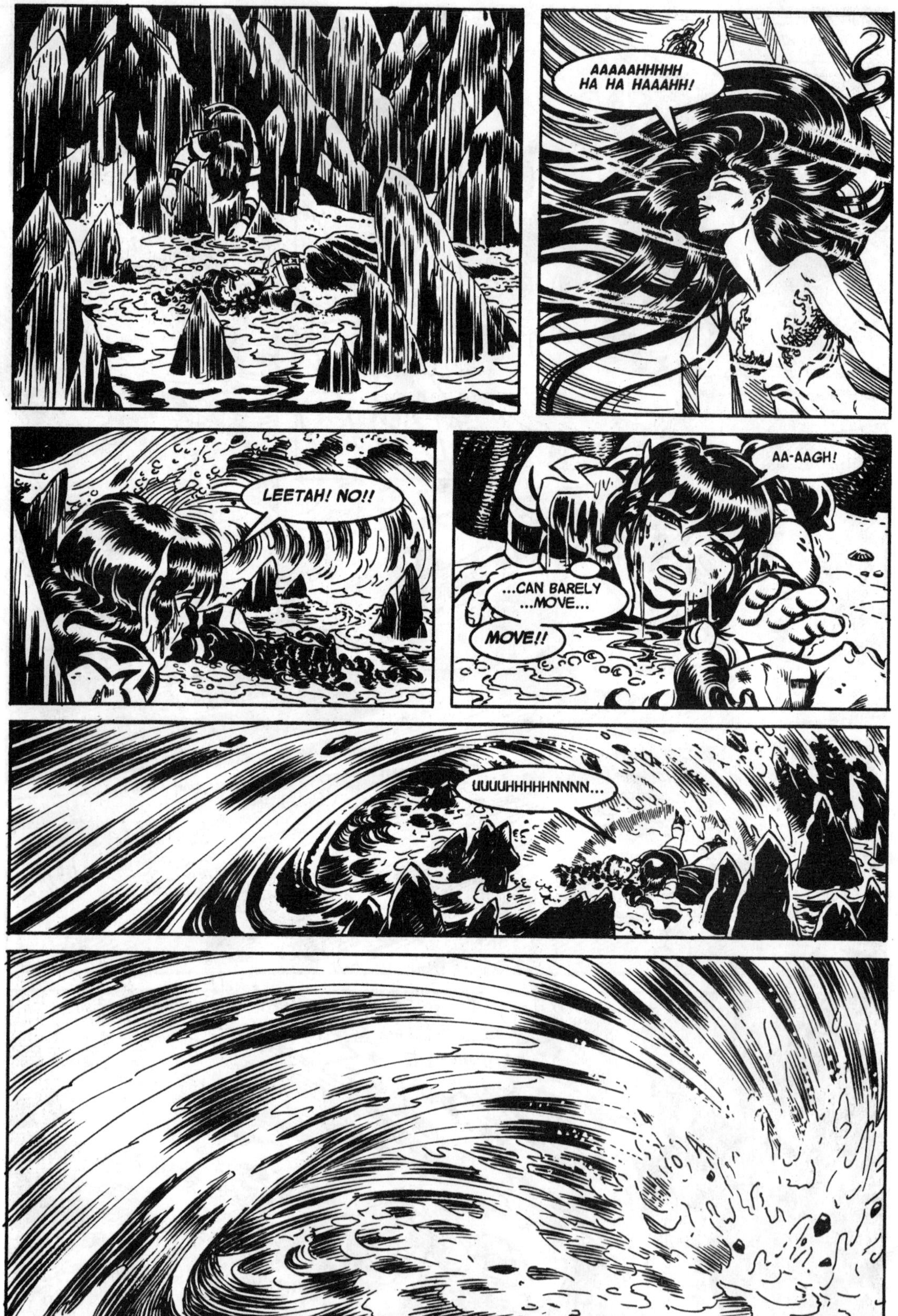
AAAAAHHHHH HA HA HAAAHH!
LEETAH! NO!!
AA-AAGH!
...CAN BARELY ...MOVE...
MOVE!!
UUUUHHHHHNNNN...

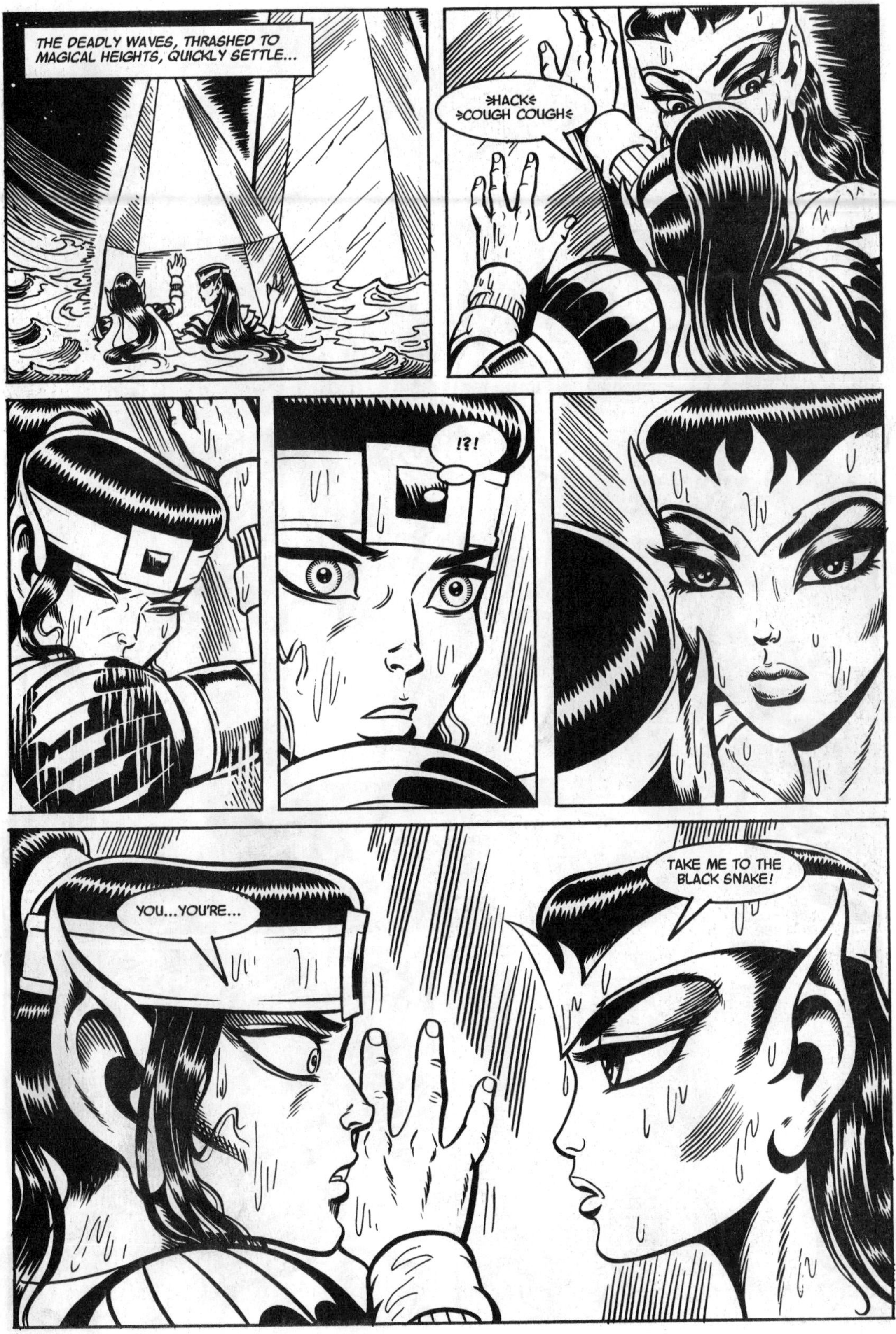
THE DEADLY WAVES, THRASHED TO MAGICAL HEIGHTS, QUICKLY SETTLE...
HACK
COUGH COUGH
!?!
YOU...YOU'RE...
TAKE ME TO THE BLACK SNAKE!

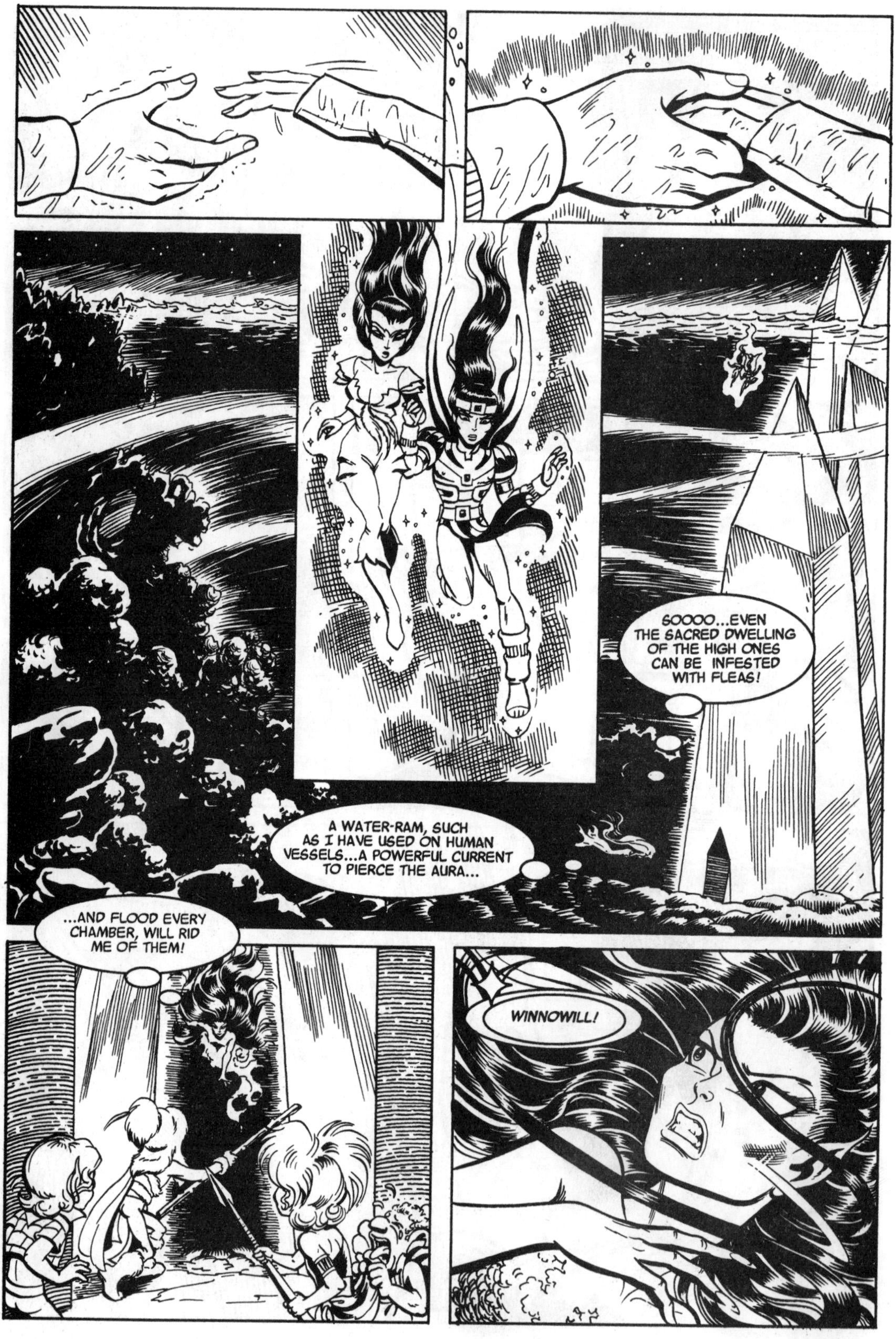
SOOOO...EVEN THE SACRED DWELLING OF THE HIGH ONES CAN BE INFESTED WITH FLEAS!
A WATER-RAM, SUCH AS I HAVE USED ON HUMAN VESSELS...A POWERFUL CURRENT TO PIERCE THE AURA...
...AND FLOOD EVERY CHAMBER, WILL RID ME OF THEM!
WINNOWILL!

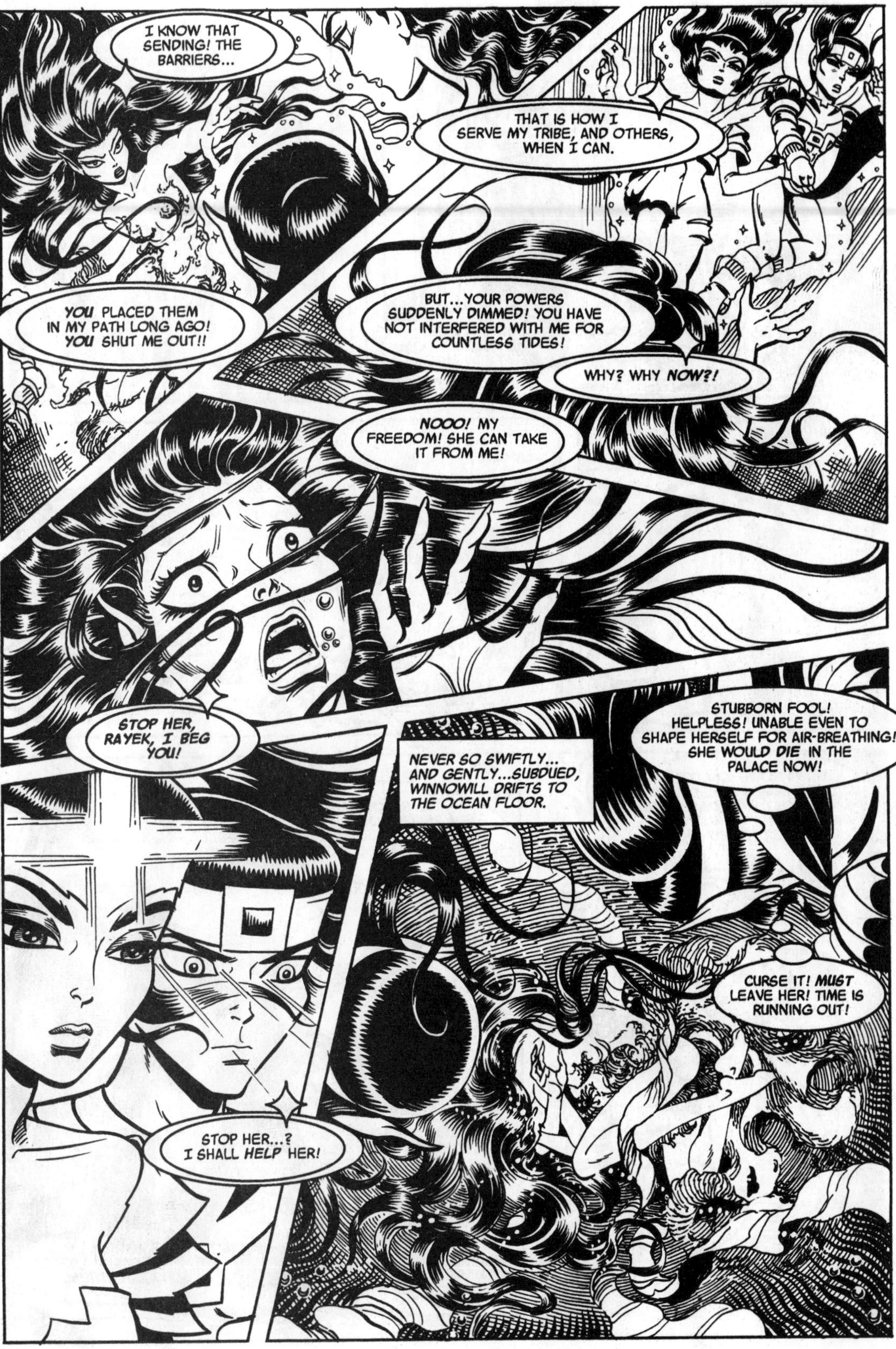
I KNOW THAT SENDING! THE BARRIERS...
YOU PLACED THEM IN MY PATH LONG AGO! YOU SHUT ME OUT!!
THAT IS HOW I SERVE MY TRIBE, AND OTHERS, WHEN I CAN.
BUT...YOUR POWERS SUDDENLY DIMMED! YOU HAVE NOT INTERFERED WITH ME FOR COUNTLESS TIDES!
WHY? WHY NOW?!
NOOO! MY FREEDOM! SHE CAN TAKE IT FROM ME!
STOP HER, RAYEK, I BEG YOU!
STOP HER...? I SHALL HELP HER!
NEVER SO SWIFTLY... AND GENTLY...SUBDUED, WINNOWILL DRIFTS TO THE OCEAN FLOOR.
STUBBORN FOOL! HELPLESS! UNABLE EVEN TO SHAPE HERSELF FOR AIR-BREATHING! SHE WOULD DIE IN THE PALACE NOW!
CURSE IT! MUST LEAVE HER! TIME IS RUNNING OUT!

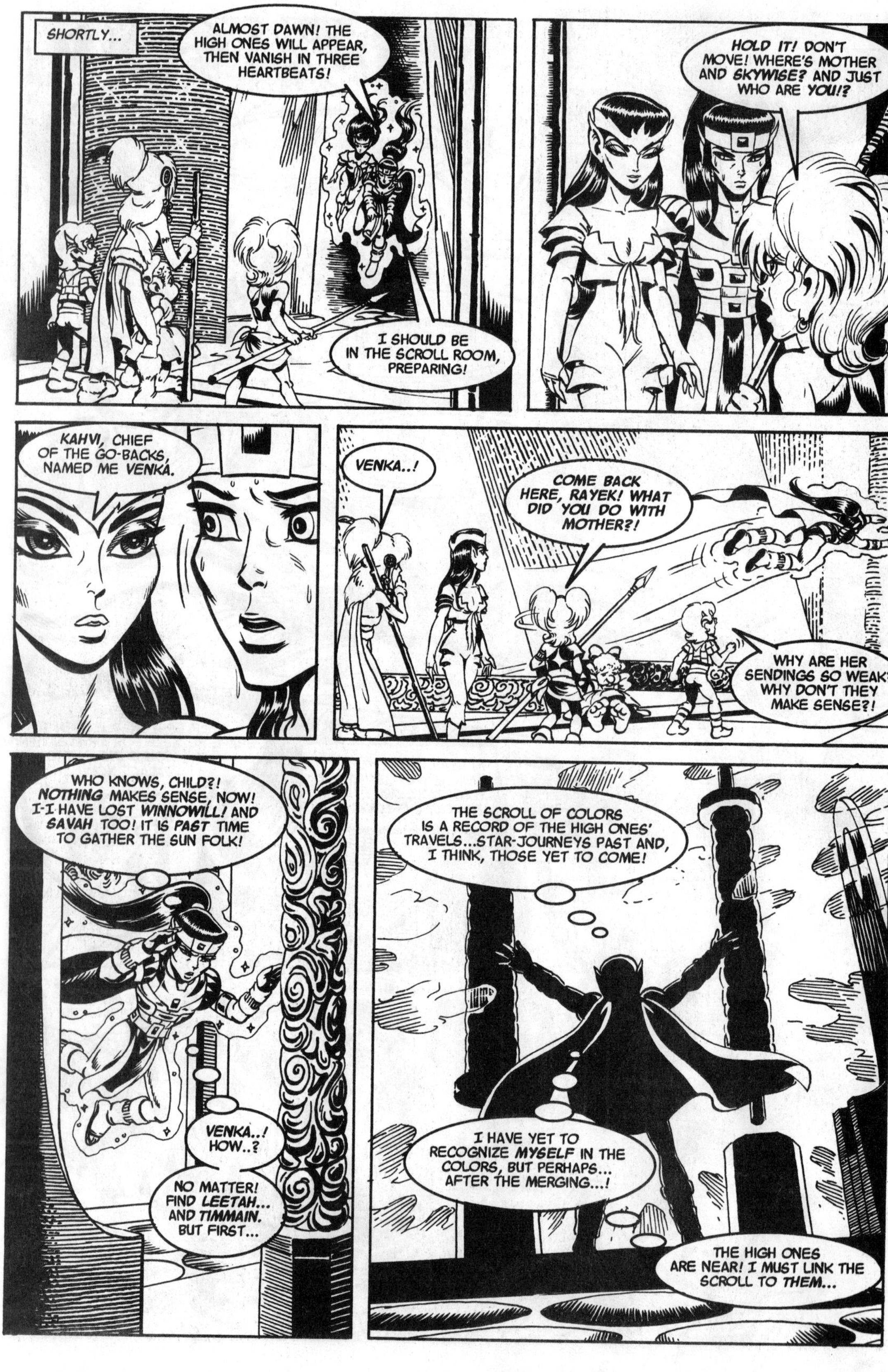
SHORTLY...
ALMOST DAWN! THE HIGH ONES WILL APPEAR, THEN VANISH IN THREE HEARTBEATS!
I SHOULD BE IN THE SCROLL ROOM, PREPARING!
HOLD IT! DON'T MOVE! WHERE'S MOTHER AND SKYWISE? AND JUST WHO ARE YOU!?
KAHVI, CHIEF OF THE GO-BACKS, NAMED ME VENKA.
VENKA..!
COME BACK HERE, RAYEK! WHAT DID YOU DO WITH MOTHER?!
WHY ARE HER SENDINGS SO WEAK? WHY DON'T THEY MAKE SENSE?!
WHO KNOWS, CHILD?! NOTHING MAKES SENSE, NOW! I-I HAVE LOST WINNOWILL! AND SAVAH TOO! IT IS PAST TIME TO GATHER THE SUN FOLK!
VENKA..! HOW..?
NO MATTER! FIND LEETAH... AND TIMMAIN. BUT FIRST...
THE SCROLL OF COLORS IS A RECORD OF THE HIGH ONES' TRAVELS...STAR-JOURNEYS PAST AND, I THINK, THOSE YET TO COME!
I HAVE YET TO RECOGNIZE MYSELF IN THE COLORS, BUT PERHAPS... AFTER THE MERGING...!
THE HIGH ONES ARE NEAR! I MUST LINK THE SCROLL TO THEM...

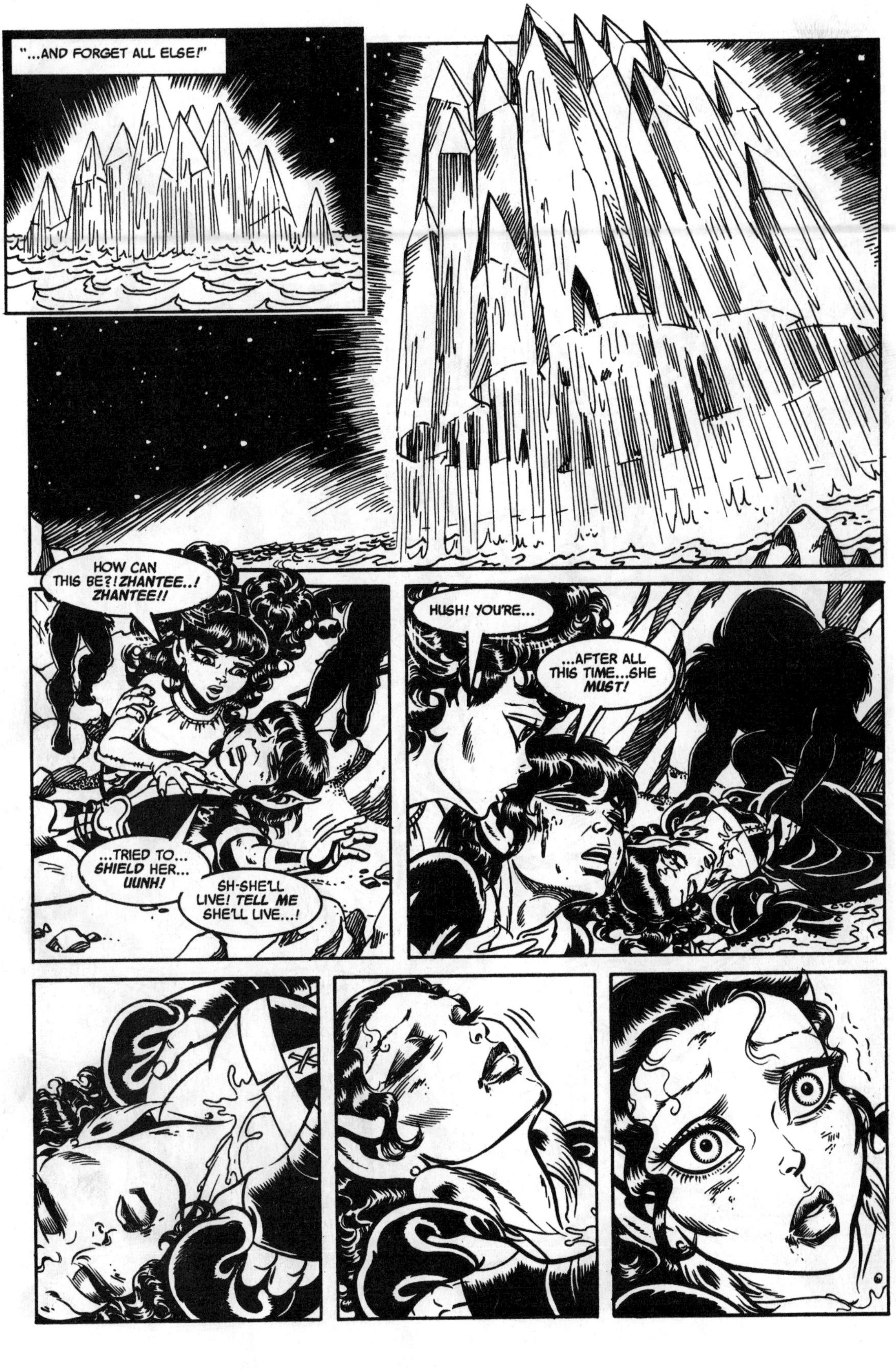
"...AND FORGET ALL ELSE!"
HOW CAN THIS BE?! ZHANTEE..! ZHANTEE!!
...TRIED TO... SHIELD HER... UUNH!
SH-SHE'LL LIVE! TELL ME SHE'LL LIVE...!
HUSH! YOU'RE...
...AFTER ALL THIS TIME...SHE MUST!

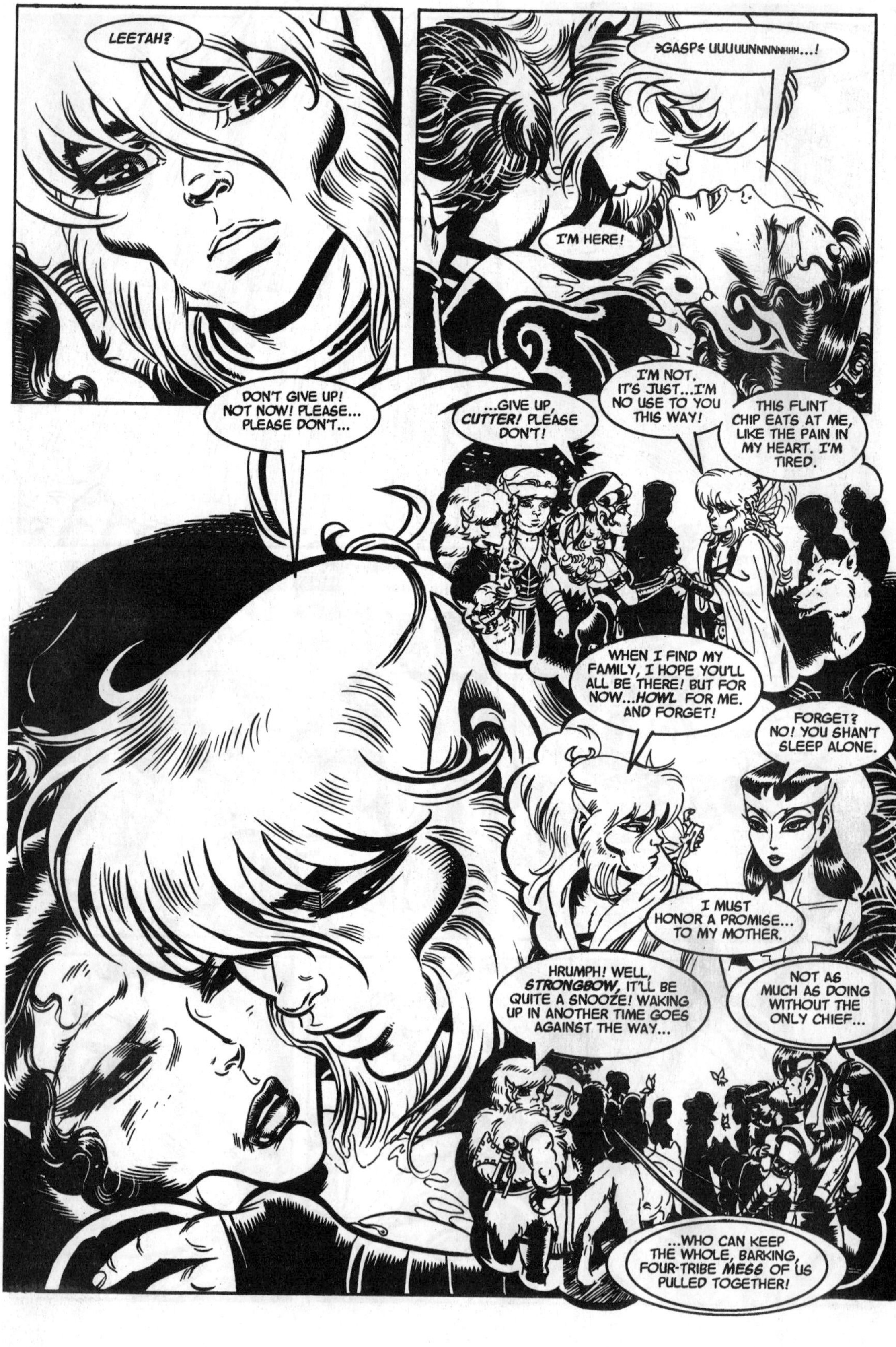
LEETAH?
≥GASP≤ UUUUUNNNNHHH...!
I'M HERE!
DON'T GIVE UP! NOT NOW! PLEASE... PLEASE DON'T...
...GIVE UP, CUTTER! PLEASE DON'T!
I'M NOT. IT'S JUST...I'M NO USE TO YOU THIS WAY!
THIS FLINT CHIP EATS AT ME, LIKE THE PAIN IN MY HEART. I'M TIRED.
WHEN I FIND MY FAMILY, I HOPE YOU'LL ALL BE THERE! BUT FOR NOW...HOWL FOR ME. AND FORGET!
FORGET? NO! YOU SHAN'T SLEEP ALONE.
I MUST HONOR A PROMISE... TO MY MOTHER.
HRUMPH! WELL, STRONGBOW, IT'LL BE QUITE A SNOOZE! WAKING UP IN ANOTHER TIME GOES AGAINST THE WAY...
NOT AS MUCH AS DOING WITHOUT THE ONLY CHIEF...
...WHO CAN KEEP THE WHOLE, BARKING, FOUR-TRIBE MESS OF US PULLED TOGETHER!

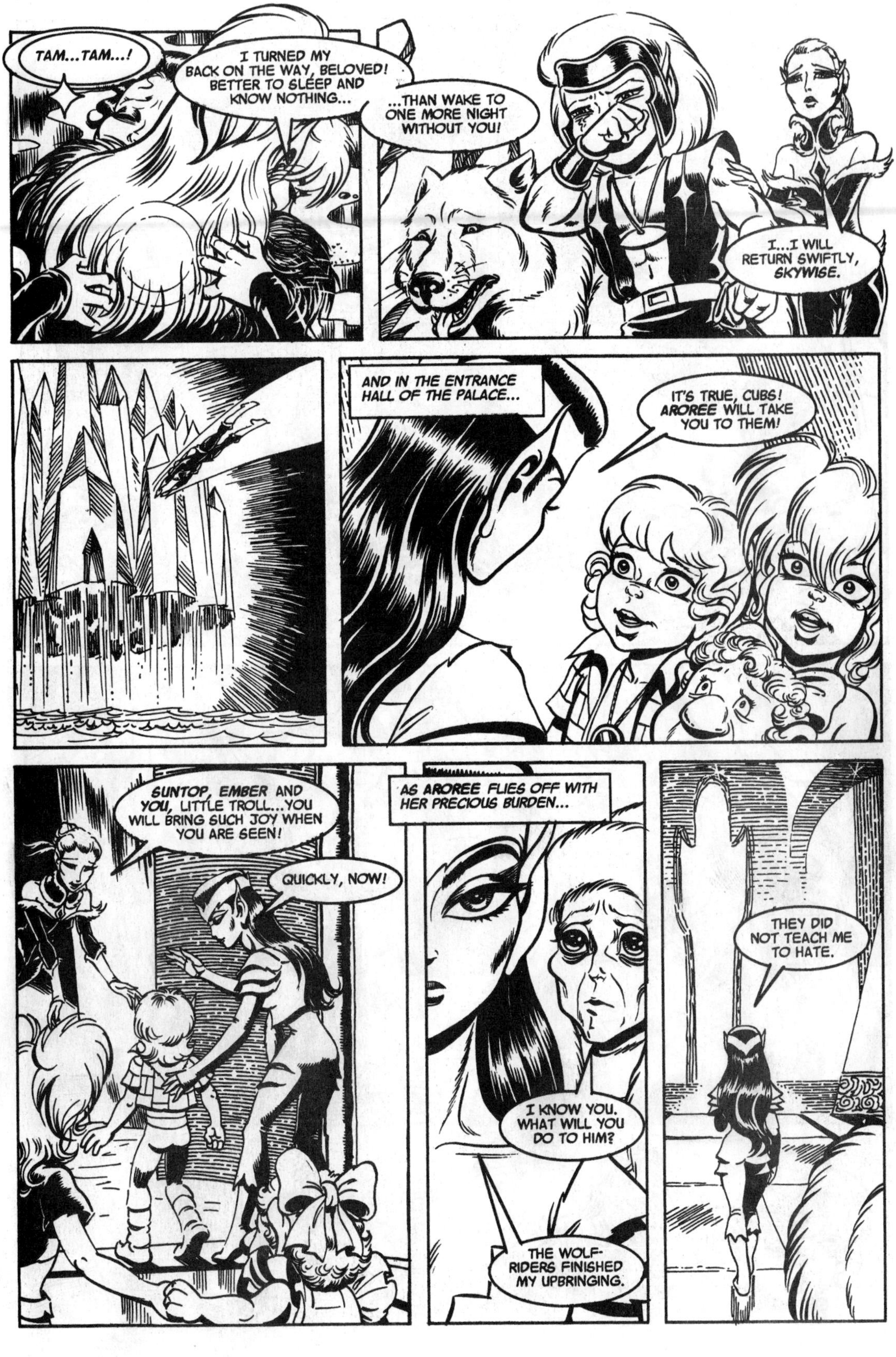
TAM...TAM...!
I TURNED MY BACK ON THE WAY, BELOVED! BETTER TO SLEEP AND KNOW NOTHING...
...THAN WAKE TO ONE MORE NIGHT WITHOUT YOU!
I...I WILL RETURN SWIFTLY, SKYWISE.
AND IN THE ENTRANCE HALL OF THE PALACE...
IT'S TRUE, CUBS! AROREE WILL TAKE YOU TO THEM!
SUNTOP, EMBER AND YOU, LITTLE TROLL...YOU WILL BRING SUCH JOY WHEN YOU ARE SEEN!
QUICKLY, NOW!
AS AROREE FLIES OFF WITH HER PRECIOUS BURDEN...
I KNOW YOU. WHAT WILL YOU DO TO HIM?
THE WOLF-RIDERS FINISHED MY UPBRINGING.
THEY DID NOT TEACH ME TO HATE.

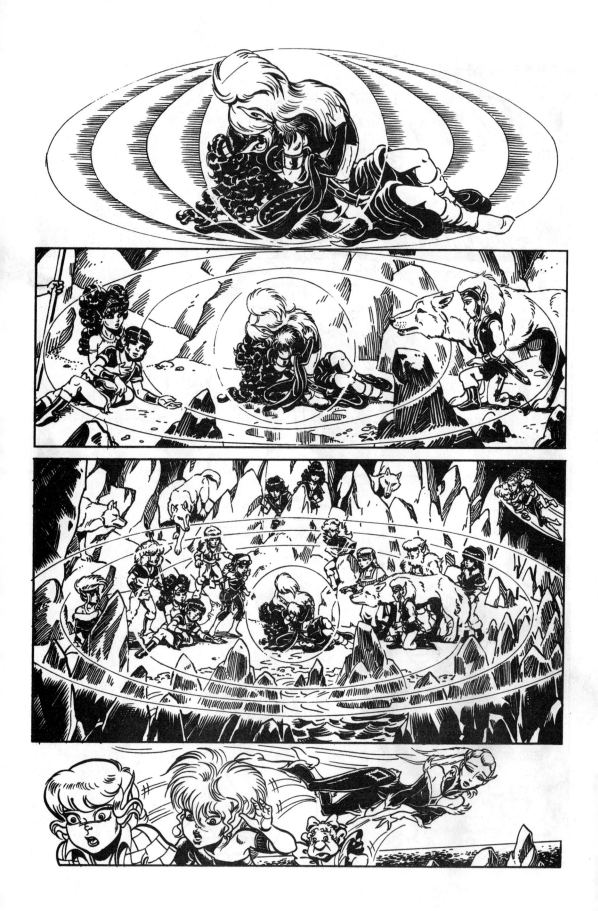

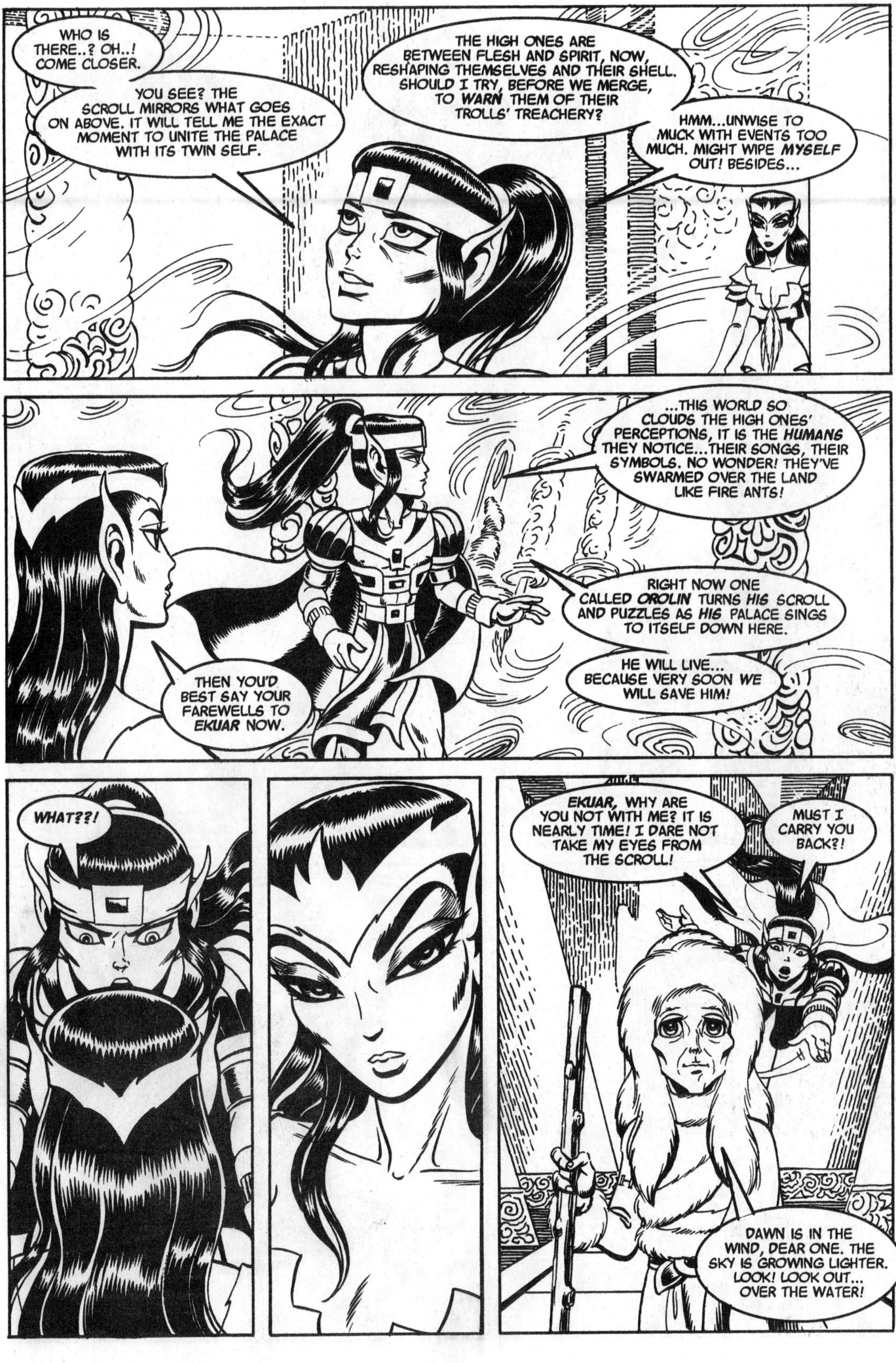
WHO IS THERE..? OH..! COME CLOSER.
YOU SEE? THE SCROLL MIRRORS WHAT GOES ON ABOVE. IT WILL TELL ME THE EXACT MOMENT TO UNITE THE PALACE WITH ITS TWIN SELF.
THE HIGH ONES ARE BETWEEN FLESH AND SPIRIT, NOW, RESHAPING THEMSELVES AND THEIR SHELL. SHOULD I TRY, BEFORE WE MERGE, TO WARN THEM OF THEIR TROLLS' TREACHERY?
HMM...UNWISE TO MUCK WITH EVENTS TOO MUCH. MIGHT WIPE MYSELF OUT! BESIDES...
...THIS WORLD SO CLOUDS THE HIGH ONES' PERCEPTIONS, IT IS THE HUMANS THEY NOTICE...THEIR SONGS, THEIR SYMBOLS. NO WONDER! THEY'VE SWARMED OVER THE LAND LIKE FIRE ANTS!
RIGHT NOW ONE CALLED OROLIN TURNS HIS SCROLL AND PUZZLES AS HIS PALACE SINGS TO ITSELF DOWN HERE.
HE WILL LIVE... BECAUSE VERY SOON WE WILL SAVE HIM!
THEN YOU'D BEST SAY YOUR FAREWELLS TO EKUAR NOW.
WHAT??!
EKUAR, WHY ARE YOU NOT WITH ME? IT IS NEARLY TIME! I DARE NOT TAKE MY EYES FROM THE SCROLL!
MUST I CARRY YOU BACK?!
DAWN IS IN THE WIND, DEAR ONE. THE SKY IS GROWING LIGHTER. LOOK! LOOK OUT... OVER THE WATER!

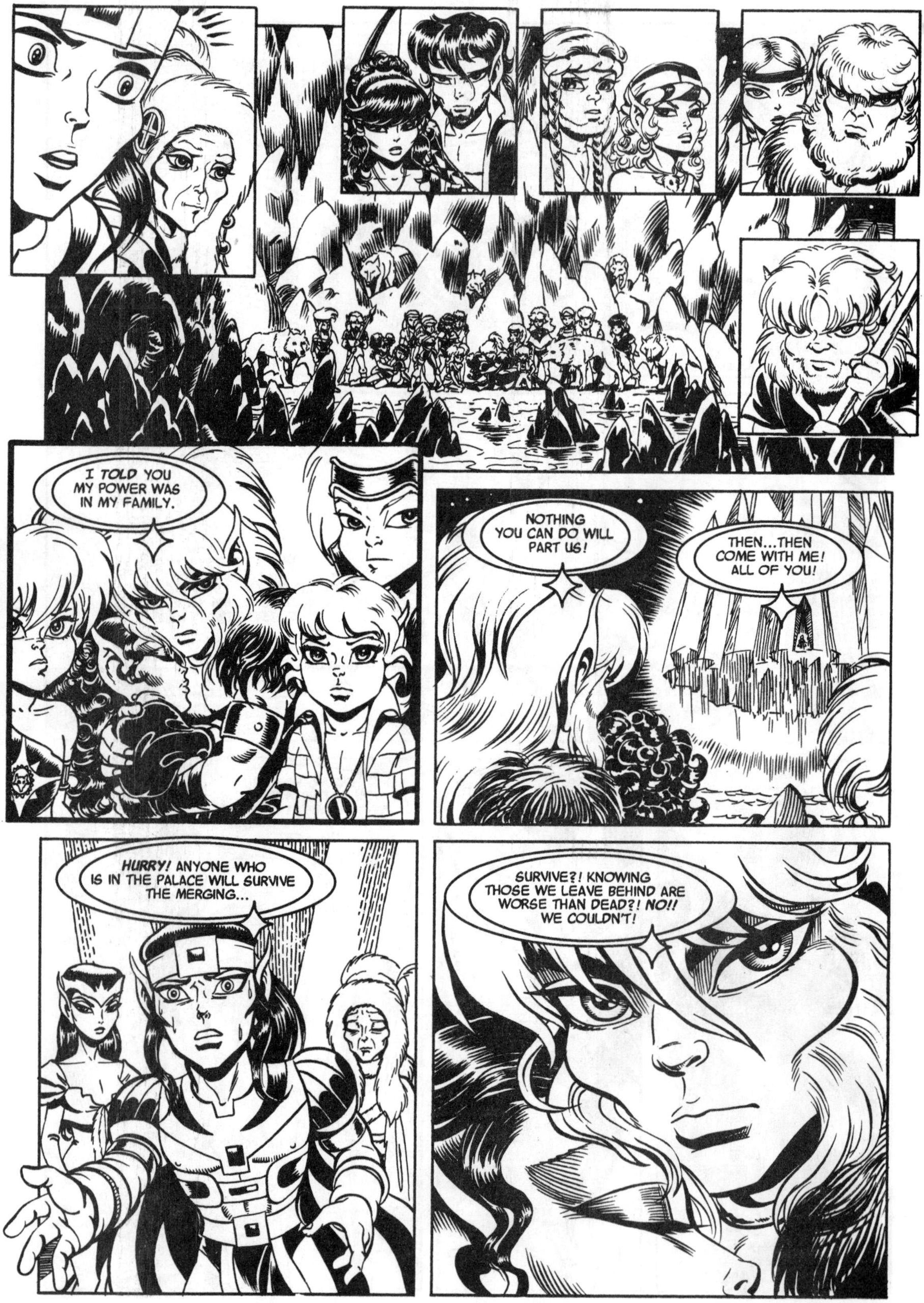
I TOLD YOU MY POWER WAS IN MY FAMILY.
NOTHING YOU CAN DO WILL PART US!
THEN...THEN COME WITH ME! ALL OF YOU!
HURRY! ANYONE WHO IS IN THE PALACE WILL SURVIVE THE MERGING...
SURVIVE?! KNOWING THOSE WE LEAVE BEHIND ARE WORSE THAN DEAD?! NO!! WE COULDN'T!

NOR COULD I.

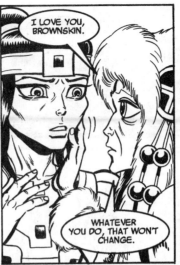

I LOVE YOU, BROWNSKIN.

WHATEVER YOU DO, THAT WON'T CHANGE.

EKUAR..!

HE-HE NEVER SAID A WORD! I DID NOT KNOW...

IT WAS EASY WHEN YOU THOUGHT WE WERE ALL LONG DEAD.

CAN YOU DO IT NOW...WIPE THEM OUT...

...WITH ALL OF THEM THERE, WATCHING?

I HAVE THE POWER TO STOP YOU. IT'S WHAT I WAS RAISED TO DO.

BUT I WON'T. IT MUST BE YOUR CHOICE.

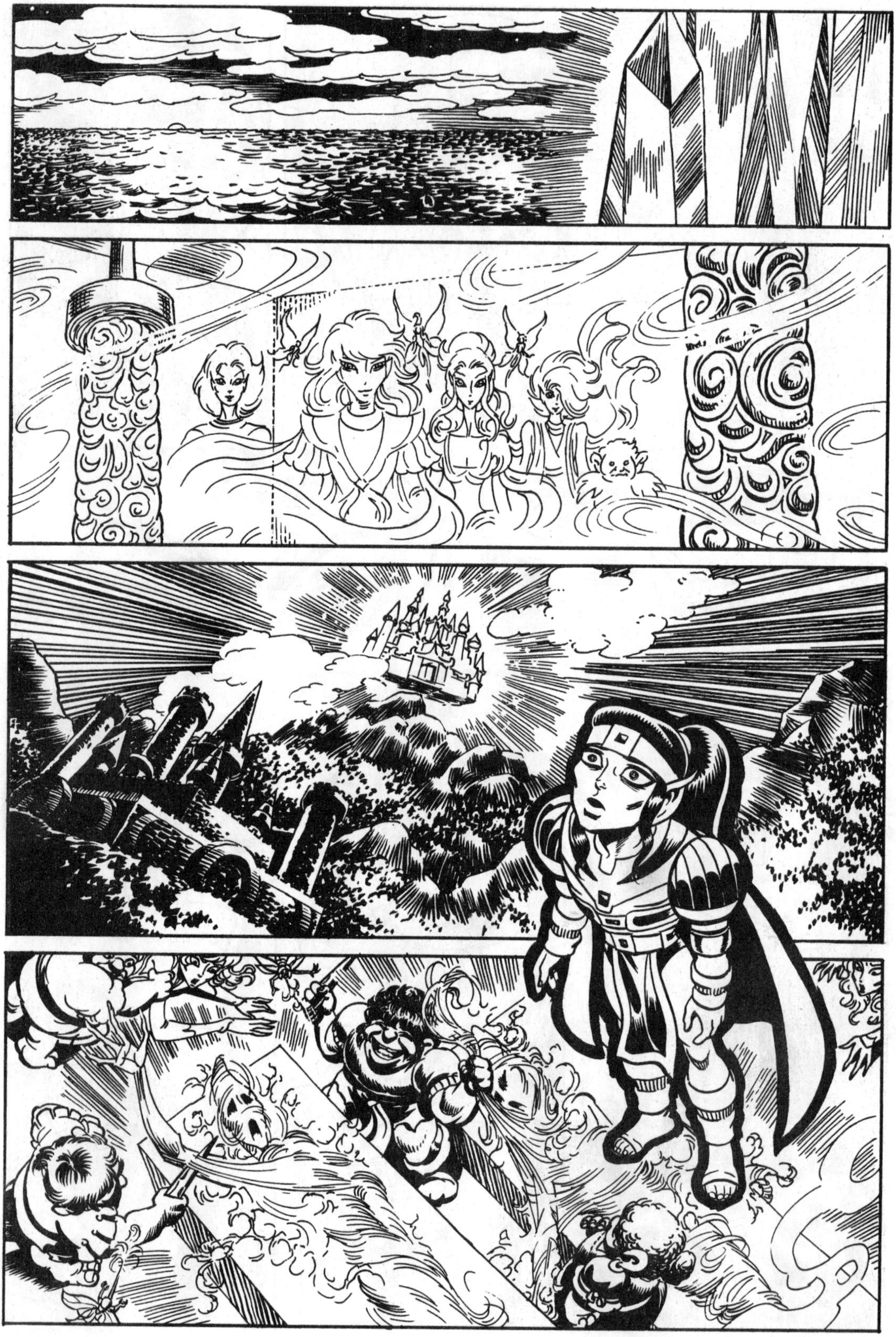

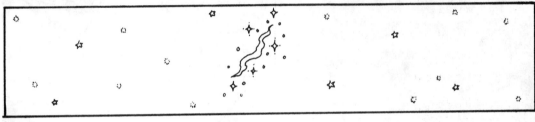

ZHANTEE! YOU ARE WELL!

...I AM! AND SHE DIDN'T EVEN TOUCH ME!

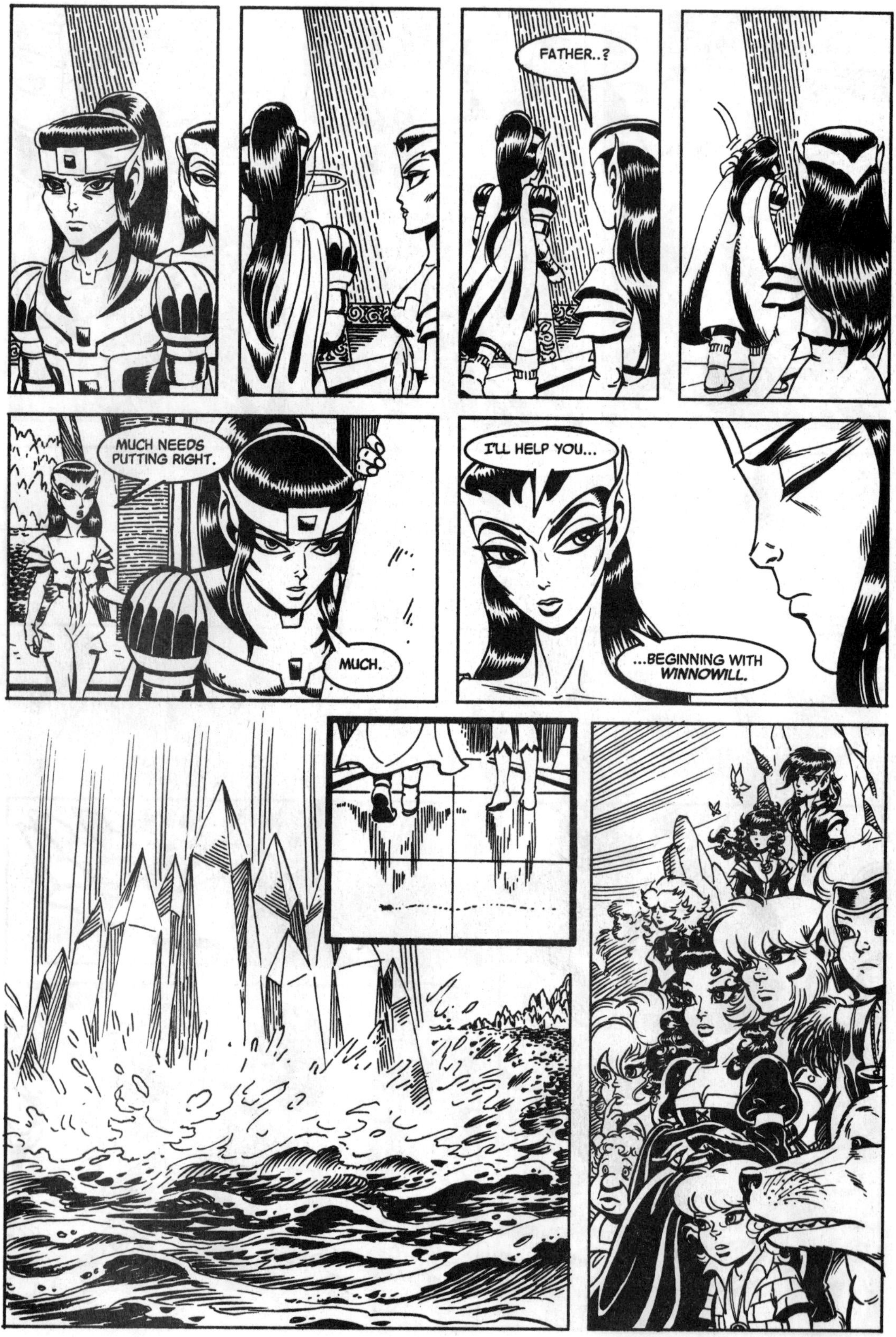
FATHER..?
MUCH NEEDS PUTTING RIGHT.
MUCH.
I'LL HELP YOU...
...BEGINNING WITH WINNOWILL.

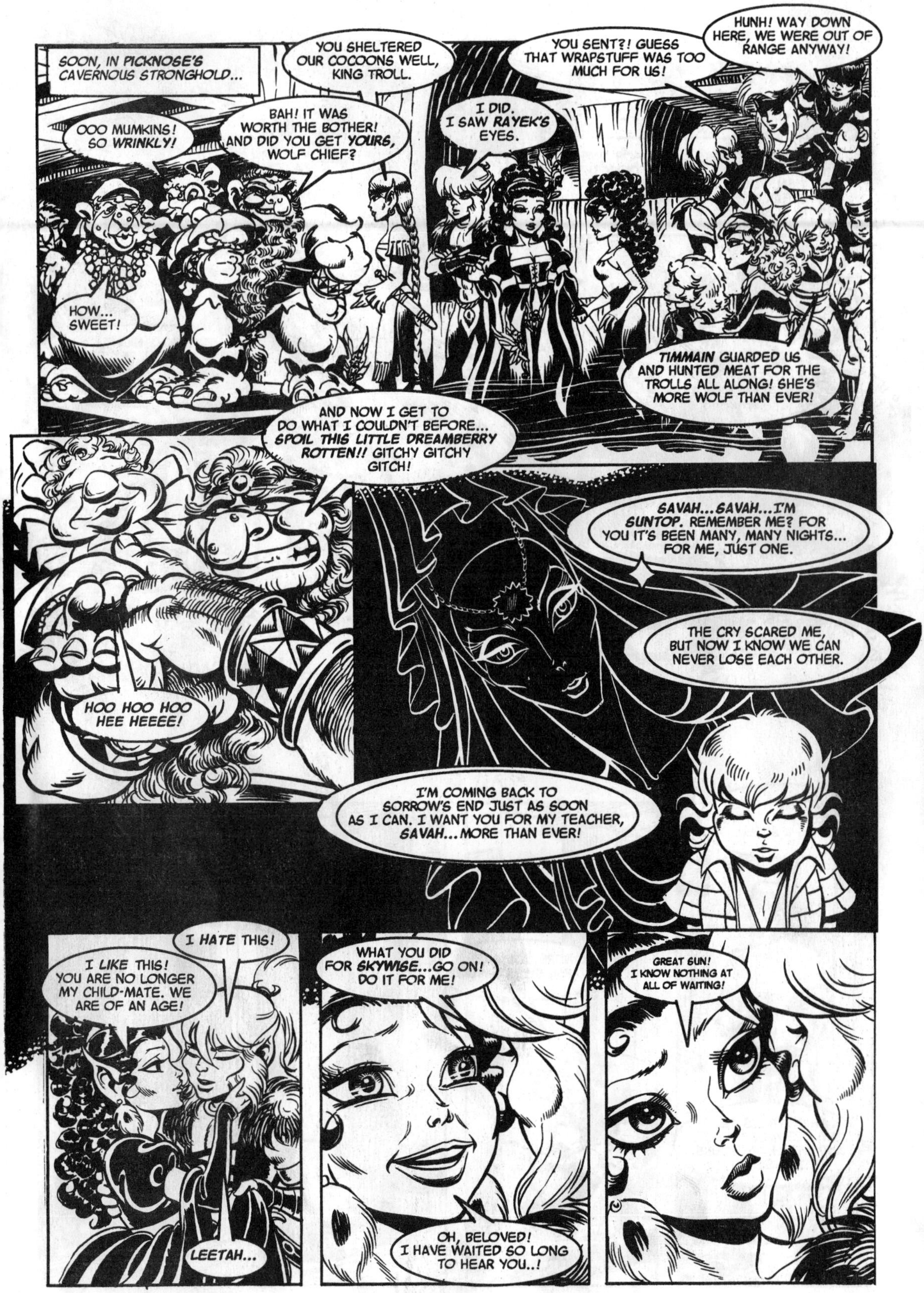
SOON, IN PICKNOSE'S CAVERNOUS STRONGHOLD...
YOU SHELTERED OUR COCOONS WELL, KING TROLL.
BAH! IT WAS WORTH THE BOTHER! AND DID YOU GET YOURS, WOLF CHIEF?
OOO MUMKINS! SO WRINKLY!
HOW... SWEET!
I DID. I SAW RAYEK'S EYES.
YOU SENT?! GUESS THAT WRAPSTUFF WAS TOO MUCH FOR US!
HUNH! WAY DOWN HERE, WE WERE OUT OF RANGE ANYWAY!
TIMMAIN GUARDED US AND HUNTED MEAT FOR THE TROLLS ALL ALONG! SHE'S MORE WOLF THAN EVER!
AND NOW I GET TO DO WHAT I COULDN'T BEFORE... SPOIL THIS LITTLE DREAMBERRY ROTTEN!! GITCHY GITCHY GITCH!
HOO HOO HOO HEE HEEEE!
SAVAH...SAVAH...I'M SUNTOP. REMEMBER ME? FOR YOU IT'S BEEN MANY, MANY NIGHTS... FOR ME, JUST ONE.
THE CRY SCARED ME, BUT NOW I KNOW WE CAN NEVER LOSE EACH OTHER.
I'M COMING BACK TO SORROW'S END JUST AS SOON AS I CAN. I WANT YOU FOR MY TEACHER, SAVAH... MORE THAN EVER!
I HATE THIS!
I LIKE THIS! YOU ARE NO LONGER MY CHILD-MATE. WE ARE OF AN AGE!
LEETAH...
WHAT YOU DID FOR SKYWISE...GO ON! DO IT FOR ME!
OH, BELOVED! I HAVE WAITED SO LONG TO HEAR YOU..!
GREAT SUN! I KNOW NOTHING AT ALL OF WAITING!

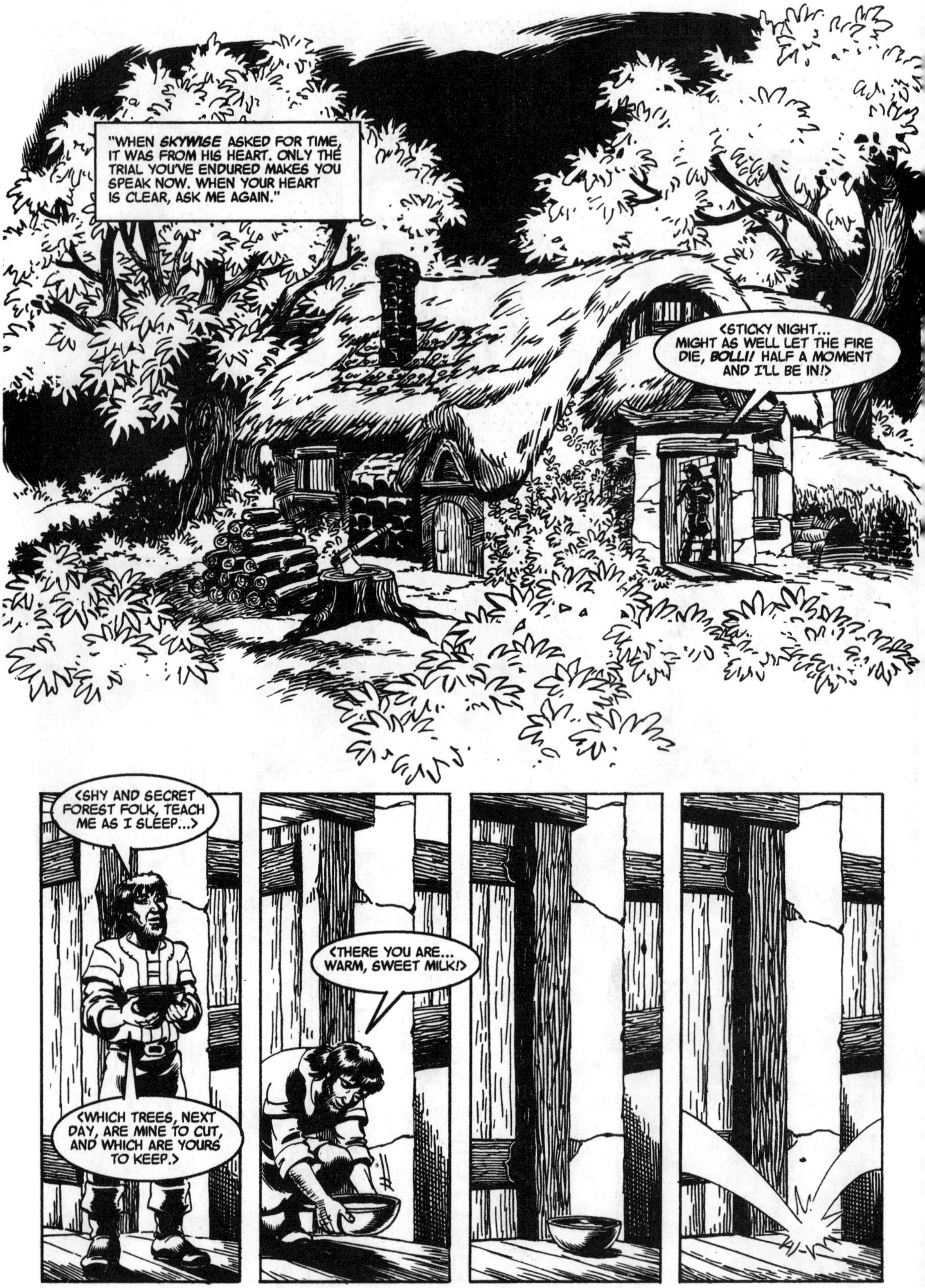
"WHEN SKYWISE ASKED FOR TIME, IT WAS FROM HIS HEART. ONLY THE TRIAL YOU'VE ENDURED MAKES YOU SPEAK NOW. WHEN YOUR HEART IS CLEAR, ASK ME AGAIN."
<STICKY NIGHT... MIGHT AS WELL LET THE FIRE DIE, BOLLI! HALF A MOMENT AND I'LL BE IN!>
<SHY AND SECRET FOREST FOLK, TEACH ME AS I SLEEP...>
<WHICH TREES, NEXT DAY, ARE MINE TO CUT, AND WHICH ARE YOURS TO KEEP.>
<THERE YOU ARE... WARM, SWEET MILK!>

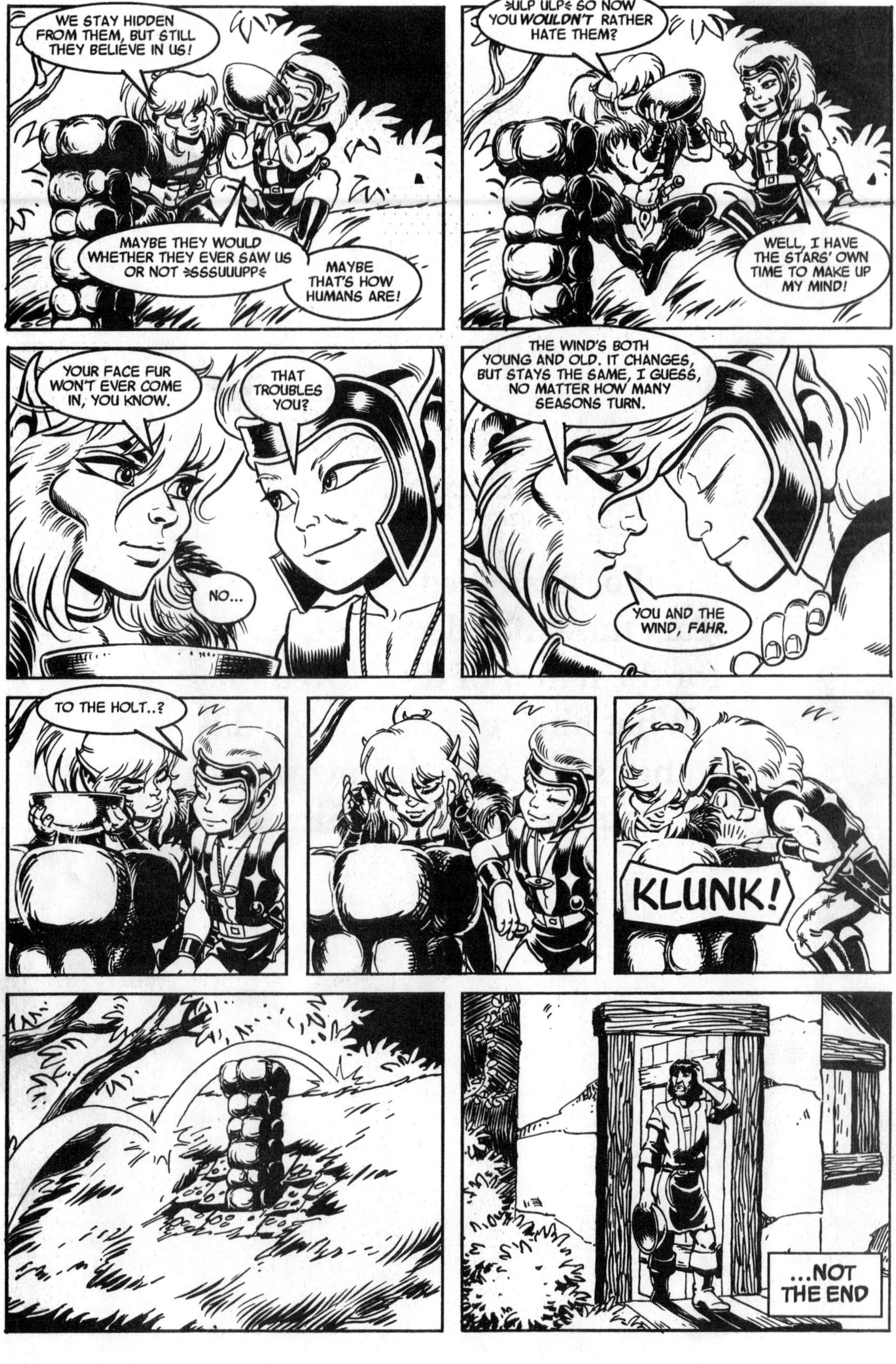
WE STAY HIDDEN FROM THEM, BUT STILL THEY BELIEVE IN US!
MAYBE THEY WOULD WHETHER THEY EVER SAW US OR NOT ≽SSSUUUPP≼
MAYBE THAT'S HOW HUMANS ARE!
≽ULP ULP≼ SO NOW YOU **WOULDN'T** RATHER HATE THEM?
WELL, I HAVE THE STARS' OWN TIME TO MAKE UP MY MIND!
YOUR FACE FUR WON'T EVER COME IN, YOU KNOW.
THAT TROUBLES YOU?
NO...
THE WIND'S BOTH YOUNG AND OLD. IT CHANGES, BUT STAYS THE SAME, I GUESS, NO MATTER HOW MANY SEASONS TURN.
YOU AND THE WIND, *FAHR*.
TO THE HOLT..?
KLUNK!
...NOT THE END

Dreams.

For nearly ten thousand
years the Wolfriders slept, waiting
for the return of their loved ones.
What hints of future strife did
they see? Learn the answer in
volume 8a, "Dreamtime."

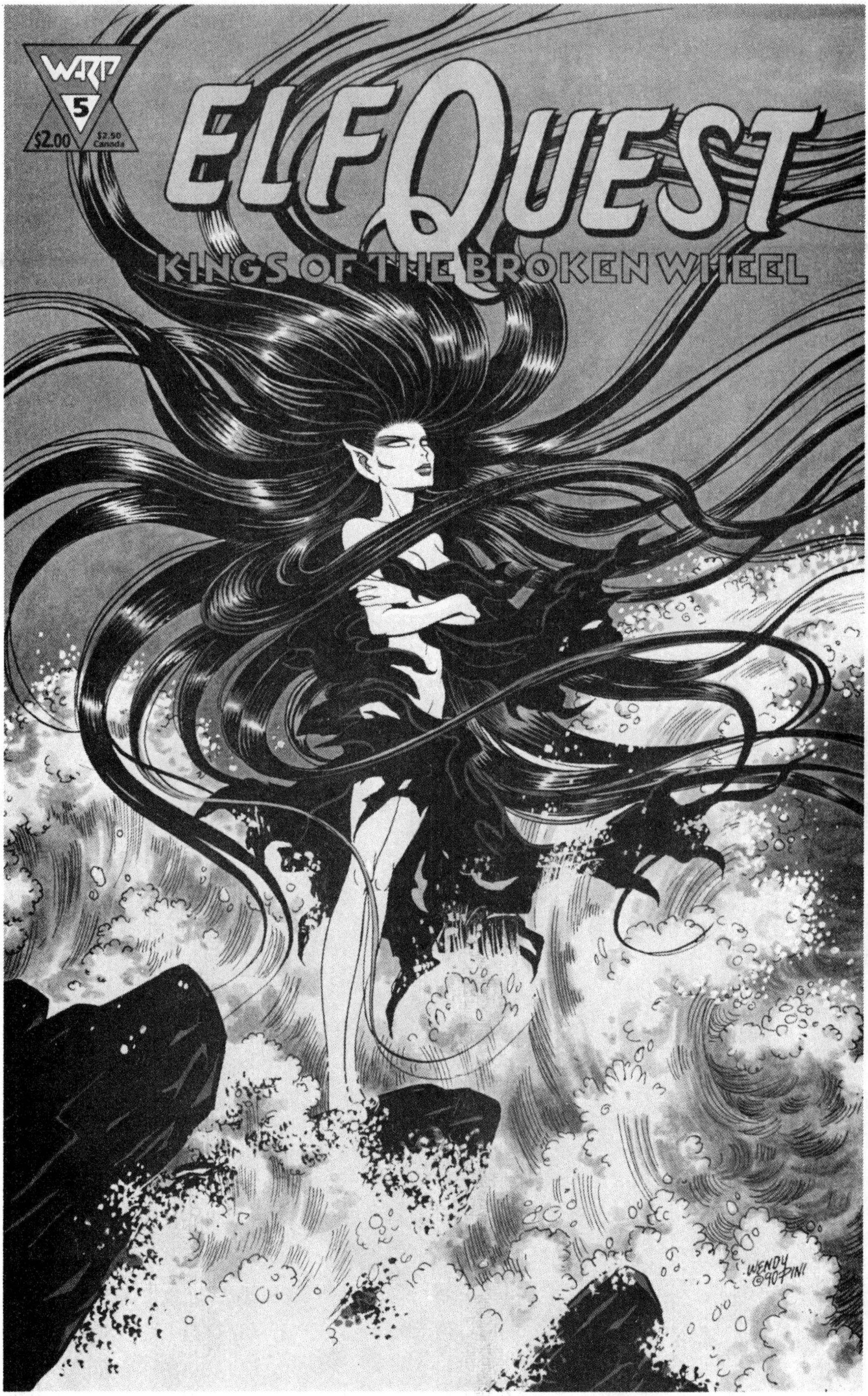
WaRP
5
$2.00
$2.50 Canada
ELFQUEST
KINGS OF THE BROKEN WHEEL
WENDY PINI ©90

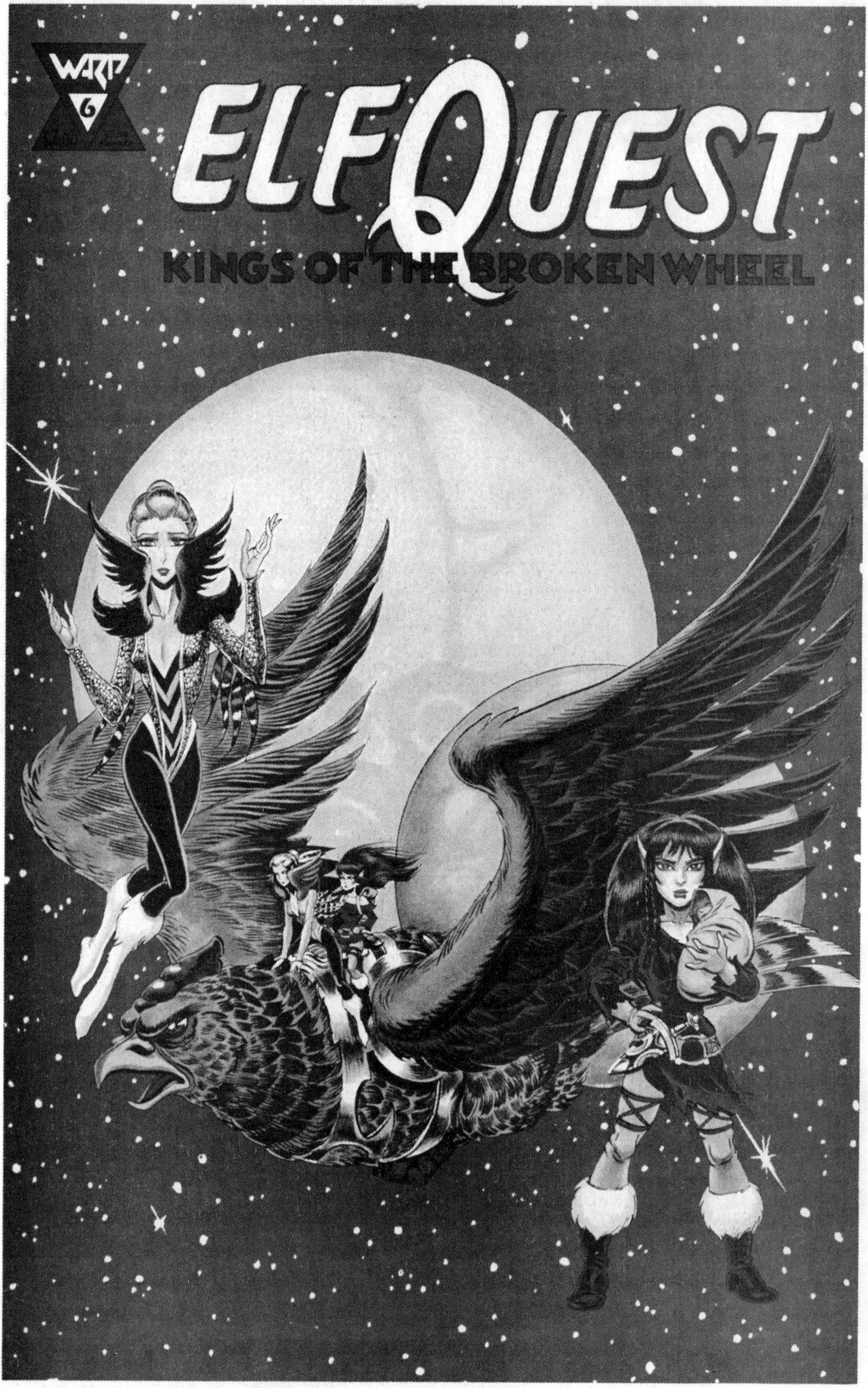
WARP
6
ELFQUEST
KINGS OF THE BROKEN WHEEL

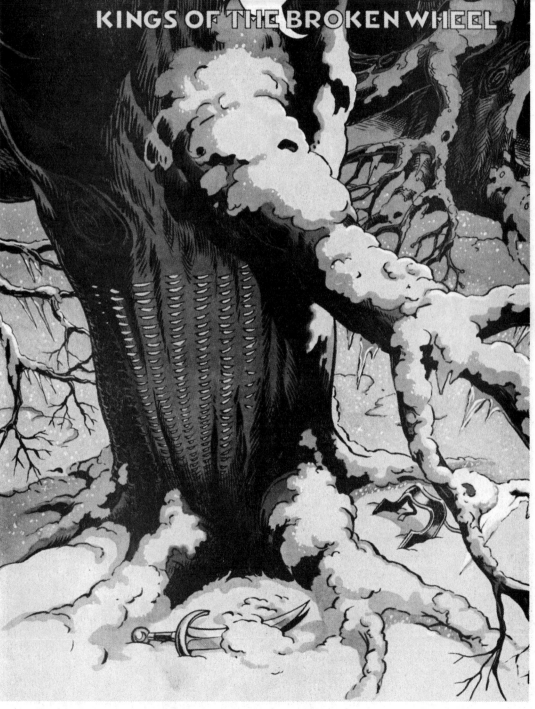

ELFQUEST

KINGS OF THE BROKEN WHEEL

7 $2.00
$2.50
in Canada

WARP GRAPHICS

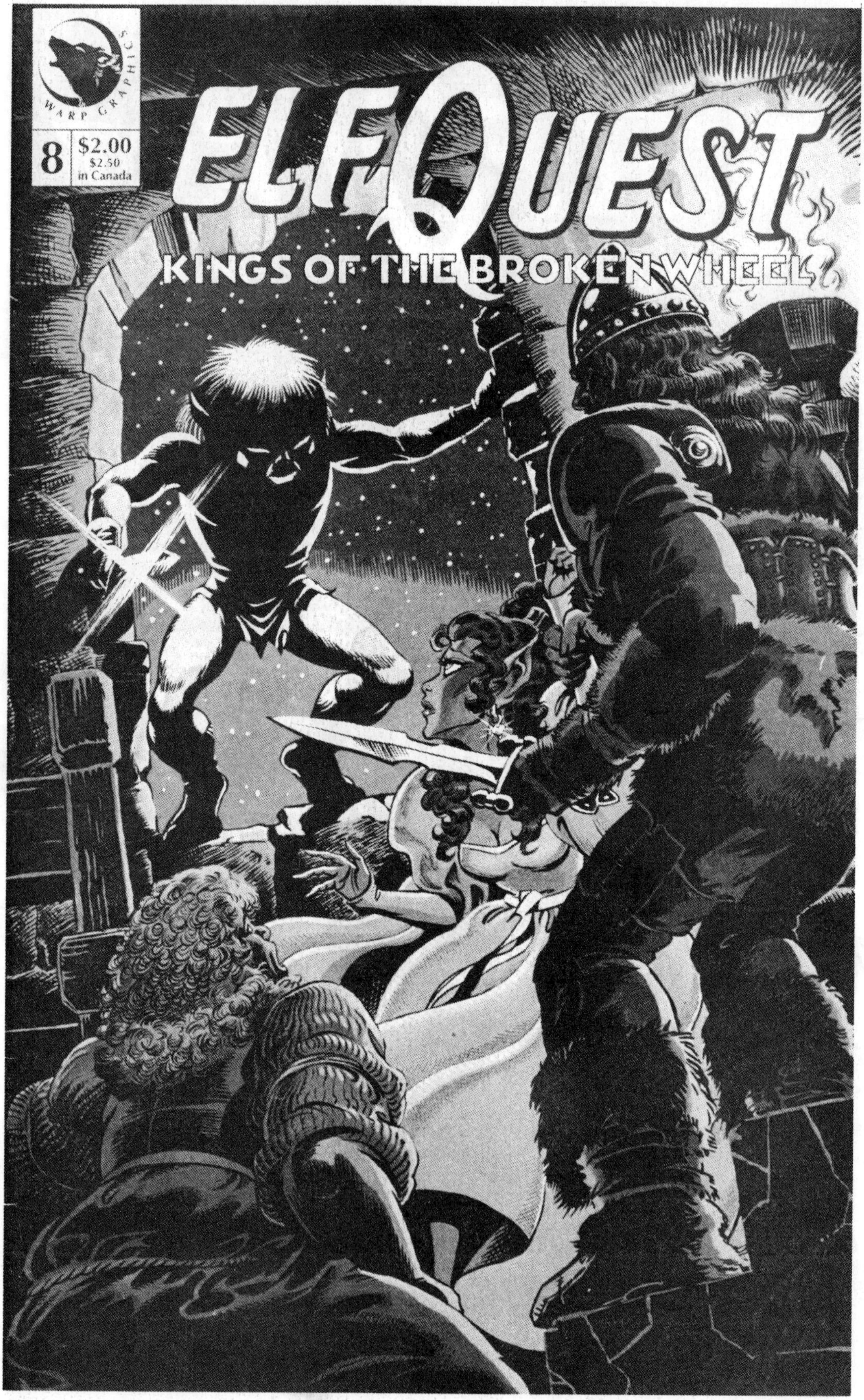

WARP GRAPHICS
8
$2.00
$2.50
in Canada
ElfQuest
KINGS OF THE BROKEN WHEEL

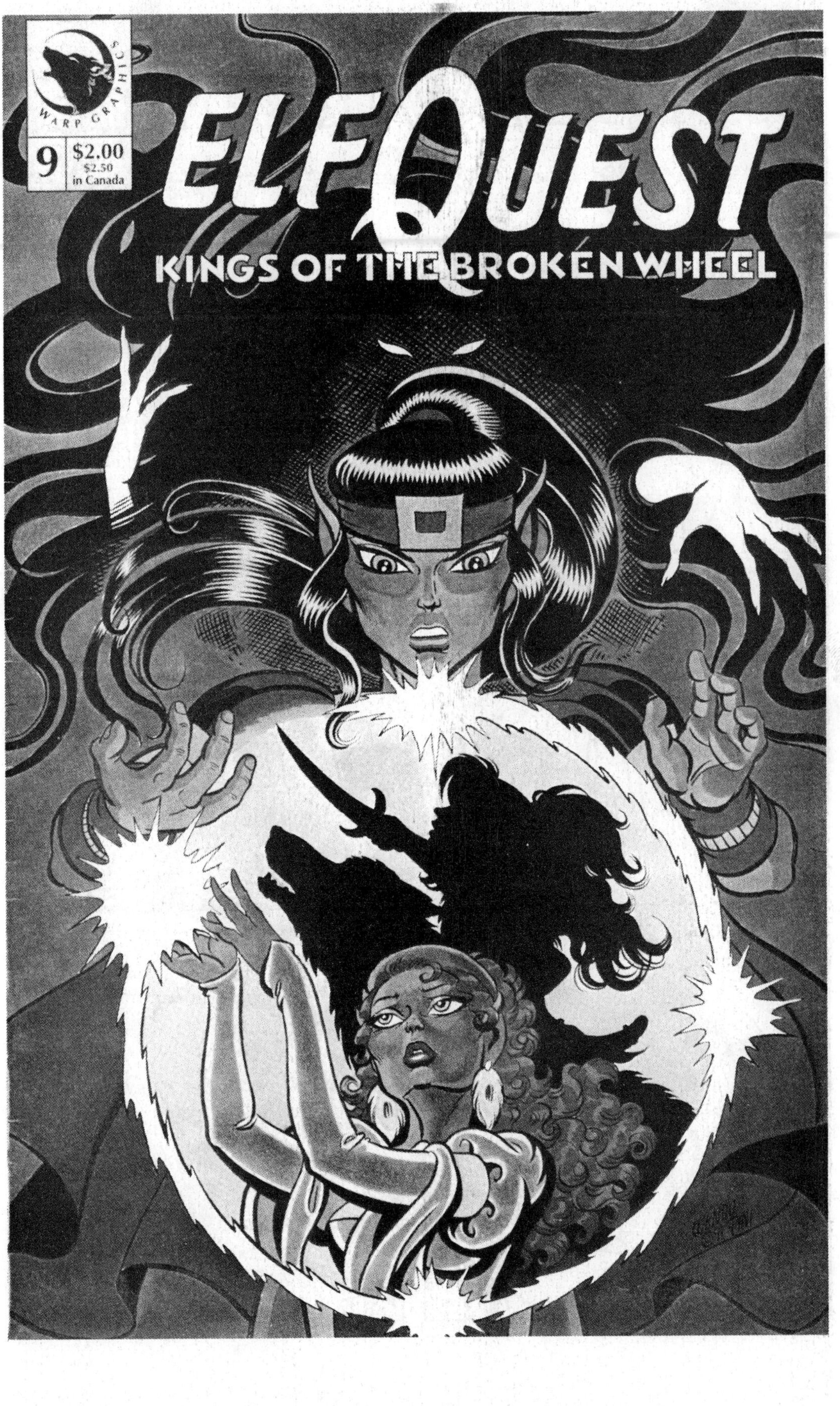
WARP GRAPHICS
9
$2.00
$2.50
in Canada
ELFQUEST
KINGS OF THE BROKEN WHEEL

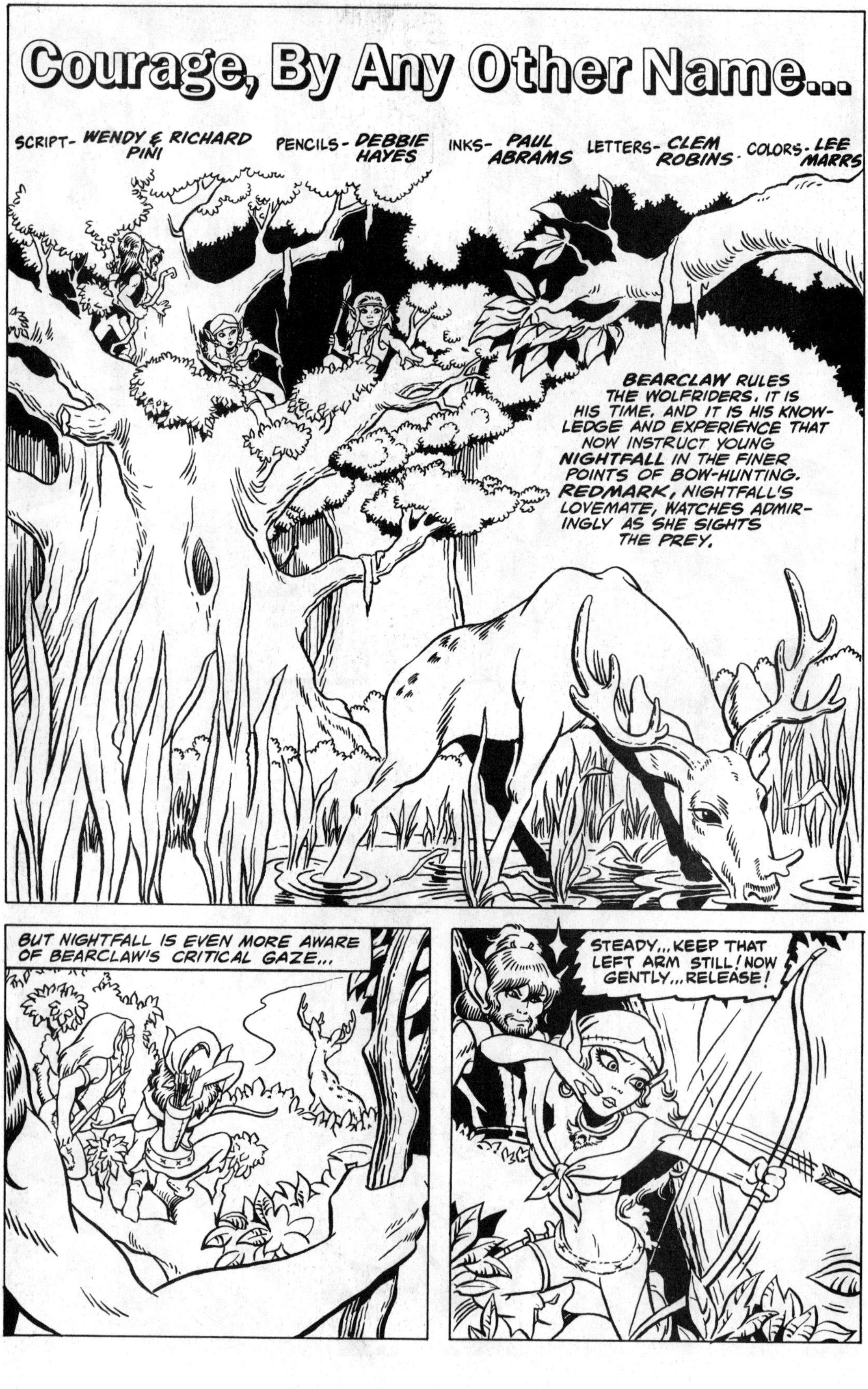
Courage, By Any Other Name...
SCRIPT- WENDY & RICHARD PINI
PENCILS- DEBBIE HAYES
INKS- PAUL ABRAMS
LETTERS- CLEM ROBINS
COLORS- LEE MARRS
BEARCLAW RULES THE WOLFRIDERS. IT IS HIS TIME. AND IT IS HIS KNOWLEDGE AND EXPERIENCE THAT NOW INSTRUCT YOUNG NIGHTFALL IN THE FINER POINTS OF BOW-HUNTING. REDMARK, NIGHTFALL'S LOVEMATE, WATCHES ADMIRINGLY AS SHE SIGHTS THE PREY.
BUT NIGHTFALL IS EVEN MORE AWARE OF BEARCLAW'S CRITICAL GAZE...
STEADY... KEEP THAT LEFT ARM STILL! NOW GENTLY... RELEASE!

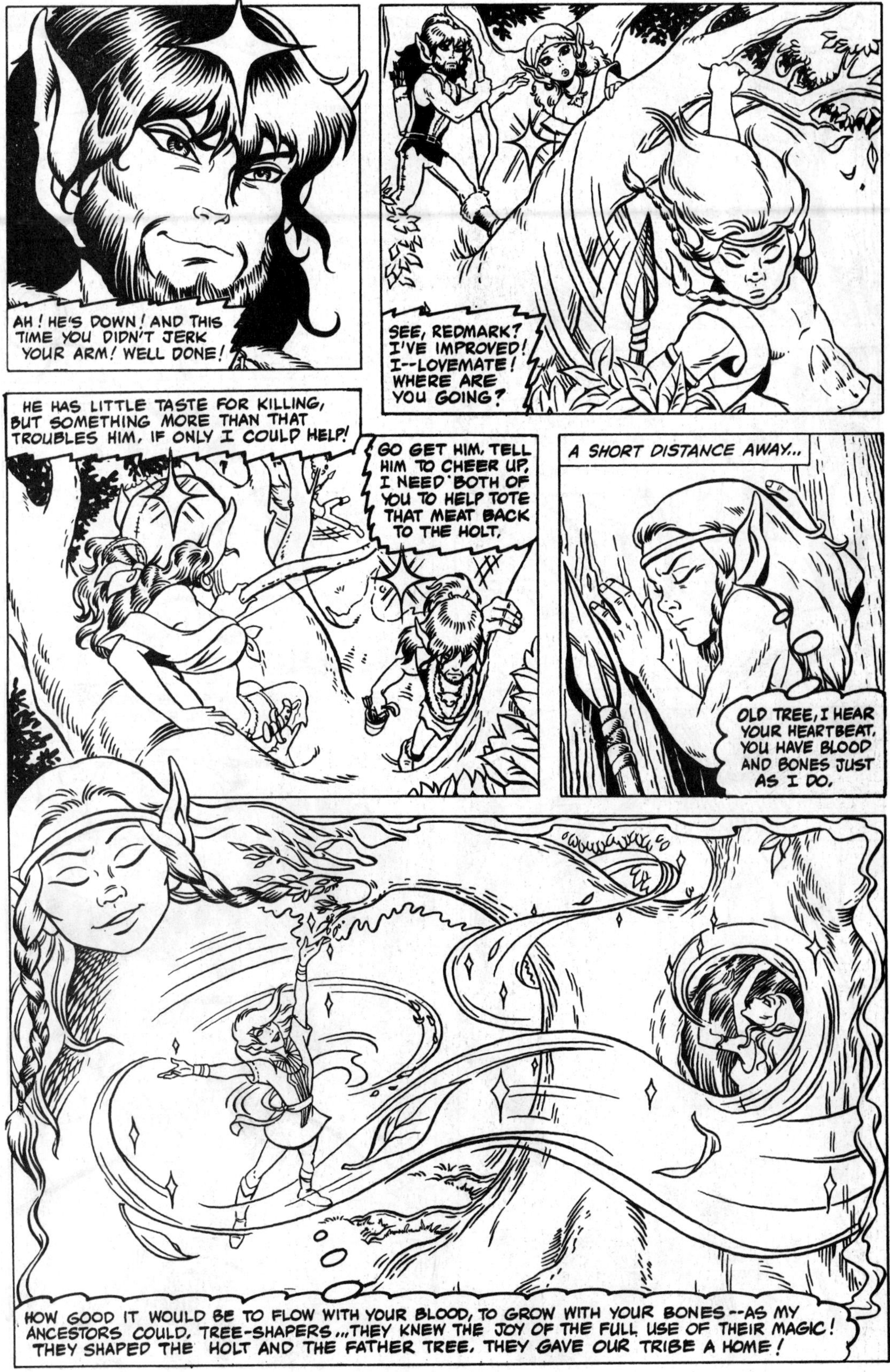
AH! HE'S DOWN! AND THIS TIME YOU DIDN'T JERK YOUR ARM! WELL DONE!
SEE, REDMARK? I'VE IMPROVED! I--LOVEMATE! WHERE ARE YOU GOING?
HE HAS LITTLE TASTE FOR KILLING, BUT SOMETHING MORE THAN THAT TROUBLES HIM. IF ONLY I COULD HELP!
GO GET HIM. TELL HIM TO CHEER UP. I NEED BOTH OF YOU TO HELP TOTE THAT MEAT BACK TO THE HOLT.
A SHORT DISTANCE AWAY...
OLD TREE, I HEAR YOUR HEARTBEAT. YOU HAVE BLOOD AND BONES JUST AS I DO.
HOW GOOD IT WOULD BE TO FLOW WITH YOUR BLOOD, TO GROW WITH YOUR BONES--AS MY ANCESTORS COULD. TREE-SHAPERS... THEY KNEW THE JOY OF THE FULL USE OF THEIR MAGIC! THEY SHAPED THE HOLT AND THE FATHER TREE. THEY GAVE OUR TRIBE A HOME!

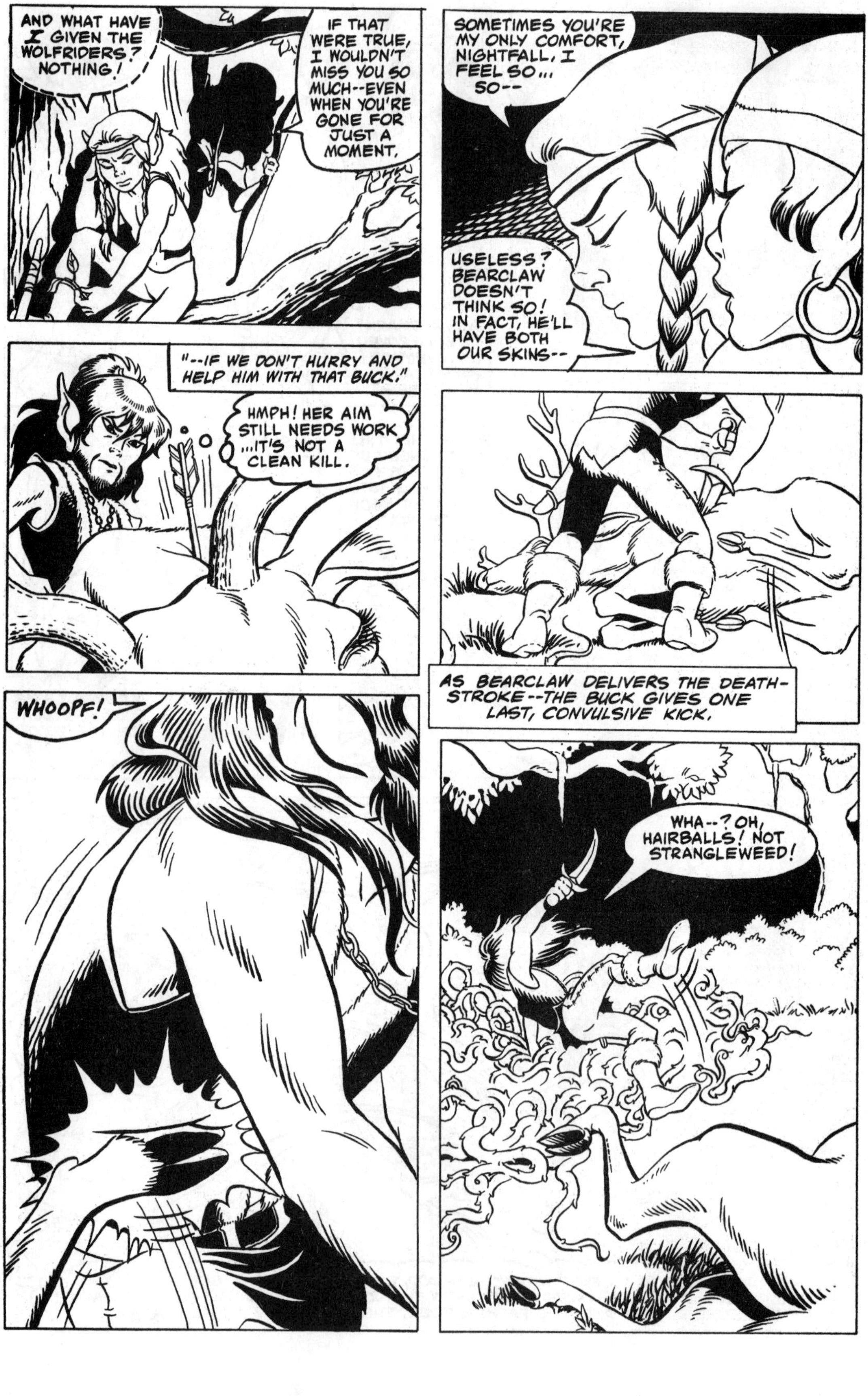
AND WHAT HAVE I GIVEN THE WOLFRIDERS? NOTHING!
IF THAT WERE TRUE, I WOULDN'T MISS YOU SO MUCH--EVEN WHEN YOU'RE GONE FOR JUST A MOMENT.
SOMETIMES YOU'RE MY ONLY COMFORT, NIGHTFALL. I FEEL SO... SO--
USELESS? BEARCLAW DOESN'T THINK SO! IN FACT, HE'LL HAVE BOTH OUR SKINS--
"--IF WE DON'T HURRY AND HELP HIM WITH THAT BUCK."
HMPH! HER AIM STILL NEEDS WORK ...IT'S NOT A CLEAN KILL.
AS BEARCLAW DELIVERS THE DEATH-STROKE--THE BUCK GIVES ONE LAST, CONVULSIVE KICK.
WHOOPF!
WHA--? OH, HAIRBALLS! NOT STRANGLEWEED!

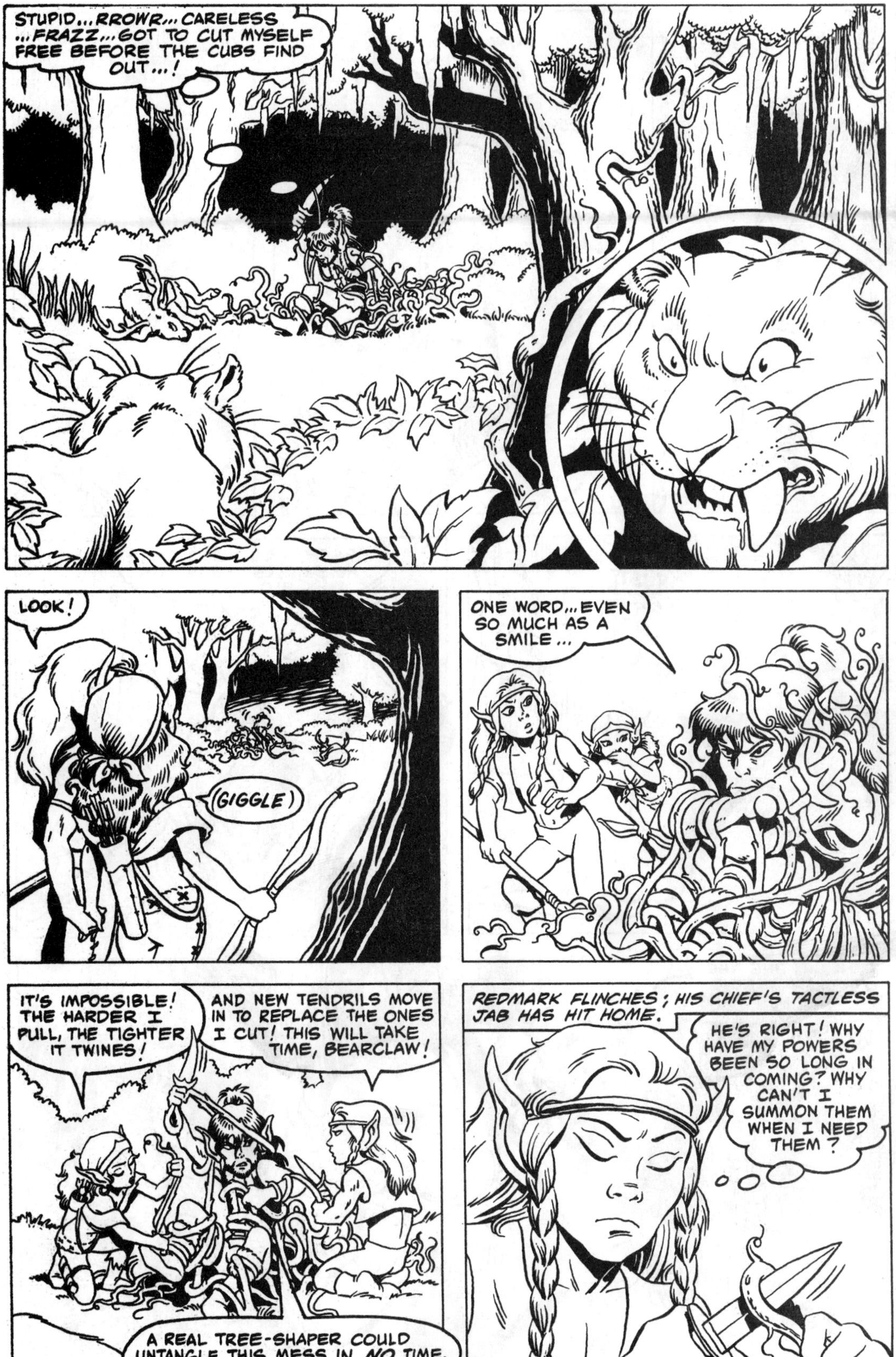
STUPID... RROWR... CARELESS ...FRAZZ... GOT TO CUT MYSELF FREE BEFORE THE CUBS FIND OUT...!
LOOK!
(GIGGLE)
ONE WORD... EVEN SO MUCH AS A SMILE...
IT'S IMPOSSIBLE! THE HARDER I PULL, THE TIGHTER IT TWINES!
AND NEW TENDRILS MOVE IN TO REPLACE THE ONES I CUT! THIS WILL TAKE TIME, BEARCLAW!
A REAL TREE-SHAPER COULD UNTANGLE THIS MESS IN NO TIME.
REDMARK FLINCHES; HIS CHIEF'S TACTLESS JAB HAS HIT HOME.
HE'S RIGHT! WHY HAVE MY POWERS BEEN SO LONG IN COMING? WHY CAN'T I SUMMON THEM WHEN I NEED THEM?

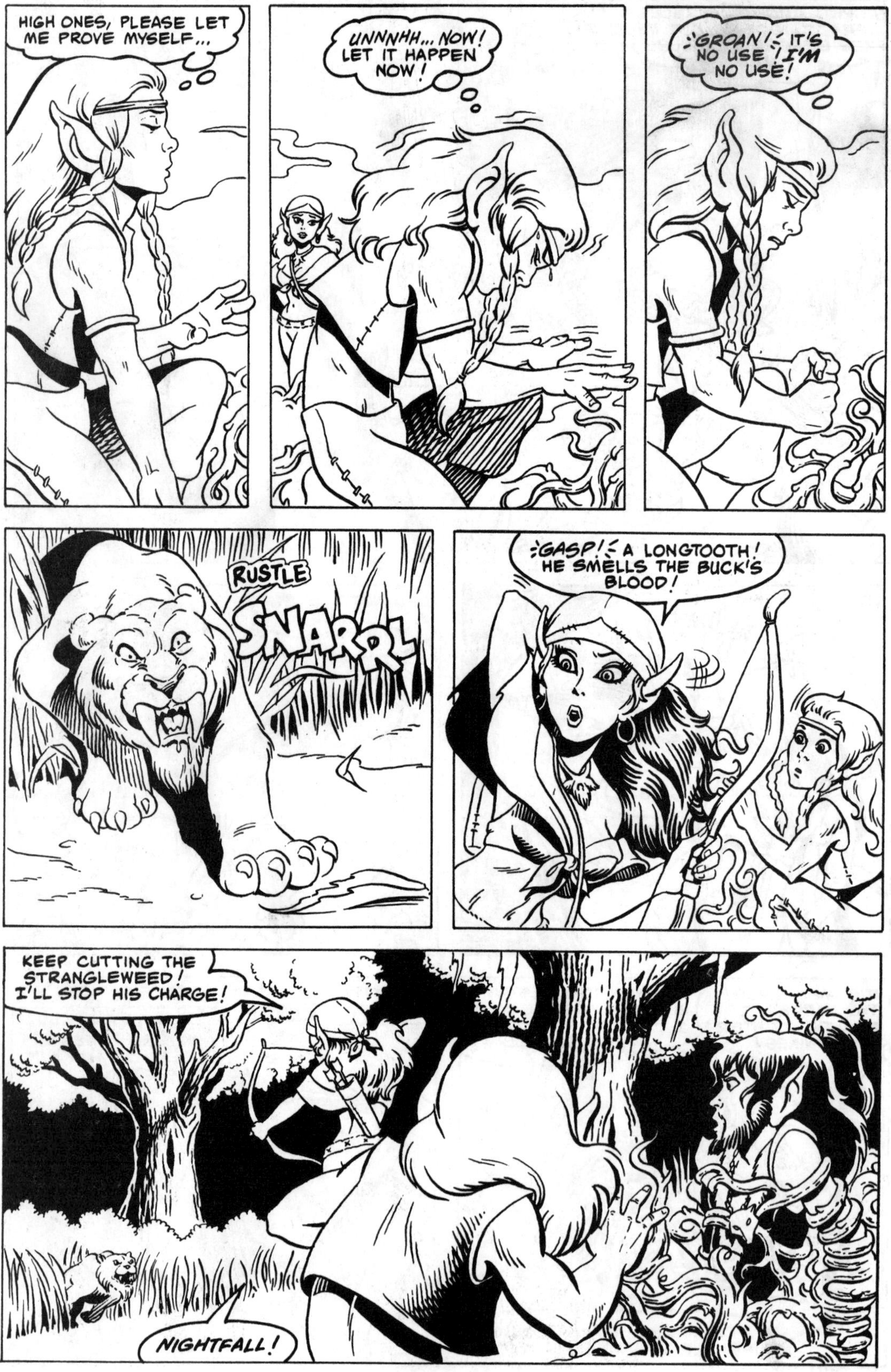
HIGH ONES, PLEASE LET ME PROVE MYSELF...
UNNNHH... NOW! LET IT HAPPEN NOW!
GROAN! IT'S NO USE! I'M NO USE!
RUSTLE
SNARRL
GASP! A LONGTOOTH! HE SMELLS THE BUCK'S BLOOD!
KEEP CUTTING THE STRANGLEWEED! I'LL STOP HIS CHARGE!
NIGHTFALL!

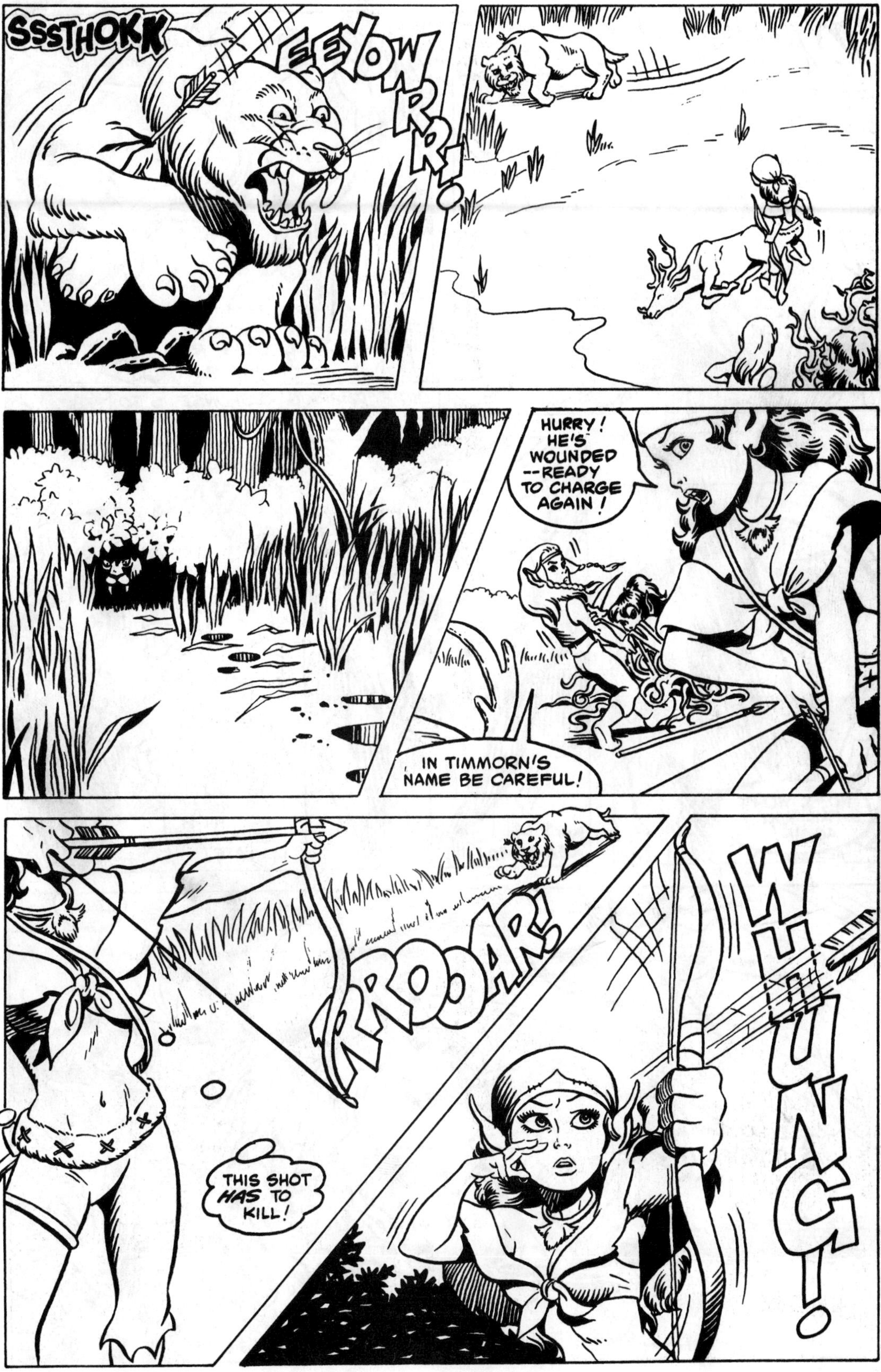
SSSTHOKK
EEYOWRRR!
HURRY! HE'S WOUNDED --READY TO CHARGE AGAIN!
IN TIMMORN'S NAME BE CAREFUL!
RROOAR!
THIS SHOT HAS TO KILL!
WHUNG!

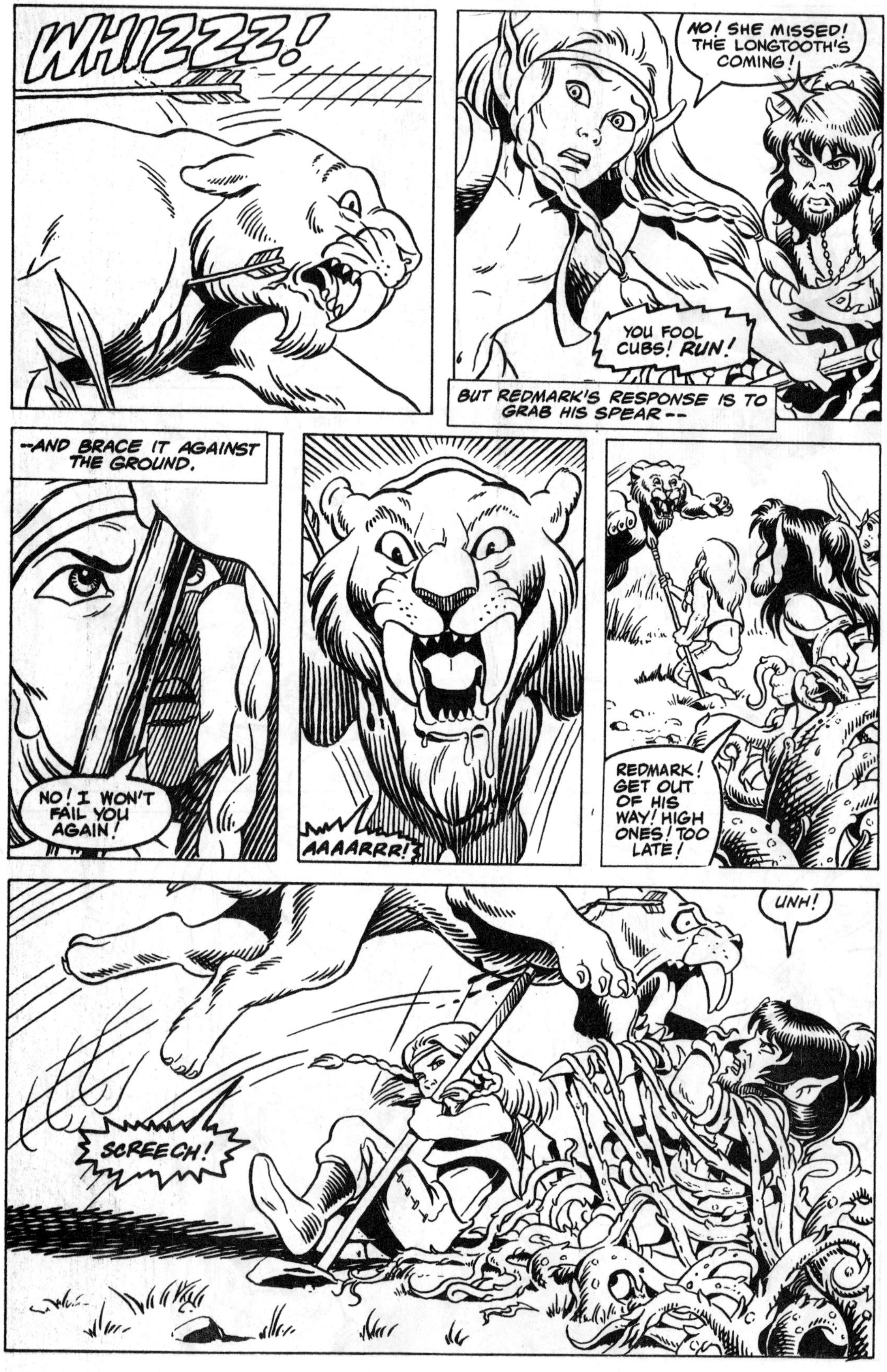
WHIZZZ!
NO! SHE MISSED! THE LONGTOOTH'S COMING!
YOU FOOL CUBS! RUN!
BUT REDMARK'S RESPONSE IS TO GRAB HIS SPEAR --
--AND BRACE IT AGAINST THE GROUND.
NO! I WON'T FAIL YOU AGAIN!
AAAARRR!
REDMARK! GET OUT OF HIS WAY! HIGH ONES! TOO LATE!
UNH!
SCREECH!

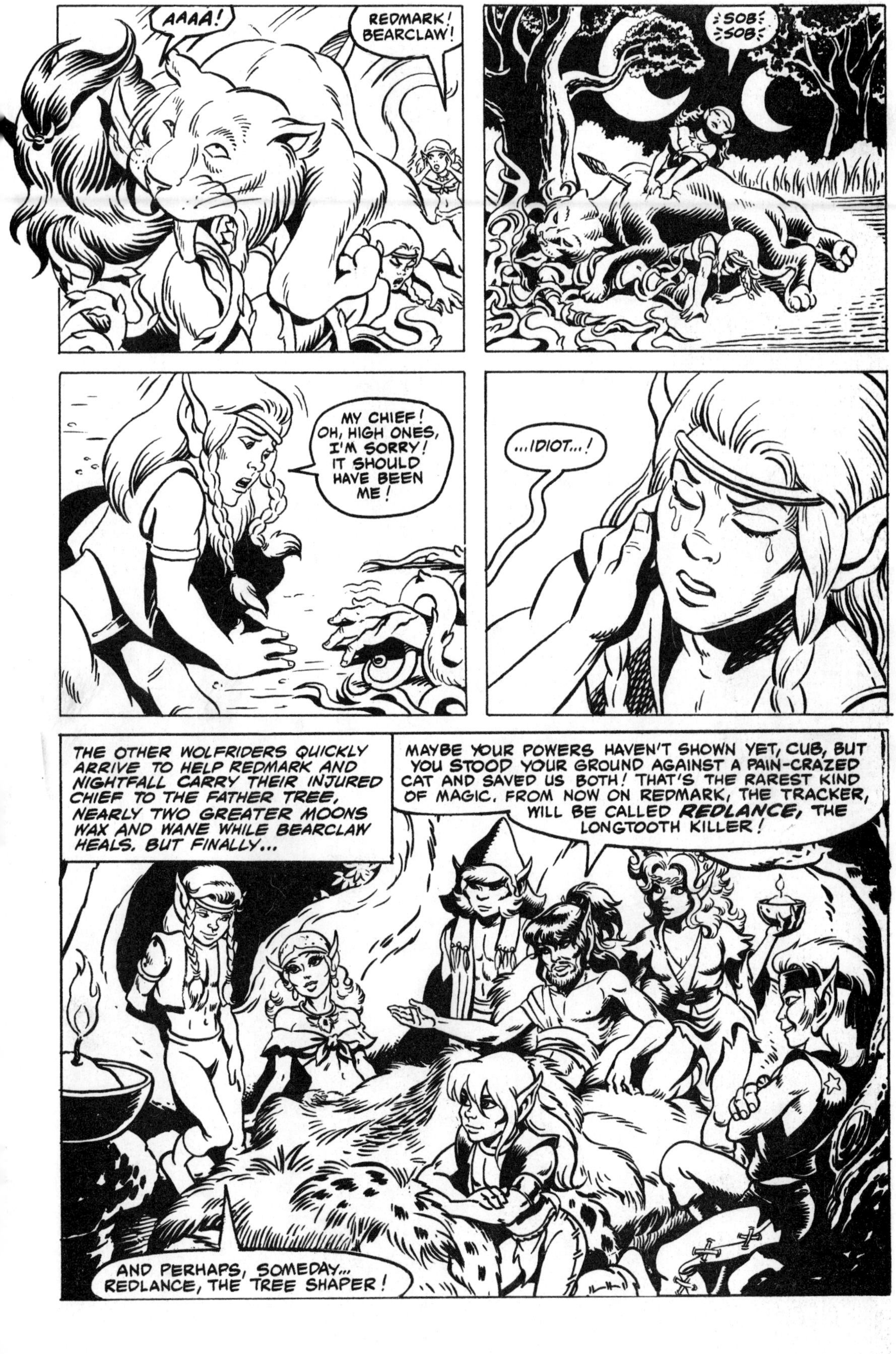
AAAA!
REDMARK! BEARCLAW!
SOB SOB
MY CHIEF! OH, HIGH ONES, I'M SORRY! IT SHOULD HAVE BEEN ME!
...IDIOT...!
THE OTHER WOLFRIDERS QUICKLY ARRIVE TO HELP REDMARK AND NIGHTFALL CARRY THEIR INJURED CHIEF TO THE FATHER TREE. NEARLY TWO GREATER MOONS WAX AND WANE WHILE BEARCLAW HEALS. BUT FINALLY...
MAYBE YOUR POWERS HAVEN'T SHOWN YET, CUB, BUT YOU STOOD YOUR GROUND AGAINST A PAIN-CRAZED CAT AND SAVED US BOTH! THAT'S THE RAREST KIND OF MAGIC. FROM NOW ON REDMARK, THE TRACKER, WILL BE CALLED REDLANCE, THE LONGTOOTH KILLER!
AND PERHAPS, SOMEDAY... REDLANCE, THE TREE SHAPER!